BOWHUNTING PRESERVATION ALLIANCE

The Scentsible Bowhunter

Rick Combs

SKYHORSE PUBLISHING

A friend recently asked me if it was fun to be an outdoor writer. Fun? Well, sometimes. Slipping on a steep trail and rolling into a big clump of prickly pears on a hunt in the Sierra Madre wasn't much fun. Nor was getting caught in a storm on the tundra with no shelter and no wood for a fire, or having an ancient outboard engine die on Hudson Bay with night falling, the temperature plummeting, and the current sweeping us away from shore. It has been an adventure, though, and at times it has been a joy. Always, it has been a privilege.

Part of the proceeds from the sale of this book have been donated to the Bowhunting Preservation Alliance, indirectly giving me the opportunity to give something back for that privilege. The funds will introduce young people to the thrill of bowhunting and expand upon bowhunting opportunities around the country. Thanks for your purchase.

Rick Combs

Bowhunting is a passion that has seen many through tough times such as the economic climate under which this book is being published. Thus we believe the contents of this work will provide many bowhunters with all they need to know to immerse themselves in the world of bowhunting. The Archery Trade Association works to put archery into every community, invites every beginning archer to try bowhunting, and wants every bowhunter to find opportunities to hunt where they live. Your purchase of this book will help provide the means for us to spread the "good news" about archery and bowhunting and ensure that, long after you've left the woods, others will experience the adrenaline rush and genuine satisfaction shared by all who've hunted with stick and string. Thanks.

Jay McAninch
CEO/President, ATA

Skyhorse Publishing books may be purchased in bulk at special discounts for sales promotion, corporate gifts, fund-raising, or educational purposes. Special editions can also be created to specifications. For details, contact the Special Sales Department, Skyhorse Publishing, 307 West 36th Street, 11th Floor, New York, NY 10018 or info@skyhorsepublishing.com.

Skyhorse® and Skyhorse Publishing® are registered trademarks of Skyhorse Publishing, Inc.®, a Delaware corporation.

Visit our website at www.skyhorsepublishing.com.

10 9 8 7 6 5 4 3 2 1

Library of Congress Cataloging-in-Publication Data is available on file.

ISBN: 978-1-61608-683-1

Printed in China

TABLE OF CONTENTS

INTRODUCTION

A routine on an early Bill Cosby record album described the very first human hunting experience. This is a memory from my long-lost youth, so I may not get it perfect, but it went something like this: Three cave men are eating grass, when the most inventive of the three (I'll call him Igor), suggests that perhaps they should kill an animal and try eating meat. Tired of eating grass, they all readily agree that this sounds like a great idea, so two of them crouch behind a bush and watch as Igor puts a stalk on a dinosaur. As Igor gets close to the dinosaur, it turns and lets out an ear-splitting roar. Igor runs for his life as his friends dive for cover under the bush. A few minutes later, when all seems calm, one of the two friends rises up carefully to peek over the bush.

"Can you see Igor?" asks the other friend.

"Yes," comes the whispered reply.

"What's he doing?"

"He's eating grass."

That has become an oft-used expression among some of my local hunting buddies. Whenever we meet back at the truck at the end of a hunt, the question is sure to arise: "Did you tag one, or are we eating grass?" We're not usually hunting dangerous game, nor, in truth, is our failure to kill an animal likely to be as serious an issue as it must often have been for hunters in preagricultural societies. However, the modern hunter's sense of frustration at the unproductive ambush, the failed stalk, the missed shot, and the trail gone cold is as real as that felt by the first hunters. That failure, as much as the occasional success modern bowhunters enjoy, is a link with ancient ancestors—and is, in fact, nothing less than a link with a vital part of being human. The sharing of that bond is one of the reasons hunters are so passionate about hunting, whether they articulate it or not.

I like to think that bowhunting in particular evokes a strong link with that essential, human part of our ancient ancestors. Bowhunting remains an up-close and personal encounter with our quarry. The case can be made that modern hunters enjoy some advantages in gear and technology, and that is certainly true. At the same time, even primitive bows and arrows represented relatively sophisticated concepts. That ability to conceptualize—call it imagination, ingenuity, or plain intelligence—is nothing new, but is itself a part of the link. It's only natural that we continue to use our imagination and ingenuity to overcome the challenges inherent in bowhunting.

The animals we hunt enjoy their own advantages. In terms of physical comparisons, humans are weak, puny, slow-moving creatures. We can't fly, and we don't climb trees very well. We see fairly well, but our hearing is poor compared to that of most creatures. Our olfactory capabilities—our sense of smell—is so poor it would inspire animals to laugh, if they had a sense of humor. (They don't, but more about that later.) The olfactory capabilities of most of the animals we hunt are so superior to our own as to put them beyond anything we can imagine. Those capabilities are widely regarded as the biggest challenge hunters face, and, in fact, they have spawned an entire industry of products that are available at sporting goods stores, as well as through mail order catalogs (not to mention every Wal-Mart in the land), and are aimed specifically at enabling hunters to over-come an animal's sense of smell or use it to the hunter's advantage. When Skyhorse Publishing approached me about writing a book on the subject of the role scent plays in bowhunting, I didn't hesitate to say yes. I've long been fascinated by the subject, and this is not the first time I've addressed it in print. So rapidly is our knowledge and our technology in this area growing that each year, new information and new products based on that information become available.

Hunting is more art than science, and to the extent it is science, it is applied science—not pure science. While a scientist, or even an academically minded reader, might find it interesting to look at the subject of scent in isolation, the hunter has a practical application in mind. For that reason, I have attempted to provide some context for the role of scent in hunting. For instance, we don't just look at the various scent glands of the deer species and the secretions they emit; we look at the role of these glands in intraspecies communications and how they affect behavior. Similarly, we don't just examine the steps hunters can take to avoid contaminating their environment with scent, but we also provide a context and a practical application by examining the use of decoys, to name one example, and the importance of handling them properly. Finally, a hunter who acquired all available knowledge about scent control could not use that knowledge most effectively without an awareness of what or how well a given species can see, or what or how well a given species can hear. For that reason, we've included at least a brief look at other sensory capabilities. It's my hope and belief that this book can contribute to bowhunters' knowledge of the role played by scent in hunting and enable them to apply that knowledge in context, in a way that will make them better bowhunters.

—Richard Combs
Cincinnati, Ohio

A quick movement or a slight sound has put this guy on the alert. If he picks up your scent, he's gone.

1

OLFACTION:

HOW IT WORKS

Is there a bowhunter who would stalk an elk or a mule deer from upwind, or who would hang a tree stand without giving a thought to prevailing breezes? Not many, I suspect, though a good case can be made that far too many bowhunters nonetheless underestimate the olfactory capabilities of big game animals. A bowhunter may not need to know how the sense of smell works to understand the importance of staying downwind of game, but beyond that basic principle, many bowhunting strategies in which scent is an issue (and without doubt, that is most of them) come down to matters of judgment. For the hunter trying to decide if the use of a given scent product is a waste of time and money or, if it is effective, when it is likely to be most effective; when to hunt a given stand in the morning and when to hunt it in the evening; when to hunt a feeding area or water hole; when to hunt close to a bedding area; and when the best choice might be to set up somewhere between the two, understanding how scent works is critical. For all but a fortunate few of us, hunting time is a limited resource to be carefully husbanded. Knowledge about optimum scenting conditions and the best times to use various types of attractant scents can be used to decide when to take off work and head for the woods, and when to wait until conditions have improved.

Olfaction, or the sense of smell, is in important ways the most direct and most precise sense. Vision is an indirect sense, entailing the perception of light reflected from an object. Hearing involves detecting sound waves created by movement, and in the case of human hearing, the sound waves must be moving between a fairly limited range of frequencies. Touch is a crude sense, and taste even more so, able to distinguish only between sweet, bitter, sour, and salty. (Taste is

80-90 percent smell.) A hunter sees movement through the foliage, but what is it? In many cases he doesn't know, and adrenalin-pumped hunters are notorious for seeing game animals that aren't there—in rare instances, with tragic consequences. A hunter hears leaves rustling, but determining the precise direction of the sound and whether it is made by a squirrel, a deer, or another hunter can sometimes be impossible. In addition to being crude, indefinite senses, taste and touch require immediate contact with the object being sensed, making their role in hunting virtually nil.

Smell, by contrast, is a very precise sense, even for humans. Biologists in the past suggested that humans could distinguish as many as 10,000 different aromas, but more recent studies suggest that the number is almost infinite. No two substances have identical aromas. One scientist has compared various substances to merchandise with bar codes—each substance has its own bar code, and the human nose/brain can distinguish between any of them. At the same time, smells are almost never forgotten. Poets have long suggested that smell is the most evocative or nostalgic sense, insisting that a rare (or for that matter common) smell from years past can elicit vivid memories from childhood or even infancy. Psychologists agree, citing lab experiments with humans and animals confirming that of all the senses, smell seems most closely linked to memory.

Admittedly some smells—especially those rarely encountered and perceived only faintly—can leave us uncertain about their origin. On the other hand, though we may occasionally not know what we're smelling, we rarely smell something that isn't there or misidentify a smell with which we're familiar. Any adult who is sure he smells a peach that turns out to be an orange, or is confident he smells a banana that turns out to be a wet dog, is probably suffering from some sort of neurological disorder.

So sophisticated is the human nose that science and industry are unable to duplicate it, or even come close to matching its capabilities. While there are several "electronic noses" on the market, their applications are extremely limited. Industries such as the perfume industry, the laundry detergent industry, the wine industry, and others still rely on panels of human judges to analyze the aromas of their products. Experienced doctors, nurses, and medical technicians can often tell by the aroma from a Petri dish or a urine sample exactly which illness a given patient is suffering from. Microscopes or chemical analyses simply confirm what they already strongly suspect. Lab technicians or chemistry teachers who smell high concentrations of toxic or explosive gasses will clear the room without stopping to consult their instruments.

Earlier we suggested that scent is arguably the most direct sense. What that means is that when you detect an odor, you are in direct contact with molecules from the source of the odor. Whether it is the smell of hot asphalt after a summer shower, an orange being peeled, or something the neighbor's dog left on your front lawn, molecules are being released into the air which make their way into the nostrils and adhere, or are "captured" by molecules on a moist patch far inside the nasal cavity. Receptors send a message to the brain, which interprets the aroma. This is a simplified explanation of the process, but it is essentially what happens.

Not every substance has an odor, because not every substance is volatile enough to release molecules into the air in sufficient quantities to be detected. Steel, for instance, does not usually have an aroma, nor does granite or certain synthetic products such as some plastics. Heat, humidity, and air pressure can affect both the rate at which molecules are released and the ability of the nose to detect them. Boiling a substance, for example, can create an aroma where it was not previously detectable, or can transform a slight aroma into a strong one. On the other end of the spectrum, low pressure on airplanes greatly reduces odors—which is one reason airplane food has little flavor.

The part of the brain that interprets smells is a very primitive part of the brain, which is probably why it so easily triggers vivid memories. That is also why it is so closely linked to instinctive behaviors. Some researchers have found, for instance, that human infants less than a week old will react adversely to certain unpleasant smells, and positively to other, apparently more pleasant, smells. There is also evidence that infants can distinguish their mothers' unique smells and even that mothers can distinguish their own infants by their smells. Women, for unknown reasons, appear to have a sense of smell superior to that of men. Smell is also related in unknown ways to emotional well-being. People with *anosmia*—a complete inability to perceive odors as a result of brain injuries or other trauma—are often emotionally depressed. And ridicule it as we might, there is evidence that aromatherapy actually works. Moods can be elevated by the aroma of certain substances such as lavender.

We can reasonably surmise that much of what is true about scent for humans is true for the more complex animals as well, which is to say that it is associated with a primitive part of the brain that involves instinct that once encountered, odors are rarely forgotten, and that certain smells are pleasant while others are unpleasant. One thing we do know is that, sophisticated as the human sense of smell may be, the sense of smell of most higher animals is vastly superior. Some researchers have claimed that the sense of smell for canines and different species such as deer, elk, and moose ranges from six times better than that of humans all the way up to 10,000 times better. But placing a precise number on the difference is not only impossible, it's almost certainly unimportant in practical terms. What is important is the awareness that most animals smell things we don't, and at much greater distances. In the case of any big game species, the nose is much larger than that of a human, and the mucous patch inside the nose that detects smell is considerably larger, as is the portion of the brain that is involved in interpreting odor. Under optimum conditions, white-tailed deer have been observed to react to human body odors from as far away as half a mile.

What are optimum conditions for detecting odors? A general consensus among scientists who have researched the subject is that the sense of smell is best when humidity ranges from 20 to 80 percent, with temperatures between roughly 40 and 90 degrees Fahrenheit, and with winds under 15 miles per hour. Extremely humid conditions, including rain, heavy snow, and even dense fog, tend to reduce dispersal of scent, often driving it to the ground. Arid conditions tend to dry out the nasal passages, preventing scent molecules from adhering to the mucous membranes in the nose. Extreme temperatures can also dry out the nasal passages, as well as affect the volatility of scent-producing substances. Wind is a trickier issue. Little or no wind means that scent disperses slowly, while high winds not only dry out nasal passages but also, presumably, scatter scent molecules widely, often swirling them around in ways that make it difficult to determine the strength or the source of an odor. Thermals are still another issue. As temperatures rise, air currents tend to rise, carrying scents with them. Conversely, falling temperatures tend to create downdrafts. In the absence of wind, such downdrafts can carry the scent of a hunter in a tree stand to the ground, where it spreads away in all directions.

Several things must happen for a smell to be perceived. First, the potential source of the scent must create odors in the form of molecules released into the air. Second, an animal must be in the path of sufficient numbers of those molecules. Third, environmental conditions must be such that the animal has the capability to trap the molecules in its nasal passages and interpret them. Environmental conditions are not typically under the control of hunters, though an awareness of these conditions and how they affect olfaction can help hunters shape their hunting strategies or make judgments about when to be patient and when to hunt more aggressively. The first two factors—the release of scent molecules into the air and the potential location of the game animal in the path of those molecules—can often be controlled, or at least influenced, by hunters, as we will see in subsequent chapters.

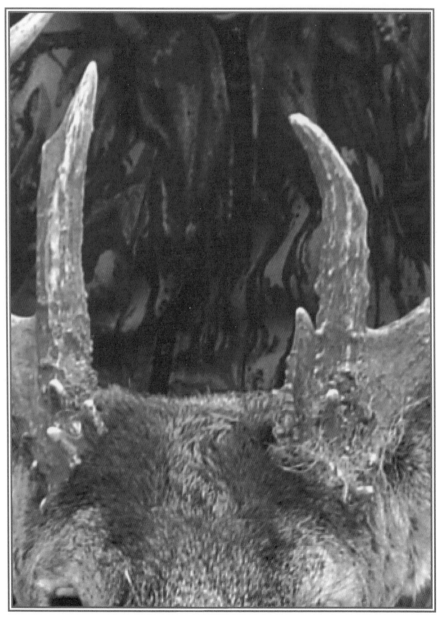

Note the shavings at the base of the brow tine. Biologists believe other deer can tell something about the health and dominance of the buck that makes a rub from scent deposited by the preorbital glands.

2

OLFACTORY COMMUNICATION

With the exception of bears, big cats, and a few others, most game species are highly social creatures, and despite the lack of a complex language, they have a lot to communicate. Animals communicate about food (usually "stay away from mine," but sometimes "come and get it"), territorial boundaries, dominance among males and among females, breeding status, and, of course, danger. They communicate in a variety of ways involving vocalizations, snorts, and other sounds, including stomping their feet and thrashing limbs and brush with their antlers. Visual cues are important forms of communication, too, and include signals such as raising or wagging their tales, staring, standing upright, laying their ears back, making their hair stand up, and others. Of all these forms of communication, though, none is more important than olfactory cues. When you consider that most of these olfactory signals can be received and interpreted for hours and sometimes days by other members of the species in the area, this olfactory communications network enables many animals to keep constant tabs on who is where—not to mention who is currently dominant among males and females, and who is in heat or in rut. It alerts them immediately to the presence of any strangers in the area, and many biologists believe it even gives them an indication of the relative health of individual animals.

Most ruminants (cloven-hoofed animals that chew cud, including deer, elk, moose, caribou, and similar animals) pay particular attention to urine. They rarely pass up fresh urine without checking it out. Deer urine, fox urine, cow urine, or even human urine—it really doesn't matter, all the deer species seem curious about it and will usually stop to scent-check it when they encounter it. These species also leave scent from various glands on various parts of their bodies. Not all glands are related to scent, and there is even some disagreement about whether or not various organs are or are not glands. Beyond that, there is some disagreement about the precise function and the relative importance of various glands. Having said all that, biologists share some widely held theories regarding the different glands that seem to be related to scent and communications, based on observations of behavior and simple deductive reasoning.

GLANDS AND SCENT

Probably the glands with which most hunters are most familiar are those of white-tailed deer. Tarsal glands are located on the inside of the hocks of the hind legs of both bucks and does. Both sexes squat and urinate on these glands during the rut, rubbing their hind legs together. Normally a buff or whitish color, the tarsals turn dark brown or black during this time. This process helps deer locate one another during the rut. Presumably, some combination of secretions from the tarsals, with the urine, offers other deer some indication of another's sexual readiness, and possibly degree of dominance and general health.

Metatarsals appear as small, whitish tufts of hair on the outside of the lower hind legs of bucks and does. Since they have no ducts, technically they are not glands, nor do they produce any known substance. Their purpose is not fully understood, but some observers speculate that they release odors to signal fear or aggression. One of the more interesting theories related to the metatarsals is that, when deer are bedded and the metatarsals are in contact with the ground, they can sense minute vibrations, alerting deer to the approach of anything walking.

The forehead gland is, as you might suspect, located on a buck's forehead between the eyes and the bases of the antlers. When a buck rubs his antlers on trees or shrubs, he leaves behind secretions from these glands as a sort of calling card, announcing his presence to other deer in the area.

Not far from the forehead glands are the preorbital glands, which are located just in front of the eye socket. Their location might suggest they are tear ducts, but they don't produce tears, although they do produce secretions that lubricate and cleanse the eyes. They also produce a waxy substance that, along with the forehead gland secretions, appears to be left behind on trees, branches, and shrubs during rubbing activity, or when bucks are thrashing their antlers in thickets. This substance has a smell similar to that of ammonia, and is strong enough to be easily detected by humans.

Whitetails also possess interdigital glands in the cleft between the front hooves. These emit odors that are left in their tracks, allowing other deer to trail them. Based on observations of the ways bucks react to the trails of does in heat, many biologists believe that the interdigital glands, as well as urine and tarsal glands, offer some indication of the breeding status of does. At the same time, when deer stomp their hooves at unfamiliar, unknown, or threatening objects in the woods, interdigital gland secretions are released in larger quantities that remain on the ground. Many biologists speculate that this scent can alert other deer to danger in the area for hours afterward.

Finally, the Jacob's gland is located on the roof of the mouth. As with many ungulates, it is used by the buck in detecting estrous females. In a behavior called the flehmen response, the buck extends his head and neck and curls back his upper lip for several seconds, which apparently intensifies olfactory stimuli and allows him to detect pheromones present in the urine of does prior to and during peak estrus.

Some, though not all, of these glands are shared by other deer species. Elk do not seem to have interdigital glands, for instance, though they do have tarsals and forehead glands that may leave scent on rubs. Since they engage in the flehmen response, they can be assumed to have the Jacob's gland. (Interestingly, cats also have the Jacob's gland and exhibit flehmen activity.) The saliva of bull elk seems to attract cows and may indicate testosterone levels. Elk also have cheek glands and belly glands. In addition, cows have rump glands. Elk seem to use some of these glands in much the same way as whitetails and engage in rubbing, as well as scraping. Elk use their antlers and their hooves in creating scrapes. When they create scrapes in wet areas, these may become wallows. Bulls urinate in these, as well as on their legs, bellies, and even necks. Then they "wallow," staining themselves dark with this mixture of mud, urine, and glandular secretions, creating an aroma that apparently attracts cows and signals to them—and sometimes to hunters—that here is a sexually mature bull elk.

Moose, too, share some of these glands and engage in similar behaviors. Moose tend to be less social and more territorial, and a mature bull moose may create a deep scrape, often referred to as a rut pit, that may be used year after year. Less is known about caribou, but they do have an interesting gland near their front hooves that appears to give off a strong warning scent when caribou rear up on their hind legs. Pronghorns (which aren't members of the deer family) have cheek glands, and seem to leave scent on various plants that they rub, and also mark territory with urine and feces. As a general rule, males of the larger deer species, such as caribou, elk, and moose, tend to distribute urine over their entire bodies, while smaller deer species disassociate from their urine, except for deliberately urinating on their tarsal glands.

Canines have a variety of glands involved in scent production, as well. Wolves,and foxes, for instance, have scent glands between their toes and a scent gland partway down their tail, often visible on the wolf as a dark patch in the fur.

As you can see, the relationships and functions of all these various glands and behaviors are complex and not fully understood. Biologists have collected some curious bits of information that may be clues to putting the whole puzzle together, but that remain mysteries for now. For instance, whitetail fawns often urinate over their hind legs and rub them together when they are frightened, whereas older bucks and does tend to engage in this behavior to display aggression or dominance. While tarsal glands, interdigital glands, and rub-urination seem to serve the same general function of sexual cues and indicators, the function of the metatarsals, shared by elk as well as white-tailed and mule deer, is less clear. It was once speculated that they released scents to warn other deer of danger, but more recent thinking suggests that deer rely primarily on visual and auditory cues such as snorting, stomping the ground, or raising the tail as warning signals.

RUBBING AND SCRAPING

Although we've made some references to rubbing and scraping, these behaviors are worth a closer look, since they are important to hunters in understanding the activity patterns of the various deer species in a given place and period of time, and in developing hunting strategies, including the use of some scent products.

Though there is some disagreement about the purposes and the significance of rubbing and scraping, biologists (and hunters) have learned a great deal about these behaviors in the last two decades or so. Rubbing activity begins in the later summer, when bucks and bulls begin to lose the velvet from their antlers. In fact, most hunters once believed that rubbing was nothing more than the means by which males of these species got rid of the velvet. That may be one function of rubbing, but it does not explain why animals continue to rub and even to rub more frequently and vigorously, long after the velvet is gone from the antlers. Most experts today accept the theory that rubs are visual, olfactory, and auditory calling cards that indicate the presence of sexually mature bucks or bulls in the area to other members of the species. The various forehead, preoribital, or cheek glands leave scent on the rubs, revealing the identity of the animal that made the rub—or that contributed to it, since in some cases numerous animals use the same rub. It is also possible that these scents, as with urine and tarsal gland secretions, offer some indication of health and relative dominance in the herd. Visual evidence alone can offer hunters some information about the size of an animal that made the rub, but whether other males and females understand the visual information (beyond an awareness that a male of the species made it) is something we can only speculate about. The noise made by a buck or bull as it rubs a tree or thrashes about in saplings certainly conveys its presence to any deer within hearing range, and seems to be an expression of dominance as well.

Scraping activity is a fascinating instinctive behavior. Though deer, elk, and moose occasionally make what appear to be haphazard, casual scrapes, a real scrape is a complex and involved routine. In the case of white-tailed deer, every such scrape is characterized by a licking branch or branches overhead. These are small limbs, usually 4–6 feet above the ground. Typically, a buck approaches a suitable area and begins nuzzling, licking, and sometimes chewing the end of the licking branch. In some cases, the buck will stand on its hind legs to reach higher limbs. All this activity deposits saliva and glandular secretions on the licking branch. Then the buck paws up the ground beneath the licking branch to clear away leaves and scratch down to bare soil. The final step is to squat somewhat, with the hind legs together, and urinate over the tarsal glands and into the scrape, often rubbing the hind legs and tarsal glands together.

There are some important differences in the ways the different species relate to rubs and scrapes. While white-tailed does often visit them, and while white-tailed bucks seem to often scent-check scrapes as they travel past them downwind, elk seem to use them primarily to get dirt, mud, urine, and secretions onto their bodies. Since they range more widely over larger areas, they are less likely to visit the same scrapes repeatedly, with some large wallows representing an exception. More territorial moose, however, not only use the same scrape, or rut pit, often, but may use the same scrape from year to year.

Interestingly, there is some controversy about whether or not mule deer engage in scraping activity at all. They certainly engage in rubbing. Much more so than whitetails, mulies spend a great deal of time displaying dominance by thrashing about noisily with their antlers among shrubs and small saplings, seemingly intent on making as much noise as possible.

PHEROMONES

Pheromones have been hot topics in recent years. Technically speaking, pheromones are chemical substances released by an individual to influence the behavior of, or produce a desired response by, another individual of the same species. Insects in particular are noted for their use of pheromones. Social insects such as bees and ants use them for surprisingly complex forms of communication, like prompting entire communities to leave nest sites in search of new ones. And many insects use pheromones as sexual attractants.

Mammals, humans included, make some use of pheromones as well. When hunters speak of pheromones, they are talking about volatile substances in the urine or glandular secretions of game animals that prompt males to chase females for breeding. In addition, some biologists theorize that pheromones in the urine or the glandular secretions of males actually prompt does into estrus, influencing the timing, intensity, and duration of the rut. In the case of less social creatures such as bears, less is known about how they communicate with scent. Bears are known to create "rubs" of a sort by biting and clawing the bark of trees, and some biologists theorize that this behavior may function in a way similar to the rubs created by the deer species. Certainly male bears can detect the scent of sows approaching estrus.

Though we'll look at this issue again in the chapter on attractant scents, we can't mention pheromones without pointing out one important aspect of these chemical signals: their volatility. Once released, pheromone molecules last for a few minutes at most, before breaking down and becoming odorless.

If we think of game animals as having a sort of wireless communication network, we're probably not too far off the mark. Between urine and various glandular secretions released into the air and deposited in scrapes and rubs, the various deer species are in near-constant contact with one another. Scent keeps them aware of the animals living in the area, as well as any others passing through, and conveys information about age, general health, social position, and breeding status. Scent probably also tells them something about where other animals have been and what they've been eating. For hunters, the question is: how can we plug into this communications network ourselves and use it to help us find game, lure animals into shooting range, or develop a successful hunting strategy?

Biologists believe that visual and olfactory cues like this big whitetail rub convey to local deer a great deal of information about the buck that made it.

Primitive hunters used wind detectors of one sort or another for thousands of years. They're still useful.

3

PLAY THE WIND

It probably wasn't long after the first creatures emerged hesitantly onto land that hunters and prey alike began playing the wind for advantage, circling to get downwind of one another. The game continues today. Knowledge and modern technology are on our side, but a vastly inferior sense of smell leaves bowhunters at a definite disadvantage. Few hunters are so confident in their scent-reduction routine that they believe they can ignore the wind. Let's assume, for the sake of argument, that you arise in the morning, shower with unscented soap and shampoo, dry yourself with a towel washed in unscented detergent and stored, until the moment you step out of the shower, in an airtight container. You remove your clothing from an airtight container and put it on carefully, pick up your gear, spray it and yourself liberally with scent killer, and head out the door. The challenge now is to get from your home or cabin without picking up foreign odors along the way—a virtually impossible task. Granted, you can (and should, if possible) wait until you arrive in your hunting area to don the clothes and use the scent killer. Still, your body begins producing odors from the moment you step out of the shower, and your body, hair, and undergarments are absorbing odors, including many that you are unaware of but that an animal with vastly superior olfactory capabilities will detect. And following such a careful scent-reduction routine is not always possible. For hunters in remote areas, (for instance, hunting from wall tents or spike camps), showering is not usually an option—nor is avoiding smoke, cooking smells, or the odors from fuel, oil, horses, mildewed canvas, or other odiferous items. Believe it: The most consistently successful bowhunters, including those who believe in reducing scent as much as possible (as well as those who don't), always take the wind into consideration in locating their stands or blinds, or in planning stalks and still-hunting strategies. Few would even consider approaching game, or a spot where game is likely to be bedded or feeding, from an upwind location. If stand hunting, they will not hunt a given stand when the wind direction is wrong for that stand. In fact, most of them will get out of a stand and move to another location if they're in a stand and the wind clearly changes direction. They are convinced that this careful attention to wind direction is a key to their success, and that careful and never-failing attention to wind direction is one of the most important distinguishing factors between consistently successful hunters and those who rarely see a mature animal.

Whether the quarry is grizzly bears in Alaska, moose in Manitoba, or whitetails in Texas, wind direction is critical. And as simple as the concept of staying downwind can be, applying it requires knowledge, scouting, and careful planning. Few hunters fully understand how the wind interacts with the land and how prey animals relate to it. Bowhunters who think using the wind is as simple as holding up a wet finger are going to get busted again and again. Unfortunately, it's not that simple, and hunters need to understand prevailing breezes, how terrain affects wind direction, and thermals. Most hunters are aware of a prevailing breeze in their area. In much of the U.S., prevailing breezes come from the southwest. We have one of the most unpredictable and violent climates in the world, largely because energy and moisture are picked up from the Gulf of Mexico, then carried by prevailing breezes to lash coastal areas with hurricanes and to carry torrential rainstorms and sometimes tornados over much of the eastern part of the country. Of course, a southwesterly prevailing breeze simply means that, on a given day, the wind is more likely to come from the southwest than from any other direction. It still sometimes comes from other directions. And prevailing breezes or not, wind direction shifts, as anyone who has ever tried to dodge the smoke from a campfire has learned. (Yes, sitting close to a campfire can create something of a vacuum or an eddy that will seem to draw the smoke, but there is no getting around the fact that wind direction often shifts.)

Adding to the difficulty of staying downwind of game is the way the terrain—hills, ridges, valleys, big rocks, and even trees—affects wind direction. An oft-cited analogy is that of water flowing in a stream. There is an obvious current, but water flows more slowly near the banks than in the deeper parts of the stream. And if you think water always flows downhill, think again. Turns in the course of the stream along with rocks, deadfalls, sandbars, and other structures cause eddies, where the current swirls and even flows against the prevailing direction. At the foot of a falls, a hydraulic is created, sometimes for the width of the stream. Water drops over the falls and goes down, then rises and flows back toward the falls, in an upstream direction, to recirculate. Buoyant objects—including, tragically, people—can be caught in these circular flows indefinitely.

Air currents move in a similar but even more complex manner, flowing around and over obstacles, turning, and sometimes flowing in the opposite direction. Eddies are formed in some places, where the air currents circle continuously. As you might imagine, a hunter in an area in which the air is swirling continuously is likely to be picked off by any game animal that moves through that area. Smart hunters avoid such areas, and some successful hunters locate their stands at or near the tops of hills, or in large expanses of flat country, for that reason. At the same time, air currents differ from water in a stream because the water in a stream, despite the temporary exceptions just cited, flows predictably in the same general direction. Air currents, on the other hand, may flow from the north one day, the southeast on another. The extent to which (and the manner in which) air currents swirl or eddy is dependent upon the direction of the wind at any given time. A stand in a certain valley may be impossible to hunt effectively when prevailing breezes blow, but a properly positioned stand might be a good spot on a day when the wind blows consistently straight down the length of the valley. Further, air currents may rise or fall as temperatures rise or fall—a phenomenon hunters often refer to as thermals. (More about this later.)

One great illustration of the fact that the terrain affects wind direction, often dramatically, can be observed by anyone at a long-range muzzleloader shooting event. Any bullet can be affected by wind, but the relatively lower velocities achieved by traditional muzzleloaders make the wind an even bigger factor. At serious shoots, flags will be placed at regular intervals of 10 or 20 yards so that shooters can dope the wind and adjust their aim accordingly. It's not unusual, especially in hill country, to see a 20-yard flag blowing left to right while the flags at 80 yards and beyond blow right to left.

Animals make use of the wind, and prefer to travel in a way that puts it to their advantage. It's important to keep in mind, though, that if they traveled only into the wind, they'd all wind up in the same location eventually. They travel into it when they can, but they also use a quartering wind, and may travel with the wind when the food source, bedding area, or other objective is downwind from them. Mature animals, in particular, tend to travel along the downwind sides of fields, forest openings, or any potential source of danger, and they often circle downwind of anything they become suspicious of. Big white-tailed bucks are notorious for bedding down near the end of a point with the wind at their backs. If the drop-off is sharp, danger cannot approach from downhill (which is also downwind in this case), and if the drop-off is not sharp, they can see or hear anything approaching from that direction, while, in either case, they will catch the scent of anything approaching from behind. Many mature game animals will select bedding areas in a similar way. Animals don't use the wind exclusively for safety, though. They also use it to keep tabs on one another, and many species are famous for scent-checking trails, food sources, and bedding areas, often moving along downwind of these locations when looking for females as the breeding season approaches.

Hunting to take advantage of the wind becomes something of a chess match, with animals attempting to use it to their advantage as hunters do the same. Given the superiority of most animals' sense of smell, this is a battle the hunter is usually going to lose, but if he doesn't play the game well, it's a battle he will always lose.

WIND AND STAND HUNTING

Game animals are not usually predictable, but their movements are far from random. Animals travel between food sources and bedding areas. They travel to water. Males travel to find females, and under certain conditions, vice versa. All else being equal, they take the path of least resistance, but all else is seldom equal. Their routes are strongly influenced by hills, streams, roads, fences, etc. Safety is always a consideration. Many animals avoid traveling in the open, for instance, though others, such as pronghorns and turkeys, may prefer to stay in the open and will avoid cover, correctly seeing it as a place in which predators hide and from which they can spring ambushes.

The serious stand hunter puts up multiple stands, which will be hunted at various times depending on the date as well as the time of day, or he uses portable stands such as lightweight hang-ons, or climbers, to access the various feeding areas, bedding areas, or travel routes. Many successful hunters, especially bowhunters, look for choke points that tend to funnel the movement of whitetails, mule deer, elk, or other species. One way to play the wind is to simply consider the prevailing breeze and hang a stand on the downwind side of the area through which the hunter expects game to travel. It's important, as we mentioned earlier, to look at the terrain and consider the possibility of eddies and other irregularities in the air currents. An educated guess can usually be made with a quick look around, but the only way to be certain is to get into the stand or blind and test the air with Windfloaters, or a similar item designed to indicate wind direction. (Milkweed pods work very well for this, by the way—pick them in the fall and put them in plastic sandwich bags, then take a pod or two along in your daypack when hunting.) Wind checkers of this sort can reveal some real surprises. In some cases, when dropped from a tree stand or other elevation, they will change course at a certain height and travel a great distance in a totally unpredicted direction.

Bowhunters who stalk game often tie a feather or a piece of thread or fine string to their quiver or some other accessory. The feather or thread will indicate the presence and the direction of even the slightest puff of wind. Wind detectors affixed to the bow or an accessory are well worthwhile for spot-and-stalk or still-hunting, but for hunting from a tree stand something that can be released into the air works better, for the just-stated reason that the air is not necessarily blowing in the same direction at ground level as it is 15 or 20 feet up a tree. Those differences in wind direction at various heights may be one reason why an animal that is directly downwind of a hunter doesn't catch his scent or, conversely, why an animal a hunter thought was upwind did catch his scent.

Taking a stand on what is normally the downwind side of the trail only works, of course, when prevailing breezes blow. That stand must be avoided when the wind blows from the opposite direction, which can be a limiting factor in the case of tree stands or ground blinds. It takes discipline to stay away from a good spot because the wind is wrong. Often, there is another option. If the spot is that hot, the hunter can create two stands, on opposite sides of the trail, funnel, or area through which game is expected to travel. What about crosswinds? In that case, hunters must use their best judgment about the direction from which they expect deer to come, and where their shooting windows are located. If the spot is really that good (if a hunter isn't confident it's that good, he hasn't done enough scouting), then it's a spot worth waiting for, and he probably doesn't want to chance ruining it. In any case, if the wind at a given time seems to be blowing toward likely bedding areas, staging areas, or feeding areas, it's probably best to avoid that stand and wait for more favorable circumstances. Hunters today do have a few options that were unavailable, or at least harder to come by, a few years ago. Tripod stands are more readily available, including some that are suitable for bowhunters. Ground blinds have improved considerably in recent years as well. Both these options free hunters from the need to find fortuitously placed trees for stands, and their mobility—especially in the case of ground blinds—enables hunters to move them quickly and easily in accordance with changes in wind direction.

Wind direction is only one factor to consider when selecting a stand site. Earlier we referred to thermals. Strictly defined, a thermal is a rising current of warm air, but hunters tend to use the term more loosely to refer to cooler, falling air currents, as well as to warmer, rising currents. It is probably not a big factor on windy days, but becomes a huge factor when winds are light to nonexistent. Thermals can affect the hunter in a number of ways. In hilly terrain, for instance, as the sun rises in the morning and the temperature climbs, air will tend to move uphill. In the afternoon, when temperatures begin to drop, air will flow downhill. Consider a stand near the top of a hill, perched uphill from a bench or a hillside trail below. In the morning, when rising air currents lift the air toward the hilltop, it's an excellent stand. Later in the afternoon, as dropping temperatures send the air rolling downhill, it can be a terrible stand.

In a flat area, rising air currents might lift a tree-stand hunter's scent beyond the range of game approaching from any direction, but falling temperatures (again, with no wind) can carry the hunter's scent straight down to the base of the tree, where it may spread out like an upside down mushroom cloud in all directions. It's bad news, especially for the bowhunter, when the Windfloaters drop slowly to the ground immediately below. Height, too, can be a factor, but we'll take a closer look at that in another chapter.

Another option, of course, is the previously mentioned ground blind. Conceivably, fully enclosed ground blinds can contain scent to some degree. More and more blinds are being manufactured with a layer of activated carbon to adsorb scent. Scent-reducing products can be sprayed on those that lack carbon. Naturally, ground blinds should be stored in areas where they are unlikely to be contaminated with the smell of gasoline, engine exhaust, paint or paint thinners, or smoke. Ideally, they'll be set up in position at least a few days prior to their use, to dissipate any smells they may have absorbed.

Not too many years ago—well within my memory, I'm afraid—hunters ventured into the woods without benefit of tree stands or manufactured ground blinds. They walked to their spot and sat, or stood, against a tree, watching for game. Few bowhunters still use this approach, though some do prefer to use natural cover or improvised blinds. In some cases, deer hunters are placed ahead of hunters who are driving deer, but, whatever the circumstances, these hunters need to give special attention to reducing scent and playing the wind.

So far we've talked about selecting a stand site, and using it, with the wind in mind. Before hunters can use a stand, though, they have to get to it. A surprising number of hunters who select their stand sites carefully give little thought to accessing them. It does little good for a hunter to select the perfect site for a stand if he alerts every animal in the area to his presence on the way to that stand. Approaching a stand without spooking game obviously requires some knowledge of the area and how game animals use it. A stand over or very close to a feeding area can be impossible to access in the morning, when game animals are more likely to be in the area. Most experienced deer hunters are reluctant to use stands that are close to bedding areas, except close to the rut, or late in the season, when it's time to pull out all the stops and hunt aggressively. Even then, many hunters think of these stands as early morning stands. They access them early, well before first light, in hopes of catching a big buck returning to its bedding area in the morning.

Regardless of whether it's a morning stand or an evening stand, hunters have to be aware of what is between their cabin, camp, or vehicle, and the stand itself. Ideally, they'll want to approach a stand from downwind. Beyond that, though, they'll want to avoid blundering through (or immediately upwind of) bedding areas, feeding areas, or large openings of any kind. They'll also want to avoid walking down trails, or through funnels of any kind, whether these are choke points between fields, trails running between streams and meadows, or crossings at creeks or fences. In short, the idea is to avoid spooking game or leaving scent in areas that game animals use regularly. It may be impossible to avoid all these situations entirely, but certainly hunters can avoid walking directly down a trail, for instance. When crossing a trail, they can step over it instead of on it. It's also preferable to avoid thickets. Wading through thick brush and waist-high weeds is not only noisy, but it also leaves scent on everything touched. If this seems to contradict the notion of avoiding trails, it sometimes does. Animals, like people, tend to take the path of least resistance, and any route a hunter chooses is one an animal might choose as well. It's a matter of judgment when the noise and extra scent left on thick brush and weeds is worse than the scent that might be left on a logging road or trail.

One highly effective route, when available, is a small stream. A wading hunter leaves little or no scent, can usually move very quietly (especially where running water masks sounds), and often is hidden as well by stream banks or thick vegetation growing along the stream edge. Another little trick many hunters use when approaching their stand is to deliberately step in droppings from game, cattle, sheep, or other animals. The idea, of course, is that this tends to cover any foreign odors that might be on the boots. It's even possible that animals will follow the scent of droppings, particularly droppings from their own species, making this technique a way of laying down a scent trail.

When feasible, using vehicles is an ideal way to access a stand, especially in ranch or farm country where game animals are accustomed to seeing vehicles and feel unthreatened by them. Depending on the type of vehicle, one hunter can carry one or more other hunters to their stands, letting them hop off as close as possible to the stand, thereby creating the smallest amount of scent contamination in the area. Many commercial hunting operations, especially those where much of the hunting is done over food plots, insist on driving hunters directly to the stand, and insist hunters not leave the stand until the truck returns to pick them up. There are usually animals in or near the food plots, and the guides would prefer to run them off with the truck, as opposed to having them spot hunters entering the area or leaving the stand. It's not unusual, especially at dusk, for a food plot to be full of white-tailed deer, but any game animal won't need to be spooked off by a hunter exiting his stand many times to associate that stand with danger and begin avoiding it or even looking into it for danger every time it enters that food plot. At the same time, this approach keeps scent contamination to an absolute minimum. The lone hunter on an ATV might not want to park his vehicle close to his stand, but even if he parks it 100 or 200 yards away, he will have avoided leaving scent up to that point.

Planning a route to a stand is almost always a matter of compromise and judgment, and there is rarely a perfect way to do it. It is always worthwhile to access a stand in as unobtrusive a way as possible, though. Hunters who always take the straightest or easiest route, without regard to wind direction or any of the other factors mentioned, are greatly reducing their chances of seeing game.

STILL HUNTING

Still hunting is practiced by some hunters anywhere there is cover and animals to hunt. Effective still hunters usually move at a snail's pace, but even moving slowly, mobility gives them the opportunity to take maximum advantage of the wind. Assuming they've scouted the area, they can, and should, plan a route that will allow them to approach trails, funnels, food sources, or bedding areas from a downwind (or quartering) position. Game animals, especially mature ones, tend to keep a careful eye out downwind, knowing they are vulnerable from that direction. As previously mentioned, big white-tailed bucks are notorious for bedding near the end of points where the wind is at their backs, alert for warnings that a predator is approaching from that direction. Other species do it, too. Still, defeating the eyes of almost any animal is considerably less challenging than defeating its nose. (One clear exception here might be pronghorns.) Still hunters, no less than stand hunters, need to be aware of the effects of terrain on wind direction, as well as thermals and other factors.

FUNNELING ANIMALS WITH SCENT

Some might consider it a risky strategy—and it is—but more than one bowhunter has intentionally used human scent to funnel deer or other species and put them in shooting range. By strategically hanging recently worn socks or T-shirts from fence posts or trees, savvy hunters can sometimes steer game in their direction, causing animals to skirt downwind of travel lanes or choose one trail, choke point, or food plot over another. For the frustrated bowhunter who knows game is moving through an area but can't quite seem to get within bow range, such a strategy might make the difference. It's not a strategy to try, though, without a thorough knowledge of how game travels through a given area.

4

GETTING ABOVE
IT ALL

Could defeating the nose of a wary game animal be as simple as getting high enough above it that any scent originating from hunters or their gear will travel over its head? Southeastern Indiana whitetail hunter Johnny Webber, who has taken more Pope & Young bucks than most hunters have even seen, is convinced that in many situations, high stands can carry a hunter's scent over the head of his quarry, and he is hardly alone. He might be in a minority, though, as numerous organizations and individuals disagree, suggesting that tree stand heights as low as 12 feet or less are more than adequate. The question arises: if height doesn't matter, why do hunters want to get off the ground at all? In fact, the case can be made (and I'm among those who would make it), that deer hunters at heights under 14 feet usually are better off on the ground. For elk, make that 16 feet. (Tree stand manufacturers' stated heights refer variously to height-to-foot platform, height-to-seat, or height-to-shooting rails, and are often unclear about which. For the sake of clarity, the numbers we're using refer to height-to-foot platform.)

The main question we want to examine pertains to height as it relates to scent, but hunters at reduced heights are well within a game animal's field of vision and have simply positioned themselves above the ground cover, where they're far more exposed and where the slightest movement is almost sure to be detected. Any scent control measures a bowhunter might take would be undermined by this greatly increased visibility. It may be true that for the firearm hunter, the better vantage point is in itself a sufficient advantage, but for the bowhunter, who must allow any potential target to get relatively close and must get to full draw without movement being spotted, the advantages of a higher vantage point alone are less important. Visually speaking, how high does a hunter have to be to put himself above the peripheral vision of game animals? I'm unaware of any scientific studies of the issue, but experience suggests to me that at heights of 16 feet or more, hunters are significantly less likely to be spotted by game. Hunters like Johnny Webber like to get even higher.

Scent is a more complicated issue, but as we've seen, air currents tend to move over the landscape in much the way water flows over a streambed. Currents flow around and over obstructions, often forming eddies and backwashes. To further complicate the picture, air currents are subject to thermals, which for practical purposes we can define as the tendency for warm air to rise and cooler air to fall. Thermals are of greater concern when the air is still, of less concern when there is a steady breeze.

Several indicators would seem to suggest that height can offer advantages in terms of scent, in some cases if not in all cases. First is the testimony of many very successful hunters who believe that height matters. Granted, it's anecdotal evidence, and not particularly scientific. On the other hand, the observations, experience, and judgment of experienced hunters are always worth serious consideration.

Various kinds of wind floaters, too, often seem to indicate that air currents may carry scent over the heads of game, at least game that is nearby. Hunters who have never used them are often amazed at what happens when they are dropped from the height of a tree stand. As we mentioned in the chapter on playing the wind, Windfloaters may move steadily in one direction, gradually falling, but nearly as often they rise, then fall, then rise again. It is not unusual to drop detectors that move off in one direction, then drop detectors two minutes later that move in the opposite direction. It's not even that unusual to have detectors that travel twenty or thirty feet at one altitude, only to turn and move in the opposite direction when they drop to a lower altitude. Sometimes, though, they maintain their altitude for some distance. In those cases, it would not seem unreasonable to speculate that any scent originating from a hunter or his gear would likewise maintain its altitude for some distance, sweeping over the heads of any nearby game. Imagine an animal approaching from downwind and stopping broadside in a shooting lane long enough for a lucky bowhunter to harvest the animal. Was it the carbon suit that caused the animal to fail to catch the hunter's scent? The scent reduction spray he applied twenty minutes earlier? The fact that he kept his clothes in a scent-proof bag and donned them only after arriving in the woods? Or did a combination of his height and prevailing breezes carry his scent over the animal's head? The answer could easily be some combination of factors, but we can't rule out the latter possibility.

Consider another possible bit of evidence. Most experienced bowhunters prefer to place tree stands on high ground, on or near the top of a ridge when possible. There are several reasons for that, but one often-stated reason is that air currents are much more predictable on hilltops, and much less likely to change directions frequently or swirl around. The preference for tree stands on high ground evolved over many years and countless man-hours of sitting in tree stands and observing that deer and other game animals were significantly more likely to detect hunters taking stands in valleys or on the lower parts of hillsides than on ridge tops or high ground. In all likelihood, the reasons stated for the difference are correct. Still, it seems very possible there is another reason. It could be that, wind direction or eddying effects notwithstanding, the scent of hunters is more likely to be carried over the heads of game animals when hunters are sitting stands on high ground, as opposed to low-lying areas.

One issue that is sure to arise when it comes to the optimum height for tree stand hunters is shot angle. The argument is that severe shot angles make it more difficult to achieve the double-lung shots bowhunters strive for. That is a legitimate concern. It's also true, though, that even from a height of 10 or 12 feet, an animal directly under the stand presents an almost vertical shot angle. Similarly, a 10-foot stand on the side of a hill may easily put a hunter in a situation of making a steep shot at an animal on the downhill side of the stand. And even on level or gently sloping terrain, the shot angle is a function of the distance from the stand, as well as the height of the stand. Predicting the precise course of travel for any game animal is difficult, but regardless of stand height, hunters should avoid putting stands of any kind right on top of a game trail, scrape, rub line, feeding spot, or other place in which animals are expected to travel or offer shot opportunities.

None of this is intended to suggest that climbing to great heights is a sure ticket to success, or that it can be a substitute for good site selection or basic hunting skills. Climbing to heights at which a hunter is uncomfortable is never a good idea, although for many hunters, this is partly a matter of how easily the stand can be accessed.

The increasing popularity of ladder stands in recent years is largely a function of an aging population of hunters who find ladder stands easier to get in and out of, and feel safer in these stands than in other styles of tree stands.

In any case, the bowhunter who can get comfortable with heights, and who is prepared to take all the necessary safety precautions, including using a safety harness at all times, may find that a height of 16 feet or more will enable him to get more shot opportunities at close-up, relaxed animals that have neither seen him nor gotten his scent.

The Division of Wildlife in many states insists that it is not necessary to climb higher than 12 – 15 feet to achieve most if not all the benefits of hunting from a tree stand. They're not alone; a number of organizations and individuals make similar statements. For the most part I suspect these statements are motivated by safety concerns. Safety is certainly a paramount interest. Climbing in and out of, as well as hunting from, tree stands is the most dangerous thing most hunters do. An alarming number of hunters will fall from tree stands in their hunting careers, and an alarming number of these falls result in serious injuries and death. Frighteningly, among the more common injuries are head, neck, and spinal cord injuries resulting in paralysis. Hunters should never climb above heights at which they are comfortable, should use only tree stands approved by the Treestand Manufacturer's Association (look for the TMA tag), and should always use a safety harness, keeping in mind that the majority of falls occur when hunters are climbing up to or down from stands. That is true regardless of the height of the stand. Serious injuries can and do occur even from reduced heights of 12 feet or less. When it comes to tree stand safety, hunters must exercise their own good judgment, and never exceed their comfort level. At the same time, many experienced bowhunters are convinced that heights of 16 feet or more—some would say 20 feet or more—offer significant advantages.

Why use tree stands if height doesn't matter? Safety is paramount, but there are advantages in getting above the line of sight. At eight to twelve feet, hunters are arguably better off on the ground.

5

YOU ARE WHAT
YOU EAT

It's no secret that hunters stink. The simple explanation for why we stink is that we perspire, and that bacteria in the perspiration cause odors. That is true, but it is also true that some of us produce a great deal more odor than do others. Further, we all smell very different. In some cases, the differences are detectable to other people. American World War II vets who fought in the Pacific noted a strong, fishy smell among captured Japanese soldiers on some islands—not surprising, since in some cases they were surviving on a diet that was limited almost exclusively to fish. In Vietnam, Vietcong and North Vietnamese soldiers could sometimes smell the presence of U.S. soldiers because their diets were relatively high in dairy products and meat. Among cultures that consume very few dairy products, people who regularly eat butter, milk, cheese, and similar products have a very identifiable odor.

The fact is that high-protein foods in general do produce more body odor. They're not the only culprits, though. The same can be said for onions, garlic, caffeine, most highly processed foods, alcohol, tobacco, and many other substances. In addition, various enzyme deficiencies, digestive irregularities, metabolic disorders, illnesses, diseases, and even injuries can cause or contribute to odors. Dogs are currently being trained to literally sniff out various types of cancer, and can even detect bladder cancer in urine. (We haven't mentioned breath odor, but the same principles apply.)

Probably the individuals with the least body odor are vegans—those who eat only fruits and vegetables and consume no meat, fish, dairy products, or eggs. One obvious way for hunters to greatly reduce their body odor, then, would be for all of us to become vegans. As my teenagers say: "Like that's gonna happen." I think it unlikely that anyone reading this book is going to radically alter his diet in order to reduce body odor. Still, there are some less extreme, perfectly sane steps we can take to help stop body odor at the source. Which of these steps hunters might consider reasonable, and which might be considered over-the-top, are matters of personal choice, but I will present some options without endorsement or censure.

While few hunters will want to significantly alter their diets, many hunters do make slight changes in their diets during hunting season. For instance, many hunters consider it to be only common sense to avoid eating garlic or onions the night before hunting. A few will go a step further and avoid eating meat the day before a hunt. There is reason to doubt, though, that avoiding meat for one day prior to a hunt will sufficiently alter body chemistry to have a significant effect.

DIETARY SUPPLEMENTS

While certain substances are known to increase body odors, others can significantly reduce them. One dietary supplement commonly recommended for controlling body odor and breath odor is zinc. Next to iron, zinc is the most common trace metal in the bloodstream. It is involved in so many bodily processes that zinc deficiencies can cause everything from inhibited growth to hair loss, delayed sexual maturation, reduced immune system functioning, cataracts, macular degeneration, and tooth decay, just to name a few. Zinc is highly involved in regulating various metabolic functions, and metabolic functions are certainly related to body odor. This could be one of the reasons zinc supplements can reduce body odor. Another reason is that zinc seems to be a natural antimicrobial. Its presence in perspiration reduces the growth of bacteria that produce odors. Zinc supplements are readily available in most drug stores, and zinc is included in varying degrees in virtually all multivitamins. Though it's a rare condition, it is possible to suffer from zinc toxicity if zinc is ingested in sufficient quantities.

Another substance commonly used in odor control is chlorophyll. Chlorophyll is the substance that makes green plants green. It has an oxidizing effect on many substances, chemically combining with molecules to eliminate odor. Chlorophyll, like zinc, is available in most drug or nutrition supplement stores and is included in a few multivitamin supplements, including Sportsmen's Edge. Nullo, another commercially available product marketed specifically at hunters, employs chlorophyll as its main active ingredient. The Body Shield Deodorant Pill from Robinson Labs includes chlorophyll, as well as alfalfa and parsley. Similar commercial products are coming out so quickly that they are difficult to keep up with, but other naturally occurring substances said to reduce odor include selenium, found in many multivitamins, cilantro, sage, rosemary, thyme, and various other herbs and spices.

Generally speaking, the same principles that apply to body odor also apply to the breath. Obviously in the case of breathing, there is no perspiration in which bacteria can form. Still, odors from inside the body—including the digestive system as well as the lungs, throat, sinuses, and inside of the mouth—are detectable in the breath. In the medical profession, certain illnesses or diseases are often associated with specific odors in the breath. Ingesting various substances can greatly reduce these odors by altering the chemistry in the mouth, throat, and digestive system. A Wisconsin company called Hunting Science produces Gum-O-Flage, a chewing gum whose primary active ingredient is chlorophyll, and Scent Shield offers a similar product called Breath Shield Deodorant Gum. The idea is to neutralize breath odor while hunting.

Simply brushing the teeth can greatly reduce the amount of bacteria present in the mouth, but some hunters worry that minty toothpastes merely replace one odor with another. Whether or not game animals associate these minty odors with hunters is a reasonable question; in areas where humans are frequently encountered, that may be a possibility. The solution to the problem might be as simple as baking soda, which is still a primary ingredient in some toothpastes. Baking soda is a mild abrasive that cleans the teeth and reduces odor by neutralizing acids in the mouth. Gargling with baking soda increases its effectiveness. Some of the odor reducers marketed to hunters for spraying on clothing and boots, etc., contain baking soda as a main ingredient, and many companies suggest gargling with the product, as well as spraying it on clothing.

Having just arrived for his afternoon post, author Rick Combs changes into his hunting clothes that he kept in a sealed bag. This is a good step to help reduce human odor when afield.

6

CLOTHES AND SCENT CONTROL

Increasing numbers of manufacturers are incorporating scent-reducing materials or products of various kinds in their clothing, and we'll take a closer look at these in the next chapter. The fact is, clothing plays an important role in scent control totally apart from any scent-reducing chemicals or materials that may be added to them, and in this chapter we'll take a look at the selection, treatment, and use of hunting clothing in general as it pertains to scent control.

Clothes are linked to scent control in several important ways. In the most basic way, clothing affects how much hunters perspire, how rapidly that perspiration evaporates, and how much of the perspiration is absorbed and held by the clothing. Cotton, for instance, is relatively light and very comfortable, but it absorbs perspiration. When it gets wet, it prevents evaporation and holds perspiration against the body, creating an ideal habitat for odor-causing bacteria. Synthetics such as polypropylene do a better job of wicking moisture away from the body, thereby creating a less ideal environment for bacteria. Some manufacturers object to terminology such as "wicking," insisting that synthetic materials do no such thing. Call it what you will—these materials do not absorb moisture, and the result is that perspiration and moisture vapor evaporate, as opposed to being trapped and held against the skin. Several companies are offering undergarments, under trade names such as Baselayers, that do an excellent job of keeping hunters dry under even the most extreme conditions. This not only helps control odor, but also keeps hunters more comfortable—cooler in warm conditions and warmer in cold weather.

LAYERING

Layering is a concept familiar to most hunters. It is a way to stay adaptable to changing temperatures and activity levels, and to stay comfortable and warm by staying dry. It is virtually impossible for hunters to stay warm in frigid conditions if they get wet from perspiration. Add a breeze and subsequent wind chill effect to the situation, and hunters who are wet with perspiration can get dangerously cold in even relatively mild conditions. Modern synthetic layers let moisture escape to outer layers, where it can evaporate, and layers can be removed or added as temperatures or activity levels change. Warmth aside, though, layering tends to help reduce body odor for the same reason it keeps hunters warm: Dry skin provides a poor environment for bacteria. A typical layering system for hunters these days might include polypro underwear and socks, a synthetic shirt and pants, a fleece jacket, possibly with some sort of wind stopping fabric, and a parka that contains a waterproof/breathable fabric or wool. At milder temperatures, the hunter might wear the same outfit minus the parka, while in extremely cold conditions, a down or heavy Thinsulate insulated parka might be substituted for the waterproof/breathable parka. In truly mild or warm weather, or in situations where hunters expect to be very active, they might eliminate the polypro long johns and wear something like Baselayers instead. Another option is to wear the Baselayers beneath the long johns for maximum wicking. Another variation for cold weather entails thin liner socks of synthetic material or silk, with an outer layer of wool socks or socks containing a blend of wool and nylon. Wool, by the way, has experienced a well-deserved rebound of late. It's extremely warm, breathes, sheds a light rain, is quiet, and does not tend to absorb odors.

Layering makes sense and is effective, but it has its limitations. It isn't always practical to be continually shedding and reapplying layers as activity levels and temperatures change. Then there is the issue of having to carry all those clothes after you've taken them off. One way to mitigate the need for adding or reducing layers is to wear vented clothing. The better garments—particularly outer garments—can be vented. Tops can be partially or wholly unzipped, sleeve cuffs can be loosened, and in some cases vents under the arms can be opened. All these can be closed for protection from wind, rain, and colder temperatures, or opened to vent moisture as activity levels increase.

LAUNDERING HUNTING GARMENTS

Any clothing can absorb perspiration odor to some extent and if not cleaned can retain odor that game will detect. Scent-free laundry detergents are among the more familiar hunting products these days, and most of them do an excellent job. Hunters should note, though, that warm water is significantly more effective at cleaning fabrics than is cold water. However, warm water can shrink, fade, or otherwise damage some hunting garments. It's important to follow the manufacturers' laundering instructions, but it's a good idea to use water that is as warm as permissible. Many scent-free detergent makers suggest cleaning the washing machine—either by running a cycle of plain water through, or running the machine empty with a little of the detergent in it prior to washing the clothes—to prevent contamination from scented detergent. The same applies to dryers. Air drying hunting clothing is not always practical or effective for a number of reasons, but the residue from scented fabric softener sheets can contaminate clothes. Sprinkling a little baking soda in the dryer can reduce that problem.

RUBBER AND LATEX

Ron Boyce, a biologist and formerly a chemist with MDR Outdoor Group, tells hunters that if they can do only one thing to reduce their scent, it should be to wear rubber boots: "Direct contact with the ground, with grass, and with weeds is the primary source of scent contamination from hunters. Just wearing rubber boots can go a long way toward eliminating that problem." Ironically, rubber boots do contribute to foot odor, since they don't allow perspiration to evaporate from the feet. Sooner or later that odor is going to get out the tops of the boots. Spraying deodorant on the feet can delay the onset of the problem. Sprinkling a little baking soda inside the boots can help, also.

Hunters who are serious about scent control generally tend to keep a pair of rubber or latex gloves in their daypack. They use these when climbing into a stand, or when handling decoys, creating mock scrapes or rubs, or setting up ground blinds.

STORAGE

From the moment clothing is cleaned and dried, it begins absorbing odors. The only way to prevent this is to seal garments in an airtight, scent-free container. Some bags are sold specifically for this purpose. As soon as the clothes are removed from the bag, they once again begin absorbing odors. Any time and effort devoted to making the clothes scent free can easily be wasted by the hunter who dresses at home before the hunt. Odors from kitchens, pets, garages, vehicles, diners, or gas stations—all these and more can, and probably will, contaminate clothing. The only way to prevent this from happening is to keep the clothes stored in the bag until you arrive at the hunt site, then change. I used to find this cumbersome, but soon learned that it works, and I am much more comfortable in my street clothes while driving to, and especially from, the hunt. Now it's just part of my routine, and at the end of the hunt I find that I look forward to getting out of my hunting clothes and back into my "civies." In many situations this isn't practical, but to the extent possible, hunters should try to keep at least their outermost garments free from contamination. If hunting out of a cabin or lodge, for instance, it might be possible to keep parkas, bibs, or pants in a mudroom or on a porch, where they are less exposed to cooking and other odors.

ULTRAVIOLET

Is it possible that bowhunters are devoting time, money, and effort to making their clothing scent free, but ignoring the fact that it glows like a neon light in the forest? The probability that deer and some other big game animals can see ultraviolet light, at least in low-light conditions, is not news—it has gained renewed attention in recent years as the U.S. garment-making industry has been all but eliminated. The bulk of our clothing, including hunting clothing, is now made overseas, primarily in Asian countries, and much of it reaches the United States after having been treated with ultraviolet brighteners, despite the best efforts of the companies that market these garments.

That word "probability" in the second sentence is not used carelessly. Not everyone accepts as fact that deer or other game animals can distinguish clothing treated with UV brighteners from clothing that is not. It is widely accepted that insects and fish can see into the UV spectrum, and that most mammals cannot. A 1992 study by biologists at Georgia State University determined that the eyes of white-tailed deer lack a filter, present in humans, that blocks out UV rays. Presumably some other big game animals with vision that is similar to those of deer in other respects lack this same filter. To my knowledge, no behavioral studies have been undertaken to test the specific ability of deer to detect UV brighteners. Various ads and demonstrations showing UV-treated clothing glowing under black lights are dramatic but hardly conclusive, since we don't normally hunt deer at night, let alone using black lights. At the same time, our fathers and grandfathers hunted deer successfully for many years, often wearing UV-treated clothing.

That is not proof that animals don't see UV-treated clothing any more than demonstrations of hunting jackets glowing under black lights is proof that animals do see UV-treated clothing.

Here is what we do know: The structure of the eyes of white-tailed deer indicates that they have the ability to see into the UV range of the color spectrum. This may allow them to distinguish UV-treated clothing from its surroundings, especially in low-light conditions, which is when deer are most active. Should hunters take this issue seriously enough to purchase UV elimination products, launder their clothing only in detergents without UV brighteners, and avoid hunting in clothing that may have been treated with UV brighteners? That is a personal decision. For hunters who insist on seeing hard evidence of effectiveness before investing their time and money in a product, the answer might be no. For hunters who like to leave nothing to chance, the answer is yes.

7

BEHIND THE LABELS: BASIC TYPES OF SCENT REDUCTION PRODUCTS

Here is the thing: dogs can be trained to find an explosive material, sealed in plastic, buried in the ground, and untouched for years. They do it routinely in war-torn areas where land mines have been used indiscriminately. For that matter, I'm still impressed when my brittany goes dashing at full speed 15 or 20 yards past a small clump of cover, only to slam on the brakes, do a 180, and lock up on point. A single bobwhite quail might be in that clump of cover—a lone, non-smoking, non-perspiring little bird that did not wash with scented shampoo that morning, or eat garlic at dinner or bacon for breakfast, or stop to pump gas on his way to the field, or—well, you get the point. Everything produces some odor, and dogs, along with most of the animals we hunt, have incredible olfactory abilities. I will refrain from enumerating all the possible sources of odor on the human body. Are you skeptical that it is possible for a hunter to truly eliminate his scent, even for a short while? I am.

The real question, I believe, is not whether it is possible to entirely eliminate odor. The real question for bowhunters is whether or not it is possible to reduce odor sufficiently to give hunters an edge they would not otherwise have. Would you wash with unscented soap every time you went hunting if it meant that on one occasion you might slip within 35 yards of a bedded mule deer buck, instead of getting picked off at 55 yards? Would you wear an odor eliminating outfit including hat and headnet day after day if it meant that sometime in the next three years a 160-class whitetail buck might stop for 3 seconds at 25 yards before running off, as opposed to turning and running without a pause when it got to 30 yards? Realistically, chances are you will never know for sure if the bear you just arrowed would have turned and run before offering a shot had you not sprinkled baking soda in your boots or used non-scented detergent to wash your parka.

It is difficult to be certain about the degree of effectiveness of these and other products in a given situation for several reasons. Little truly independent research has been done on the subject. Scent, as we have seen, is a matter of volatile (gaseous) molecules being carried through the air to the sensory organs, in this case nasal passages, of an animal. While the technology and methodology may exist to determine the concentration of these molecules in a given controlled area, few independent labs with the necessary resources have to date had sufficient motivation to conduct the kind of research that would provide useful information to hunters. Further complicating things, hunters are dealing with biology and uncontrolled conditions, not machines in a lab. A machine may indicate the concentration of various molecules in an enclosed space, but that does not tell us how those molecules behave in a forest or on a prairie. It also doesn't tell us at what level of concentration a given species under given circumstances can detect those molecules, or how it will react to various concentrations of them.

What hunters have mostly relied upon, then, is common sense and anecdotal evidence accumulated by hunters in the field. I'll confess a bias: I'm highly skeptical of common sense. For thousands of years common sense told us the earth is flat and the sun circles it. Science came along to tell us the earth is round and it circles the sun, and I'm inclined to go with science. Having said, that I would nonetheless point out that I am sure I will smell my hunting partner more quickly, from further away, and with a more noticeable reaction, after a week in elk camp than was the case on the first day of the hunt. Is it unreasonable to suspect that the same is true for most game animals? Anecdotal hunting evidence is far from perfect, but it is evidence and should not be ignored, especially in the absence of other evidence. And anecdotal evidence suggests that scent reduction can make a difference. Virtually every consistently successful bowhunter I know makes some effort to reduce or control scent in some way.

Not all the anecdotal evidence available on the subject comes from hunters. Among the more convincing sources of evidence are trappers. Though I've done very little trapping personally, as a hunter I've long been fascinated by it. If hunters are concerned about odor control and the use of scent, successful trappers seem to be obsessed with it. Evidence from trappers strikes me as particularly convincing for the reason that trapping by nature tends to reduce or eliminate many of the variables involved in hunting. For instance, if I'm hunting an elk wallow, a bull approaches, stops momentarily, then retreats into the brush, any number of things might explain the behavior. Did he catch my scent in the air? Did he come across scent I left on the ground as I approached the wallow? Did he see me? Hear me? Did another animal scare him off or warn him of my presence? I will probably never know. In the case of trapping, most of these variables would not apply. Some trappers run trap lines daily through the season, and almost all of them over the years experiment with a variety of locations and trap sets. Further, much as most of them enjoy trapping, trapping is hard work, and many trappers are looking for supplemental income. They tend to do what works, with as little wasted time and effort as possible. The fact that almost all of them are convinced careful scent control is a major factor in their success is telling.

Somewhere out there, perhaps, is a consistently successful bowhunter who pays no attention to scent control. I just haven't met him. Imperfect though the evidence may be, thousands upon thousands of hunters have logged countless hours in the field and have come to the conclusion that taking some measures to reduce scent while hunting is worth the effort and the expense.

SOURCES OF ODOR

When hunters talk about controlling odor, they are talking about two things. One involves the odors with which they or their clothing and gear may be contaminated, including soaps and shampoos, shaving creams, lotions, ointments, smoke, gas fumes, oils, mothballs, foods and beverages, cooking odors, and any other substance that hunters or their gear may come in contact with. For that matter, the clothing or gear may itself emit odor. The sources of most of these odors are clear enough. They are in our kitchens, our bathrooms, our garages, basements, and even storage sheds. When we leave home, they may be in our cars and trucks, in the diners we stop in for breakfast, in the gas stations where we stop for gas. Sometimes, they are just plain in the air around us.

Another type of odor is the one produced continuously by hunters' bodies and their breath, or more specifically by various secretions and the action of bacteria on these secretions. Most perspiration is produced by eccrine glands that cover the entire body, and has little if any odor, consisting primarily of water and a few salts.

Apocrine glands, however, produce perspiration that is much higher in fats and proteins. These fats and proteins, along with hair, dead skin, and other detritus form a rich medium for bacteria, and it is the action of these bacteria on the fats and other ingredients of perspiration that causes most body odor. In effect, apocrine glands are human scent glands. Most are located in the armpits and the pubic areas. (Interestingly, some of us have more apocrine glands than do others. Asian populations, for instance, have far fewer apocrine glands, and in some cases none at all. In Japan, body odor is considered a medical condition.) It is no accident, of course, that the areas of the body containing apocrine glands tend to be covered in hair. Hair contributes to an environment favorable for the formation of odor-causing bacteria, and holds odor. Laugh if you like at those hard-core trophy hunters out there who shave their underarms during hunting season—I know I do—but they may be on to something. I haven't yet got up the nerve to ask them if they shave their groin areas, also.

We can speculate about whether body odors or contaminant scents are more important, and which of these odors animals may or may not associate with humans or with danger, but the simplest and safest course of action for any hunter concerned about scent control is to try and keep all odors to an absolute minimum. Knowing how best to do this requires a basic understanding of how various scent reduction products work. Though manufacturers like to imply that their products will reduce or eliminate any form of scent, the fact is that some are better suited to reducing body odors at its source, while others are better suited for applying to clothing and other gear. At the time of this writing, scent control is a rapidly growing part of the hunting industry and new technology, much of it borrowed from medical and other applications, is developing so rapidly that it is difficult to stay abreast of it. Much of what follows is to some extent a sort of snapshot of the industry as it exists today.

Start Clean, Stay Clean

There is no scent reduction product that cannot be overwhelmed at some point. Scent control begins with getting clean and staying as clean as possible, and it only stands to reason that the cleaner the hunter, the less chance for any scent control product to fail. In fact, the scent-control regimen of some very successful hunters is as simple as washing themselves and their clothing thoroughly in scent-free soaps or detergents. Starting clean is easy enough, but staying clean is more challenging. What often happens is that hunters work up a

Whenever possible, keep hunting clothes in sealed containers until it's time to hunt. Apply scent reducers right before hunting.

sweat getting to their stand (or into their stand). Leaving off the parka or jacket until getting settled into a stand can alleviate that problem. Increasing numbers of bowhunters prefer ladder stands and ground blinds, partly because we bowhunters are an aging population. In the process, they are discovering that not only are ladder stands and ground blinds easier and safer, but getting into them is also quicker and quieter, and does not require working up a sweat, especially compared to climbers.

THE CHEMISTRY BEHIND THE PRODUCTS

Essentially, there are three types of commercially produced products intended to reduce odors. These are 1) antimicrobials, designed to prevent the formation of certain odors by killing or inhibiting the growth of bacteria that cause these odors, or by neutralizing acidity 2) products designed to prevent the formation of the gas molecules that form odors, or which create a chemical reaction such as oxidation, to destroy odors, and 3) products with materials such as activated carbon that adsorb odors. Some products combine two of these types of scent control, and by using various layers of clothing or different types of scent control products, many hunters simultaneously employ all three.

Sodium bicarbonate—more commonly referred to as baking soda—is famous for its ability to control odors by neutralizing acids, including the acids present in perspiration. It has some antimicrobial properties in that its presence creates a less inviting habitat for many types of bacteria, and it absorbs moisture, which creates an environment in which bacteria can thrive. It is the active ingredient in a number of the scent control products being marketed to hunters. If the product suggests you can gargle with it, there is a good chance its active ingredient is baking soda. The best way to use many of these products is to apply them directly to the skin after showering. Apply them everywhere, if you like, but pay special attention to the areas that perspire the most. Plain baking soda can be useful, either as a deodorant (mix it with a little corn starch to keep it from clumping), as a toothpaste, or a mouth rinse. For hunters who cannot (or prefer not) to line-dry clothes, a few tablespoons of baking soda in the dryer can reduce odors present in the dryer.

Most common deodorants are antimicrobials, including the unscented products marketed to hunters. Antiperspirants differ from deodorants in that they clog the pores to prevent perspiration, as opposed to acting on the perspiration. Though they might contain zinc or aluminum or other ingredients that have an antimicrobial effect, they prevent body odor primarily by preventing the perspiration on which bacteria thrive.

A number of herbs, minerals, and other substances are claimed to have deodorant effects, in some cases by acting as antimicrobials. Many people are interested in these because of allergies to ingredients often found in commercial deodorants, or because the commercial products cause irritation, or because they have concerns about the long-term health effects of deodorants. Determining the validity of claims made on behalf of "natural" deodorants is difficult if not impossible, and most of the evidence is purely anecdotal. The lack of scientific evidence supporting many of the claims may simply be an indication that there are no organizations sufficiently motivated to spend time and money researching the effectiveness of, for instance, coconut oil, as a deodorant. Coconut oil is among the substances sometimes touted as a deodorant, along with chlorophyll, sesame seed oil, aloe, and various "crystals" and minerals, often containing bauxite, alum, or zinc. Chlorophyll and zinc in particular have long been touted as natural deodorants, and we'll take a closer look at them in another chapter.

Another antimicrobial is silver, which is increasingly being used in clothing. The U.S. army has for some time issued to infantrymen socks with silver in the fabric to control the growth of bacteria that give rise to a number of foot ailments. In more recent years, several makers of hunting garments offer socks and undergarments incorporating silver. The idea, again, is to prevent the growth of the bacteria that cause body odors.

Stopping odors by controlling the conditions that create them is one approach; another approach entails a chemical interaction with substances to prevent volatility, or destroying odors as quickly as they form through oxidation. As we have seen, odors are formed when substances release molecules into the atmosphere. Some substances are not volatile. Steel, for instance, is not volatile and normally has no odor. A chemical reaction that controls volatility—that is, one that stops the release of molecules into the air—prevents odors. Many of the scent reduction products that are sprayed onto the skin, clothing, or gear, operate by reducing volatility or creating other chemical changes that prevent the formation of odors.

Finally, there are the products that adsorb or absorb odors. Manufacturers like to point up the differences, but from the hunter's perspective it matters little. Technically, adsorption refers to a process in which molecules cling to the surface of other molecules. Absorption, on the other hand, refers to a process in which molecules are actually drawn into or contained within other molecules. Doubtless the best known of these products (in the hunting industry) exists in the form of carbon-impregnated clothing. Any bowhunter who has looked at an ad for these garments probably has a basic understanding of how they are supposed to work. Tiny carbon granules trap and hold odor molecules, preventing their release into the air. Eventually the granules are full up, and can contain no more odor molecules. An application of heat releases some, if not all of these molecules, freeing the carbon granules to trap odors again. The use of activated carbon has long had industrial and military applications, usually for controlling or neutralizing toxic substances of various kinds. The military often issues carbon clothing to personnel in areas where there is the threat of chemical weapons. It works.

The use of carbon clothing for odor control is more controversial. In industrial applications, carbon that has adsorbed its capacity and will be re-used is heated at temperatures that would destroy any garments. In military applications, carbon clothing is issued in airtight containers, and is intended to be used once, then discarded. The argument is often made that the temperatures to which carbon clothing is exposed in clothes dryer are insufficient to achieve the desired results. The case made by the manufacturers of these garments is that heat at these temperatures, while it may not entirely eliminate the scent molecules trapped by the carbon, will eliminate enough of them to enable the garment to work as intended. In addition, to some extent time may be substituted for temperature. By exposing carbon clothing to moderate temperatures for longer periods of time, we can achieve the same results as if we exposed it to higher temperatures for a short period of time.

Critics also suggest that to be effective, carbon must have scent molecules forced through it under pressure, or the scent molecules will simply find their way around the carbon molecules. Put an air filter in the middle of a room, as one argument goes, and it will have little if any effect. Put it in ducts or vents where air is forced through it, and it can work. This does not explain how carbon clothing protects military personnel from toxic chemicals, though it may be a simple matter of the concentration of carbon used. (That is, if the carbon particles are sufficiently concentrated that molecules cannot get around them, they can be effective.) The arguments about carbon clothing go back and forth. In recent years, lawsuits have been filed against the makers of carbon hunting clothing, and in at least one case, a ruling has been made. It was the kind of ruling that enables both sides to claim partial victory. In plain English, it seemed to suggest that some of the ads on the part of the carbon clothing companies had to be toned down. The implication is that the product may be useful, but claims of 100% effectiveness (as in "Forget the wind, just hunt") were excessive.

CYCLODEXTRINS

Harnessing technology to control odors is a relatively recent phenomenon in the hunting community, but major industries ranging from the medical industry to companies involved in food, sanitation, household cleaners and detergents, and others have long experimented with technical means of reducing or eliminating odor. One fairly recent development along these lines has been the increasing use of cyclodextrins for odor control. (Probably the best known product currently using cyclodextrins is Proctor and Gamble's Febreze, a popular household odor eliminator.) In addition to reducing or eliminating odor, cyclodextrins can actually store and deliver odor (such as perfumes), and have also been used to release and store medications gradually into the body over time.

In layman's terms, here is how they work. Cyclodextrins are complex molecules, similar to sugars, and are shaped much like a doughnut. They tend to join together in strings that form tubes or hollowed out cones. The exterior is hydrophobic (repels water), while the interior is hydrophilic (attracts water). In addition, they can be ionically charged to create an electrostatic attraction with other molecules. The effect is that they attract and absorb other molecules (including the volatile molecules that are the source of odors), storing them in their hollow cavities. Eventually, of course, all the cyclodextrins are full of molecules. When this happens, additional cyclodextrins must be applied to the source of odor, at least in the case of sprays such as Febreze. In the case of clothing that contains cyclodextrins in the fabric, the odor molecules can be removed simply by washing and drying the garment.

Sound too good to be true? The scent control industry is highly competitive, and every product has its critics, many of whom make other products, or are on the payroll of those who do. There is a great deal of protective secrecy, rumors fly everywhere, and lawyers make a lot of money initiating or defending suits. Getting solid, unbiased information is difficult, and manufacturers often start to sound like politicians: "I'm sorry, but I can't discuss that while it's in litigation."

So far, the criticism sometimes heard regarding cyclodextrins is that they are good at containing certain odor molecules, not so good at containing others. So, for instance, cyclodextrins may be good at containing body odor, but may not eliminate odors of frying bacon. Or they might be good at eliminating the odor from the dog that rubbed against your leg on your way out the door, but not at eliminating campfire smoke. Dan River, the company that makes No-Trace hunting clothing, insists that the cyclodextrins in their clothing will effectively reduce body odor as well as external contaminants that may contaminate hunting clothes. Who is correct? It is true that a given cyclodextrin may attract and hold certain odor molecules, and not others. It is also true, however, that to some extent cyclodextrins can be tailored to work for a variety of molecules. It may be possible to make use of a variety of cyclodextrins to operate on a variety of odors. As a case in point, Proctor and Gamble claims that Febreze is effective on a wide range of household odors, from pet odors to cooking odors to cigarette smoke.

Just how much odor can cyclodextrins absorb? As of this writing, No Trace is the only brand of hunting garments making use of cyclodextrins. "If you sit for awhile in a truck that just smells strongly of gas fumes," concedes No Trace's Dewey Knight, "you could end up out in the woods hunting before the No Trace has an opportunity to absorb all the odor." Normally though, continues Knight, you can hunt up to a week before you'll need to wash the clothing to reactivate its scent reducing properties. "Of course that is under typical hunting conditions," Knight explains. "If you're very active and the weather is warm and you're sweating a lot, that time might be reduced." In any case, the same things can be said for most any odor reduction process on the market. All can be overwhelmed with very heavy odors, and the performance of all of them can be affected by activity levels, temperature, humidity, and other factors.

The fact that cylcodextrins have been used for some time, and continue to be used, in the medical and pharmaceutical industry as well as in other industries, suggests that they have some legitimacy. In fact, cyclodextrins have been tested by the scientific community, including specifically the use of cyclodextrins in clothing. Two tests I'm familiar with were conducted at the University of North Carolina, and by the Journal of Inclusion Phenomena and Macrocylic Chemistry. The limitation of these studies, and others like them, is that they examined the ability of cyclodextrins to increase the effectiveness of flame retardants, and to hold for release various kinds of perfumes or antimicrobials. Specific tests of their abilities to absorb odors were not to my knowledge conducted, although the tests that were conducted yielded positive results and could be construed to indicate that cyclodextrins in clothing are—or at least have the potential to be—effective odor reducers.

As always, hunters will doubtless conduct their own tests on these products, and will arrive at their own conclusions about whether or not this technology works. The tests will be less than scientific. On the other hand, they will be conducted in the only arena that truly matters to the hunter, which is out in the woods in the presence of game. And, scientific as any more formal tests might be, it is probable that the only way to know for certain if such a product can defeat the super sensitive noses of game animals is to wear them in the presence of game animals and observe their responses. For sure, what we can say at a minimum about cyclodextrins at this point is that they represent a promising technology for helping hunters with the most challenging aspect of big game hunting

BLINDS

Blinds haven't traditionally been thought of as scent reduction products, so I've given them their own category. When I say "traditionally," I mean that few hunters would associate blinds with reductions in scent—but that's not to say the thought has never occurred to any hunters. In recent years, with the growing popularity of commercially produced, fully enclosed blinds, a number of hunters have suggested that these blinds could help contain scent. Use of such ground blinds is increasing in popularity, but they have not been commonly used long enough to accumulate the kind of anecdotal evidence that has built up around other scent reducing products.

Still, it doesn't seem inconceivable that blinds could afford some degree of scent control, if only because they block the wind, thereby preventing it from carrying at least some scent downwind. More recently, some blind makers have been offering in blinds the same carbon-impregnated fabrics that are offered in hunting garments. Short of that, hunters are well-advised to avoid contaminating blinds with foreign odors to the extent possible. Hunters generally prefer to set up blinds at least a few days prior to hunting from them, mostly to allow game to become accustomed to seeing them in the environment. It could be, though, that allowing the blinds to de-odorize, or the game to become accustomed to their odor, is at least as important as visual considerations. Many hunters also pile dirt, leaves, sticks, and other debris around the base of the blind, to aid in preventing the escape of odor from inside the blind. Whether blinds are designed with scent reduction in mind or not, it only makes sense for bowhunters using ground blinds to keep scent considerations in mind.

WHAT DOES SCIENCE SAY?

Many readers aren't old enough to recall the controversy in the 1960s and 70s surrounding the health effects of smoking cigarettes. Suffice it to say that there was no shortage of scientists and even medical professionals willing to state for the record that there was no evidence supporting the notion that cigarettes increased the likelihood of contracting cancer. Sadly, many of them continued to maintain that position in the face of mountains of evidence to the contrary. Much of the public didn't know what to believe. That issue has been resolved by time, of course. Maybe a better comparison is the more current controversy surrounding global warming. Unless you happen to be a climatologist, you are more or less in the position of having to choose which scientists you believe. The science of scent reduction— at least as it pertains to its practical applications in hunting situations—is still in its infancy. There are arguments and counter-arguments, with experts testifying for and against the efficacy of different scent reducing products.

In the only truly independent scientific study of scent control I have found—at least as it might have some relevance to a hunting situation—Dr. John Shivik of the National Wildlife Research Center extensively tested the ability of seven search dogs to find people wearing carbon-impregnated clothing, compared to their ability to locate people not wearing such clothing. The people were placed in blinds, the dogs were allowed to sniff a piece of fabric previously handled by the people in the blinds, and dogs and handlers were then given specified amounts of time in which to locate the subjects. In all but one of 42 trials, dogs found all the test subjects within the allotted time. Dr. Shivik found that persons not wearing carbon suits were detected from slightly greater distances, but did not find the differences in distance to be statistically significant. While noting that he believed it possible for individuals to put on sealed carbon suits in such a way as to remain undetectable to dogs, his overall conclusion was that for practical purposes, carbon suits are ineffective.

If you think that settles the issue once and for all, you are not a scientific thinker.

In fairness, if we are going to be truly scientific in our approach, we have to concede that the results of one test are never conclusive. It will be interesting to see if other researchers can duplicate these results, or if they arrive at different conclusions. As a side note, it is significant (though not surprising) that Shivik did observe significant differences in the time it took dogs to find subjects, and these differences were related to barometric pressure, humidity, and the variability of the wind. Shivik also speculated that one probable source of contamination of the suits was that wearers handled them in putting them on. Bowhunters using these suits might want to consider wearing rubber gloves when donning them.

Scent-Lok's Glenn Sesselman also makes an interesting point in regard to this study. Search dogs, he points out, are trained to detect a faint odor, then follow that odor as it grows stronger until they reach the source. A wild animal is not seeking the source of the odor, and if it is faint will not seek the source of it (assuming it isn't food or a female in heat). In most cases the animal will simply not react at all to a very faint odor.

Scent-Lok has funded several studies of their product, including at least one study in which it was compared to another product and found to be superior. The study was conducted by professors at the University of North Carolina, which is internationally renowned for its college of textiles. Laboratory testing indicated that Scent-Lok fabric was very efficient at adsorbing a wide range of odors and, perhaps most significantly, that it could in fact be regenerated sufficiently in an ordinary clothes dryer to remain effective for repeated use. The public has every right to be skeptical of studies that are not independently funded and conducted. In fairness, though, it should be pointed out that the academics conducting these studies are more than credible scientists, and that when they present their findings they put their reputations on the lines. Further, such studies are expensive. Few outside the industry are likely to invest the time, money, and human resources necessary to conduct a truly scientific study of this issue.

The criticism may be raised also that a study conducted in a lab is not necessarily a predictor of results outdoors. Fair enough, but this really only points to the limitations of science. A very large part of what defines scientific methodology is control of variables so that valid comparisons can be made. Laboratories offer a great deal of control. Operating in the outdoors makes control of variables such as temperature, wind velocity and direction, and humidity (to name only a few), extremely difficult or impossible.

In time, we may accumulate sufficient evidence to convince any rational, educated hunter that a given type of scent reduction product does or does not work. In the meantime, it would behoove hunters to keep an open mind on the subject. The more serious and consistently successful hunters I know tend to employ at least some of these scent-reduction products, and some use them all. They wash with unscented soaps, apply unscented deodorants, wear scent-reducing clothing of one type or another, or use scent reducing powders or sprays. None that I know totally ignore wind direction, and most take it seriously.

My own experiences, which I present here as neither less nor more valid than those of any other experienced hunter, are inconclusive. I am convinced that reducing scent is possible and that it makes a difference. How much of a difference is not clear. Depending on circumstances, I use some or all of these products. I have been detected by game when following a rigid scent control regimen. I have also had game downwind of me for extended periods of time, and remained undetected. In addition I have observed, as have many hunters, that game animals at times appear to detect an odor, but not to a degree that causes them to bolt. The head comes up, perhaps, and they appear to change from a relaxed state to a tense state. They look around, as if looking for the source of a faint odor. It could be that they detect an odor, but think it is at some distance, or are simply unable to locate the source of it. I've even had deer snort, or jump and run a short distance, only to stop. On more than one occasion I've had the opportunity to arrow animals that I'm sure were aware of my presence, but couldn't locate me. It is not unreasonable to speculate in these situations that keeping scent to a minimum is the difference between an animal that becomes alert to possible danger and remains in the area long enough to provide a shooting opportunity, and one that bolts instantly.

Based on all this, I am inclined to continue using scent reducing strategies unless and until more extensive scientific studies convince me they are ineffective. My feeling, which appears to be in accord with the thoughts of many experienced hunters, is that getting within bow range of mature big game animals is sufficiently difficult that I want any edge I can get.

8

COVER SCENTS

Behavioral scientists have observed that white-tailed deer can distinguish between as many as twenty different scents simultaneously, and it seems reasonable to assume that most of the species we hunt have similar capabilities. There is reason to wonder if it is even possible to fool a game animal's nose by attempting to cover one scent with another. Before you give up on the idea of cover scents, though, you might want to consider this question: Why do most dogs seem to delight in rolling in the foulest, rottenest, most disgusting carcasses or other sources of odors they can find? Biologists tell us this behavior is common to wild as well as domesticated canines, and many theorize that the behavior is an attempt to mask scent, as an aid in stalking prey. Along similar lines, why do canines, felines, and other critters often kick dirt over their droppings, if not to reduce or mask scent?

If it is true that animals engage in these behaviors to cover their scent, then thousands upon thousands of years of evolution would seem to support the notion that it is indeed possible to mask scent to a degree that will make a hunter less easily detected by his prey. While it seems unlikely that scent can be entirely eliminated in this manner, perhaps it can be reduced to such a degree that it cannot be detected for as great a distance, or as quickly, by a prey species. Or perhaps the mixture of aromas causes a momentary hesitation, giving the predator a few extra seconds that can make the difference.

Native Americans were known to sometimes apply cover scents of one sort or another. Some tribes routinely sat in the smoke from campfires, convinced this cover scent gave them an edge when stalking into bow range of their quarry. They may not have understood scientific methodology, but they hunted almost daily all their lives, and for generation after generation depended on successful hunts for their very survival.

On a recent South African hunt, Wilhelm Greeff of Zingelani Safaris strongly urged me to burn cattle or zebra dung near my blind as a cover scent, insisting that it made a difference. Jim Litmer of Third Hand Archery products was in camp.

"We kept dung burning on and off all day outside our blind near a waterhole," Jim told me one night over dinner. "When the dung was burning, game came in. When the dung wasn't burning, no game came to the waterhole. At one point three rhinos came in and decided to stay awhile. They hung around until the dung burned up, and soon after that they spooked and ran off." My own experience was not quite so conclusive, but I can report that numerous species of game came to the waterhole I was watching while the dung was burning, including zebras, waterbuck, kudu, and numerous warthogs.

WHAT KIND OF COVER SCENT TO USE?

This is a more complicated question than it might at first appear to be. Typically, cover scents attempt to produce a strong smell that is common in the environment. Earth scent, pine scent, and the urine of common creatures such as foxes and raccoons are probably the most

Did a cover scent encourage this bear to come into bow range? It's impossible to be certain, but positive results are hard to argue with.

popular cover scents. Usually, earth and pine scents are sprayed on or attached to an item of clothing in the form of wafers or patches, while urines are usually applied a few drops at a time to boot soles before entering the woods, to prevent deer from readily discerning the trail. As in the case of food scents, some hunters feel it's important to use cover scents that are common to the area. Dirt would seem to be a common element, but, would a generic dirt scent closely resemble everything from the red clay of Georgia, to the sand of the South Carolina Low Country, to the fertile loam of the Midwest?

What about the use of urine from predators such as foxes? While some studies indicate that animals may react negatively to the urine of predators, even more studies suggest otherwise. Then too, although the urine of various species may have different odors depending on what they have eaten, urine does tend to break down quickly to the point at which, according to biologists, all mammal urine soon smells basically the same. More than a few successful deer hunters routinely apply fox urine to their boots before entering the woods.

Still other hunters scoff at the notion that an animal is put on the alert by, for instance, the scent of pines in an area where there are no pine trees. My own take on this is that since it is easy to use a scent that is common to the area being hunted, why not do it, just in case. Here is another consideration: If half the hunters in the woods are using earth scent (or pine scent, or fox urine), might not a deer learn to associate that scent with hunters? In the West, many hunters, especially elk hunters, hunt from spike camps, where they usually spend at least some time sitting around campfires. Like their Native American predecessors, some successful modern hunters are of the opinion that the smell of smoke acts as an effective cover scent. Most of us have heard stories about hunters who smoke cigarettes on deer stands, putting a smoking butt in the fork of a tree just long enough to shoot an approaching deer, then finishing the smoke before climbing down to take up the trail. Happily, I quit smoking years ago, but I can confirm the truthfulness of those stories, having done that very thing myself. Could cigarette smoke be a cover scent?

Assuming cover scents can work, whether or not smoke (or any other scent) can act as a cover would probably depend upon whether or not deer have learned to associate the smoke, or other scents, with humans, and more specifically with danger. It seems unlikely that animals in more-or-less remote areas would make that connection— although if they experience pain or a threat from one smoking hunter, the association could be made quickly. At the same time, deer that often come into contact with people, whether in heavily populated suburban areas, farm country, or areas where they are subject to heavy hunting pressure, would be quite likely to associate the smell of smoke with humans.

COVER SCENTS VS. SCENT REDUCERS

I have spoken with one manufacturer that specifically recommends against using cover scents in conjunction with scent reducers. Most don't address the issue, while others insist that it makes perfect sense to do so. Many scent reducers work by absorbing scent, adsorbing scent, or chemically interacting with substances to prevent odors from forming. All these products have a capacity. Products that absorb or adsorb odor molecules at some point are filled up, and become ineffective until they are cleaned or reactivated in some manner, and products that oxidize or in some similar chemical reaction neutralize scent are in effect "used up" in the process. It would seem to make no sense to invest in, for instance, a Scent-Lok suit, then spray pine scent all over it. The Scent-Lok will absorb the pine scent, counteracting its effectiveness. What's worse, the carbon particles in the Scent-Lok will reach capacity and then fail to adsorb any additional odors. In the case of some spray-on products, it is possible to reapply them frequently. Still, it would not seem logical to use a cover scent, then use a product that will attempt to neutralize that scent. If the scent reducer succeeds, the cover is not working. If the cover scent succeeds, the scent reducer is not working.

Some scent reducers, such as most soaps, detergents, and deodorants, work primarily as antimicrobials, preventing the formation of bacteria that cause body odor. In that case, the two products might be used in conjunction, since the cover scent would not prevent the scent reducer from killing bacteria and in this way preventing body odor. Another way to use cover scents involves placing them slightly downwind, where they can provide cover without fighting scent-reducing products.

9

ATTRACTANT SCENTS

The 140-class whitetail was more than 100 yards out when Kentuckian Jason Strunk first spotted it crossing a bean field. Though it was far-off and moving in the wrong direction when he lost sight of it, Jason cautiously stood up, lifted his bow from its holder, and turned in his tree stand. When the buck came around a bend in the logging road about two minutes later, Jason waited for the right moment, tooted on his hands-free grunt tube to stop the buck in a shooting lane, and loosed a perfectly aimed arrow. Not ten seconds later, he watched it drop. How did Strunk know that buck was headed his way? He had laid down a scent trail with a drag rag on his way into the stand less than an hour before, starting at the far edge of the bean field and circling carefully to his stand. When he saw the buck cross the field with its nose to the ground, he knew it was following his scent trail.

There are scents on the market designed to attract not only whitetailed deer, but mulies, sitkas, blacktail deer, elk, bear, wild hogs, moose, all the North American wild canines, bobcats, cougars, and even small game and furbearers such as rabbits, raccoons, and skunks. There is no question that game can be lured into shooting position with scents. What is equally clear is that scent doesn't always work. And when it does work, just why is a controversial issue.

Realistic hunters aren't really expecting to find something that always works. They're looking for something that gives them an edge—something that makes the odds against scoring on any given day a little lower. How many times would you use scent for one opportunity at a good buck?

The issues for hunters are what kind of scents work, when do they work, and when (and why) do they often not work? Attractant scents can be divided into several categories, though there may be some overlap. These are food scents, sex scents, and curiosity scents. Urine can also be a category of its own. Though it is often considered a sex scent, and might also be considered a curiosity scent, we'll explain why we list it as a category of its own when we get to it. Why do I say there may be some overlap among these categories? Until we can get inside an animal's head, we really have no way of knowing for certain what motivates it. Was it hungry and fooled by that bottled apple scent, or was it curious about a strange new smell it had never encountered before? Was that rutting elk fooled by the cow-in-heat scent, or was it curious about something that vaguely resembled the scent of a cow-in-heat but wasn't? Some would argue that any time animals respond to a bottled or synthesized scent, they are responding mostly from curiosity. And of course some hunters would say, "Who cares why they come in, just so they come in?" Manufacturers themselves recognize the overlap. Many refer to their scents as lures. The ingredients are something they prefer to keep secret, but they often indicate that the lure contains a mixture of ingredients designed to appeal to hunger or curiosity or both.

FOOD SCENTS

First let's distinguish between "food" and "food scents." In states such as Texas, where baiting deer is perfectly legal, hunters may put corn, apples, beets, or similar foods out as bait, and it seems reasonable to assume deer that encounter the bait for the first time are responding to smell. Bears, too, are hunted over bait in some states and Canadian provinces.

That is not what we are talking about, however. By "food scents," we are referring to bottled scents made from concentrates or synthetic odors, or solid mixtures that are volatile enough to produce food scents that can be detected from some distance, or various products that are heated or even boiled to produce scents intended to resemble foods. An interesting issue related to food scents is the oft heard caution about using the scents of foods that do not occur naturally in a given area. We'll examine this again in the chapter on animal intelligence, but essentially the idea is that a deer that suddenly detects the scent of, say, apples, in an area where there are no apple trees, will react with suspicion, or will sense in some way that something is not right and will avoid the area.

As in the case of similar concerns about cover scents, many biologists, and some hunters, scoff at that idea. In their opinion, the idea that a deer catches a whiff of corn in an area where there is no corn-field and is suddenly on the alert or suspicious that something is fishy, is just ridiculous. Deer are very wary, or so goes the reasoning, but they're not that complicated. They don't think that way. If it smells like something good to eat and they're hungry, they'll check it out. If the smell is unfamiliar but not threatening, they may or may not react with curiosity.

We can speculate about why animals respond to certain foods at certain times, and others at other times, but ultimately it's something only the animals themselves know for certain. It's probably often associated with seasonal factors, or the amount of sugar, protein, or other nutrients present in a given food source at a given stage of ripeness. The bottom line for many hunters, though, is that putting out a food scent is unlikely to do any harm, and can sometimes be the ticket to success.

CURIOSITY SCENTS

Most animals, especially deer, are curious to some degree, which is the idea behind curiosity scents. Animals investigate their environment, and one of their chief instruments of investigation is the nose. Whitetails have been referred to as one-hundred-pound noses that run around smelling everything in the woods. Given their curiosity and their reliance on their noses, it's not surprising that deer will, on occasion, approach the source of a strong, unusual, or unknown aroma to check it out.

What exactly are curiosity scents? In the case of commercially produced scents, that is a difficult question, since manufacturers are highly secretive about the formulas they have developed, if their ads are to be believed, after years of research. In a University of Georgia study involving the use of motion-activated cameras placed over a variety of scents, the numbers of deer attracted to car polish rivaled the numbers attracted to several kinds of urine and food scents. (Of course, who is to say the deer were not reacting to urine and food scents out of curiosity?)

SEXUAL ATTRACTANTS

Sexual attractants don't just get game animals excited,they get hunters excited. No mystery there—when you consider that close to and during the rut is the one time, for many species, when even the most cautious, trophy-class animals allow their obsession with estrous females to make them vulnerable, it's not surprising that hunters would seek to take advantage of that vulnerability. Probably the most commonly used sexual attractant is doe-in-heat urine, which may be placed on the ground, used to saturate a rag or a wick and hung from a tree, or even sprayed into the air. Hunters also frequently use doe urine to lay down scent trails, saturating a rag that can be dragged, or a pad that can be worn on a boot sole.

Dominant buck urine, too, is popular. The idea is that bucks detecting the scent of another buck in their area will feel challenged and will seek out the buck to chase it off. Still others theorize that dominant buck urine can attract and hold does in a given area. It has been demonstrated that does can determine the difference between subordinate and dominant bucks simply by smelling their urine. Though we tend to think of the bucks as seeking the does, does will frequent areas containing dominant bucks, and especially in those areas where the buck to doe ratio is in good balance, does may travel outside their home ranges to find dominant bucks.

Among the better trophy hunters I know are several who begin placing dominant buck scents in various forms throughout their hunting area, usually late in the summer, though sometimes earlier, and in one case year-round. The theory is that this brings more does in the area, and keeps them there, and in turn more bucks are drawn into that area as the rut approaches. (More about this approach in subsequent chapters.)

Earlier we suggested that urine could be considered a category in itself. Here is why: ungulates, including deer, tend to be fascinated by urine of any kind. It seems to be a means of communication within the species, but may also tell deer about other species, including predators, in the area. There is some controversy regarding how deer react to the urine of predators, but regardless of how they react, they do seem drawn to check out urine. Ordinary doe urine is a commonly used scent. Many hunters believe that it doesn't make sense to use doe-in-heat scent before any does are likely to be in heat, but there are some other reasons not to use it. One reason is that it tends to repel does. The hunter looking primarily to cull does from a local herd or put venison in the freezer probably doesn't want to repel does. Beyond that, some hunters theorize that does attract bucks, so why drive away does?

The whole issue of how deer react to human urine has generated the widest possible response from hunters. At one extreme are the hunters who use bottles or other devices to avoid contaminating their

More than one whitetail buck has followed a hot scent straight into the lap of a waiting bowhunter.

hunting location with the smell of human urine. At the other extreme are hunters who intentionally "contaminate" their stand sites with human urine, deposit human urine in scrapes, and even create mock scrapes with human urine, in the belief that it attracts deer. A number of more-or-less scientific studies in recent years have examined deer response to a variety of scents. The studies aren't always conclusive, but they do tend to point in a couple of interesting directions. One of these is that deer herds confined in pens don't always react to smells the same way wild deer do. The other is that neither penned nor free-ranging deer appear to have strong aversions to human urine, and may exhibit some curiosity about it. The bottom line is: Human urine may or may not attract deer to some degree, but it doesn't seem to repel them. Leave the urine bottles at home and let fly from your tree stand if you want.

Urine is not the only way deer convey sexual messages to one another—various glandular secretions, such as those deposited by bucks on rubs, may serve a similar function, along with the tarsal glands. A buck in rut can be smelled, even by the inferior noses of humans, for some distance under the right conditions, and any hunter who has picked a buck up by the hind legs to lift him into a pick-up truck, or who has ridden in an SUV with a buck behind the seat, is intimately acquainted with that aroma. Various commercial producers have attempted to bottle or mimic tarsal gland scent, and more than a few hunters like to trim off the tarsal glands of a tagged buck, to use as a lure. Many hunters freeze them in plastic bags for repeated use.

PHEROMONES

We can't address the issue of sexual scents without taking a look at pheromones. Pheromones are organic chemical substances used by various species to communicate with one another, or to produce any of a number of instinctive responses. Many insects, in particular, are known to use pheromones heavily. Pheromones may enable an ant to tell its community the location of a food source, for instance, or allow a colony of bees to coordinate an exodus from a hive to establish a new colony elsewhere. They also stimulate sexual activity. Insects aren't the only species that make use of pheromones. Mammals do, also.

Hunters became very excited about pheromones, more specifically the volatile substances produced by females in heat to produce sexual responses in males. A buck or a bull detecting these pheromones will instinctively react to them—every time. Hunters who first learned about pheromones thought that they had hit on the holy grail of deer hunting: A scent that would invariably cause any buck to come to the source of the pheromones. Their hopes were dashed, however, by another incontrovertible fact: After they're released by the deer, these pheromones last for anywhere from 15 seconds to, at most, six minutes. They work for animals in heat because animals in heat produce fresh pheromones continuously.

Does this mean that, as a practical matter, there is no such thing as doe-in-heat scent? Some experts would argue that that is indeed the case. Consider, though, that scientists have identified at least 93 substances in the urine of a doe in heat. It seems entirely possible that a buck can tell a doe is in heat even without the pheromones. Will a buck respond to a doe even if the pheromones aren't present? We can't say with any certainty, but experiences like those of Jason Strunk suggest that a buck will, at least sometimes, follow a trail of doe-in-heat scent, regardless of what the ingredients may be and regardless of whether or not it contains pheromones.

TIMING

When is a good time to use scents? In the case of curiosity scents, arguably any time, since curiosity is not seasonal. It seems unlikely, though, that a buck eagerly seeking a hot doe—or a doe being pursued by a randy buck—would stray far from its route to check a smell out of curiosity. It also seems unlikely that a deer heading for a dinner of alfalfa, corn, or clover would delay getting dinner to check out a strange aroma. Nonetheless, any hunter who has spent time in the woods knows that deer aren't always chasing or being chased by other deer, nor are they always making a beeline for the nearest preferred food. Deer take their sweet time, most of the time, and tend to amble along slowly, browsing and grazing as they go.

When it comes to using food scents, timing raises some interesting and complex issues. As a general rule, most hunters, and even some manufacturers, recommend using food scents early in the season, pre-rut, and late in the season, post-rut. Why? Because the periods immediately before the rut, and during the peak of the rut, are the prime times for doe-in-heat scents or dominant buck scents.

To my knowledge, no one has done any sort of scientific (or, for that matter, unscientific) study to determine if doe-in-heat or dominant buck scents outperform food scents during the rut. Most manufacturers have little incentive to pursue such an inquiry; the status quo is that hunters use food scents on some hunts, sexual attractants on others. Why limit sales to one or the other?

How often have you heard that the best way to hunt bucks during the rut is to hunt where the does are? If that's sound advice, wouldn't it make perfect sense to attract does to your stand with food scents? Perhaps in some updated edition of this book, we'll have an answer to that question.

But the issue of when to use a given food scent is much more complicated than whether or not food scents are or are not more effective than sexual attractants at various times in the season. While it's true that deer like a variety of foods, it's also well documented that at any given time, deer have a preferred food and will often pass up other foods to get to it. Further, their priorities change, sometimes from one day to the next. Deer may pass up any food source available to get at alfalfa in late summer or early autumn. Later they might switch to soybeans, passing up alfalfa to get the beans. When the acorns fall, deer will abandon every other food source to get to them. Though they readily eat the acorns from red oaks, they seem to prefer the less bitter white oak acorn. Why these changing preferences? Availability has something to do with it, but in many cases, it's a matter of what is ripe. And some plants—especially broadleaf green plants such as the brassicas that are so popular these days in food plots—become sweeter after a frost or two. They may literally be ignored one day, and sought after to the exclusion of nearly everything else the next day.

What does all this have to do with food scents? Neither corn scents nor apple scents are likely to be at their most effective if acorns are dropping in the woods. And while all this might seem to suggest that acorn scents should be effective any time, there is the fact that deer seem to prefer foods with varying amounts of protein or sugars depending on the time of the year and whether they are bulking up with protein or seeking high-energy foods with more sugars.

Timing as it pertains to the use of sexual scents would seem to be a more straightforward matter. Though there is some evidence that the scents released by bucks can actually stimulate does to come into heat, the timing of the rut is fairly predictable. A doe, as every deer hunter knows, will run from a buck until she is good and ready to stand still for him. At the same time, it is unlikely that a buck would respond to a doe in heat if not for the increased level of testosterone that courses through his veins as the rut kicks in. That would suggest that the best time to use dominant buck or doe-in-heat scent would be the period leading up to, and during, the time that the rut takes place, beginning when bucks begin frequently scraping, rubbing, and cruising for does, and very late in the season when testosterone levels have dropped.

Proper Use

Many bowhunters use an attraction scent in the hope that wandering deer will hit the scent stream and follow it to the source, where they are waiting to loose a well-aimed arrow. Others, though they would welcome such an occurrence, have more limited expectations. Their hope is that a deer passing by will stop to sniff or lick the source of the scent, pausing long enough and in a correct position to give them a perfect shot. In either case, it only makes sense to put the source of the scent in a spot that is comfortably within bow range, in the open, and likely to position the deer for a broadside shot.

It also makes sense to use the wind very carefully. It's a tricky situation—on the one hand, you want to position the scent source upwind of areas you expect deer to move through, while on the other hand you don't want them to get your scent. Obviously this is a situation in which scent control (reduction of the hunter's scent) is extremely important. In other circumstances, it is possible the target will be passing by upwind, but in the case of using attractant scents, game will be in a more-or-less downwind position. The trick here, aside from maximum personal scent control, is to position the scent source neither directly upwind nor downwind from the hunter, but crosswind. Ideally, game will hit the scent stream prior to being directly downwind of the hunter and follow it in without ever hitting the hunter's scent stream.

Hunters use a variety of media for conveying scent, including various wicks, drag rags, boot pads, liquids, gels, and homemade devices or concoctions. Which is the most effective may depend to some extent on current conditions. One consideration, according to Jamis Gamache of HeatWave Scents, is weather. "The use of liquid- based scent when it is raining or if temperatures are extremely cold is minimized greatly," explains Jamis, "because the scent is diluted with the rain or the liquid freezes. A better type [of] device would be a scent-impregnated wafer in which the scent is built into the device."

When conditions are favorable, Jamis believes aerosol sprays can disperse scent better than can a liquid on a wick. A few years ago, Jamis became sufficiently sold on heated scents that he formed his own company, HeatWave Scents. It's no secret that heat increases the volatility of most substances, which means, in effect, that it makes odors stronger. Not that you have to be a chemist to understand that fact.

"Think of it this way," says Jamis. "After a long day of hunting, you walk into the house and there is a hot pot of chili on the stove. You know right away when you walk in that something smells great. The next day you walk in and the leftover chili is still on the stove but is not heated. You practically need to stumble over it before you realize it is there. The same holds true for game scents. By heating or atomizing the scent, it produces a much stronger aroma, which is more apt to attract game to your hunting area."

At the beginning of this chapter, I made reference to laying down a scent trail with drag rags. Usually this is a rut-hunting strategy, and the attractant is doe-in-heat urine. I know at least one hunter who makes it a point to always step in deer droppings when he comes across them on his way to his stand, and claims to have taken a nice buck that followed that scent to his stand. Would food scents work? I know of no one who has tried it. I'd be inclined to think it could be very effective for bear hunters, but I, for one, would be leery of putting a food scent on any part of my body in bear country. One technique that I see increasing numbers of deer hunters using involves soaking a drag rag with liquid scent, putting it on the end of a stick, and by that means laying down a trail that is not directly in their own footsteps. It can't hurt, and some hunters are convinced that it makes bucks less likely to detect the hunter's scent.

Earlier I made reference to some serious trophy hunters who begin making mock scrapes and putting out dominant buck scent in the summer, and sometimes year-round, in the belief that it attracts and holds does and bucks in an area. We'll take a closer look at that in the chapter about mock scrapes and rubs.

10

NATURAL VS. SYNTHETIC SCENTS

On a hunt in the mountains of Virginia several years ago, I stepped out of a pickup truck, said good luck to my hunting companions in the backseat, and watched momentarily as the guide drove off down the logging road, leaving me in the predawn stillness of a crisp fall morning. It was the end of October and the perfect time, it seemed to me, to lay down a scent line to my stand using a drag rag with a little doe-in-heat scent. I removed the bottle of scent from my daypack and, in the darkness, attempted to squirt a little onto my drag rag. Nothing came out. I shook it a few times and squeezed again with my fingers. Still nothing. Finally, I squeezed with my whole hand. The entire top of the bottle burst open and doe-in-heat scent sprayed all over me. I gathered my gear and began walking toward my stand, and soon heard something walking in the dry leaves behind me. I stopped and it stopped. I began walking and again I heard it, unmistakably following me. Eventually I was able to make out a forkhorn buck, following about 40 or 50 yards behind me. It left when I climbed into my stand, but later came back and hung around all morning. It ran off when I climbed down at lunchtime to make my way back to the logging road for the ride back to the lodge. The truck came along, with several other hunters inside, and stopped. I climbed in. The truck went about ten yards and stopped, the door flew open, and I flew out. I had to ride back to the lodge in the bed of the truck.

Being the scientific type that I am, I deduced several things from this experience. First, that the forkhorn buck sure was interested in something about me, and my best guess is that the doe-in-heat shower I took by the logging road had a lot to do with it. Second, you want

Most camo is effective. Some patterns excel in one specific habitat while others, like the pattern above, are more all-purpose.

to avoid contaminating yourself or your gear with that stuff if at all possible, but sometimes it is not possible.

I bring this up because it represents one of the arguments in favor of synthetic, as opposed to natural, scents. The near certainty of occasional contamination is definitely on the con side for natural scents, and on the pro side for synthetics, which tend to be easier to handle and less offensive, at least to humans.

Scents of nearly any kind can be synthesized in laboratories. Are these inferior or superior to natural scents? Contamination and convenience of handling aside, there are other issues to consider. On the pro side for synthetics, the argument is that certain natural substances, particularly urine, break down into other compounds, including ammonia. The ammonia smell is perfectly natural, and hence, arguably, a good thing. Soon after it is bottled, though, bacteria begin breaking urine down into unnatural compounds—unless special measures, including the use of preservatives, are used to prevent this. And preservatives, or so goes the argument, have their own unnatural scent. Synthetic scents, on the other hand, won't break down. And they're easier to use, since hunters needn't worry about when they were produced, or how they are stored, or how long they will be effective after the package is opened.

On the negative side for synthetic scents, some question whether or not it is possible to produce a synthetic scent that will fool an animal's nose. An animal will not have the same reaction, according to this line of reasoning, to a synthetic as opposed to a naturally produced scent. Animals that respond to a synthetic scent, according to this position, are reacting out of curiosity, and not because they are genuinely fooled.

Here is another controversial issue concerning the use of natural urines: Some products contain not deer, elk, or moose urine, but the urine of cattle or sheep. In fact, some cow- or doe-in-heat products actually contain the urine of cattle or sheep in heat. Hunters were scandalized to make that discovery, but it's not all that clear they should have been—for one simple reason: Target animals respond to them, and no scientific evidence to date proves that the urine from real does is more effective than the urine of other ungulates in heat. To further cloud the argument, recent studies indicate that the pheromones that get bucks and bulls (not to mention hunters) so excited are not present in urine, but in vaginal secretions. In a University of Georgia study, white-tailed bucks, when given a choice between vaginal secretions of estrous does and the urine of estrous does, ignored the urine and went in the direction of the secretions virtually every time.

Once again, we get into the motives of animals. Certainly the argument can be made that whether or not we truly fool an animal's nose, or whether it is reacting to a sexual stimulus or simply out of curiosity, doesn't matter. All that matters is, does it respond? To my knowledge, no scientific studies have been completed regarding how animals react to natural versus synthetic scents, or fresh urine deposited by animals in the wild as compared to urine bottled on a farm and used weeks or months later.

11

WHAT ANIMALS SEE AND HOW THEY SEE IT

Judging the trophy status of bears can be notoriously difficult, even when the bear is close. When my guide on a British Columbia spot-and-stalk bear hunt whispered that the bear we had just glimpsed slipping through a stand of stunted pines 30 yards or so away was not quite the trophy black bear we were looking for, I relaxed. When the bear passed through an opening and paused momentarily to look our way, the guide got a better look at his big, square head and small, wide-set ears and changed his mind.

"Go! Go! Go!" he whispered frantically, pushing me forward. "That's a good bear! Get up there!" The bear turned and dropped into a small ravine, and I quickly nocked an arrow and began moving forward. Thinking the bear was probably running full speed in the opposite direction, but keenly aware it could also be moving in our direction, I brought my bow to full draw as I approached the lip of the ravine. I peeked over carefully and spotted the bear, hardly 10 yards away and broadside. It lunged forward a few steps toward a thicket, then, inexplicably, stopped and stared in my direction. I don't believe animals think, but if I were asked to caption a photo of that situation, the caption would be "Wait a minute. I'm a bear. I'm not the one who is supposed to run." In one motion I put the sight pin behind the bear's shoulder, touched the release, and watched the fletching disappear in the sweet spot.

That was the first day of a weeklong hunt, and I spent most of the rest of the week photographing bears. It was a remote wilderness area, early enough in the spring that the big boars were just coming out of hibernation, and they were hungry. On several occasions over the next few days, with the guide sitting beside me toting a .45 caliber carbine, I sat photographing bears from close range. In each case, the experience was similar. The bear would raise its head from time to time to look at me, then go back to eating. When it "huffed" at us, or got inside 25 yards or so, the guide would tap me on the shoulder and we would slowly back away.

Many hunters assume bears have poor vision, but recent studies suggest they see color, and many biologists are convinced their vision is at least as good as ours. Hunters observe that bears seem to glance at them and then look away, and assume the bears don't see them. My experience in British Columbia, and numerous similar experiences since then, convinced me that, in most such cases, the bears do see the hunter. In a remote wilderness area, though, bears seldom encounter humans, and are not likely to be threatened by anything but a bigger bear. I suspect they see hunters, but just aren't intimidated by them. Many animals, including canines, perceive staring as a threat and will turn their eyes from another animal if they don't want a confrontation. Hunters often think that because a bear looks at them and then looks away, it hasn't seen them. That may be, but it could also be the bear is simply avoiding the kind of long, intense stare that for many species is a prelude to a fight. In less remote areas, where bears come into more frequent contact with people, especially in areas of heavy hunting pressure, they do seem more likely to run without hesitating.

Regardless of how their vision compares to that of humans, the vision of most species rarely compares to their sense of smell. While defeating the olfactory abilities of most game animals is somewhere between difficult and impossible, defeating their eyes is usually less challenging—the obvious exceptions that come to mind being pronghorns and turkeys. (Fortunately for bowhunters, turkeys have virtually no sense of smell.) The vision of pronghorns is often compared to that of 8X binoculars and, like most animals, they are quick to spot motion. Moose and wild hogs are often cited as having poor vision, but even they are far from blind, and the hunter who underestimates their vision is going to be seen by them sooner or later. Every hunter has been spotted by a wary old buck or a smart doe as the hunter crossed a field or other opening, made their way down a logging road, or, for that matter, still hunted through a hardwood forest. The hunter whose tree stand has him silhouetted, or which simply leaves him exposed with inadequate cover, is likely to be spotted as well.

A number of strategies can help hunters evade the eyes of their quarry, but before we examine some of these, let's take a close look at exactly how animals see and what their optical capabilities are. Generally speaking, vision occurs when light enters the eye and is absorbed by various specialized cells at the back of the eye. These cells transmit signals to the brain, which interprets the signals as sight. Color is a function of the wavelength of light reflected from the objects we see. The entire spectrum of wavelengths includes ultraviolet at the short end and infrared at the long end. Humans and other primates are rare among mammals in that they have very sophisticated color vision, and can see the entire wavelength with the exception of the extremes at both ends. We cannot normally see either infrared light or ultraviolet light.

Structurally, most mammals' eyes differ from a human's in several important respects. At the back of the eyes of all mammals are two kinds of light-sensitive cells: rods and cones. Rods function in very low light and allow some degree of night vision. Cones operate in brighter light and allow daytime vision and the perception of color. Human eyes have three types of cones, which are sensitive to short wavelengths (blue), middle wavelengths (green), and long wavelengths (red). Most species of mammals have more rods than humans, but fewer cones. This suggests they have better night vision, but poorer daytime vision. The specific cones they lack are those that perceive the longer (red) wavelengths of light. Both physiology and behavioral studies suggest that most mammals can see shades of blue and green, but not red and, like some color-blind humans, they probably cannot distinguish between green and red. Large mammals have larger pupils than humans, to admit more light, further improving their vision in low light. In addition, they possess a reflective layer at the back of their eyes called a tapetum. (The tapetum is what shines so brightly in the headlights of a vehicle.) This reflective membrane further increases the light available to the eye, again improving night vision. We mentioned earlier that humans cannot see the ultraviolet end of the color spectrum. That is because we have a filter that blocks almost all ultraviolet light. One advantage of this is that it enables us to see fine detail better than most animals. Because most mammals lack that filter, they can probably see better in the UV spectrum than we can, but they do not perceive small details well.

What does all this mean, in general terms, for the hunter? To begin with, it means hunters needn't hesitate to wear blaze orange in most situations. Where legal, the blaze orange camo patterns are probably effective. The issue of UV vision, as we indicated in an earlier chapter, has to do with the fact that most modern detergents have

UV brighteners in them, to make clothes appear whiter and brighter. The concern is that hunting garments that have been washed in detergents with UV brighteners will be highly visible to game animals. An entire industry has sprung up to provide hunters with special, non-UV detergents and spray-on products developed to remove UV residues from clothing that has been exposed to it. While I'm not aware of any independent studies proving that deer readily distinguish garments washed in UV detergents, their ability to see that portion of the color spectrum suggests that, in low light, they probably can see such garments better. Using the products designed to eliminate it certainly can't hurt, and might very well make a difference.

All the data available about how animals see is useful, but like all scientific information, it leaves some questions unanswered and leads to even more questions. Here is one that I have long pondered: If game animals have superior low-light vision, why have I, on so many occasions, been able to approach very closely to grazing deer when heading to my stand or leaving it in low light? Apart from remaining downwind of them and pausing whenever they raised their heads, I took no particular efforts to conceal myself, and have often managed to walk to within 20 or 30 yards of deer, usually when they were feeding in groups. Even more mysteriously, this seems to happen not in the darkest situations, but on those occasions when I'm late getting to my stand—before sunrise but after first light—or when I've left a stand early in the evening, after sunset but well before hard dark. I've even had deer approach me in such low-light situations, seemingly out of curiosity. On one occasion I arrowed a big Kentucky doe that approached me in a meadow at dusk. She appeared to spot me from nearly 100 yards out. When I knelt and nocked an arrow, she sneaked in, stopping several times to bob her head and paw the ground, but eventually approached to within 40 yards and offered me the shot. Never have I walked up on feeding deer like this in broad daylight. I've discussed this phenomenon with many hunters including, most recently, well-known white-tailed deer hunting expert (and my publisher) Peter Fiduccia. Peter, along with many other experienced hunters, has made the same observation.

Despite this puzzling behavior, the tendency of many pressured species to become almost exclusively nocturnal, together with their ability to run full speed through thickets on the darkest night, indicates that, as the physiology of their eyes suggests, they see very well indeed in low light. How well do they see in the light of day? I suspect they see better than many hunters give them credit for. Turkey hunters like to say that a deer sees a man in the woods and thinks he's a stump, while a turkey sees a stump in the woods and thinks it's a man. There is some truth in that old saw, but I suspect it has more to do with the tendency of deer to rely more on their keen sense of smell than on any inability to see well. Most game animals that have not been heavily hunted, or that are simply not alert, will probably not see a motionless hunter standing against a tree or behind a sapling. Once alert, any animal, even bear and moose, is quick to detect the slightest movement and will probably spot the human silhouette, or the unconcealed face or hands of a hunter. And, as increasing numbers of hunters are learning, deer, bears, elk, and even moose will learn to look for hunters in tree stands.

Aside from the fact that most animals, once alerted, can use their eyes very effectively, experienced hunters have learned that one way to increase their success ratio is to avoid overhunting the same spot. Perhaps more to the point: Don't continue to hunt a spot from which you have you have been picked off. Any game animal that has been spooked in a given location will be extra wary for some time when approaching that location. They will learn to avoid certain spots. In the case of deer, there is some evidence that they communicate alarm with their interdigital glands, leaving scent on the ground that other deer immediately recognize as a danger signal, putting them on alert. Many hooved game animals have similar glands and engage in similar behaviors, and it is possible that most herd animals have similar means of alerting one another to danger.

One of the more efficient—and effective—game/hunting operations I've been fortunate to hunt with is at Enon Plantation, a well-known bow-only deer hunting plantation in Alabama. The fact that it is bow-only is incidental; any hunting operation could benefit from similar practices. Hunters at Enon routinely see numerous deer on each morning and afternoon hunt. What's more, the deer tend to venture into food plots during daylight hours on a regular basis, and usually seem to be relaxed. At the opposite extreme, I've hunted at operations in which plenty of tracks and other sign indicated the presence of deer in good numbers, but they're rarely seen venturing into food plots during the day, and when they do, they are extremely wary. How does Enon do it? I observed two ways. First, there are numerous tree stands over a large area. No stand gets hunted frequently, and, because of the wide choice of stands available, there is never a temptation to hunt a stand for which the wind direction is not right.

Second, Enon controls how stands are hunted. Hunters are driven directly to their stands, which they can access by taking only a few steps. They are asked to remain in their stands until a vehicle returns to pick them up, and told that only then should they leave the stands. Because of this approach, any deer that are in or close to the food plot (and there are usually at least a few), run off at the approach of the truck. They never see the hunter enter or climb down from the stand. Even when a hunter sticks a deer, the folks at Enon suggest he remain in his stand, awaiting the arrival of the vehicle before taking up the trail. These precautions mean that not only are hunters rarely seen entering or leaving their stands, but also they don't contaminate the area with scent. If the guides at Enon suspect a stand has been com-promised—if a hunter reports deer looking up and spotting him, for instance—they either relocate that stand or give it a long rest. The result is that deer at Enon travel more during daylight hours, and tend to be relaxed most of the time.

MOTION DETECTORS

We've seen that few animals have good color vision, and that their enhanced night vision tends to come at the expense of an ability to see details. On top of that, the placement of their eyes on either side of the head gives them a very wide field of view, but decreases their depth perception. They make up for these disadvantages by being motion detectors. As every bowhunter knows, one of the chief challenges of bowhunting is drawing the bow without being seen. Nearly every bowhunter has a story or two about a trophy that was in range but picked up the movement and bolted when the hunter started to draw his bow. Bowhunters learn to wait before drawing until their quarry's head is hidden behind a tree or brush, or at least until its attention is focused elsewhere. There are several ways hunters can minimize the problem of having their movements spotted. The obvious one is over-looked by more than a few hunters: Don't move. In a society that val-ues productivity over just about everything else, standing still, sitting motionless, or even walking very slowly can be a near impossibility for many modern hunters. Hunting situations may at times require moving fast, but the hunter who cannot remain nearly motionless for long periods is at a real disadvantage, and probably spooks game he never knows is there.

There are two keys to remaining still. The first is comfort, and the second is relaxation. We'll look at these in another context later in the book; for now, suffice it to say that both are underrated. However, the hunter who is not comfortable will have to rely on a tremendous amount of discipline to remain motionless, and the hunter who cannot relax totally in the outdoors will be a less effective hunter.

CAMOUFLAGE

It's a rare hunter these days who ventures afield without camouflage clothing. Even our guns, bows, and gear are camouflaged. Now and then someone makes the observation that, as recently as a generation ago, hunters, including the most successful ones, ventured afield without camo clothing. That is only partly true. While they may not have worn the kinds of patterns that are popular with hunters today, they tended to avoid light-colored clothing, preferring darker colors, often green or brown. Red was a commonly seen color, too, often in plaid. The old-timers understood that game animals did not seem to distinguish red, and felt that plaid tended to break up a hunter's outline. I also recall, from my earliest childhood hunts with my father, being admonished to wear gloves and to keep the bill of my hat low over my brow to keep my white face shaded.

By the same token, our fathers' generation also didn't hunt from tree stands and rarely, if ever, used the kind of fully enclosed ground blinds available to hunters today. Few experienced modern hunters would deny that tree stands or ground blinds offer significant advantages in many hunting situations.

One well-known outdoor writer of my acquaintance, who also acts as a guide on frequent occasions, enjoys hunting without camo. He wears dark clothes and takes other measures to avoid being spotted by game. He gets an extra kick out of tagging animals and ribbing his hunting buddies who are dressed head-to-toe in the latest camo patterns.

The real question, though, is not whether it is possible to tag a trophy animal while not wearing camo. It most certainly is. The question is: Does wearing camo clothing and using camo gear give the hunter an advantage, if not in every situation, at least in some of them? While I would not hesitate to go hunting without camo if there was no camo available to me, I'm also inclined to seek every edge I can get, especially when bowhunting. It's just too darned hard to get within bow range of a trophy animal to do otherwise.

Breaking up a hunter's outline and wearing dark, nonshiny clothes are important, but if I could camouflage only one part of me, it would be my face. Second choice would be my hands.

On a hunt with my friend Vince in Tennessee several years ago, I paused before entering the woods to put some camo paint on my face and hands when I noticed Vince grinning at me. I had to laugh, because I knew exactly what he was grinning about.

"I guess you don't need any of this," I said.

"No, I don't think I do," he said.

Vince, if you haven't guessed, is black. Apparently he found it amusing to watch a hunter pull what looked like a makeup kit from his daypack, flip it open to the mirror in the lid, and start applying camo paint to his face.

The fact is, though, unless you have a very dark complexion, you need to cover your face and hands with camo paint or a head net of some sort. A hunter can be wearing camo head to toe, but if his skin is white and his face and hands are not camouflaged, they will shine through the woods like a full moon on a cloudless night.

Since there are no limits on how much camo I wear, I generally wear it head to toe. Does the pattern matter? In many situations, it probably doesn't. I will wear any pattern as opposed to none, but when I head out west to hunt sage country, I try to wear a pattern that blends better with the lighter colors of that area—if possible, one designed to imitate sage. If I know I'll be hunting primarily in spruce forests, I wear a pine pattern. The fact is, I do 80 percent of my hunting in mixed hardwood forests, and have found patterns, such as the popular Mossy Oak and Realtree, to be effective in environments ranging from southern swamps to northern forests to wide-open prairies. Still, more than once I've been caught in a camo pattern that seemed far too dark, too light, too green, or too brown for the area in which I was hunting. There are some excellent all-round camo patterns available, such as ASAT, which tend to reflect the colors around them and conceal hunters in every imaginable environment.

Camouflaging gear is probably less important than clothing, the exception being blinds or anything that shines or is highly reflective. Some blinds, though printed in camo patterns, are made from fabrics that will shine in the sun.

Remaining undetected by game animals is far more than a matter of wearing camo, climbing trees, or hunting from blinds. (Later we'll look more closely at hunting from tree stands as well as ground blinds.) Whether avoiding the eyes of the hunter's quarry is instinctive or learned behavior could be the subject of a good debate, but a surprising number of hunters take little care to remain unseen. A few years ago a book high on the bestseller list was, *Everything I Need to Know I Learned in Kindergarten*. I cannot quite say that I learned everything I need to know about hunting in kindergarten, but that is about the age at which my education as a hunter began. My father took me along with him hunting in the woods of southwestern Ohio and southeastern Indiana, and the basic lessons I learned on those outings are things every hunter should internalize. I can almost hear my father's voice when I think of them:

"When you come to a field or an open area in the woods, don't walk through the middle of it. Skirt around it. If you have to walk through it, don't waste time; get through it in a hurry."

"Walk in the shadows and out of the sunlight as much as you can. When you stop to look around or take a break, stay in the shade."

"Be careful about brushing against saplings and small trees when you walk, and don't hold on to them when you climb up a hill. An animal will hear and see that sapling shake for a long ways through the woods."

"Try not to walk down ridgelines or stand out on points, where you'll be exposed."

"Avoid walking down game trails and logging roads if you can. Animals use them, too, and will spot you. They'll also pick up your scent long after you've gone."

"You can usually get away with slow movements, but rarely with quick ones. When you look around, turn your head slowly. If you've got to scratch or get something out of your pocket, do it slowly."

"When you stop, stop behind cover that will hide you, but that is not too thick to prevent shooting."

"Use the terrain as much as possible—ravines, hills, creek bottoms, even large rocks or downed trees—to move without being seen."

"Keep in mind the time of day, the time of year, and the weather, to avoid spooking animals. Don't walk through a likely feeding area or bedding area at a time when you might expect game to be there."

"A man standing upright can be seen for a long ways. Stay low when approaching game—hunker down at a distance, drop to your knees as you get closer, and crawl if you need to get very close."

To the experienced hunter, these behaviors are automatic, and require no thinking. And yes, I can think of numerous hunting situations that represent exceptions—times when shaking a sapling, moving quickly, or walking down a logging road might be the right thing to do. They're good general rules, though, and most hunters would be better hunters for following them unless there is a good reason not to.

CONCEALING TREE STANDS

It's surprising how many hunters spend hours scouting and picking the perfect location for a tree stand, but give little consideration to keeping the stand hidden. Make no mistake: Game will spot hunters in tree stands. In fact, it happens all the time. Sometimes the easiest way to understand how to do a thing is to look first at how not to do it. Let's take a look at the worst-possible tree stand setup. We'll assume we're dealing with a deer-hunting scenario here, since the great majority of tree stands are used by deer hunters. The same reasoning could apply to other species that might be hunted from a tree stand.

Our hypothetical stand is ten feet high, on the side of a medium-sized tree with no limbs until about twenty-five feet up. It's on the side of a hill, facing uphill, with a well-used trail straight ahead, and a cluster of scrapes off to the right, which in this location is to the south.

Problem one with this stand is that it is not high enough. I say this as someone who is not all that comfortable with heights. Height matters. Sorry to all those who want to think that eight, ten, or twelve feet is high enough—it's not. Ask yourself this: If height does not matter, why are we climbing trees anyway? Actually there are several reasons, but the main one is to get above the normal line of vision of deer. Deer can and will learn to look up into trees, but it is not something they routinely do. By getting above their normal line of sight, we can more often remain unseen by deer. It's that simple. How high is high enough? Opinions vary, but my own experience tells me that at somewhere above 15 feet, a white-tailed deer becomes less likely to spot a hunter, and the likelihood decreases further at 20 feet or above. Experimenting with deer I did not intend to shoot, I have literally waved my arms and remained unseen by deer when I was hunting from 20 or more feet. And yes, I have also been spotted at that height and higher, and yes, I have taken deer from stands as low as eight feet. Over the years, though, I have been spotted far more often at heights below 15 feet.

Some hunters would argue that fifteen feet is an adequate height, and a few of the best deer hunters I know would suggest that the magic number is closer to 25 or even 30 feet. But I do believe this: the bowhunter at less than 15 feet is better off on the ground. On the ground, he can use terrain and cover to his advantage. Perching 10 or

12 feet up in a tree simply makes him more visible to his quarry, unless he is fully enclosed in a blind. (In which case, why bother climbing the tree?) Though our focus here is on visibility, many hunters also believe that when they are at greater heights, deer are less likely to catch their scent. The theory, which we addressed in an earlier chapter, is that in some situations the hunter's scent will be carried over the head of deer approaching close to the stand.

A related problem with our hypothetical tree stand is its location on the side of a hill. In hill country it's not always possible to avoid such a location, but the hunter needs to keep in mind that, even if he is 20 feet up a tree, deer on the uphill side will, at some point, be at eye level. That may be unavoidable, but a hunter should at least see to it that a trail, logging road, scrape, or rub line is well below eye level, to decrease the likelihood of deer walking by the stand at that level. A stand facing east is not necessarily a problem, but the hunter should be aware that if he plans to hunt this stand in the morning he may, depending on the steepness of the hill, find himself looking directly into the sun. Morning stands facing the rising sun to the east, or evening stands facing the setting sun to the west, can leave the hunter nearly blinded for a good while on clear days, and can be downright uncomfortable.

Hunters are often advised to position stands in such a way that deer are more likely to be looking into the sun, but I have some doubts about the soundness of that advice. First, the primary consideration—far and away—is wind direction, and the likelihood seems low that the perfect setup with regard to wind, among other factors, will position hunters so that deer are likely to be looking into the sun to see the stand. What's more, if the sun is behind the hunter, he is likely to be casting a long shadow. If concealment behind the hunter has him completely shaded, this is not a problem. But if so much as the top of the head or one arm is at any time touched by sunlight, the hunter's slightest movement will be exaggerated by a giant shadow on the ground. It's far better if no portion of a hunter's shadow extends into the area where he expects to see deer. Finally, our hypothetical tree has no limbs until the twenty-five-foot mark. That is just the kind of tree many of us look for when using climbing stands, but it leaves us hanging out there in the great, wide open, where deer—especially mature deer—are almost sure to spot us. Drawing a bow without the movement being picked up can be all but impossible in a stand of this sort. In this kind of stand, even the absolutely motionless hunter can and probably will be seen by deer, unless he is at heights beyond the comfort and safety level for most of us.

There are fixes for that problem, including various camo skirts designed to conceal hunters in tree stands. Trimming limbs and properly positioning them around the stand with wire or nails can help address the problem, in areas where hunters have permission from landowners to do this. There are also artificial limbs on the market that can be used in these situations to help provide concealment. Also among products that can be useful here are umbrellas such as Eastman Outfitters' Sta-Dry Umbrella. From the perspective of a deer looking up, these provide a background to which hunters can blend in, and simply keeping hunters shaded makes them less visible. Decoys can be useful, too, by helping to keep the attention of an approaching deer on the decoys and away from the hunter, though decoys in themselves are no substitute for some degree of concealment.

Many hunters turn an otherwise excellent stand into something less than that by overpruning. Some judgment is called for here. It's an exercise in frustration to sit in a stand with inadequate shooting lanes that require an animal to stop and position itself in one of two or three spots for the hunter to have a good shooting opportunity. At the same time, overpruning can call attention to the hunter and leave him exposed. There is a happy medium between adequate concealment and adequate shooting lanes, and only good judgment and experience will tell the hunter when that point has been reached.

EYE CONTACT

Is eye contact an issue in concealment? Though some hunters might scoff at the idea, most veteran hunters have reached the conclusion that many prey species understand that when eye contact is made, they have been spotted. More than a few hunters have stopped to scan a nearby deadfall or thicket, only to have an animal that was hidden there bolt the moment eye contact was made. Among many species of animals, staring is recognized as a threat, and animals, including most canine species, will show submissive behavior to a dominant member of their own species by turning their heads and looking away. More often than not among canines, two animals staring at one another is the first step toward more overtly aggressive behavior which usually leads to a fight. It doesn't seem at all out of the question that prey species should have evolved in such a way that they recognize—through eye contact—when they have been spotted.

Hunters have developed some interesting approaches to this

A good ground blind might be the ultimate in concealment, hiding movement, and even reducing sound and scent.

problem. One, of course, is to avoid staring (at least when the quarry is close) by not looking directly at the animal, but looking to one side instead. Ultimately, it's difficult for a hunter to avoid looking at what is about to become a target. My friend Chip Hart, with whom I co-host The Big Outdoors radio program in Cincinnati, swears by glasses, developed specifically for the purpose, that allow hunters to see perfectly while completely hiding their eyes with a camo pattern. Many hunters—and I confess to doing this myself on occasion—try to squint in such a way that they can still see, but the whites of their eyes are mostly hidden. It would be difficult to prove that these methods work, but it's hard to imagine they can hurt.

We've already mentioned that most animals are great motion detectors. The best concealment is unlikely to work if a hunter makes exaggerated movements. It's important that the stand be arranged in such a way that movement can be kept to a minimum. That limb partway around the tree trunk might be suitable for hanging a day-pack on, but only if it can be accessed without requiring gynmnastics. It could be that I fidget too much, but I frequently access my daypack for water, snacks, calls, or other items. Bows and rifles, too, should be in easy reach. Holders attached to stands work very well. My own preference when bowhunting is the EZ Hanger, but there are similar devices that can be affixed to the tree over the hunter's head, with the bow hanging immediately in front. With this arrangement, a hunter can get his bow in hand with only the slightest movement. Still other hangers and organizers are available for hanging calls and other accessories. There is nothing worse than frantically digging around in a daypack or a pocket for an item that has become suddenly very necessary.

One of the more interesting approaches to reducing the likelihood of being spotted in tree stands involves the use of dummies. I've seen this trick used most often in tripod stands where concealment options are limited, but it can be used in any tree stand. A simple, homemade dummy of some sort (usually consisting of an old jacked stuffed with pillows or straw, with an improvised head wearing a hat) is left in the stand when it is not occupied. The idea, of course, is that a deer spotting the stand will become accustomed to the general shape of a hunter in it, and will not react to the real thing. I can't speak to this from personal experience, never having tried it, but it seems like a good idea.

GROUND BLINDS

The first hunter probably used ground blinds of some sort. Even four-footed predators will remain hidden behind deadfalls, thickets, or trees, waiting to pounce on any prey species that walks by. Humans simply improve on that tactic by, in effect, creating their own dead-falls, thickets, or trees. They can considerably improve on the "blinds" that occur naturally, and enjoy the huge advantage of being able to put them wherever they want them. (That is only an advantage if they know where to put them, but we'll get to that later.) The corollary to this is that prey species have learned that predators like to use cover for setting up ambushes, and many of them have learned to avoid danger areas, or to pass by them with extra caution. A young goose or turkey might wander close by a big tuft of grass or a row of standing corn, but older ones will usually give them a wide berth, preferring to remain out in the open where they can see all around.

Deer and some other game animals are a little different in that they often prefer thick cover for concealment, relying heavily on their keen sense of smell to avoid danger. Still, mature animals are wary enough to be cautious around anything new or unnatural in their environment. This suggests two keys to success in using a blind for hunting: (1) make sure it's not "new," (2) try to make it appear as natural as possible. Both things are very doable for the hunter willing to take a little time. Making it not "new" is as simple as setting it up in advance. Even a blind set up in the middle of a wide open meadow or pasture is something animals will become accustomed to if they see it repeatedly. How long that takes depends on how often the animals pass by it, and probably a little bit on the individual animal itself and how wary it is. Longer is better, but the hunters I know who are consistently successful from ground blinds prefer to have a blind in place at least several days before hunting from it. That is not always possible for any of several reasons, and in any case, that strategy tends to negate one of the chief advantages of using a ground blind, which is mobility. Many of today's newer blinds, which are designed to be set up and taken down very quickly, allow hunters to observe ever-changing travel patterns and take advantage of their observations by setting up a blind for an ambush.

This leads us to the other key to success in using a ground blind—making it appear as "natural" as possible. I use the term "natural" here, because it is the kind of jargon with which hunters are familiar. On a farm in South-Central Ohio is an abandoned barn. It's surrounded by thick, second growth penetrated only by a network of well-used game trails. I have used that barn as a blind on several occasions. There is also a rusted-out, old pickup truck in the corner of a field close to where a logging road enters the field, and I have spent a few hours sitting in that truck, too. There is nothing natural about either of them, but deer accept them as part of the landscape because they have been there a very long time. Making a blind appear natural is mostly a matter of breaking up an unnatural silhouette. Cover behind the blind helps, but it can be important to have some cover in front of the blind, as well. In many spots it is possible to set the blind up in such a way that some natural cover is all around it, and that may be sufficient. In other cases, hunters will have to manipulate the habitat a little. A log or limb on the ground in front of the blind can help anchor it and keep it from flapping, as well as break up an unnatural straight line along the ground. Additional concealment can be had by leaning a few limbs, real or artificial, against the blind. Many blinds have ties at strategic locations to facilitate this process. By backing off and looking at the blind, it's not hard to tell when the silhouette is less discernible. As with providing concealment for a tree stand, some judgment is in order. The idea is to provide concealment while insur-

The ears and the body language of this buck suggest something is approaching from across the clearing. Is it another buck?

ing that adequate shooting lanes are available.

Keeping blinds shaded can be helpful here. Aside from the fact that blinds in direct sunlight can get uncomfortably warm in all but the coldest weather, sunlight will make any unnatural aspects of the blind more visible. Also, as we mentioned earlier, some fabrics reflect sunlight, creating a very unnatural shine. When a given environment or location requires setting up a blind in the open, it becomes increasingly important that it remain there for some time before being hunted. While a fully enclosed blind can go a long way toward concealing hunters, sharp-eyed game animals can still pick them off if they can see inside the blind. One way to avoid that is to keep the interior of the blind dark by putting it in the shade. Better still, many newer blinds have black interiors for this purpose. A hunter wearing camo or dark clothing, whose face and hands are covered, will be virtually invisible from outside the blind unless he gets very close to the opening. This is another advantage of comfortably large blinds. It can be impossible to stay back from the opening in a smaller blind, and a smaller blind may even require that the arrow be extended outside the window, which is a real disadvantage.

There is some concern that shooting windows can be problematic in blinds with black interiors. From outside the blind, these windows, when open, appear as large black spots, and there is reason to believe that many animals shy away from these—in fact, the folks who developed Double Bull blinds are convinced that this is the case. They recommend keeping the shoot-through camo mesh netting in place. Hunters inside the blind can see through the netting, but from the outside the netting blends in perfectly with the camo pattern of the blind. I've shot through them on numerous occasions and noticed no loss of accuracy. There is one important limitation, though. Not all mechanical heads will work with shoot-through netting, since the netting will open the heads prematurely. In general, L-shaped or wing-blade mechanicals won't work, while other designs such as the Rocket Steelheads will work. I would highly recommend trying any mechanical heads before shooting them through the netting in a hunting situation. String trackers will not work with the shoot-through netting.

Finally, there is the issue of scent and ground blinds. Some hunters have suggested that ground blinds tend naturally to reduce scent, since they block the wind and may tend to contain some scent inside the blind. A few of the newer blinds actually include the same carbon-impregnated fabrics as Scent-Lok suits. At least one blind I'm aware of—Scent-Tite—is sealed and actually vents the hunter's scent through a tube high into the air. I've never used a Scent-Tite blind, but have seen some impressive demonstrations in which deer, following a bait trail put down for demonstration purposes, walked completely around the blind, eating as they went, and showed no awareness of the people in the blind.

12

THE SILENT HUNTER:
WHAT ANIMALS HEAR
AND
HOW THEY HEAR IT

On a spring turkey hunt in southeastern Indiana many years ago, I sat along a treeline looking over a pasture that rolled away almost to the horizon. There was a tiny black spot moving across the field in the distance, and my binoculars confirmed it was a gobbler. I yelped as loudly as I could with a diaphragm call, and a few seconds later, the gobbler went into full strut, then it gobbled several times in rapid succession. I couldn't hear him gobble, but I could see him extending his neck to do it. I was convinced it was coincidence, but soon learned, as I continued yelping intermittently, that he could hear me clearly. The big tom was walking across the pasture scratching and pecking at cow pies—a common occupation of turkeys in pastures, since cow pies typically contain bits of undigested corn or other grains, as well as grubs, worms, and other little critters. About five seconds after every series of yelps, without exception, the gobbler went into full strut, gobbled, or both. He took his time coming my way, and it was a good fifteen minutes before I could hear his faint gobbles in the distance.

I never tagged that gobbler. When he got within 100 yards or so, a hen intercepted him and led him off into the woods. It was an interesting and educational encounter, though. The wild turkey's hearing ability is especially amazing when you consider the tiny size of its ear openings and the fact that is has no external ears at all. After that day,

I always hunted turkeys as if at least one gobbler could hear my calls at any given time, whether I was hearing a response or not, and I'm convinced I became a more patient and more successful turkey hunter as a result. In more recent years, I've tried to take the same approach with any quarry I might be calling.

Just how well do game animals hear? For whatever reason, the subject has drawn less scientific attention than how well they smell or see. Most of the research that has been done on animal hearing has been done with the aim of producing devices to prevent car-animal collisions. The focus of those studies has involved primarily the frequency ranges to which white-tailed deer respond, and the short answer to the question is that their hearing is very similar to that of humans in terms of the frequencies they hear, with some biologists suggesting they can hear slightly higher frequencies. For the hunter, it may be sufficient to know that most game animals hear sounds at slightly greater distances than do humans, and that they seem better equipped to pinpoint sounds both in distance and in specific location.

As hunters, we do have this going for us: The woods are usually full of sounds. Birds chirp, squirrels bark, chipmunks whistle, sticks pop, leaves rustle, limbs squeak, streams gurgle, and the wind sighs through the trees. And, at least in the places where most of us do most of our hunting, vehicles pass by, planes fly over, dogs bark, roosters crow, chain saws rumble—as often as not, it's downright noisy out there. At a certain level of noise—on a very windy day, for instance— animals feel vulnerable and tend to bed down. Short of high winds, they will move normally. They will react to the constant sounds around them in much the same way as will a hunter. They will tune out the bird song or the leaves rustling in a breeze. They will be startled by any sudden loud noise that is close by. Unlike human hunters, they are not at the top of the food chain, so they will almost certainly run from it. They will register other sounds that are not overly loud or do not originate from very close by, becoming more alert and waiting to determine the source with their sense of smell, or visually. They might even assume the sound was made by another deer. They are alert to certain sounds—coyotes or wolves howling, dogs barking, a flock of crows raising a ruckus—and can certainly associate them with danger. They will also learn to tolerate certain sounds that might otherwise cause alarm, if the sounds are regular and tend to emanate from the same area. A dog barking from the same yard every day, for instance, is something animals learn to ignore, while the same dog

Which shot would you take? I'd go for the top one. Both offer broadside shots, but the buck is busy feeding in the top shot. The lower shot shows the buck alert, ready to flee at any odd noise or movement.

Old timers say a deer sees a man in the woods and thinks it's a stump, while a turkey sees a stump in the woods and thinks it's a man. Despite excellent vision, turkeys are more easily fooled by blinds than are most game.

Jim Litmer of Third Hand Archery with a fine warthog. Warthogs are extremely quick, but this one didn't manage to jump the string.

Recent studies suggest bears see color. Author is convinced that often they are aware of a hunter's presence, but aren't intimidated.

Which game animal has the best all-around sensory perceptions? With excellent sight, an amazing sense of smell, and keen hearing, a good case can be made for the Cape Buffalo. In a situation like this, you want to have complete trust in your PH.

Prey animals sense their vulnerability at waterholes and tend to be extremely wary.

Like bears and the wild hogs with which they often share habitat, javelinas have an excellent sense of smell, but possess poor vision and only average hearing. The bowhunter who stays downwind can often stalk within bow range.

Pronghorns mostly rely on their vision, but don't underestimate their other senses.

Reasonably good vision and superior intelligence are the only edge we have over the game we pursue. Good African trackers put both to use in developing skills that most hunters have to see to believe.

Fooling the eyes is much easier than fooling the nose. Notice how the bare hand stands out in this otherwise well-concealed hunter.

barking from an unexpected location will cause nervousness or fear.

Animals can probably learn to distinguish humans moving through the woods from other critters simply by sound, but only because careless humans make sounds that differ from those of any other creature. Only humans consistently crash through the underbrush, and only humans walk with a constant, regular cadence. Hunters who refrain from making either of these sounds by picking their path more carefully, by varying their pace, and by stopping frequently to look and listen, can often avoid being "made" by alert animals. It is certainly possible to walk quietly through the woods, stepping softly and avoiding the sticks and rocks that betray our location. Most hunters simply don't bother. And I am amazed by the number of hunters who talk in the woods. The human voice is very distinctive, and carries over great distances. To some extent remaining unheard in the woods is, like remaining unseen in the woods, a matter of instinct or early training. For those who have the instinct or the early training, there is a natural tendency to remain quiet in the woods.

RIG FOR SILENT RUNNING

Years ago I was among the last handful of young men to be drafted into the U.S. Army. The war in Vietnam was winding down rapidly, and I was fortunate enough to serve my time here in the states. I didn't know that would be the case when I was in training, though, and I have a very vivid memory of one particular training exercise at Fort Knox. My platoon, in full field gear, made its way on a ten-mile hike through the woods by moonlight. Boots stomped the ground, steel helmets clanked, canteens gurgled, loose ammunition rattled, and hardly a minute passed without someone feeling an irrepressible urge to say something to the man in front of him or the guy behind him. I made a mental note to myself to look for a desk job or try to get into the sniper program, because I didn't think my chances for survival in combat would be very good if my buddies were as noisy as this bunch. In retrospect, I have to assume that more advanced training was in store for anyone headed for a combat zone, and that that training would include learning how to move quietly.

Hunters are not normally in life-or-death situations, of course, but they do have a need to be quiet. In part, that means learning how to move quietly through the woods. It also means having the right gear and using it correctly, beginning with the right clothing. The standard for comparison is wool. Wool has several advantages to recommend it, including its ability to shed moisture and retain some insulating ability when wet, but wool is also normally a very quiet fabric. It doesn't swish when the wearer walks, and it doesn't make loud scraping or zipping sounds when a stick, thorn, or other object rubs against it. Fleece is another relatively quiet fabric, which is one reason for its popularity with hunters. Cotton, depending on the weave, can be quiet, and can be a good choice for mild-weather hunting. Until a few years ago, rain gear was unavoidably noisy. Newer blends of waterproof breathable fabric, especially when combined with fleece or wool, can be very quiet. Whatever the style garment, testing for quiet is easy enough. If it doesn't swish or make excessive noise when rubbed together, and if it doesn't scrape loudly when a thumbnail is rubbed over it, it's probably acceptable for hunting. Just keep in mind: On a quiet day in the woods, even the slightest rustle of clothing can cause a nearby game animal to bolt.

Buttons are the quietest closures. Zippers, if they don't have to be accessed too often, might do. Velcro is noisy. Clothing aside, the hunter who heads into the woods without making some preparations with silence in mind is probably going to sound a little like my platoon at Fort Knox. Fanny packs and daypacks are great items, but unless packed properly, loose items will rattle in them, liquids will gurgle, and metallic buttons will click. Combine these with a tree stand and a bow, and the noise intensifies. Quieting these items doesn't require a course in engineering—just the time to assemble everything, walk around with it for a minute, and take the necessary steps to ensure that it can all be worn or carried together quietly.

Most hunters have a story or two about the big buck or bull that almost was, and in many cases, the difference between filling a tag and another "one that got away" story comes down to a tiny detail. The sound of an arrow being drawn over a noisy rest, a release aid clicking against the bow riser, a jacket sleeve swishing as an arm is raised—all these sounds and many others have saved more than a few animals from winding up on a plate or on the wall. The hunter who pays attention to those details will still probably lose an opportunity or two to unpredictable noises. The hunter who doesn't will surely spook many animals, some of which he will never know were there.

Earlier we made reference to the fact that carrying tree stands through the woods can compound the difficulty of moving quietly. The need to silence a tree stand, though, doesn't end when it comes off the back. Even worse than rattling through the woods en route to the stand location is rattling, squeaking, or creaking when in position on the tree. Tree stands seem to get better every year, and the days of metal scraping metal and chains rattling with every movement are fortunately over, for the most part. Still, it's worthwhile applying a little oil (or better still, grease) to all moving parts of the stand before hanging it. Some hunters customize their stands, and quiet them further by applying carpeting, which has the added benefit of comfort and warmth.

HEARING AND HUNTING TACTICS

Should an animal's hearing ability be a factor in hunting strategies? Still hunting, for instance, can be enjoyable and effective, but on a crisp, dry fall day in the Midwest when hardwood forests are carpeted with leaves, still hunting is not the best option. Even moving at a snail's pace—which is generally the proper pace for still hunting—the hunter is going to make noise that will alert game, possibly for hundreds of yards. On the other hand, game animals have the same problem. The hunter on a stand can often hear deer approaching from great distances under such conditions. Getting to and from the stand without creating a commotion is difficult. Hunters can sometimes wade along the edges of lakes or ponds, or use creeks or creek bottoms, to avoid wading through dry leaves. This is a situation in which walking along the edge of an open field, or even crossing the middle of one, can be the best approach. If the stand is not far from a creek or a field edge, it is not difficult to keep a path open to the stand in order to approach it in complete silence. Hunters with ATVs can keep a path clear over fairly long distances through the woods. Granted, even at mid-day, such path-clearing activities might alert game; if so, better to alert game while clearing a path at mid-day than when walking to a stand to hunt.

When the woods are damp, or when a steady breeze maintains a constant level of noise, it is a great time for still hunting. Such conditions are also great for hunting standing corn. Deer often bed in standing corn, and when a light breeze tends to cover movement and sounds, the careful hunter can sometimes slip up on deer in their beds. The technique is simple, which is not to say easy. The wind must be coming from a direction that enables the hunter to move across (as opposed to down) rows while simultaneously moving more-or-less into the wind. The hunter steps very carefully and slowly from one row to the next. At each row, he leans his head forward slowly into the next row, looking up and down the row. When the field is crossed, the hunter can retrace his steps quickly downwind, move over 30 or 40 yards (depending on visibility in the corn field) and start again, eventually working through the entire field.

A pair of compact binoculars can be helpful. Seldom will the hunter see an entire deer, or even a large portion of it. More often he will spot a patch of brown or white fur, or catch the flick of an ear or tail. It's often impossible to be sure how the deer is oriented, or which part of it is visible. The trick is to move very slowly into position or wait for the deer to stand or move. Often, a stone or clump of dirt tossed into the air to come down on the other side of the deer will cause it to stand, turn, or turn its head. Getting into such a position can take hours or days—then again, getting a shot opportunity from a stand can take hours or days, too. Cornfield stalking is an exciting way to hunt deer, particularly for those hunters who prefer not to sit in a stand.

BODY LANGUAGE AND HEARING

In his book *Whitetail Strategies*, Peter Fiduccia devotes an entire chapter to interpreting deer body language. It's interesting and useful stuff, and I'd like to reference a portion that is relevant to the subject of this chapter.

If you're watching a doe and both of its ears are forward, Peter points out, the doe is probably alone. However, if one ear rotates toward the back, she is probably listening for deer that are following her. It could be a pair of yearlings or another doe, but of course it could be a buck, too.

Those large, cupped ears help deer pinpoint the location of sounds, and they will often rotate them toward the source of a faint or distant sound. Keeping an eye on those ears, and watching for something to approach from the direction they are pointed, only makes sense.

Peter is talking about white-tailed deer, but the same points apply to many other species, including mulies, elk, and moose. Watching their body language, and particularly the position of their ears, can not only tip a hunter off when (and from where) other animals are approaching, but can also give an indication of whether the animal is relaxed— and likely to stick around awhile and offer a perfect shot— or nervous and likely to bolt any moment or jump the string.

Calling

An in-depth look at all the various vocalizations and other sounds that can be used to bring game into bow range is beyond the scope of this book, but there are some general aspects of calling having to do with hearing in general, and the superior hearing of most animals in particular, that we can take a look at.

One seeming difference between the hearing of animals and humans is the superior ability of most animals to course sound—that is, to hear a sound from a distance and know exactly where it is coming from. This can work to the hunter's advantage, enabling him to bring game in from long distances. The downside is that hunters are often spotted, usually because they continue calling as the animal gets close. This is why experts at calling virtually every species almost invariably recommend the following: When you see or hear that an animal is moving in your direction, do not call. The objective of calling is to bring the animal to you; if he is headed your way, why risk spooking him or revealing your location by continuing to call? If he stops for awhile, changes directions, or appears to be leaving the area, then by all means, call again. Sometimes aggressive calling in this situation can turn an animal around. For the same reason, most experts recommend calling quietly at first, in case an animal is close by. Then step up the volume. As an animal approaches, reduce the volume and frequency, stopping altogether when he gets close, or when you can see that he is moving your way. Ideally, he will move into range looking for the source of the sound, as opposed to looking right at the source of the sound.

Never forget that game animals hear better than you do. There are times to pull out all the stops and call loudly, frequently, and aggressively. That is rarely the way to start out, though. A quiet call can be heard by animals for a long distance when the woods are still. Even the subtle sounds—simulating an antler rubbing gently against a tree or a cow moose urinating into water—can be heard for surprising distances. Calling in breezy conditions is another matter. This naturally calls for more volume, especially since the hunter should be downwind of where he expects game to be.

String Jumping

"String jumping" is a misnomer. "String ducking" would be a more accurately descriptive term, although even that would be somewhat misleading. What happens, as slow-motion video reveals clearly, is this: A tense or very alert animal, upon hearing the various sounds associated with the release of an arrow, and possibly in some cases the sounds of the arrow itself approaching, crouches in preparation to spring forward and run. In many cases the animal turns as it drops. The arrow flies over its back. As a side note, I suspect that string jumping accounts for a fair amount of high hits, in addition to misses. I've taken several whitetails with liver shots that I suspect resulted from the deer dropping and turning at the release of the arrow. Whether the result is a clean miss or a high hit, the whole sequence takes place so quickly that, in many cases, it isn't clear to the shooter what happened. On a number of occasions I've been in hunting camps watching video footage of the day's hunt, along with a dejected hunter recounting the story of a disappointing miss, only to discover that what the hunter thought was a poor shot was actually on target. The problem was that the target moved out of the way. String jumping occurs less frequently than it once did because today's bows are faster and quieter than their predecessors. It is still a very real phenomenon, though, and bowhunters should do everything they can to reduce, if not eliminate, its occurrence.

Not all animals are capable of jumping the string, but among those notorious for doing it often are white-tailed deer, pronghorns, and various of the African plains game. Significantly, string jumping is most likely to occur at ranges of between 20 and 30 yards. Closer than that, and animals rarely have time to jump the string before the arrow arrives. At distances beyond 30 yards or so, the sound is not heard, or perhaps it is not loud enough and close enough to result in the same reaction.

The very fact that animals rarely jump the string at very close ranges belies the oft-heard assertion that it is not possible to shoot an arrow fast enough to prevent an animal from jumping the string. Since the noise is even louder at very close ranges, the only reason animals don't successfully jump the string at close ranges is that the arrow arrives more quickly. The argument is often heard that, since the speed of sound travels at roughly 1,100 feet per second, and the fastest arrow at less than 400 feet per second, it is not possible for the arrow to arrive before the animal hears the sound of the shot. True enough, but that does not take reaction time into account. As amazingly fast as some animals can react, they are not instantaneous. More and more experienced bowhunters are convinced that a very fast arrow can reduce the incidence of string jumping.

Increasing arrow speed makes sense to the extent it can be done comfortably, safely, and without sacrificing accuracy. On the other hand, it always makes sense to reduce the noise generated by shooting, and it is usually possible. Newer bows are designed with silence in mind, and most come from the factory with various sound-deadening materials installed in the risers, in the limb pockets, or on the limbs. Stabilizers, string silencers, and aftermarket silencers such as Limbsavers and similar products can all reduce noise. Accessories such as quivers, sights, and rests are often sources of noise. These should be tightened down with products such as Lok-Tite. Small silencers are available for quieting noisy accessories, but in some cases, accessories that rattle or produce a lot of noise should simply be replaced.

Some arrows sound like buzz bombs flying downrange, and it seems hard to imagine that these cannot prompt string jumping. The sound is usually not apparent to the shooter, by the way. The best way to check for excessive arrow noise is to have someone stand well off to one side as you shoot. Feather fletching tends to be louder than vanes, but vanes that are slightly detached, bent, curled, or perforated even slightly can be surprisingly loud.

13

THE SIXTH SENSE

Do deer and some other species have a sixth sense—some way of perceiving the presence of a hunter that goes beyond the ordinary five senses? It's impossible to prove they don't, of course, but is there scientific evidence that they do? In fact there is, though the relevance of any sixth sense to hunting is not clear.

Biologists have long known that birds and some other migratory animals are able to migrate over long distances to precise locations with unerring accuracy. Experiments performed on some birds (sometimes involving surgical procedures) have indicated that the ability is visual, and that the birds can apparently see lines of magnetic radiation that surround the earth, and can use these in order to navigate. Of course, the ability to see things, such as infrared or ultraviolet, is not so much a sixth sense as a visual capability that extends to colors or types of energy humans cannot see.

Then there are pigeons. Biologists have determined that pigeons, which share and, in some cases, exceed the navigational ability of other birds, do not rely on vision for navigating. Instead, it appears they have magnetic materials in their beaks, connected to the brain via specialized nerves. These materials somehow act as a sort of internal compass by means of which pigeons can navigate. Clearly this is a form of sensory perception humans do not have, and it would not be unreasonable to label it a sixth sense.

According to one current theory, deer and some other animals possess the ability to perceive various forms of electromagnetic radiation, including the electromagnetic radiation produced by humans. The fact is that every living creature produces some amount of electromagnetic radiation. The question is, can it be perceived by other animals? Given that heat is one form of electromagnetic radiation, the short answer to the question has to be yes. So is light, so anyone who has watched fireflies flickering over a meadow has perceived electromagnetic radiation produced by another creature. The theory that is being proposed, though, is that deer and some animals are able to detect more subtle forms of electromagnetic radiation, explaining why they sometimes seem to detect the presence of a hunter when conditions (at least in the opinion of a given hunter) make it unlikely they could see, hear, or smell the hunter.

This is the basis for the HECS (Human Energy Concealment Systems) line of hunting clothing, which is designed to block most of the EMR produced by the human body. Does it work? HECS designers suggest that independent studies offer evidence of its effectiveness. The authors of these studies are not listed on their products or their website, but in fairness, the same could be said for many hunting products making similar claims.

Here are the objections with which I've become familiar to the claim that animals can perceive subtle forms of electromagnetic radiation: First, many biologists insist the amount of EMR produced by humans is so tiny that perceiving it from any distance would be impossible. Second—and what strikes me as more convincing—is the argument that, in the case of a deer, for instance, the deer itself is emitting EMR, and this would interfere with the ability of the deer to detect EMR from another creature. (On the other hand, we emit heat, but that doesn't stop us from detecting the heat emanating from another person, at least at a very close range.)

At this writing, the product is relatively new. Over time, anecdotal evidence will accumulate. Ideally, the sources of the studies done in the past will be revealed, along with detailed information about how they were conducted. Even more ideally, the studies will be peer-reviewed and similar studies will be conducted by other researchers. If the past is any indication, hunters shouldn't be holding their breaths waiting for any of that to happen. As is so often the case, consumers will have to use their own judgment about what seems plausible to them and make their own observations about whether or not a product works. In the meantime, an open mind with a healthy dose of skepticism is probably the best course.

Author Rick Combs tagged this Iowa bruiser using decoys, grunts, and attractant scents.

14

DECOYING BIG GAME

"We've got to try the horse suit. The horse suit never fails."

That is what Jay Liechty of Grim Reaper broadheads said to me as we watched yet another herd of pronghorns race off across the North Dakota grasslands. We had spent the better part of two hours glassing the herd and a couple of satellite bucks on its periphery. Eventually we circled the herd and stalked carefully for half a mile or so, then crawled on our bellies through mud and wet grass, dragging our bows and a couple of decoys behind us. We managed to get within 80 yards of the pronghorns before popping up the decoys but, after showing some initial curiosity, the entire herd decided to retreat over the far horizon. They didn't like the decoys, perhaps, or they spotted something suspicious, or maybe they caught our scent. Pronghorns rely more on their eyes and less on their noses than most big game, but hunters who think they can ignore a pronghorn's formidable sense of smell are making a mistake.

Jay was joking about the horse suit, though I think if he had had it with him, we'd have been ready to give it a try—this being the tail-end of a week spent trying unsuccessfully to tag a North Dakota prairie goat. The horse suit was actually an outfit Jay had put together for goose hunting, and with it he and a hunting buddy had managed to sneak within shotgun range of flock after flock of honkers near Jay's home in Provo, Utah. The horse suit was fairly elaborate, right down to a real tail that could be swished from inside. That suit had become legendary among waterfowlers in the region. "About the only time it didn't work," Jay explained, "was when there were real horses or cattle in the field. They would go bonkers, and that would spook the geese. Otherwise, it almost always worked." We discussed the use of cow silhouettes, which Jay had also used with some success by hiding behind them and pushing them forward slowly to get within range of geese, but the cow silhouettes were not as effective as the horse suit, in Jay's opinion.

In case you're worried that this is going to be a chapter about using horse suits and cow silhouettes to fool big game, it's not. The focus will be on using more traditional types of big game decoys, with reference to scent considerations as they apply to decoying. I bring up Jay's experience with horse suits and cow decoys because they illustrate two of the best reasons I can think of for using decoys: (1) they work, and (2) they can be a lot of fun.

Those two reasons are not unrelated, of course. Successful hunts tend to be more fun than unsuccessful hunts, and certainly using decoys can boost a hunter's success rates. That's not what I'm talking about, though. Decoys are fun because when they provoke a reaction, it's often an intense reaction. In many cases, animals seem to be aware that something is not quite right with this stiff, slightly strange-looking creature, but they can't quite figure out what it is. Or perhaps they are just reacting to the fact that the decoy represents a stranger in their midst. Most game animals, particularly herd animals, are accustomed to being familiar with other members of their species in their areas. Strangers are seldom welcome, and often create a situation in which a new pecking order must be established. Animals often engage in head bobbing, hoof stomping, snorting, or various scraping or rubbing activities in the presence of decoys. Sometimes they approach a decoy, run off, then sneak back in. Now and then, they charge it. Males may attempt to mount female decoys.

Decoys don't always work, any more than any other strategy always works. Like calling, rattling, stalking, or most other hunting tools or strategies, decoying deer, elk, moose, or pronghorns works just often enough to make it worthwhile. Decoys offer several advantages. First, and most obviously, decoys can bring game into range that would otherwise be out of range. In addition, they can cause animals to linger in the area, allowing hunters more time to assess the trophy potential of a buck or a bull, and increasing the likelihood of shot opportunities while providing more time for careful shot placement. At the same time, decoys can distract an animal's attention from the hunter, making discovery less likely. Finally, a decoy can help position an animal properly—in a shooting lane, at the best angle. All these advantages are critical to bowhunters.

A recent successful experience using decoys is one that I'll relate because I think it illustrates some of the advantages of using decoys, along with some typical decoying strategies. I was hunting whitetails at Thunder Valley Outfitters in southern Iowa with my friends Steve Bailey and Steve Lorenzo of Renzo's Decoys. It was early November. The weather had been unseasonably warm, with little deer movement, but temperatures dropped nicely the night I arrived, and everyone in camp was optimistic bucks would be cruising or chasing does.

Flight delays and a missed connection meant that I didn't arrive in camp and get to my bunk until around three in the morning and, exhausted from an entire day of travel, I slept in. I got to my stand a little after noon. The stand was near a hilltop in rolling, wooded country, though there were crop fields nearby. I made my way to the stand carrying two of Renzo's silhouette decoys, a buck and a doe. At Steve Bailey's suggestion, I put the doe in a bedded position, with the buck behind her. In order for deer to be able to see the bedded doe, I put them in a fairly open area near a logging road. That meant they were over my left shoulder, somewhat behind me, but the stand was positioned in such a way that I could easily turn to make a shot in that direction. I placed a white handkerchief doused with doe urine in a slot made for that purpose on the doe decoy's rump. Bailey is a strong believer in scent-control, and at his insistence I used rubber gloves when handling the decoys. I climbed into my stand and noted that a slight but steady breeze was coming from my left.

I had been in the stand a little over two hours when a doe approached from the left, moving with the wind at her back. She crossed in front of me about 15 yards out, and was almost past me when she spotted the decoys. Immediately she stopped and stared intensely at them. She bolted and ran off, directly away from me, for about 60 yards, then stopped. Again she stared at the "dekes" for some time, then began approaching them cautiously, stopping now and then to bob her head or stomp the ground. Eventually she wandered off again, but she never got more than 70 or 80 yards away, seemingly fascinated with the decoys. About fifteen minutes later, another doe came through from the same direction, with much the same reaction to the decoys as the first, though she never bolted. Instead she began browsing off to my right, directly downwind from me and about 30 or 40 yards from the dekes.

But this one had a buck following. The buck came along a couple of minutes later, and I judged it to be about a 140 class—a definite shooter. It was watching the doe, which may be why it never spotted the decoys. It stopped behind a deadfall not 15 yards away. When the doe it was following moved off, the buck followed at a fast trot. My grunts were to no avail—it was moving too fast for a shot when it crossed my shooting lanes. When the doe stopped about 70 or 80 yards away, the buck stopped too. I could see the tops of its white tines shining through the woods. Discouraged at having a nice buck pass by so closely without offering a shot, I began trying to lure it back into range by grunting.

After the second or third grunt, I heard an answering grunt—not from the buck I was watching, but from another buck somewhere off to my left. He grunted in response to my every grunt, and then I saw him, walking stiff-legged in my direction. I estimated him to be in the 160 range, and began struggling to control my breathing. I'll admit I might have been shaking just a little bit, too. I came to full draw as he approached, waiting for him to step into a shooting lane. He didn't oblige. He stopped behind the same big deadfall as the first buck, a little further out at 25 yards or so, but this one saw the decoys. The moment he spotted them, he began grunting more steadily, then putting on a show by thrashing around at several nearby saplings, along with the limbs of the deadfall. When I couldn't hold at full draw any longer, I let down as slowly as I could. Perhaps because his attention was fixed on the decoys, he didn't spot the movement.

The extra time gave me a chance to calm down a little and get my breathing under control, but I was worried. There were two does and a buck all more or less downwind from me. The doe and buck pair remained where they had stopped about 70 yards away to my right, and the first doe had wandered back toward the decoys and was no more than 30 yards from me, directly downwind. I was convinced that one of them would soon catch my scent and send the whole gang running off through the woods.

The bruiser buck showed no sign of stepping into my shooting lane. Intent on displaying his dominance to the decoys, he continued to punish the saplings around him. He did shift around some, though. I leaned off to my right a little and found an opening the size of a soccer ball through the deadfall. When the buck shifted position a little more, he moved into the opening and offered me a shot that was almost broadside, quartering toward me slightly. It wasn't the ideal shot for a bow, but convinced that the other deer were going to catch my scent, and confident I could put the arrow through the opening where I wanted it, I came to full draw, put my top sight pin tight behind the buck's shoulder, and loosed the arrow—and was rewarded with the solid "whack!" that every bowhunter lives to hear. I saw the fletching disappear in the sweet spot as the big buck kicked, turned, and bolted down the hill. He disappeared over the lip down into a ravine, scrambled up the opposite slope about ten feet, stopped, and tipped over backwards. He's not yet back from the taxidermist as I write, but I gross scored him at just under 160.

I'll never know for certain, of course, but I'm convinced the decoys made the difference on that hunt. They did not bring the buck in—he came from a direction that would not have allowed him to see them until he was fairly close—but they did hold him in the area. Without them, I suspect he'd have behaved much as did the first buck, running past me in pursuit of the doe without offering a shot.

TYPES OF DECOYS

Essentially, there are two types and two genders of decoys. The types are full-bodied (3-D decoys) and silhouette decoys. There are variations on those themes, including some very solid silhouettes that are on the heavy side, and some very lightweight foam decoys that are three-dimensional.

We'll look at gender first. With some exceptions, if the quarry is not a trophy but meat for the freezer, the choice is a no-brainer. Females tend to avoid males, particularly as the rut approaches. It is true that females of some species may actively seek out males when they are in heat, especially in areas where male-to-female ratios are close to even, but as a practical matter, the great majority of females already have a suitor or two in hot pursuit as soon as they approach estrus. Females are generally far more likely to avoid, than to approach, a decoy that looks like a male of the species.

Most decoyable big game animals are social creatures to a degree, with a high amount of curiosity and a definite pecking order. Females will often approach female decoys, or decoys resembling young-of-the-year. I won't pretend to fully understand their motives, but their posture and body language when approaching female decoys suggest a desire to figure out who this stranger is, along with an inclination to demonstrate dominance in the pecking order, or at least establish which is to be the dominant of the two.

When the quarry is a trophy, some hunters are convinced that a buck or bull decoy works better than does a doe or cow decoy. In my experience, does or cows produce more consistent results throughout the season. Males in the pre-rut and rut are actively seeking females, and while it is true that males are naturally inclined to demonstrate dominance toward other males, they're often more interested in love than in war. A buck in hot (or even not-so-hot) pursuit of a female will often ignore another male. Still, bucks and bulls can be very effective, especially during the pre-rut phase when rattling, grunting, and bugling are effective. Some buck and bull decoys are smallish in body size as well as rack, to decrease the likelihood that any passing buck or bull will be intimidated by the decoy and shy away from it. Big bucks and bulls will sometimes ignore very small ones, so the best bet is probably to use a decoy that approximates the average buck or bull in the area being hunted.

On the other hand, more than one hunter has watched with amusement as a male attempted to mount a female decoy. Hunters can add wagging tails (more about this later), or appropriate scents to present the image of a female that is ready for action. Since bucks and does tend to be segregated most of the year (with the exception of pronghorns), does probably are most effective for bucks only during or close to the rut, though hunters should keep in mind that a male of any species that is in hot pursuit of a doe or cow in heat is unlikely to leave her to pursue another doe or cow. For that reason, decoying with either male or female decoys is usually more effective on animals during the phase when they are pursuing or seeking females that are approaching estrus, as opposed to the days when females are standing for males and mating is taking place. When most females have been bred, decoying with female decoys can again be effective for a short period as males continue to seek estrus females.

An obvious way around the problem of whether to use doe or buck decoys when trophy hunting is to use one or more of each, as I did with the Iowa buck. If a buck is annoyed at the sight of a strange buck in his area, he is (assuming the rut is at or near full swing) also likely to be enraged by the sight of a strange buck with a doe.

Choosing between full-bodied and silhouette decoys is largely a matter of personal preference. Each has its advantages and disadvantages. The full-bodied decoy is exactly that—full bodied and three dimensional, fully visible from any direction. Some hunters believe full-bodied decoys offer more realistic presentations, but that is debatable. They do offer greater stability in windy conditions. The downside to many of these decoys is that they are relatively heavy and cumbersome to carry. The best decoy in the world will not be   effective if a hunter stops using it because he gets tired of lugging it around. This may not be an issue for hunters using ATVs, hunting stands over food plots or logging roads to which they can drive.

Silhouettes have the obvious advantage of being lighter and easier to carry—a real advantage for deer and pronghorns, a practical necessity for elk and moose. Silhouettes fold up and can be carried on belt hooks in some cases. A related advantage is that hunters can easily take two, three, or more silhouette decoys to their stands, something that is difficult to do with the heavier, full-bodied decoys even when hunting the most accessible stands. Strong winds can be problematic for many silhouette-type decoys.

Whether the lack of three-dimensionality is a weakness or a strong point is a debatable issue. Steve Bailey suggests—and I have seen behavior that would tend to confirm it—that putting out several silhouette decoys arouses curiosity in deer, and presents the illusion of movement. A deer circling several properly positioned silhouette decoys will find decoys alternately appearing and disappearing as it circles. Further, in terms of realism, some modern silhouette decoys are essentially life-sized photographs of the animals they represent. From a distance, they can be virtually indistinguishable from the real thing.

HUMAN DECOYS

Call them gimmicks if you like but so are game calls, scents, and more commonly used decoys. Native Americans—and no doubt other hunters before them—used crude, human-looking decoys to corral herd animals into box canyons or other areas where they could be easily speared, arrowed, or snared. The Nunamiut of Alaska corralled caribou into bays where hunters hidden in kayaks would encircle and spear them. The only current use of human decoys I'm aware of is the homemade decoys some hunters put in their tree stands. Deer and other species get pretty adept at picking off hunters in tree stands. Something as simple as a sack of grain or a big pillow with a hat perched atop it means that when a real hunter is sitting in the stand, he is less likely to be noticed.

LOCATING AND POSITIONING DECOYS

Decoys obviously won't work if they are not seen, which suggests using them in more-or-less open areas. Food plots, meadows, and prairies are good bets for decoys, as are logging roads or mature, open woods where visibility is good for long distances. I have experienced situations, such as the Iowa hunt previously recounted, in which deer did not see decoys until they were within bow range, but the decoys still proved useful for distracting the attention of deer from me, as well as for keeping the deer in the vicinity until a shot opportunity presented itself. Having said that, it still only makes sense to try to use decoys and position them in such a way as to make them visible for long distances.

There are exceptions, but decoys tend to work best when positioned upwind, which is the direction most hunters are going to be facing in any case. Bowhunters naturally need to keep the decoys in close. Some experts recommend as close as 10 yards, but I've found myself handcuffed a few times when using decoys that close, and have come to prefer setting them up at 15 to 20 yards. It's an easy matter to pace off or measure the distance, so the decoys can serve as benchmarks for estimating the range of approaching game.

To some extent, hunters can influence shot position, and even the route game will follow getting to the decoys. Males tend to approach male decoys from the front, female decoys from the rear. Female decoys tend to approach other female decoys from the front or side. The logical positioning of the decoy, then, would usually be broadside to the hunter—assuming the use of one decoy. If several are being used, positions can be varied. In fact, if the decoys are silhouettes, it is important that positions vary so that animals can see at least one decoy from any direction. By placing decoys strategically near deadfalls or other kinds of cover, it may be possible to further influence the approach taken by game, but keep in mind that if the cover is too large it will prevent the decoy from being seen from certain directions.

DECOY TRICKS AND TACTICS

Placing decoys in highly visible locations increases the likelihood they will be seen, but does not guarantee it. Further, stiff, motionless decoys are not entirely natural and may even suggest alarm or aggression to deer—especially decoys in the "heads up" position. Adding motion to decoys is one of the easiest and most effective strategies the hunter can use. It will increase the likelihood that decoys will be spotted and, once they have been spotted, some motion will tend to put game at ease, increasing their confidence and the probability that they will come in for a closer look at the decoys.

Author, publisher, and Woods 'N Water television show host Peter

Fiduccia makes another excellent point about the importance of motion in white-tailed deer decoys. Peter has observed that when deer spot decoys from some distance, they tend to get over their initial nervousness when motion is imparted to the decoy. However, if deer moving by a stand suddenly spot decoys from close range, they tend to be startled and often become very nervous—a nervousness that they often don't get over.

Peter began experimenting with decoys many years ago and, being the unorthodox hunter he often is, came up with some very unorthodox—but effective—methods of decoying deer. Some of his early experiments involved putting a shoulder-mount doe on one side of a tree and hanging a stuffed deer rump on the other. This was effective, if clumsy to carry. Noticing that the rump itself seemed effective, he soon eliminated the shoulder mount and began using the rump alone. Eventually—partially because of the ribbing he took for carrying around a deer rump and partly out of concerns for safety— he eliminated the hindquarters, too, except for the tail, which he could carry safely, discretely, and easily. And it worked!

Here's the approach Peter came up with: he collects deer tails during the season, cleans and brushes them, secures them between two pieces of cardboard with a rubber band, and sticks them in the freezer. A few weeks prior to the next season, he removes them from the freezer, cuts a hole in the cardboard near the top, and airs the tails out. He hangs a tail about 10 or 20 yards from his stand, at a height of a little over two feet. It's important that visibility be sufficient that deer can spot the tail, but not so wide open that the tail is obviously disembodied.

The key to the success of this simple decoy is motion. Peter attaches about 30 yards of string to the tail, with the other end attached to his wrist if he is on the ground, or his ankle if he is in a tree stand. The most effective technique seems to be to occasionally wag the tail slowly, and slightly. Fast or exaggerated motions are to be avoided. Peter has found that the tail alone can bring deer into bow range, hold them in the area, and in many cases position them for a shot.

In more recent years, Peter has begun experimenting with the use of full-bodied decoys as well. Movement for these is important, too.

Peter is a great believer in total simulation, sparingly using scent with his decoys when the time is right. He also uses grunts and rattles in combination with decoys. Peter believes it's important to avoid calling aggressively when using a decoy. The idea is to get a buck's attention and lure it in, not intimidate it with aggressive tactics.

There are battery-operated tail waggers and other devices designed to create movement in decoys, and these can be effective where legal. At the other end of the spectrum, a white handkerchief simulates a deer tail and will move in a breeze. White tissue paper can work even better if properly secured, since even the slightest puff of a breeze will cause it to move.

MOVEMENT AND BODY LANGUAGE

Steve Bailey has logged more than a few hours observing and videotaping big game animals interacting with decoys, and has learned a few tricks in the process. Like Peter, Bailey emphasizes the desirability of putting some motion into decoys, not only to get their attention, but because it tends to relax animals and give them confidence. This may be in part because it makes decoys appear more natural, but Bailey is convinced also that animals often signal other animals with movement. White-tailed deer, for instance, may acknowledge one another's presence simply by wagging their tails as they feed. The head position of decoys can also be important.

"I never use a heads-down, feeding doe decoy alone," Bailey explained to me in a recent conversation. "When deer approach that decoy, they expect some acknowledgement of their presence. A decoy that remains motionless in that grazing position can get deer stomping and snorting, and sometimes it will just drive them crazy. But put an alert, heads-up decoy in the mix that seems to be looking at them and recognizing their approach, and they'll usually relax and come on in."

SPECIAL SCENT CONSIDERATIONS

The same scent considerations that apply to any hunting situation apply when using decoys, but proper use of decoys involves some additional scent considerations and opportunities. First, virtually every decoy manufacturer recommends that big game decoys be handled with plastic gloves, to avoid contaminating them with scent. Handling them with gloves will make little difference, though, if the decoys are already contaminated with unnatural scents by being stored in a garage, for instance. Decoys should be periodically washed with some sort of scent-free detergent and stored in plastic bags, to keep scent contamination to a minimum.

Most hunters use decoys as part of an attempt to appeal to all the senses—sight, sound, and smell. It's not unusual for bucks to approach the sound of grunting or rattling, only to hang up at some distance when they are unable to spot the source of the sounds. By providing that source in the form of one or more decoys, especially when used in conjunction with the appropriate scent, a fairly elaborate but, from the buck's perspective, common and fully expected scenario can be created. While using estrus scents or dominant buck scents can be very effective, it is important not to contaminate decoys with these scents, which will linger for long periods of time. Instead, scent should be carefully placed near the decoys, or on rags or tissues that can be hung from decoys to replicate a tail. Renzo's decoys feature openings specifically designed for placement of a scent-containing film canister, as well as openings at the rear from which "tails" can be hung. With a little ingenuity, virtually any decoy can be made to accommodate similar scent-laden materials. The fact that white handkerchiefs or tissues will move in the slightest breeze adds attention-getting motion and a heightened sense of realism, as well. Again, it's important that decoys not come in direct contact with these scents, which may contaminate them.

DECOYING PRONGHORNS, MOOSE, AND ELK

Though some of the same principles apply to decoying pronghorns, moose, and elk as to decoying white-tailed deer, the tactics most commonly employed in decoying these species differ sufficiently from deer that they merit a separate discussion. Typically, decoying these other species involves a combination of spot-and-stalk techniques with decoying. Let's look first at pronghorns. Though pronghorns are herd animals and naturally curious, decoying is a very low-percentage tactic, with the exception of a window of opportunity leading up to the rut. In much of the pronghorn's range, this usually occurs for a week to ten days beginning sometime in mid-September, though, as with whitetails and other animals, that can vary from year to year by as much as a week. When the timing is right, decoying can be an exciting and effective way to hunt pronghorns.

Its effectiveness stems from several facts. First, pronghorns are very visually oriented and tend to inhabit areas in which they can take advantage of their formidable eyesight, which is often compared to 8X binoculars. Second, pronghorn bucks are obsessed at this time of year with corralling, and defending from other bucks, as many pronghorn does as possible. Though it's not uncommon to see a buck and a single doe, it's more common to see a buck and a harem of does, sometimes as many as twenty or thirty. In addition to the herd buck—

and this is especially true for larger harems—it is common for one or more less dominant bucks to stay on the periphery of the herd, sometimes watching it from distances of several hundred yards. These satellite bucks search for any opportunity to sneak in and run off with one or more does, especially those that stray a little from the herd. Between corralling errant does, many of which are constantly attempting to escape, and running off satellite bucks that approach too closely, herd bucks often stay frantically busy racing over the plains. Any time they leave the herd to corral an errant doe or chase off a satellite buck, other satellites are prone to take advantage of their absence. It's a tough life being a pronghorn buck during the rut.

Though pronghorns have been observed to respond to decoys from as far away as 400 yards, the comfort zone is usually about 200 yards or less. Hunters who can slip in to that range and get a decoy up without being spotted stand an excellent chance of getting the buck to respond. Responses vary from bucks that charge full tilt at the decoy to those that sneak in cautiously, or even circle to get downwind. In either case, some bucks will approach within 20 yards or less, but most will hang up momentarily at anywhere from 30 to 60 yards before stopping momentarily, then dashing off. More often than not, the bowhunter must, at a critical moment, judge range (no easy task on the prairie, where little exists to provide a sense of scale), draw, take aim, and loose an arrow in a matter of seconds. It is a challenging style of bowhunting, and one in which the bowhunter who has not practiced to shoot well at extended ranges is even further handicapped. That challenge, though, along with the way that events tend to suddenly develop in a hurry, is what makes this form of hunting so rewarding to increasing numbers of bowhunters.

Slipping into that comfort zone is the first challenge, and requires conditions allowing for a stalk. Some pronghorns are simply unapproachable and are best left for another day, when they venture away from the flat, wide-open spaces to an area near hills, ravines, drainages, higher grass, trees, or even hay bales to provide cover for the stalk. More often than not, hunters will find it necessary to crawl on their bellies, sometimes for extended distances, to have a chance at success. The bigger the herd, the more eyes are watching and the more difficult the stalk. Silhouette decoys come in very handy here, as crawling with full-bodied decoys is difficult at best. When hunters manage to get within the desired range of 200 yards or so, they must wait patiently until pronghorns are not looking their way before

Bears (along with other animals) learn to be timid or to be bold, depending on frequency of contact and amount of hunting pressure.

quickly raising the decoy into position. Pronghorns are not the smartest of animals, but they are smart enough to be spooked by something that looks like another pronghorn popping up out of the ground. Hunters can, however, get away with a little movement, since pronghorns expect to see some movement when looking at another pronghorn.

A typical tactic involves a two-man operation, with one raising the decoy while the shooter remains behind him and the decoy. Many decoys have openings through which approaching pronghorns can be watched, or they can be watched carefully from under the decoy. While some movement will be tolerated, looking over or peering around the decoy should be avoided. An electronic range finder can be more than helpful in this situation. Doe pronghorn decoys can be effective, by the way. A particularly aggressive herd buck may venture short distances to round up another female. Satellite bucks can be particularly vulnerable to a carefully placed doe that appears to be alone and not part of the herd. As with whitetails and most other species, dominance is not determined by size alone. It is not unusual for a satellite buck to be larger than a herd buck.

The key to successfully decoying pronghorns is patient persistence. It's necessary to assess each situation to determine if an approach is possible. When an attempt fails and the pronghorns flee, they will be more difficult to approach in the future. Better to keep moving and glassing and concentrate on higher-percentage opportunities than to waste time on low-percentage situations. At the same time, most attempts will fail. Keep at it, and eventually things will come together to result in a shot opportunity, assuming the window of the rut doesn't close first.

Unlike pronghorns, elk and moose tend to rely primarily on sound to locate prospective mates or challengers. Scent is a factor, too, but decoying elk and moose is most typically done in conjunction with calling. The usual strategy is to get their attention and hopefully bring them to the area with calls, then use the decoy to bring them even closer while focusing their attention away from the hunter. As with pronghorns, decoying elk and moose sometimes involves stalking close enough to get within their comfort zone, then using the decoy. Stand hunting for both moose and elk has gained popularity slowly but steadily in recent years, and there is no reason decoys cannot be used effectively in these situations. Theoretically, as with deer and pronghorns, either male or female decoys can be effective, depending to some extent on the phase of the rut. In practice, cow decoys tend to be used more frequently when hunting elk, while bulls are more commonly used by moose hunters.

Moose are known for relatively poor vision, so it's important that moose decoys be placed in highly visible locations—something that is not always easy to find in the tag alder thickets they often stick close to. One reason bulls seem to make more effective decoys is that the antlers are more visible, because of their size and lighter color. Among the more commonly used and at the same time most effective decoys is a pair of boat paddles crossed over the head of a hunter to simulate moose antlers. Hunters sway back and forth slowly with the paddles rising above the thickets, flashing in the sun, to get the attention of a bull at surprising distances. Then, too, hunters can thrash the paddles around to create a ruckus that simulates a show of dominance and adds to the illusion.

There are practical reasons behind the preference for cow elk decoys, including the fact that the size of elk antlers make them difficult to simulate (not to mention hard to maneuver through an aspen thicket) with an elk decoy. Then too, some hunters reason that a bull elk is far more likely to leave his herd temporarily to round up another female than to go off after another bull.

SAFETY

There is one limitation, though, and that is the issue of safety. Many hunters will not use big game decoys of any kind when gun seasons are open, but the photorealistic silhouette decoys in particular should never be used during gun seasons. Carrying decoys in and out of the woods should be done carefully, with the decoys covered. Some decoys feature blaze orange coloration on the ears or other visible areas—a good idea, since deer can't see it but hunters can.

Assuming safety and local game laws are kept in mind, the only limitation on the use of decoys is the imagination of the hunter using them. They're effective, and they add an exciting and often entertaining element to bowhunting.

IMAGINATION

Hunters have been using decoys of one sort or another since spears and maybe rocks were the weapons of choice. At the same time, decoying—especially decoying species other than white-tailed deer—seems to be in its infancy. That is the case because the effectiveness of decoys appears to be limited only by human imagination. I began this chapter by recounting Jay Leichty's experience using a two-man horse suit as a decoy of sorts. Cow decoys have been used in a similar way to approach game of all sorts. Several of Renzo's customers returned from a caribou hunt and called Steve Bailey to report that, while using simple, unaltered cow elk decoys, they had managed to walk into a herd of caribou on two occasions during their hunt. Caribou are a species we haven't looked at in this chapter for the simple reason that there is little modern-day experience decoying them. We haven't mentioned musk ox, either. Would a pronghorn decoy at a water hole encourage wary pronghorns to come in? Bailey indicates that he has used elk decoys at wallows or water holes, but finds they work better if he places them at some distance upwind from the water hole, as opposed to right at the water hole. He also reports some success using white-tailed doe decoys to bring mulies into alfalfa fields or other feeding areas. He used white-tailed decoys only because there are no mulie dekes available on the market, and in fact the market for them may not be big enough to encourage the manufacturing of mulie decoys. That is true for a number of species, but there is no reason creative hunters can't make their own decoys. And what about confidence decoys for big game? Would a goose or a heron decoy on a pond encourage big game to come in? Could a coyote decoy on a heavily used trail encourage deer to use an escape route in which a savvy hunter is waiting? We're still learning.

15

HOW SMART ARE BIG GAME ANIMALS?

Several years ago on an Ohio whitetail hunt, I observed something that nearly caused me to fall out of my tree stand. I was set up close to an apple orchard, and in the course of the afternoon several does, along with a smallish eight-pointer and a forkhorn, filtered in from the adjacent woods to eat apples. I had enjoyed watching them for maybe ten minutes when the eight-pointer began scratching behind his ear with his hind leg, like a dog. Nothing unusual about that, but suddenly the buck got his hoof caught in his antlers, began staggering across the orchard like a man with his foot caught in his trousers, and fell over. Not only did I almost fall out of my stand laughing, but all the other deer in the orchard began hooting, guffawing, and pointing at the hapless buck.

Well, not really. The young buck really did hang his hoof in his antlers and fall over, but I made up that part about all the other deer laughing at him. As far as I can tell, neither white-tailed deer nor any other game animals have a sense of humor. Nor are they, in my opinion, capable of embarrassment, shame, guilt, or worry, though I don't doubt they experience fear and probably something equivalent to contentment. Some biologists believe they react to things on an almost entirely instinctive level, with no cerebral processing. Their reactions are triggered when certain thresholds are reached. For instance, an odor is perceived at a certain level and the animal turns and runs without processing the information, or the odor does not reach that level and the animal does not react. Not every biologist shares that perspective, and in any case, there is solid evidence that most animals are capable of learning.

We've looked at the phenomenal olfactory capabilities of the game animals we hunt, along with their keen sense of hearing and their vision, which in many cases provides them with a distant early warning system, a wide field of view, and a well-developed ability to detect motion. Perception, though, is arguably meaningless without the capacity to make sense of all the input and react intelligently. Knowing—or at least being able to make an educated guess about— how and why animals are most likely to react to various scents in different contexts can save a hunter time, energy, and money (on products), as well as improve his hunting strategies.

Exactly how smart are big game animals? Several factors complicate any exploration of that subject, beginning with the fact that every hunter wants to think his quarry is a challenging and worthy adversary, and part of being challenging and worthy is being smart. We've already looked at anthropomorphism, which is the tendency to attribute human motives or characteristics to animals. Giving animals credit for more intelligence than they possess is certainly among the more common forms of anthropomorphism. As an example, my children tell me that my Brittany knows its name, but I'm doubtful. I don't believe that dogs know what a name is. I suspect my dog has learned that when he hears the sound "Jasper," he is about to get some sort of attention, or is about to hear some other sound, such as "Hunt 'em up!" or "Stay!" or "Fetch!" which he wants to respond to, or has

Mock scrapes aren't difficult, but creating them requires knowledge and caution if they're to have any chance of success.

learned he must respond to.

I know, I know . . . there is nothing like a scientific attitude to take the fun out of things. Some of my pet-owning friends even find my attitude offensive, feeling that I am in some way failing to show proper respect for my dog by underestimating its intelligence. My own feeling is that part of respecting any animal is recognizing that it is not a person. Go ahead and believe that your dog has a great sense of humor if you want to. Keep in mind, though, that anthropomorphism has its downside, not the least of which is that for many people, the next step beyond attributing human emotions and reasoning ability to animals is giving animals moral equivalency to humans, or even moral superiority. For hunters, a more likely downside is that we will develop hunting strategies based on misunderstandings of behavior.

Another complication is that "intelligence" is notoriously difficult to measure. Are deer as smart as dogs? Are moose as smart as elk? Wild turkeys illustrate the problem here very well. Many turkey hunters—and I am an avid turkey hunter myself—will tell you that turkeys are very smart, indeed. They say this because they find turkey hunting challenging, and because, on many occasions, they have been defeated by turkeys in one way or another. On the other hand, wild turkeys are completely baffled by a woven wire fence, and if they have never encountered one (or in some cases, even if they have), they can be observed to walk into the fence, bounce off it, and walk into it again repeatedly. Eventually they will fly over it or walk around it, but it seems to take some time to figure that strategy out. This behavior does not suggest a high level of intelligence. Turkeys are challenging to hunt, I would suggest, not because they are intelligent, but because they are extremely wary, have excellent vision, possess amazingly quick reactions, and lack curiosity—that is, they tend not to seek confirmation of anything suspicious in their environment, but to avoid it if it's at a distance, and run or fly from it if it's close. (Does the fact that turkeys are noticeably less challenging to hunt in areas where turkey hunting pressure is light, and correspondingly much harder to hunt in areas where they are regularly hunted, indicate they are smarter than we think? It might, but then again, it might just mean that they become warier when hunted.)

That game animals are capable of learning, there can be no doubt. Exactly what and how much they can learn may always be the subject of debate. A thorough discussion of animal psychology is beyond the scope of this book, not to mention the expertise of this writer. Still, a basic understanding of how most animals learn (and how they don't learn) can be helpful in forming judgments about how they are likely to respond to a given situation or hunting strategy. Some behaviors are simple reflexes, hardwired into an animal's physiology. Most animals will be startled by a sudden loud noise, for instance, and will jump or run in response. Other behaviors are instinctive; in some cases instinct is clearly at work, while in others it can be difficult to distinguish entirely between what is instinctive and what is learned. For instance, when a robin builds a nest, that appears to be entirely instinctive behavior. The care that a doe gives her fawn may appear to be instinctive, but deer that are raised in isolation from all other deer may not care properly for offspring. Does that have had offspring in the past are likely to provide better care than those giving birth for the first time. Both these phenomena suggest that caring for young is at least partially a matter of learning, as opposed to instinct.

Other behaviors are more clearly a matter of learning. A deer that has never encountered a certain food—corn, for instance—will probably not respond immediately to the sight or smell of corn. Eventually, after some exposure, deer will sample the corn and learn that it is indeed a desirable food. Behavioral psychologists speak in terms of various sorts of conditioning, but a common factor with regard to how most animals learn is association. Essentially, through experience, they associate one thing or event with another thing or event. The association may be positive or negative, but it has little to do with any sort of logic or abstract reasoning. For instance, when I was in my teens, I bought a beagle pup. The pup had never been outside the kennel in which it was born, with the exception of twice-daily romps around a fenced-in yard. I made the mistake of putting it on the floor of my car in the backseat, and the bigger mistake of bringing along a relative who smoked cigars. Not surprisingly, the pup got sick. After that, it got sick every time I put it in the car. In fact, simply putting the dog on a leash and leading it toward a car made the pup drool, foam at the mouth, and begin vomiting. The moment the dog believed it was about to be put into a car, it was sick. It associated cars with illness. Curing it was a long and difficult process that involved first allowing the pup to become comfortable in the bed of a motionless pickup truck, and rewarding it with a treat. Eventually, it wanted to get in the bed of the pickup truck. Over time, I drove the truck slowly with the dog in it, gradually increasing the length of each trip. Soon I was able to entice the dog into an automobile to get a treat. There were some setbacks along the way, but over time, the dog learned to associate automobile rides not with being sick, but with getting a treat, and eventually with going hunting. After that, it was difficult to keep the dog out of a vehicle.

Humans can form such associations, too. They are often the basis for phobias of various kinds, or other irrational fears. However, our ability to use logic and abstract reasoning enables most of us to understand when such an association is irrational, and as a result, we can often get over it. One of my children gets sick when she reads in the car. She understands that it is reading in a moving vehicle that makes her ill, and not simply being in one. If she weren't capable of that kind of understanding, she might very well associate illness with the car and, like my beagle, become ill any time she thought she was about to get into a car.

What does all this have to do with bowhunting? A lot, I think.

Will a white-tailed deer react negatively to the smell of cigarette smoke? It is possible that deer have an instinctively aversive reaction to any amount of smoke. I've never observed them running amok when a farmer burns trash in his yard, though. And some deer attractant scents are made in the form of smoke, which carries curiosity or food scents downwind to attract deer. I suspect that how a deer—or an elk, or most other animals—reacts to cigarette smoke depends on whether or not that animal has learned to associate the smell of cigarette smoke with humans. No doubt many have, in areas where they occasionally come in contact with humans. In remote areas where contact with humans is rare, such an association would be unlikely. To take this a step further, imagine animals that come into such frequent contact with nonhunting humans that they have no fear of them. In that case, they may associate cigarette smoke with humans, but since they would not associate humans with danger, they would not associate cigarettes with danger.

How will a deer react to the scent of apples? Quite possibly, a deer will not react to the scent of apples at all if it has never encountered an apple. Assuming, though, that deer are familiar with apples, many hunters suggest that it would be a mistake to use apple scent (or any other attractant scent) in a location where there are no apple trees, or where the deer have never known apples to be present. Perhaps so, but that would require a level of fairly abstract reasoning that I am doubtful deer possess. I simply do not believe that a deer in that situation will stop to wonder if it is strange to be smelling apples in an area where there are no apple trees. (Actually, I doubt that a deer has any concept of "strange" at all.) The deer simply smells apples. If he is hungry and wants apples, and if that takes priority over the alfalfa field he is headed for, the doe he is following, or any number of other factors that influence his behavior, then he will come in to eat apples.

Similarly, is it a mistake to use estrous doe scent months before any does in the area are likely to come into heat? Probably, but not because a buck detecting the scent will consult a calendar and decide that something is wrong. It's a mistake because it's a waste of time—testosterone levels have probably not yet reached the point at which a buck is likely to respond to a doe in heat.

Here is another scenario: you're deer hunting, and a big buck walks by your stand, 30 yards out. You overestimate the range and put an arrow just over his back, at which point, predictably enough, he runs off. Do you abandon that stand? Some experts may disagree, but I say no. The buck has no idea what that arrow is, or where it came from. He may have been startled or experienced a momentary sense of danger, but he felt no pain and nothing gave chase. It seems unlikely that, based on that sole experience, the buck will avoid the area. On the other hand, if a buck's behavior suggests that he smells or sees a hunter in the stand, it may very well be time to abandon that stand, at least temporarily. The deciding factor is, did the buck or did it not associate that particular spot with danger?

A representative for Bio-Logic feeds once said to me, "I hope we never really figure deer out. It will take the fun out of hunting them." He's right, of course. On the positive side, I don't think we're all that close to totally figuring out deer, or any other animals. I suspect there will always be room for debate about the kinds of issues we've looked at in this chapter. In any case, an inquiring mind, a healthy dose of skepticism, and a continuing interest in how animals learn and respond to their environment can enhance a hunter's enjoyment of hunting while giving him an edge other hunters won't achieve.

16

CREATING MOCK SCRAPES & RUBS FOR WHITE-TAILED DEER

My apologies (and condolences) to those few bowhunters who rarely or never hunt white-tailed deer. This chapter will focus on whitetails for two reasons. One is that an overwhelming majority of bowhunters hunt whitetails. The second and main reason, frankly, is that all this attention to whitetails has resulted in a great deal of scientific information about the natural history of white-tailed deer. The truth is that most of the deer species, including elk and moose, engage in some form or degree of rubbing and scraping activities. And while rattling, calling, and using scents can be used with varying degrees of success with most of these species, not a great deal is known about the importance of scrapes and rubs in terms of hunting tactics, partly because these tactics are not often attempted. The reasons they aren't often attempted include the fact that, in some cases at least, other approaches have been demonstrated to be very effective. A lot of hunters—and I admit to being among them—always prefer spot-and-stalk hunting over stand hunting when spot-and-stalk is at least equally effective. Also, many species of deer range over larger territories than whitetails. Almost any animal can become habituated to certain sources of food, water, or other requirements, but in the case of many species, a hunter who stands in one spot waiting for game to revisit a given scrape or rub may wait for a very long time.

Having said that, well-known Western outdoor writer Mike Schoby has written about how his friend Taro Sakita moved to the Northwest from New York and began adapting Eastern whitetail hunting tactics—including the use of rattling, grunting, using scents, and creating mock scrapes—to the black-tailed deer. Locals ridiculed him, and Schoby himself was highly skeptical, until Sakita began taking big blacktails with some regularity. It turns out that, during the rut at least, these tactics were very effective on blacktails. No one had ever tried them. It's quite possible that the use of mock scrapes or rubs could, under the right circumstances, be effective on other deer species as well: Coues deer, blacktails, mulies, and moose. If so, learning more about how these tactics are used with success when hunting white-tailed deer can serve as a starting point for experiments with other species.

If hunters are to have any hope of effectively creating mock scrapes and rubs, they must have a thorough understanding of what scrapes and rubs are, and how deer use them. There is still a great deal we don't know about the subject, even as it pertains solely to white-tailed deer. Biologists are gathering information continually, though, and in recent years some good, scientific studies have been undertaken that have enriched our knowledge and resulted in some surprising insights. Like all good scientific studies, they have also raised new questions.

Here is a more-or-less conventional way of looking at scrapes: in the weeks leading up to the peak of the rut, white-tailed bucks, especially mature bucks, paw away leaves, sticks, and any debris on the ground to expose fresh earth. They then stand over the exposed area and rub-urinate, a behavior that entails rubbing together the tarsal glands on the hind legs and urinating over them into the scrape. This deposits urine, along with tarsal gland secretions, into the scrape. Does will visit the scrapes, and bucks will return at intervals to freshen the scrapes and check to see if does have visited. When they detect the scent of a doe that is in or approaching estrus, they will then take up the trail.

"Serious" scrapes—that is, scrapes that are likely to be visited repeatedly—always have a licking branch overhead at a height that is easy for the buck to reach. (Licking "twig" might be a more descriptive term, since they are usually the very ends of small branches.) Bucks will rub their forehead and preorbital glands against these lick-

Creating mock scrapes and rubs offers some advantages, but many hunters prefer to take advantage of the real thing by adding dominant buck or doe-in-heat scent.

ing sticks, presumably depositing glandular scent on them, and will also lick and chew on them, depositing saliva. Scrapes at particularly desirable locations may become "sign-post" scrapes. These scrapes will be used by more than one buck, and will become enlarged, sometimes to the size of garbage can lids or bigger.

A few decades ago, when hunters first began to understand the nature of scrapes and what they signified, they understandably became excited. The thinking was something like this: Here is fresh sign, created by a mature buck, and he visits this spot regularly looking for does. All I've got to do now is put my stand downwind from this scrape and wait for Mr. Big to come along. If the scrape was a very large signpost scrape, that was even more exciting. Not one buck, but a number of bucks were using the scrape. Among the first observations hunters made after a few years of scrape hunting was that bucks didn't always go directly to scrapes, but often seemed to scent check them from some distance downwind. That required the relatively simple adjustment of moving the stands farther downwind from the scrape. An earlier, more frequently made observation was that bucks weren't visiting the scrapes at all during the many hours hunters spent watching them from nearby tree stands. Scrape hunting, it turned out, was not a route to guaranteed success. But how could this be? The scrapes were fresh, and in some cases showed regular activity. Clearly, the scrapes were being visited mostly, if not exclusively, at night.

WHAT BIOLOGISTS SAY

As biologists began studying the phenomenon of scrapes and scraping activity, they put together more pieces of the puzzle. Some of the early studies, instructive as they were, later proved flawed with regard to certain behaviors, for a very simple reason: They were based on observations of captive deer during daylight hours. Captive deer, as it turned out, did not always exhibit the same behaviors as free-ranging deer, nor did deer behave the same during the day as during the night.

Two more recent studies have greatly added to the store of knowledge about scrapes. The first was a two-year study completed in the fall of 1999, and was reported by wildlife biologist Karen Alexy of the Quality Deer Management Association in Watkinsville, GA. Alexy's team installed motion-activated video cameras to observe the behavior of a population of free-ranging deer at a 3,460-acre location in northeast Georgia. The team located six active scrape sites, four along field edges and two in forests, and placed the video cameras near the scrapes. Floodlights with red lenses were programmed to turn on at night. The results of this study confirmed some of what was already believed true, but also offered some surprises.

One unsurprising result: 85 percent of all scraping activity occurred at night. (Actually, some hunters might have guessed, based on their lack of scrape-hunting success, that the number would be higher.) More surprisingly, while previous research on captive deer suggested that only dominant bucks perform all the behaviors associated with scraping activity, the Georgia study indicated that many bucks worked the same scrapes, including yearling bucks, and that younger bucks engaged in all the same scraping activities as mature bucks.

Does were often seen visiting scrapes, sometimes using licking branches, but since the researchers were unable to distinguish one doe from another, it was impossible to tell how often a given doe visited a scrape, or whether a given scrape was visited repeatedly by the same doe or by a number of different does.

It was no surprise that most of the scraping activity occurred in the two-to-three-week period leading up to the rut, and that scraping activity dropped off sharply after the peak of the rut.

While some scrapes were visited by as many as thirteen bucks, others were visited by only a few. An even bigger surprise was that two of the scrapes that were less than 300 yards apart were visited by entirely different groups of bucks, with only one buck visiting both groups of scrapes. One conclusion the researchers reached was that the notion of a single buck creating a scrape line seemed unlikely.

The area under study was hunted, which led to an interesting sidenote: Hardly any of the mature bucks of three and a half years or older that were taken by hunters during the two-year period were ever seen on video, though several of them were taken within a few hundred yards of scrapes being monitored. The researchers speculated these bucks may have been monitoring the scrapes from downwind.

A less exciting but possibly very useful bit of information is that bucks visited scrapes far more often than they marked them with rub-urinating or the use of licking branches. The researchers suspect this indicates that the scents left at the scrapes endure for fairly long periods of time, so it is not necessary for bucks to mark them frequently.

During roughly the same time period that this study was being undertaken, the Institute for White-Tailed Deer Management and Research studied deer reactions to mock scrapes. Research Associate

Ben Koerth set up the mock scrapes on an 8,000-acre hunting club in East Texas during the pre-rut period of late October, using a variety of approaches. These included: (1) no scent, (2) mock scrapes with rutting buck scent, (3) mock scrapes with doe-in-heat scent, (4) mock scrapes with a combination of rutting buck and doe-in-heat scents, (5) rutting buck scent on the ground with no mock scrape, and (6) doe-in-heat scent on the ground with no mock scrape. These various scent stations were monitored by infrared-triggered cameras. A total of twenty-five stations were monitored, five for each type of scent.

The results were interesting, beginning with the observation that the various scent stations did, in fact, attract deer. Does and fawns were attracted to the scrapes, but the majority of visits were from bucks.

Before you get too excited, though, consider the other observations. First, deer showed almost no inclination to revisit a scrape after they discovered it. Only one buck was observed to revisit the same mock scrape, and he did it one time, five days after his first visit. Further, only one buck visited more than one of the twenty-five mock scrapes in the area.

Koerth's study revealed several other interesting bits of information. For one thing, he put his scrapes in areas of high traffic that he thought were sure to yield quick results. When several of the scrapes got no visitors, he found that by moving them only a few feet, he soon began to get photographs of deer visiting those locations.

Another useful observation: Deer visiting the scrapes did not spend a great deal of time at them. They stopped briefly and moved on.

With regard to which types of scents received the most visitations, the main distinction appeared to be between the mock scrapes made in conjunction with scents, and the scents applied alone, without the scrapes. While deer visited all the stations Koerth created, they were more inclined to visit those using a combination of the scrape and the scent. Presumably, the scrape itself is a visual cue, while the scent is an olfactory one.

Also of interest: In a follow-up study Koerth used human urine, buck urine, and doe-in-heat urine in mock scrapes and discovered that deer came to the human urine as readily as to either of the other scents.

Koerth's conclusions with regard to the use of scents and mock scrapes were as follows: Scrapes and scents can be useful to hunters. Deer probably react to them mostly from curiosity. They will move a short distance to investigate them when they encounter them, but are unlikely to respond to them from long distances and are unlikely to change their normal travel patterns to approach them. Their best use is probably to bring deer that pass near them into a shooting position and keep them there just long enough to enable an alert hunter to get off a shot.

Like all good studies, Koerth's study raises almost as many questions as it answers. The study was not intended, as Koerth concedes in his report, to compare one commercially produced scent product to another. Instead, he simply purchased the first scents he encountered, assuming he could buy enough to use the same scent for all his scent stations. This raises one very important and obvious question: Could other scents, perhaps because of better initial quality, better quality control, or greater freshness, have produced better results?

Another issue: Koerth observed that moving the stations for distances as little as a few feet made an immediate and dramatic difference in the numbers of deer visiting that station. What is not clear is why changing the location by such a small amount made such a difference. The assumption is that deer were not willing to change their travel patterns by even a short distance, but perhaps there were other reasons. We don't know if, for instance, the original mock scrapes lacked a licking branch overhead. If so, simply moving the scrape a short distance to a location with a licking branch overhead might be the reason for the increased visitation, as opposed to the new scrape being closer to a habitual path of travel. Licking branches aside, there might be other factors we are not aware of that cause deer to prefer one location to another for scrapes.

Another question is raised by the limitation of the cameras being used. If it's true that bucks often travel downwind of scrapes, scent checking them from a distance, is it not possible—perhaps even likely—that bucks that visited a scrape one time were not photographed repeatedly because they tended to scent check it from downwind after the initial visit?

All these questions and more might be answered by future studies, but in the meantime, it's not unreasonable to theorize that the use of mock scrapes and scents might be analogous to the situation of bringing an animal to a call. Experienced turkey hunters, for instance, are well aware that it is much easier to call a turkey to a place the bird wants to go. That does not mean calling isn't effective; it simply means that the location from which the call is made is an important factor in the likelihood of successfully calling in a turkey.

Using quality optics to scout from a distance is the best way to locate game without disturbing it.

HOW IT'S DONE

Certainly many hunters use them, and some excellent hunters swear by them. Creating the mock scrape itself is as simple as scraping up debris to expose bare earth, then applying deer urine or, as increasing numbers of hunters do, urinating in the scrape themselves. Naturally hunters will want to take extra care to avoid contaminating the spot with their own scent, including wearing rubber gloves.

The more complex aspect of creating an effective mock scrape is choosing a suitable location. Hunters, like Ben Koerth, have observed that moving a mock scrape even a short distance can make the difference between deer using the scrape or not using it. Beyond positioning the mock scrape along a route that deer want to use anyway, another key factor is the licking branch. It's usually a waste of time to establish a mock scrape in a spot lacking a licking branch overhead.

That doesn't necessarily mean that hunters must look around for a licking branch before thinking about making a scrape. In fact, one of the more effective techniques hunters have hit upon in developing mock scrapes is to cut off the licking branch over a real scrape, and position it over a spot where a mock scrape is to be made. Not only is the lack of a licking branch resolved, but the licking branch put in place is one containing the natural scent deposited by bucks.

Why not simply hunt over the real scrape? It might be in a spot lacking suitable trees for a stand, for one thing. Or the trees that would otherwise be suitable might be upwind of the prevailing breeze. Or the location might be difficult to access, or in a valley with swirling breezes, or too close to a bedding area, or less than ideal for any number of reasons. By creating a mock scrape, the hunter is attempting to influence a buck to come to a particular spot that the hunter finds advantageous, as opposed to hunting a spot that might leave the buck with all the advantages.

Many hunters believe it's important to keep a scrape fresh, which means freshening it regularly, at least every few days. There's an easier way, though and it might solve several problems at once. By using a scrape dripper, most of which release scent as the temperature rises, hunters can avoid the necessity of repeatedly visiting a scrape to freshen it. Scrape drippers are widely available at sporting goods stores as well as in hunting supply catalogs, and there are two additional advantages to using drippers. First, since hunters needn't repeatedly approach the scrape to freshen it, they avoid the possibility of contaminating it with foreign odors. Finally, as we've observed, most scrape activity, including simply scent-checking scrapes, occurs at night. There is little doubt that deer can determine how much time has elapsed since scent was deposited in a scrape. It is possible that by releasing scent into the scrape only during daylight hours, in time a buck can be influenced to check the mock scrape during the day.

Some granular products—MDR Group's 24Seven products are ones that I'm aware of—are designed to release scent gradually over time, and compared to liquids that might soak into the ground or be washed away, tend to be relatively weatherproof. They're good for up to a week between applications.

RUBS

Perhaps even more exciting to deer hunters than a fresh scrape is a fresh rub, especially if the rub is on a large tree. More so than large tracks or even scrapes, rubs are clearly the work of bucks. And while large bucks will often rub saplings or small trees, it is unusual for a small buck to rub a tree with the girth of, say, a telephone pole. A rub on any solid tree with a diameter of 8 inches or more was most likely made by a big buck, particularly if the tree is deeply scored.

As with scrapes, rubs are both a visual and an olfactory cue for deer. Bucks deposit the scent from their forehead and preorbital glands in rubs, but rubs are even more visible than scrapes. In areas where vegetation is not overly thick, a rub can be seen for long distances through the woods. In heavily traveled areas including funnels, staging areas near food sources, or bedding areas, hunters can sometimes stand in one spot and see numerous rubs, or a line of rubs trailing off into the forest.

While I've yet to come across a scientific study of rubs or mock rubs, anecdotal evidence suggests that mock rubs can work. As is the case with scrapes, location is critical. Bucks simply are not going to take a route they are not naturally inclined to take just to investigate a new rub, though they will certainly travel a short distance to check it out, and may provide an excellent shot opportunity as they pause to investigate it.

Most hunters who create mock rubs use a simple file to rub off the bark. (Keep in mind that this practice will likely be illegal in public hunting areas, and should be done only with the permission of landowners.) Several companies offer forehead gland scent compounds of one sort or another to use on mock rubs as well as licking branches over scrapes. Naturally, hunters want to wear rubber gloves and take the usual precautions to avoid contaminating a mock rub area with their own scent.

HOW TWO SUCCESSFUL HUNTERS USE MOCK SCRAPES

Some hunters are so sold on the use of mock scrapes that they begin using them months prior to the rut. I know of at least one case of a hunter who uses them year round. The effectiveness of what they are doing might be controversial, but these hunters are not off the wall, and can present perfectly defendable reasoning for what they do. While biologists point out that scraping activity generally begins in earnest a few weeks prior to the rut, and tapers off rapidly after the peak of the rut, they are not talking about the entire package of scraping behavior. Scraping is essentially a marking behavior, and the fact is that deer—bucks and does—engage in some marking behaviors year-round. They make occasional scrapes, although they're not as obvious as scrapes made during the rut, and they frequently tend to nuzzle and lick branches. And, of course, they urinate. These behaviors allow deer to keep tabs on other deer in the area, probably telling them something about the health and social status of these deer.

Dave Parrot is a longtime hunter in central Ohio, not far from where the world-record Beatty Buck was taken. For years, Dave has begun creating mock scrapes in mid-to-late summer, and he is convinced that he sees more trophy bucks on his hunting property as a result.

Dave's theory—and there is scientific evidence supporting it—is that does can distinguish mature, healthy, dominant bucks from lesser bucks, and that does seek out dominant bucks and will gravitate to areas where dominant bucks live, at least in areas where the herd is healthy and relatively well-balanced. As the rut approaches, bucks seek out does. Dave believes that his early mock scrapes with dominant buck urine attract and hold does, which in turn attract and hold dominant bucks as the rut approaches. Developing hard, scientific evidence to prove Dave's theory would be difficult, but it's hard to argue with success, and Don has certainly taken his share of big bucks over the years.

As an outdoor writer, I've met more than a few hunters who are obsessed with white-tailed deer, but none who are more fascinated with whitetail behavior than Ron Boyce, formerly of MDR Outdoors Group. Talk to Ron and in a short while, you'll get the impression he considers the whitetail woods to be one big laboratory. Ron is convinced he can significantly increase the amount of deer traffic in his area by creating mock scrapes using any of several scents.

"The first thing I want to know when a hunter asks me how to use a scent product," Ron explains, "is: What are you hunting? Do you want meat for the table? A buck? A trophy buck?"

Ron's favorite tactic is to begin creating numerous mock scrapes in a given area in late summer. Using rubber gloves and the other accepted methods of keeping his own scent to a minimum, Ron will freshen his scrapes every five days or so, observing carefully to see which scrapes are getting attention. He starts with Early Buck, an MDR nondominant glandular scent, along with Branch Magic, because he's convinced these will attract the interest of any deer. Later, as the rut approaches, he will switch to a dominant buck or doe-in-heat scent if his target is a trophy buck. Branch Magic is a gel containing extracts from the preorbital glands of bucks, and Ron spreads this on licking branches over the scrape.

"Deer have definite preferences when it comes to licking branches," says Ron. "In the Northeast where I hunt a lot, hemlock is a popular species. But whatever the species, deer tend to prefer live branches over dead ones, and they also prefer branches that slope toward the ground, or which are at least parallel to the ground. Rarely will they use a branch that goes upward."

The relative effectiveness of mock scrapes and rubs continues to be a controversial subject. The limited number of truly scientific studies examining scrapes and mock scrapes reveals some interesting information, but one or two studies can never be conclusive, and they leave many questions unanswered. At the very least, it seems clear that deer, including mature bucks, will often stop to investigate a mock scrape they encounter. Since mock scrapes can be strategically located, this could provide a hunter with a shot opportunity he might not otherwise have. How many hunters would be willing to create a mock scrape just to increase the odds of a close, broadside shot at a buck moving by his stand? My guess is that any hunter who has ever had a really good buck move past his stand within range but without offering a good shot opportunity would be inclined to give it serious consideration. And if hunters like Dan Parrot and Ron Boyce are right, mock scrapes can do more than simply cause a buck to stop in a shooting lane.

17

OUTDOOR THEATER

One species may rely more on vision, another on smell or hearing, but all prefer to confirm their perceptions with multiple sensory inputs whenever possible. I might wake up in bed at night and think I hear the crackle of fire, or be pretty sure I smell smoke, or wonder if that flickering light is caused by a flame. Put all three perceptions together, though, and I am dialing 911.

What's that got to do with hunting? In an earlier chapter, I recounted the story of an Iowa hunt on which I took a 160-class whitetail. It was one of the most exciting and rewarding deer hunts I have ever experienced, and as I climbed down from the stand, recovered my arrow, and started down the hill for a closer look at my prize, I couldn't help but reflect on the fact that for a total elapsed time of nearly forty minutes, two does and a buck had milled around downwind of my stand, at ranges varying from 15 to 80 yards, and not one of them had picked up my scent. Prior to heading out to my stand, I had showered with scent-free soap and shampoo, and sprayed myself all over with a scent eliminator before toweling off. After getting out of the truck, a few hundred yards from my stand, I opened up my sealed plastic bags and put on my outer hunting clothes and rubber boots. Finally, I sprayed myself again with a scent eliminator before making my way to my stand. Using rubber gloves, I carefully positioned a Renzo's bedded doe decoy and a standing buck decoy. I sprayed a little doe-in-heat scent on a white kerchief and hung it in a slot for that purpose on the doe's tail. In the course of the hunt, I did a fair amount of grunting. Was the scent reduction regimen the reason I had remained undetected by three deer milling around all that time directly downwind of me? Was it the grunting that brought the second buck in and the decoys that caused it to remain in my vicinity, thrashing a deadfall in an obvious display of dominance until it turned enough to give me a broadside shot? Did the doe-in-heat scent on the kerchief seal the deal? I think all of these things might have been factors, though I can't prove it. Still, everything came together in a way that provided me with a shot opportunity. None of the things I was doing appeared to hurt, and at least one of them brought about the desired results. Or was it the combination?

Many hunters have observed animals that didn't notice decoys, or tended to hang up and observe them warily from a distance until a breeze (or the hunter himself) imparted a little motion to a decoy, at which point the animal dropped all caution and approached with confidence. Other hunters have tipped the balance by imitating the sounds of a moose urinating in water, a turkey scratching in leaves, or a buck rubbing a sapling. None of these tactics alone is likely to bring an animal into bow range, but used in conjunction with other sights, sounds, or smells, they can make all the difference. The idea is to create a scenario that is as natural and realistic as possible, and that appeals to more than one sense.

As I indicated in a previous chapter, I'm hardly the first hunter to engage in a variety of visual, auditory, and olfactory strategies in an attempt to create a convincing scenario. One part of the equation that is sometimes overlooked, though, is the importance of leaving the environment as undisturbed as possible. Wary game animals are usually intensely aware of any changes in their environment and tend to steer clear of them. On an African hunt, I was bowhunting over a water hole when I saw a steinbuck at about 50 yards. Steinbuck are famous for their ability to get all the water they need from the food they eat. They rarely, if ever, come in to a water hole. This one had found a salt block some previous hunter had put out, and spent a fair amount of time at it. That night I had a tracker move the salt block about 20 yards closer to my blind.

The next afternoon, right on cue, the steinbuck came in. It stopped at the edge of the clearing, stared intently at the spot where the salt block had been, then proceeded to circle the clearing from a good distance before wandering off. The next day I saw it again. This time it appeared to spot the relocated salt block. Again it circled the clearing, staring intently all the while at the salt block, then left. I never saw it again. I'm inclined to think that in time, the steinbuck gained the confidence to approach the salt block and begin using it, but the point is that the one small change of moving the salt block 20 yards made the steinbuck sufficiently wary that it refused to come in for at least two days. Creating a natural and familiar scenario is half the equation. The other half is putting up blinds sufficiently far in advance to give animals an opportunity to accept them as part of the environment, keeping pruning to a minimum (and doing it in advance whenever possible), and avoiding contaminating the area or any decoys used with scents that are foreign to the area.

It can be a lot of work to create the scents, sounds, and sights that will overcome the natural caution of a game animal—particularly a trophy-class animal—and cause it to come close and offer a shot. Often a little creativity works. Moose hunters sometimes hold canoe paddles over their heads when they spot bull moose in the distance. Apparently the paddles flashing in the sun resemble the antlers of a rival bull sufficiently to bring the animal in. (Clearly moose don't see all that well.) We already mentioned the trick of pouring water into the shallows of a lake or river to imitate a urinating moose—a familiar sound in moose country. This often works like a charm. We also

Maps and aerial photos are good starting points, but there is no substitute for boots on the ground.

Under the right circumstances, vehicles are a great way to cover a lot of ground and scout without disrupting game patterns.

mentioned Jay Liecte's famous horse suit. He used it to approach geese, but who is to say it couldn't work on bigger game? Some hunters use cow decoys in a similar manner. Confidence decoys are another possibility that big game hunters seldom use, but heron, crow, or turkey decoys in a clearing or near a water hole could be the final touch that convinces a pronghorn or a trophy whitetail that all is safe. Outdoor theater can be a lot of work, but it can be a lot of fun, too. And when it works, it's very rewarding.

18

LOW-IMPACT SCOUTING

"The place I'm taking you to," outfitter David Mann explained as we bumped along dirt roads in the predawn darkness, "is a part of the ranch where turkeys have never been hunted." Mann's Horns & Thorns Outfitters, not far from Del Rio, Texas, had been hosting deer hunters for years, but this was his first experiment with turkey hunters. The stars were still fading in the west when I stepped out of the truck, and before the sounds of the truck had entirely died away, I was amazed to hear a Rio Grande turkey gobbling. I tried to check the time, but couldn't see my watch in the dark. The gobbler was some distance off, and as the promise of a beautiful South Texas spring morning began to spread across the eastern horizon, I started to make my way toward him. Stopping and looking around I realized that, far away as the gobbler seemed to be, the prickly pear and mesquite around me didn't provide adequate cover for any movement. I dropped to the ground and began calling from where I was.

Fifteen minutes later, I was tagging the big Rio. I had hours to kill until David came back in the truck to pick me up for lunch, so I made my way to a tripod deer stand and climbed up to have a place to sit, not to mention a great vantage point. Before David was back in the truck I had seen seven gobblers, six of which I was sure I could have stuck. There were half a dozen gun hunters in camp, and most of them came into lunch carrying one of the two Rios the ranch allowed. Interestingly, within a few days the big birds were gobbling less and exhibiting the kind of wary behavior hunters learn to expect from turkeys.

I've had similar experiences with turkeys elsewhere, and with other game whenever I've been fortunate enough to hunt in remote or unpressured areas. Pronghorns are skittish by nature, but it is easier to stalk a pronghorn that has never been hunted than one that has, and the same can be said for bears, whitetails, and probably most other game animals. Assuming game is present in huntable numbers and the weather is stable, few factors have a bigger impact on game movement and behavior in general than hunting pressure.

What's that got to do with scouting? Well, animals cannot distinguish between hunting and scouting. (It is true they can often distinguish between predatory and nonpredatory behavior, but we'll look at that as it relates to scouting later in this chapter.) A sudden intrusion by people into their habitat, or a sudden increase in the frequency of such intrusions, can easily alter the behavior of many game animals. (There is some interesting correspondence between early frontiersmen such as Daniel Boone, Simon Kenton, and others lamenting the fact that elk in Kentucky suddenly became difficult to stalk, and wondering what could be the reason. It apparently never occurred to them that a sudden influx of settlers shooting at every elk they saw might have some effect on the behavior of the elk.) Especially in the case of trophy-quality game, which got that way by being naturally wary or by surviving and gaining experience, heavily hunted animals may alter their activities after even a very limited amount of contact with people. White-tailed deer are notorious for becoming almost exclusively nocturnal in response to the presence of hunters moving through their home ranges, but the same can happen with many other species. Even wild hogs can become extremely wary and almost exclusively nocturnal in response to pressure. The question is how to go about scouting without decreasing our chances of encountering game when we're hunting.

THE PARANOID HUNTER

You've heard it before: "If you want to kill a big buck, hunt where the big bucks are." Something similar might be said about any species we are hunting, but even hunters whose goal is meat for the table, herd management, or a just plain fun hunt want to maximize their opportunities. That means knowing where the game is likely to be at a given time and knowing where might be the best places from which to intercept it, and that means scouting. Scouting is important to hunting success and worth some risk of spooking game. Hunters need to accept that risk. The idea is to minimize it, not eliminate it. I say this because I have encountered hunters—usually deer hunters—who are so concerned about spooking game that they hardly scout at all. How many times have you heard the following, or some variation of it: "A hunter is lucky to see a big buck once. The odds of seeing him a second time are extremely remote." Possibly so, but the odds of seeing that big buck even once are extremely remote if someone ("someone" being the hunter or a guide) hasn't scouted the area enough to know that a big buck is in the area, and to learn something about where that buck goes and when. A lack of knowledge about how game uses the local habitat and where to hang tree stands or set up blinds, or which areas to glass, or how to approach a given area for still hunting, is more likely to result in an unsuccessful hunting season than is occasionally spooking game when scouting.

NO-IMPACT SCOUTING

It's a perennial topic in the outdoor publications: how to scout using aerial photos and topo maps. Frankly, without for one moment questioning the usefulness of topo maps and aerial photos—both of which I use from time to time—I think these approaches are oversold as a means of scouting for most hunters in most situations, for the simple reason that in my experience, there is no substitute for getting your feet on the ground. Hunters preparing to hunt large tracts of unfamiliar territory would do well to study maps and aerial photos to orient themselves, become as familiar as possible with the terrain, and eliminate areas that lack suitable habitat or that might be inaccessible. Could be we're talking about semantics here, but all that strikes me more as a prelude to actual scouting than to scouting itself. Wildlife relates to the trees, shrubs, ravines, drainages, ridgelines, undercut banks, and edge habitats in an intimate fashion that topo maps and even the best aerial photos can usually only hint at.

WHEN NOT TO SCOUT

I don't want to belabor the obvious, but when it's not necessary to scout, hunters are better off not scouting. If you know you will be hunting whitetails or turkeys on a 300-acre tract of land that you have hunted for years, chances are you know the feeding areas, the bedding areas, and the travel routes. You've observed scrapes and rub lines in the same areas for years. You have stands hung, or know where you will put them. You know roosting areas, strut zones, and maybe even a dusting spot or two. Why muck around in your hunting spot?

Granted, habitat can change over time, especially in farm country. You will want to be aware of which fields are planted in corn or soybeans, and which are left fallow or enrolled in CRP, and any major changes may require some scouting to see how game movements may have changed in response.

Best Times to Scout

Scouting is a little like hunting in that, for many of us, the best time to scout is when we can. Given options, though, one of the best times to scout is late winter, right after the season closes, or early spring. Spooking game is not normally a concern then, since the season won't be in again for at least six months, often longer. At the same time, the lack of foliage and undergrowth makes game trails, rubs, and other sign much more visible. There is nothing like snow to reveal the recent movement patterns of game. Hunters should be aware, though, that travel and feeding patterns can and often do change from season to season. Especially in the case of animals that migrate seasonally—elk moving from higher to lower altitudes, for instance—finding game or game sign in late winter or early spring is no guarantee that game will be present in fall or early winter.

The best time of day to scout depends largely on the species being scouted, and perhaps even more so on the purpose of scouting. If the primary purpose is to familiarize yourself with the area, to confirm the presence of huntable populations of game in the area, to locate feeding areas, bedding areas, travel routes, and potential locations for stands or blinds, the best time to scout is probably midday, when most big game animals tend to be least active. This minimizes the likelihood of direct confrontations.

There are exceptions to this. The serious trophy hunter can examine tracks, rubs, and other sign to make educated guesses about the quality of game in an area, but ultimately the only way to determine the presence of real trophies is to spot them, and that usually means being out and about when game is out and about. Though hunters may not be concerned about spooking game during postseason scouting, scouting at other times should be undertaken with a plan and with methods intended to reduce the risk of spooking game and thus altering their behavior.

Take Advantage of Optics

There are several things hunters can do to minimize their impact while scouting. One of them is to try and observe game whenever possible from a distance. Every serious hunter should own one decent pair of binoculars and, if he is hunting mountains, plains, or tundra, a spotting scope. In the wide open spaces of the western states, it's not too difficult to move cautiously from one observation point to the next, spending some time at each scanning with binoculars or spotting scopes. In the East, hunters familiar with an area can observe pastures, meadows, crop fields, or other feeding areas from hilltops or by simply taking up a position along a field edge earlier in the day, before animals are actively feeding. In many areas, hunters can observe fields from roads. This is not only low-impact, but it's also extremely efficient, allowing hunters to cover a great deal of ground in a short period of time. Unpredictable as they are during hunting season, white-tailed deer often establish very predictable patterns in late summer. In fact, it's not unusual to see even mature bucks feeding in open fields in late August through September in much of the U.S. Savvy trophy hunters will take advantage of this, watching likely areas and targeting several trophy bucks to hunt when the season comes in. Depending on when the season opens in a given area, it's likely those bucks will no longer be on a predictable summer pattern. It's also likely they will remain in the vicinity where they were spotted, at least until the rut cranks up and they begin cruising for hot does. Even then, their core area will often remain the same. They'll simply enlarge the amount of territory they cover in their ramblings, as opposed to leaving it for extended periods.

Scouting from a distance is not always an option, especially if a hunter is unfamiliar with an area or needs to locate specific spots for stands or blinds. It only makes sense, in those situations, to take the same precautions when scouting as when hunting. Wear camo, follow a scent-free regimen, and try to take advantage of wind direction and thermals to stay downwind of game. To the extent possible, avoid traveling along game trails or logging roads.

WALK-AND-TALK SCOUTING

It may be a cliché to compare the woods to a church, but I can't help it. I was raised that way. My father taught me that from the moment we stepped into the woods we were hunting, and that meant we spoke very little, and then in a whisper. Even when I'm taking a hike in the summer and hunting is the farthest thing from my mind, I find myself instinctively speaking in quieter tones and avoiding creating disturbances when I step into the woods. Nonetheless, there is another approach to scouting that is popular with increasing numbers of bowhunters. This method is based on the fact, referenced earlier, that game animals seem capable of distinguishing between predatory and nonpredatory behavior. The theory behind this approach is that if hunters amble along through the woods as if they were walking through the park, moving at a steady pace, talking, and generally making no efforts to hide their presence, game animals will hide and let them walk past, or will move away from them, often circling around to get behind, but will not be overly alarmed. A variation on that theme entails scouting from an ATV, and it is true that game animals often pay little attention to vehicles. My friend Johnny Webber does a great deal of scouting from his ATV, which enables him to cover a lot of ground very efficiently.

Not every expert accepts that this approach to scouting does not spook game, particularly trophy-class game. That debate aside, scouting in this way does have some serious limitations. Finding and evaluating sign such as tracks, rubs, wallows, or scrapes, as well as locating and assessing food sources and bedding areas or spots for stands or blinds, all requires more than a stroll (let alone a drive) through the woods. For hunters who wish only to confirm that no major changes have taken place in their hunting area, or who are entering the area only to hang a stand or build a blind in a pre-determined location, this approach might make perfect sense. Another factor here is the extent to which game in a given area is accustomed to human activity. In suburban areas or farm country, where animals are accustomed to hearing and seeing humans, walk-and-talk scouting might make sense. In a more remote area where human activity is limited, any contact with people is likely to alarm game.

GAME TRAIL CAMERAS

The next chapter is an in-depth look at game trail cameras and their use, but we can't discuss scouting without some refernce to them. Game trail cameras have gone from novelty items to an industry in their own right in a matter of five years or so. The appeal is obvious: They are a very low-impact way to determine the quality of animals in a given area, as well as learn a great deal about game movement patterns. It doesn't hurt sales any that they are a lot of fun. High-end cameras offer video footage, and there are several systems on the market that will transmit images to a computer or, for that matter, multiple computers. One such system that I have some experience with is Buckeye Cam, which transmits a wireless photo to a base station in a house, cabin, barn, etc., up to a couple of miles away. From there, with an Internet connection, it can be sent along to a computer or, for that matter, any number of computers as an email. Multiple units can be monitored in real time from a desktop computer in a home or office, or from a laptop virtually anywhere wireless service is available. Variations on such systems include sending photos to a website, where anyone with the password can log on to view them, or sending photos directly from cameras via cell phone signals. The downside of that system is that the camera must be in range of a cell tower, but it is a very convenient and effective system when a cell tower is located within five miles, give or take a mile depending on terrain.

Hunters who think they're going to find an intersection of heavily used trails, or a staging area or similar hot spot, set up a camera, and sit back a week or two later to view a lot of game photos are often disappointed. On the other hand, not seeing game in a supposed hot spot is useful information in itself. Using several cameras can save a lot of time, but budgets are limited for most of us, and that is not always an option. Even one camera, though, can provide a great deal of information, including not only data about trophy quality, but game numbers, travel routes, feeding areas, and other habits. For instance, over time the camera may reveal that a certain animal is only in the vicinity of the camera at night, and never during daylight hours. One photo of a trophy-class animal during daylight hours might well be worth several such photos taken at night.

INTEGRAL SCOUTING

The best hunters I know seem not to think of scouting as something separate from hunting, but as part of hunting. Most consistently successful trophy hunters insist that they spend more time scouting than hunting, with some suggesting that the ratio of scouting to hunting should be as high as 5 to 1. Given that the opportunities to get afield are limited for all but a few fortunate hunters, that is a tall order. The hunter whose outings are limited to occasional weekends and a few precious vacation days may be understandably reluctant to spend more time scouting than hunting. Still, whatever their circumstances, all bowhunters would do well to keep in mind that the likelihood of success is to a high degree related to the time they have invested in scouting, and that a few days of hunting in a carefully selected spot is probably worth a few weeks of hunting in a spot that was hastily chosen.

It's also important to remember that, though preseason scouting is essential, scouting doesn't end when the season begins. Every hour spent hunting is, or should be, an hour spent scouting as well. The most effective bowhunters hunt their spots with all the confidence merited by good scouting, and they exercise the patience to give that spot a fair chance. At the same time, they know that animals change habits in response to weather, seasonal patterns, hunting pressure, and other variables, which means adaptability is at least as important a quality as is patience. Stand hunting can require a great deal of discipline and patience, so perhaps it's not surprising that some hunters can become totally inflexible as the season progresses.

The story of one of Johnny Webber's better whitetail trophies is a case in point. With friends and family, Johnny is surprisingly generous about sharing information and hunting spots. He shared with two hunting buddies some information about a local hunting spot, and even directed them to a drainage that he thought a couple of good bucks were using regularly. They hunted the spot two weekends in a row. When he saw them later and asked them how their recent hunts had gone, they were enthusiastic.

"Both of them," Johnny later told me, "said that on their first day out, they saw the same big buck moving up the next drainage over, about 100 yards out. And one of them saw a different big buck the next day. They went back to the same spot the following Saturday, and both of them saw that first buck again, moving up that same drainage. They went back Sunday, and you know what they did? They took their climbers right back up the same trees. Neither of them moved over to that drainage where they had both seen bucks. I had a day off that week, so I went and took my climber up a tree in that drainage the bucks were using, and killed a 160-class that evening."

Few bowhunters—or so I would like to think—are as "disciplined" as Johnny Webber's two friends. Still, most of us are guilty of falling into ruts, if you'll pardon the pun. I spent more days than I'd like to admit hunting the edge of an oak-covered bench on a south-central Ohio hillside, racking my brains to figure out why a heavily used trail that showed so much sign in the form of tracks, droppings, and rubs should be so unproductive. In subsequent seasons, I discovered what should have occurred to me much sooner: Deer walked along the edge of that bench regularly until the leaves fell, after which the area was totally exposed. In the course of a few days every fall, use of that trail, at least during daylight hours, went from heavy to almost nothing. Changes in preferred food sources, decreasing foliage, different weather patterns, hunting pressure, and other factors all affect game habits in ways that make scouting a neverending process for the bowhunter.

19

GAME TRAIL CAMERAS

We've looked at the differences between human visual capabilities and those of most game animals, but one factor in that equation that is difficult to measure is that of alertness. Hunters know they rarely get away with any movement, for instance, if they are within bow range of a mature animal. On the other hand, how many animals do we overlook because we're just not able to remain alert every moment?

Game trail cameras are constantly on the alert. (Some are actually more alert than others, but more about that later.) They never sleep, and unlike hunters, they aren't just visitors; they "live" out there with the game animals we pursue. Next to radio telemetry and GPS tracking studies, hunters have probably learned more about the behavior of game, deer in particular, from game cameras than from any other source. Not only that, game camera "studies" are easily conducted by any hunter and are applicable to the specific game they are hunting and the specific areas they hunt.

I unwrapped my first game trail camera with much excitement. I already had a perfect spot in mind for it, a place where two heavily used trails intersected. Both trails were pocked with tracks, and this being late October, there were numerous scrapes and rubs in the vicinity. One of the trails ran through thick cover along a fence on a ridge top. The other trail crossed it at right angles where a large hole in the fence clearly funneled deer. I strapped the camera confidently to a big hickory tree about 15 feet from the hole in the fence, facing it, and left it there for almost two weeks. I was surprised when I saw that there were only four photos on the camera, and even more surprised to see that all four photos were of me, taken as I left the camera and again when I approached to check it. I repositioned the camera to face the other trail, but the results were the same.

I repositioned the camera several times over a period of two months or so before I captured my first images: a doe and its yearling, and a hen turkey with her two offspring from the previous spring. I could have gotten images more quickly by putting the camera near a feeder, or along the edge of a food plot, but I knew deer were using the feeder and the food plot; I wanted to find out where they were traveling between feeding and bedding. What I learned about white-tailed deer and interpreting sign using that camera and others over the next few years was invaluable. And while some of it only served to confirm what I had learned from other sources, there is something about learning it for yourself that drives a point home and makes it unforgettable.

One thing I confirmed: Deer are unpredictable. Not that the unpredictability of deer was a news flash to me. It's just that I hadn't realized how unpredictable they normally are. To a given mature buck, for instance, walking a mile is the human equivalent of leaving the family room to visit the refrigerator. Two miles is nothing. Distance aside, there is another big difference: The buck would rarely go from the family room to the kitchen via the same path. A mature buck that is under little or no pressure might occasionally be observed in the same area for several days running, maybe even a week or so, though that is the exception and not the norm. A buck that is aware of hunting pressure is unlikely to be even that predictable.

Another lesson: sign can be (and I think usually is) misinterpreted. It is one thing to distinguish fresh tracks from older tracks. Distinguishing week-old tracks from month-old tracks is beyond the ability of all but the most expert trackers, and even expert trackers would have to be keenly aware of the weather over that period of time to make an educated guess about the age of the tracks. Also, game trails are visible for long periods of time after they are last used. It doesn't take much to make a visible trail. Game cameras have proved to me that some apparently "heavily used" trails aren't that heavily used at all.

Studies have suggested repeatedly that most scrapes and rubs are never revisited, and my experience with positioning game trail cameras near rubs and scrapes certainly confirms that to my satisfaction.

All this is probably beginning to sound as if game trail cameras are of little use, but that is not the case at all. It's important to keep in mind that while a lack of photos might be less exciting than a photo of a trophy buck or bull, it is data nonetheless. Knowing where game is not is one step toward finding where it is, and eliminating an area from consideration can save a great deal of time that might otherwise be wasted in an unproductive stand. Further, that process of elimination increases the chances that each subsequent location will result in photos depicting our target species. At that point, we begin to learn not only something about the numbers and quality of animals frequenting the area, but where they travel and, almost equally important, when they travel to or through a given area. Most deer hunters have on more than one occasion excitedly put up a stand in response to smoking fresh droppings, tracks, rubs, and scrapes, only to be mystified when hours turn to days spent unproductively in that stand. No doubt in some cases, the mystery was as simple as a spot that deer just don't use during daylight hours. A game trail camera can go a long way toward identifying such spots, as well as spots that are frequented during the day.

WHAT TO LOOK FOR

Film cameras are still available, but digital is the way to go. The savings in film and processing alone can pay for a digital camera in a season or two, sometimes faster if you have multiple cameras and use them regularly. Then too, digital images are available instantly; film must be retrieved, taken to a processor, then picked up. Invariably, and for any number of reasons, some images will reveal no animals, while others may be so badly over- or underexposed as to be useless. You pay for those images along with the others, in time as well as money. In the case of digital cameras, you erase those images in a few moments.

Cost is always a factor. What do you get for greater cost? Possibly a faster trigger. Probably higher resolution, better color, and a generally all-around superior image quality. Maybe greater durability—or so go the claims. One important thing to keep in mind when considering cost is the fact that multiple cameras are much more useful than one camera. Monitoring one spot at a time can reveal very useful information, but is a slow way to collect data compared to monitoring a feeding area, a stream crossing, and a rub line all at once. The cost savings of a less expensive camera can allow a hunter to buy two or three cameras for the cost of a single very expensive camera. Let's ignore prettier packaging, celebrity endorsements, and a product that is advertised heavily, and look at more important factors such as trigger speed, image quality, and durability.

TRIGGER SPEED

Advertising has increased awareness of trigger speed in recent years. Prior to that, more than a few hunters retrieved images from their trail cameras only to stare in consternation at photos of trees, feeders, meadows, or food plots devoid of any kind of animal. Photos can be triggered by things other than animals, but what often happens is that an animal walking by the camera is out of the picture by the time the photo is taken. Trigger time can range from a fraction of a second to as much as six seconds. As technology improves and the market grows, prices are coming down on trail cameras, and at this writing more and more cameras are advertising speeds of a second or so. It could well be that in a few years, trigger speed will be a minor consideration, since even the less expensive models are trending toward faster triggers. If you already have a camera with a slower trigger speed, try positioning it near feeders, fence openings, stream crossings, or in such a way that you expect animals to linger in the area or walk directly toward the camera, as opposed to passing by in front of it.

IMAGE QUALITY

Increasing numbers of hunters are finding that, in addition to being useful hunting tools, trail cameras are a lot of fun. Assuming you are interested only in information, image quality is probably not a major factor. Much of the competition among game trail cameras currently seems to be in the direction of higher MPs (megapixels), which is, in simple terms, a measure of the camera's potential resolution, or the sharpness of the image. If you want to know how many deer are entering your food plot, including how many bucks and how big they are, a 2 or 3 MP camera will do that and more. Keep in mind, too, that if you will be viewing your images primarily on a computer, higher MPs are not normally a factor, since the resolution of your computer monitor is limited.

So what are the advantages of higher (4, 5, 6 MP) game trail cameras? If you want to try and get professional quality photos that you can print, there may be a real advantage. (Keep in mind that there is more to getting professional quality images than having a 5 or 6 MP camera. However, good resolution is a starting point.) Also with higher resolution, it is possible to zoom in on small, distant, or less distinct objects in a photo. It is conceivable that this ability might in some instances yield information that would not otherwise be available. In my own experience, if the goal is simply to identify and monitor the quality of big game animals in a given area, lower MP cameras will do the job just fine, and for significantly less cost. With a little luck, in a few years manufacturers will turn more of their attention away from megapixels and toward faster triggers, more sensitive activation, and better flashes that will cover wider areas without washing out objects that are closer to the lens. In the meantime, if you are not interested in making large color prints of your game trail photos, you can save a little money by staying away from the high-resolution cameras.

DURABILITY

No doubt some trail cameras are tougher than others. This may be a factor for some hunters, depending on where and how the cameras are used. Having experimented with half a dozen of the more popular models for several years now, I've yet to have one that failed to perform. I don't handle my trail cams carelessly, but I don't baby them or take special precautions with them, either, and have even managed to drop a couple of them.

RANGE

This is really two issues: distance from the camera (out in front and peripherally) at which game will trigger the shutter, and distance at which the flash sufficiently illuminates the subject to capture a usable image in low light. The importance of range really depends on how and where the camera is used. A camera with a trigger range of 20 feet, for instance, used near a food plot, would fail to be triggered by animals wandering by at 25 feet or more, while a camera with a limited flash range would reveal only darkness or a pair of eyes reflecting the flash.

FLASH VS. INFRARED

Flash photos offer better quality in low light, but there is some concern that the flash spooks game. It is not difficult to find evidence supporting the claim that camera flashes spook game—or that it doesn't. Photos of herds of whitetails grazing calmly in a greenfield at night, often including multiple photos taken in rapid sequence, are strong evidence that many deer are not spooked by flash. Other sequential photos reveal deer jumping and vacating the area rapidly in response to camera flashes. It is possible that some deer that are initially spooked by camera flashes learn that they are not a threat and quickly tune them out. Some manufacturers recommend mounting the cameras higher in a tree, the theory being that animals will accept the flashes as lightning, which is a natural phenomenon. Maybe so, but then again, perhaps this is yet another classic case of anthropomorphism. It seems unlikely animals have any concept of lightning, or of the difference between a natural and unnatural phenomenon, or that a flash originating from up in the sky would not spook them, while a flash originating from three feet off the ground would.

If you think the solution to the problem is as simple as using an infrared camera, you might want to think again. Many users claim that the red glow of the infrared array (which contains some white light) spooks game as well, and they provide photos of jumping whitetails as evidence.

NOISE

I have spent a fair amount of time sitting in blinds photographing various species of animals, and never once do I recall an animal spooking from the sounds made by my camera. There have been several occasions when I fully expected this to occur, and more than once I have had animals react to camera noises by raising their heads, pausing as they walked by the blind, and so forth. None have bolted.

Having said that, I don't doubt that, under the right conditions, a nervous animal might very well be spooked by camera noises. I report my personal experience only by way of keeping things in perspective. I do not believe that in most situations, with most animals, barring a defective camera that makes an unusual amount of noise, camera noise levels are a big issue. Most game trail cameras that I have experimented with have been reasonably quiet, with the exception of some of the older model film cameras.

POWER

Power sources for today's trail cameras range from simple alkaline batteries at one extreme to solar panels at the other. In between is a range of rechargeable batteries of various kinds, as well as twelve-volt and lithium batteries. Which power source makes the most sense for you depends largely on where, how, and when you will be using them. At warmer temperatures, most cameras will operate for two months or so on a variety of battery types. In colder temperatures, that time period will be greatly reduced. This may not be a big issue if you are in a position to check cameras and change or recharge batteries frequently. If not, you'll want to look at twelve-volt or lithium batteries, which tend to last longer.

MEMORY AND ACCESS

Digital trail cameras can be plugged directly into computers, but that requires removing the camera from its location or carrying a laptop computer into the woods. A far more convenient method entails using two smart chips. For as little as thirty dollars, you can purchase a couple of the smaller chips. How many images these will hold depends in part on the resolution of each image, but at a moderate resolution, even a small chip should hold hundreds of images. For a little more money, larger chips can store thousands of images. Remove a chip from the camera periodically and replace it with a fresh one. The removed chip containing images can be inserted into a camera, which can be wired to a computer, or it can be inserted into readers developed specifically for the purpose, the readers then being wired to a computer. Upload the images, delete them from the chip, and next time you're in the woods, remove the chip in the camera (assuming the camera indicates it has recorded images) and swap the chips out. Larger chips are available at greater cost, and these can be useful if you expect to record a large number of images, either because you are in a game-rich area or your visits to the camera are infrequent.

Several game trail cameras currently on the market transmit photos, either via direct transmission to a computer in a home or cabin nearby (which can then automatically be emailed to a specified address or uploaded to a website), or via cell phone signal to specified email addresses, websites, or even cell phones. Each of these has its advantages and disadvantages. The cost is significantly higher than is the case for other game trail cameras—generally in the $1,500 to $2,500 range—but costs are coming down. Most of these systems can accommodate several cameras simultaneously. Among their advantages, such systems can be monitored without the need to visit the camera, saving time and avoiding any concerns about leaving scent or otherwise spooking game. They also offer the capability to continuously monitor locations.

CAMERAS THAT TRANSMIT

Several game trail cameras on the market transmit photos instantly (well, quickly at least) to computers, websites, smartphones, or all three. Some will transmit simultaneously to a number of different email addresses. At least one I'm familiar with (Buckeye Cam) transmits directly to a computer that must be within a mile or so of the camera (or cameras). This computer then transmits the image to other locations. Others—Smart Scouter is one, and Moultrie makes another with which I'm familiar—transmit via cell phone signals to any location anywhere in the world. This means locations are currently limited to areas with cell phone coverage, but as cell towers are appearing all over the landscape, more and more areas are included. Smart Scouter offers a booster system that can put marginal areas into range. And technology is on the way that utilizes satellites instead of cell phone towers, at which point presumably even remote wilderness locations could make use of these cameras.

They offer a number of advantages, in addition to the fun of receiving regular and real-time emails of photos of game on your computer or smartphone. For one, they tell you what is going on yesterday, today, and even right now, as opposed to two weeks ago. That in itself is worth a lot. Second, they let you see what is going on without the need to actually visit the camera. That means that 1) you save on gas and time spent visiting the camera, which is especially useful if your hunting spot is thirty or sixty miles from your home, and 2) you needn't be regularly spooking game and contaminating your hunting area with scent to retrieve your photos. This latter point is especially important when your quarry is a trophy animal, since trophy-quality game is much more sensitive to and less tolerant of human intrusion in their areas.

This technology doesn't come cheap. On the other hand, prices are coming down steadily, and these cameras are already less expensive than some of the higher-end nontransmitting digital cameras. There is a monthly subscription fee, but these costs are coming down as well. One option: Several hunters who hunt the same area can split the costs of one or two cameras and a subscription fee, and all will receive the photos. The technology is improving each year, and having personally used the Smart Scouter camera for a season, I can say that it works well, assuming your hunting area gets a cell phone signal.

WHERE TO PLACE A TRAIL CAMERA

Few hunters, I suspect, need a tutorial on where they might want to put a game trail camera. Game feeders or food plots are obvious possibilities, along with trails game might use getting to these areas. Game trails in general, especially where they intersect, are good possibilities, as are wallows or watering holes, funnels created by fences, stream crossings, crop fields, and so forth. Any areas where sign is abundant in terms of tracks, droppings, and rubs and scrapes are good possibilities. To some extent, where to place cameras depends on what you are trying to learn and how many cameras you have. Let's say its July, you have one camera, and you want to find out by opening day how many big white-tailed bucks are on your 200-acre hunting lease. If you have a feeder that is being regularly visited, that's a good place to start. If it's been a dry summer and you have a pond or stock tank, that is an obvious location. On the other hand, maybe you live nearby, visit regularly, and are already confident that there are several good bucks frequenting the place. You know the area like the back of your hand and have a pretty good idea where the bucks are bedding and where they are feeding. You are probably more interested in determining their travel patterns as quickly as possible. In that case, funnel areas or heavily used trails might be better sites for your cameras. Of course, if you have multiple cameras, you can monitor feeding areas, water holes, and trails simultaneously.

There are some other considerations when it comes to specific camera placement. Many manufacturers of game trail cameras warn against placing the cameras with an east-west orientation, since the rising or setting sun can trigger the camera. Similarly, boulders, cliff faces, large rocks, and even some large trees can trigger some cameras if they are in a position to absorb heat from the sun on clear days. Hunters who find their cameras are regularly producing image devoid of animals should look carefully to see if any of these factors could be the culprit. Moving the camera short distance, or even simply reorienting it slightly, can solve the problem. Finally, it can be helpful to orient the camera toward the direction from which you expect animals to approach. An animal walking steadily past the camera at right angles will be too quick for some triggers, and an animal hurrying by will probably be too quick for even the fastest camera.

THEFT PREVENTION

There is no getting around the fact that using game trail cameras entails leaving a fairly expensive item out in the woods where it is vulnerable to theft. The first means of defense is to decrease the likelihood of detection as much as possible. Game trail cameras often sport camo patterns, and those that don't tend to be drab green, brown, or gray in color. Beyond that, it only makes sense to position cameras away from areas often traveled by humans to the extent this can be done without compromising the camera's effectiveness. Totally hiding the camera is not really an option, since the view finder and lens must be clear of obstructions to detect game and get a clear photo. On the other hand, it is certainly possible to use natural vegetation to conceal the camera as much as possible without obstructing its view, and even artificial camo such as fake leaves or camo fabrics can be used to make it less detectable.

Here is one advantage of infrared over flash cameras, since a flash bulb going off instantly reveals to any passerby that there is a camera nearby, along with its location. This is also an area where cameras that transmit images to websites, email addresses, or cell phones can really shine.

A few years ago on a hunt with some folks from Buckeye Cam, a representative from that company was discussing with me some of the early experiments with their system, which was one of the first of its kind. They were surprised one morning to come to the office, log on to their website, and find a series of photos of what was clearly a young man approaching their camera and removing it from the tree to which it was attached. The young thief took the camera home, and a quick examination revealed a sticker attached to the camera with the company website on it. He logged onto the website and quickly learned that in all likelihood his photo had been taken as he approached the camera and transmitted to an email address or other website. Later that day, the employees at Buckeye Cam answered the door to discover the young man they had seen in the photos, sheepishly handing them the camera and mumbling something about "finding" it.

Placing cameras in difficult-to-reach spots, such as high up in a tree, can certainly reduce the likelihood of detection while discouraging theft even if the camera is detected. There are disadvantages to that approach, since placing and retrieving the camera or memory chip will be more difficult. In addition, the camera will have to be placed very carefully to be sure that it will cover the area desired, in terms of both range and ability to detect animals. Stout cables and locks can discourage spontaneous theft and are worth using, though the determined thief can always find a way to get past a cable and lock. In the final analysis, the best way to discourage theft is probably to avoid public areas, or areas where human traffic is likely, and to conceal the cameras as well as possible.

The bottom line on game trail cameras is that they can be very useful, and their usefulness is multiplied given time and/or multiple cameras. They can provide information about the numbers and quality of animals in a given area, as well as providing useful data about the changing travel patterns of animals. On top of all that, they're a lot of fun.

20

A WALK ON THE WILD SIDE

Anthropomorphism, as we have seen, is the term biologists use in reference to our very strong, but perfectly natural, tendency to attribute human characteristics or motivations to animals. At the more extreme level, it leads to depictions of animals that talk, possess subtle senses of humor, and engage in complex reasoning. Almost all of us are guilty of it to a lesser degree, though. For instance, we might assume a dog is wagging its tail or a bird is singing because it's happy. Bass anglers talk about "triggering" strikes with lures that make nonfeeding fish angry. In fact, many biologists think dogs wag their tails to communicate submissiveness, anxiety, or indecision. The best evidence suggests that a bird sings to declare territories, and who knows if fish experience anger? (And if they do, would eating the source of their anger be a likely response?)

Up to a point, this natural tendency is harmless but, as hunters, it limits our understanding and knowledge of the animals we hunt. A case in point: When I was a youngster, old-timers told me repeatedly that smart old bucks would let does and fawns precede them down the trail, while the bucks hung back to make sure the coast was clear. They said this with complete confidence, and I'm sure they believed it. It's not an unreasonable conclusion to reach, based on their observations that does and fawns were seen a lot more often than bucks, and that in many cases when they saw does run or walk by, a buck came along a few minutes later. Today's hunters are far more inclined to interpret this behavior as a simple case of bucks following does that are in estrus, or about to come into estrus. Most available evidence would support the modern theory. Does this better understanding of deer behavior improve the strategies hunters use when deer hunting? Absolutely.

There are obvious limitations on our ability to perceive the world from the point of view of the animals we hunt, but to the extent we can use our superior imaginations to do so, it might be a useful experience. First, we need to remember that animals rely on their sense of smell in much the same way humans rely on their sense of sight. Our instinctive reaction, if we hear something or smell something, is to look for the source of the sound or smell. If we smell smoke, for instance, we will probably need to see the fire before we run from it, unless the smoke is very thick. In a similar way, any noise that is not loud enough to startle us will probably cause us to look for the source of the sound. The tendency is to confirm with our eyes anything we hear or smell.

THE NOSE KNOWS

Most animals, too, will look toward the source of a sound or smell, but game animals will often try to confirm what their eyes and ears tell them by using their noses. Every experienced deer hunter has had a deer spot him, then proceed to circle downwind only to bolt the instant its nose confirmed what its eyes had already made it suspect.

Because game animals rely on their noses in much the way we rely on our eyes, it could be that the best way to understand their perceptions is to compare them to our own vision. For instance, imagine that you can not only see extremely well at great distances, but that if you look in the right direction, you can see through any object. Naturally, anything you hear or smell that might be a threat would prompt you to circle at a safe distance until you could look through any intervening obstacles to visually confirm the threat. That might sound like a stretch, but when you consider that under the right conditions game animals can detect the source of an odor that is half a mile or more upwind, the analogy is probably not far off the mark.

Now imagine that you have the ability to see not only what is happening at a given moment, but that images of events that have transpired hours or even days before are visible. The more recently the event occurred, the more vivid the image, and the more time that has passed since its occurrence, the fainter the image. You see not only what is happening right now, but the coyote that walked down the path two hours ago, the pair of wild turkeys that scratched the area for acorns three hours ago, and the hunter that climbed down from the tree and walked out of the woods the evening before. In a very real sense, that is what most animals can do with their sense of smell. Their noses tell them not only what is happening upwind of them, or on the ground around them, at a given moment, but what happened over a preceding period as long as two days, with at least a rough idea of when the events occurred. No wonder most game animals seem to be constantly on the alert!

SIGHT AND SOUND

To their prodigious sense of smell, we need to add a couple of other abilities that we humans lack. We've looked at visual and auditory capabilities in greater depth in previous chapters, but we'll briefly review here a few specific differences in vision and hearing. First, in terms of hearing, many game animals have the ability to precisely locate the source of a relatively distant sound. A human, for instance, hearing the bugling of an elk, will have little more than a general direction and a guess about the distance of the elk. If it doesn't continue bugling as the hunter approaches it, his chances of finding it are slim. On the other hand, a bull elk hearing the single mew of a cow

Bowhunting is all about getting up close and personal. There is no denying, though, that extending your effective range provides more shot opportunities.

elk can, if sufficiently motivated, move into a position very close to the cow. And though the vision of many game animals is in some respects inferior to that of humans, most are able to detect motion at least as well as, and probably better than, humans. Further, most game animals have much better low-light vision than do humans. Since their eyes tend to be located on opposite sides of their heads, they have a field of view much wider than that of humans and are able to see not only what is in front of them, but far around on either side. Finally, as we have seen, they can see ultraviolet light, which can give them advantages in certain situations.

The result of all this is an animal that can "see" for great distances, and can even "see" through objects in the right direction; is excellent at spotting motion; can see well in the dark; has a huge field of vision, with the ability to see anything that is not almost directly behind it; can locate a source of sound precisely from a great distance; and has an uncanny ability to know not only what is happening at the moment, but much of what has happened over the preceding hours.

VULNERABILITIES

Are any of our quarries' sensory capabilities inferior to our own? Among mammals, few animals other than primates see color well, though some recent studies suggest that bears see color. Most hoofed animals seem to perceive some shades of blue, but are blind to shades of red and green in much the way some humans, mostly men, are red/green color-blind. Resolution for most animals is inferior, meaning that they do not see detail as well as humans. We have mentioned that mammals generally have a wider field of view, since their eyes are farther apart, but there is a downside to that: They lack good depth perception. The lack of visual acuity, along with some degree of color blindness and poor depth perception, means that camouflage can be highly effective in defeating the eyes of game animals. As our grandfathers knew, any patterned clothing that breaks up the human outline can make the motionless hunter difficult for deer or other game animals to detect.

Visual vulnerabilities aside, the strength of their other senses, along with near-constant wariness and incredibly fast reflexes, means that getting within bow range of most truly wild animals is a formidable undertaking. Despite all that, game animals are not supernatural creatures. They do have some chinks in their armor, and hunters have demonstrated repeatedly that no animal is truly unstalkable.

With a full awareness of the sensory capabilities as well as the vulnerabilities of the animals they pursue, bowhunters can accept the challenge of bowhunting knowing that, though they will lose the battle more often than they will win it, they can achieve success over time.

21

INCREASING RANGE

Clearly, increasing effective shooting range can help a bowhunter defeat the nose, the eyes, and the ears of his quarry. For several reasons, the chances of remaining unscented by a bedded mulie are better for the bowhunter who can shoot from 40 yards than for the one who must stalk to within 20 yards. An eye, a shape, an exposed patch of skin, even a movement that might be spotted by an elk at 18 yards, might not be spotted at 38 yards. And a piece of blind fabric rustling, a button clicking, or a shirt sleeve swishing may turn a nervous pronghorn inside out at 15 yards, but not at 30 yards.

Not every bowhunter has a desire to increase his or her range. My friend and fellow outdoor writer Tom Cross lives in the heart of Ohio's big buck country and has some impressive trophies on display in his home. Tom hunts whitetails using just about every legal method, but among his favorite weapons are a beautiful flintlock musket and a Black Widow recurve bow. In Tom's opinion, the recurve is strictly for close-range use.

"How close is close?" I once asked him.

"Oh, about 15 yards or less," he answered matter-of-factly. Tom is well aware that there are bowhunters who are proficient with recurve bows at ranges beyond 15 yards, but that doesn't bother him in the least. Big eastern white-tailed bucks are notorious for spending most of their time in thickets, where a shot beyond 15 yards is unlikely to be an option. Tom takes his Black Widow into the thickets after them. And Tom would argue, as do most bowhunters, that getting close to game is part of the challenge, and part of the special thrill, of bowhunting. That is the irony of modern bowhunting. On the one hand, we embrace it because of the challenge and the thrill of getting close. At the same time, part of the challenge is shooting well, and the natural tendency for most bowhunters who shoot well at 20 yards is to begin practicing out to 30 yards. When they become proficient at 30 yards, many will begin practicing out to 40 yards, and so on.

More years ago than I like to remember, I sat in a tree stand by an Alabama greenfield at dusk and watched three bucks emerge from the opposite side of the field to walk single file in my direction. The first buck was a forkhorn, the second a smallish six-pointer, and the third a respectable eight-pointer that easily made my "shooter" list at the time. The field was 80 yards wide, and when the bucks were less than half-way across, they turned and began walking broadside. Because I knew the width of the field, I was confident they were 50 yards out, give or take 2 or 3 yards, and I considered my maximum range at the time to be 40 yards. I came to full draw on that third buck, hoping the light would be insufficient for my sight pin and I would be spared a difficult decision. The light was adequate, and I could see the sight pin just fine. I settled the 40-yard pin just over the buck's back, and when he paused to look behind him I came very close to touching the release. In the end, I let him walk. For the rest of the hunt, though, I couldn't stop thinking about the fact that for a couple of other hunters in camp with me, a 50-yard shot at a broadside whitetail would be routine. I vowed that I'd never again let a P&Y buck walk by me at 50 yards because I couldn't shoot consistently well out to that range. Not long after I was home, I began practicing regularly at 50 yards.

There are bowhunters who object to shooting at longer ranges, insisting that it is unethical to shoot game beyond a certain specified distance. I have to admit, I've never fully understood their logic. Granted, it is unethical for a bowhunter whose maximum effective range is 20 yards to loose an arrow at an animal standing at 30 yards. On the other hand, as an outdoor writer I often find myself in the company of 3-D target-shooting champions and other people in the industry, some of whom can consistently produce grapefruit-sized groups at 80 yards with broadheads. I see no reason why such a bowhunter should have to limit his shots to some arbitrary distance of 40, or even 50, yards. Ultimately, each bowhunter must decide for himself the range at which, under hunting conditions, he can shoot with confidence.

Having said all that, on occasion I have encountered bowhunters with a tendency toward overconfidence in their own abilities. In fact, I have more than once been downright amazed to find myself standing side-by-side with a hunter who is shooting poorly even as he boasts about his shooting prowess. It is an interesting psychology, and one that invariably prompts me to think: "Dude. I am standing here watching you spray arrows all over the target. How can you boast about your shooting ability with a straight face?"

Short of this sort of delusional behavior, most of us do need to remind ourselves regularly that there is a huge difference between shooting paper or 3-D targets and hunting. The best bowhunters I know regularly take shots at targets that they would never consider taking at game. First, of course, is the all-important fact that a poor shot at a target is unlikely to result in anything worse than a lost arrow, while a poor shot at game risks wounding an animal that may never be recovered. Beyond that is the fact that, unlike target shooters, rarely are hunters able to concentrate on perfect shooting form while standing flat-footed and spending as much time as necessary on the shot. The better 3-D shooters let down from full draw as often as 20 percent of the time because the shot doesn't "feel" right. That is perfectly allowable, and is even good strategy, on the 3-D course, but won't work very well in a hunting situation. The hunter is in many cases cold, tired, stiff, or worn out, and if none of those situations applies, he is probably going to be very excited.

For all those reasons, I've never bought the old "paper plate" theory of bowhunting. Over the years, countless thousands of novice bowhunters have been told to practice until they can hit a paper plate every time at 20 yards, then head for the woods to hunt. If you consider, though, that those paper-plate-sized groups are probably going to open up in the less-than-ideal conditions of hunting, shooting paper-plate-sized groups at 20 yards seems inadequate. Fortunately, today's gear is more forgiving and easier to shoot, and most novice bowhunters, with a little coaching from a good pro shop, can soon shoot much better than 8-inch groups at 20 yards.

HOW TO GET THERE

Maybe you've heard the old joke about the tourist in New York who asked a local how to get to Carnegie Hall. The answer: practice. When it comes to extending their range, the answer isn't always so obvious to bowhunters. That is probably because, in theory, a bowhunter who can shoot 2-inch groups at 20 yards can shoot 4-inch groups at 40 yards, and 8-inch groups at 80 yards. Nice theory, but it doesn't hold up. In fact, the bowhunter who shot only at 20 yards, and who in time achieved 1-inch groups at that range, would find that he would still be unable to shoot 8-inch groups at 80 yards, and probably wouldn't shoot 4-inch groups at 40 yards, either. To a lesser degree, the opposite is also true. A bowhunter who shot exclusively at 30 yards until he could shoot 3-inch groups at 30 yards might assume that his groups would be tighter at 20 yards, but would probably need some practice at 20 yards to significantly and consistently get tighter groups. Similarly, some bowhunters shrink their bullseyes at closer ranges, theorizing that if a 2-inch bullseye at 20 yards appears to be the same as a 4-inch bullseye at 40 yards, consistently hitting the 2-inch spot at 20 yards will enable them to consistently hit the 4-inch spot at 40 yards. Shrinking that bullseye may well tighten their groups, but they will likely be disappointed when they switch to the 40-yard range. The fact is, as countless bowhunters have discovered, shooting at extended ranges is the one and only way to become consistently proficient at those ranges.

SPEED KILLS

For years bowhunters debated the relative merits of forgiving, quiet bows as opposed to fast bows offering a flat trajectory for longer-range shooting. No doubt some will disagree, but I'm convinced that the issue has become moot. Advances in technology, materials, and bow design have in recent years resulted in bows that are faster, quieter, and more forgiving than their predecessors.

Speed itself is still an issue, though, for one reason: Shooting accurately with broadheads becomes increasingly difficult above certain speeds. Depending on a number of factors, that speed might be as low as 250 feet per second or as high as 280 feet per second, but somewhere in that range—probably closer to 250 fps than to 280 fps for most bowhunters—the setup with broadheads becomes significantly less forgiving. One response to that has been the growing popularity of mechanical, or open-on-impact, broadheads. The controversy surrounding mechanical heads is another issue altogether, but bowhunters who use them to compensate for the fact that their bow is not tuned adequately for the speeds at which they wish to shoot might be making a mistake. Poor arrow flight doesn't necessarily mean decreased accuracy with mechanical broadheads, but it can reduce penetration, since an arrow that hits the target at an angle will slap sideways, robbing it of energy. Furthermore, a poorly tuned bow is a less forgiving bow, and bowhunters need all the forgiveness they can get in hunting situations.

Finally, there is one other speed-related issue. If bow A is more efficient (read faster) than bow B, then bow A might reach speeds at a draw weight of 60 pounds that bow B can only reach at a draw weight of 65 pounds. The bowhunter who can reach his desired speed at 60 pounds as opposed to 65 pounds can practice longer without fatigue, can hold at full draw longer when a situation demands it, and is less likely to develop the kind of shoulder or arm problems that plague far too many bowhunters, even forcing some to give up the sport altogether.

There is always a temptation, especially when the object is longer-range shooting, to boost draw weight in order to get a flatter trajectory and reduce the incidence of range estimation errors. There is something to be said for that, and certainly there is nothing wrong with working one's way carefully up to a heavier draw weight. The hunter who shoots regularly can turn the limb bolt a quarter turn or so once a week, and in doing so will increase draw weight without even feeling it—up to a point. The fact remains, though, that after 40 yards, even at relatively high speeds, an arrow will begin to drop rapidly, and knowing the distance (to plus or minus a couple of yards) becomes critical. When the distance is such that it must be known precisely, some of the advantages of higher speeds are negated. Boosting draw weight beyond the point of comfort is likely to result in less accurate shooting at all ranges, not to mention an increased risk of arm and shoulder problems. In some cases, hunters who increase their draw weights begin to ocassionally creep forward into the valley (as opposed to pulling hard against the wall), in which case their arrow speeds become inconsistent, defeating the purpose of increasing the draw weight.

Though we tend to credit improved bow designs for today's faster bows, the fact is that arrows have gotten significantly lighter in recent years. Decreasing arrow weight is another way to boost speeds significantly, and with today's quieter bows and sound-dampening accessories, this usually doesn't result in unacceptable noise levels. There are a couple of caveats with regard to decreasing arrow weight. First, consider the quarry. For deer, black bears, and smaller game, any of the more popular arrow shafts currently on the market should prove adequate. If the quarry is elk, moose, grizzlies, or some of the larger African game, the lightest arrows may not consistently result in adequate penetration. Second, light arrows with light broadheads and plastic vanes can result in inadequate FOC, or weight forward of center, which makes for an unstable and inaccurate (or even dangerous) arrow. Information about determining FOC is readily available on the Internet and elsewhere, but for hunting purposes FOC should probably be no less than 11 percent, and something a little higher than that may prove more forgiving.

Consistency in arrows—in weight as well as in fletching style, length, straightness, and other variables—becomes critical at extended ranges. The same applies to alignment of broadheads and nocks. Bowhunters determined to significantly increase their maximum effective shooting range are well advised to purchase a grain scale and an arrow spinner, and use them regularly to keep arrows as consistent and as near-perfect as can be achieved.

RANGE FINDERS ARE THE KEY

I still recall being on bivouac in basic training at Fort Knox, and being designated the step counter. In those days, a platoon leader would actually appoint someone to count steps as we made our way from point A to point B. It was a crude way to measure distance, to be sure, but far better than nothing. Also in those days, the U.S. Army conducted tests of the ability of individuals to judge distances. The theory was that with sufficient practice, soldiers could be trained to improve their ability to estimate distances for purposes of marksmanship and artillery. The results were disappointing, the conclusion being that even with a great deal of training and practice, the best that could be expected from human range estimators was a margin of error of 15 percent between 50 and 100 yards or so, after which the range of error began to increase rapidly. Granted, range estimation is better at shorter ranges, but for bowhunters, even an error of 10 percent can be the difference between a quick kill and a poor hit.

Now, of course, modern electronics tell us precise locations and measure long distances accurately to within a few feet. When it comes to bowhunting, modern electronic range finders have extended the potential maximum effective range of even the most accomplished bowhunters. There is simply no way a bowhunter can shoot accurately at long ranges without knowing the distance. On spot-and-stalk hunts, I've taken to putting my binoculars in my daypack or a belt pouch, and putting my range finder on my bino-harness. I'm not usually in a rush to use my binoculars, but often I need the range finder right now. On many hunts, a range finder can be more important than binoculars.

EXTENDED-RANGE BROADHEADS

A broadhead may perform flawlessly at 20 yards or at 30 yards, but poorly at extended ranges. Joel Maxfield of Mathews Bows routinely tests broadheads by shooting them at extended ranges of 80 or even 100 yards. "If it shoots accurately at those distances," Maxfield once explained to me on a Saskatchewan bear hunt, "then it's a good broadhead."

Mechanical heads generally fly well at any distance, and the better ones may be good candidates for extended-range shooting. Some mechanicals require more energy to penetrate effectively, though, which makes them poor choices for long-range shooting, since energy levels decrease with distance. Large, traditional cut-on-contact heads are rarely good candidates for extended-range shooting, but certainly there are a number of replaceable-head broadheads, and a few cut-on-contact styles, that fly straight enough for long-distance shooting, assuming the shooter is capable. Among the latter, G5's Montec broadheads and NAP's Hellrazor hold up well at extended ranges.

Few bowhunters are fortunate enough to have as much time as they would like to tune their bows to perfection and to practice shooting. Proficiency at 60 yards requires more practice than proficiency at 40 yards, and proficiency at 40 yards requires more practice than proficiency at 30 yards. At some point for most of us, demands of family and career must take precedence, and we must be content with the maximum range we have achieved. In the final analysis, bowhunting is all about up-close encounters. There is no denying, though, that increasing effective shooting range can be a significant advantage for those who have the desire and the time available for practice. When it comes to bowhunting, whatever our maximum range, we can all embrace the challenges that are unique to our sport.

22

WEATHER
OR NOT

In my home state of Ohio, people like to say, "If you don't like the weather here, wait a few minutes and it will change." They say that in Alabama, too, and in Maine, and in Oregon, and probably in Siberia. They don't say it in San Diego or the Caribbean, but since there is little hunting to be done in either place, who cares?

The point is, changing weather is a reality for hunters almost everywhere. The most successful hunters are weather watchers, not only because weather patterns greatly affect the movement patterns and the behavior of game animals, but because weather can also affect the ability of game to see, hear, or smell, sometimes increasing their vulnerability to hunters. (At the same time, animals often recognize their increased vulnerability and respond by becoming more wary or even lying low and not moving.) Conversely, weather can give all the advantages to game and make hunting more difficult. Deer hunters often refer to the "October lull," when whitetails are notoriously difficult to hunt, presumably because they move very little, at least during daylight hours. I don't doubt for a moment that whitetail movement is reduced during daylight hours in October, but I have to wonder if there aren't other factors at work that might be equally important in explaining why filling a whitetail tag is so notoriously difficult through most of October. To begin with, temperatures on a typical October day through much of whitetail country are optimum for scent conditions, being neither extremely hot nor extremely cold—though they are warm enough to make a hunter perspire, particularly if he is sitting in the sun or using a climber stand. Humidity levels are not so low as to reduce scenting ability, nor so high as to drive scent to the ground. And October is usually dry, and the ground is deep in newly fallen leaves, which means that it is nearly impossible to walk through the woods to a deer stand without making a racket. Put those things together and the result is often a sweaty hunter, out during optimum scent conditions, who has just made a terrible racket getting to his stand.

FRONTS

My friend and well-known writer/wildlife biologist C. J. Winand is a self-proclaimed "deer geek." C. J. is a stickler when it comes to maintaining a scientific approach to wildlife behavior. As a hunter, though, he still gets excited by his observations. I spoke with C. J. recently at his home in eastern Maryland about weather and deer behavior.

"Listen," C. J. said. "Right before Ivan hit—Ivan was our last big hurricane—I saw bucks coming out of nowhere, bucks that I had never seen before. They hadn't shown up on any of my cameras, or at any of my feeders, or anywhere. And suddenly, there they were. The same thing happened before our other big hurricane. . . ."

C. J. hastened to point out that he was skeptical that other weather patterns significantly affected deer movement, but there was no doubt in his mind that a rapidly changing barometer meant increased deer movement.

"And is there scientific evidence for that, like telemetry studies?" I asked.

"We're past radio telemetry," he explained. "Now we use GPS and satellite tracking, and the amount of data we can collect is scary. And from Maine to Florida and points in between, the data show the same thing—that deer movement increases when the barometer is falling and a storm is approaching. I've seen one study in Texas that did not come to the same conclusion, but they looked at data only on the day of the event, and not the day before. I'm convinced if they had analyzed the data starting twenty-four hours before the weather change, they'd have produced the same results."

A great deal has been written about how game animals seem aware of approaching weather fronts, typically feeding heavily as a cold front or storm activity approaches, lying low through the worst of the weather, then becoming active again as the storm or the cold front passes and weather begins to stabilize. Much of this activity seems to be related to barometric pressure, with activity levels peaking when the barometer is rising or falling rapidly. It only makes sense for hunters to take advantage of such information as much as possible. Hunting ahead of a front, as the barometer is dropping, can be phenomenal, with game seemingly everywhere. Similarly, hunting can be excellent after a front moves through, the barometer is rising, and conditions are moving toward normal. The problem is that few of us have the luxury of hunting only when conditions are optimum. We hunt when we can. We do usually have some control over precisely where and how we hunt, and knowing how weather affects game can help us adjust our strategies accordingly.

RAIN

Years ago, on a hunt at Alabama's Bent Creek Lodge, I sloshed along a muddy logging road behind well-known guide Larry Norton. It had been raining for days, and we were taking advantage of an early-morning break in the weather to get afield. "I see you're optimistic," I whispered as we stopped by a greenfield to catch our breath.

"How do you mean?" he asked.

"Well, you're not wearing any rain gear."

"I never wear rain gear unless I'm duck hunting. A wool jacket will turn a light rain."

"What if it rains hard?"

"If it rains hard, I go home."

He had a point, of course. In a real deluge, game doesn't move much anyway, so being out is arguably a waste of time. It's also true, though, that many grazing animals prefer wet greenery, and will take advantage of wet weather to feed actively. Then too, during most hunting seasons, rainy weather is usually cooler weather, which is preferred over warm weather by almost all game. A certain amount of moisture in the air makes for good scenting conditions, especially when compared to dry, hot conditions that dry out the nasal passages. On the plus side for hunters, rainy conditions and fog do not disperse scent well, tending to cause it to fall to the ground. And rain will certainly wash away contact scent that is left on trails. Rain also makes for quiet footing. Wet leaves are silent. All in all, while hard, continuous rain usually tends to minimize game movement and make hunting a miserable waste of time, wet weather in the form of a steady drizzle, intermittent showers, and those periods immediately following the cessation of rain can be excellent times to hunt. (The exception here is hunting game over water holes. In that case, the hotter and drier the conditions, the better the hunting.)

STRING TRACKER

An unavoidable issue for bowhunters in wet weather is the fact that blood trails can be washed away. Many bowhunters simply refuse to hunt when rain threatens, and that may be the wisest course, especially when hunting in thick, brushy, or wooded areas where locating an animal without the ability to track it is an unlikely prospect. Other hunters limit themselves to close-range shots, the reasoning being that they will not have the benefit of a blood trail in the event of a marginal shot, or in a situation in which they cannot be sure about the shot and will not have the option of waiting overnight to begin tracking. Still another option is the use of a string tracker. Many bowhunters reject string trackers on the grounds that they rob accuracy, but, if properly used, they will not significantly affect accuracy inside of 25 or 30 yards, and current models are very effective. In my experience, string trackers mounted on a bracket above the arrow (as opposed to being mounted in the stabilizer hole) work well for hunting from tree stands or ground blinds. (Don't try to shoot through camo mesh windows with a string tracker, though.)

WINDY CONDITIONS

A light breeze is something animals are accustomed to, and it has little effect on their behavior or their sensory capabilities. Animals on the western plains are less bothered by wind than animals in other places, since near-constant wind is a fact of life on the plains. Harder winds are another matter altogether, and at some point even animals on the prairie are made nervous by high winds. Small wonder, since hard, gusty winds take away much of their ability to detect predators. Scent conditions are difficult in hard winds, and spotting movement is tough since trees, grasses, and pretty much everything but rocks are in motion. Hearing is affected, too, by the constant noise of the leaves and grass rustling, not to mention by the sound of the wind itself. If the winds are stiff enough, game will lie low and move little.

Behavior is affected by the wind before movement is shut down altogether, though. Game may continue to move, but will tend to be warier than usual, super alert, and, in some cases, they will mill around nervously. For the bowhunter, of course, the wind poses the additional disadvantage of degrading shooting accuracy. Bowhunters usually respond by limiting themselves to close-up shots. At the same time, getting that close-up shot can be easier, for all the reasons mentioned. Windy days can be great for still hunting, even in areas where still hunting is usually a low-percentage tactic.

BITTER COLD

"Bitter cold" is a relative term. What a hunter in the lower Midwest calls bitter cold might be mild in Saskatchewan. Most game animals in most climates will react negatively to a sudden precipitous drop in temperatures, particularly if temperatures are unseasonably cold. Often they'll bed down and hardly move for as long as two or even three days. The thing about the cold, though, is this: Animals must consume many more calories in cold weather than in mild weather if they are to maintain their body temperature and survive. In the case of game animals that may become largely nocturnal in milder weather, that means they can no longer limit their activity to the night, but must move about during the day. In the coldest weather, many species must eat at least twice a day. For the bowhunter able to tough out the challenges of hunting in extremely low temperatures, cold can be an ally, as hunger forces even the wariest, most secretive trophy animals to get out and move to feeding areas during hunting hours. Apart from the need for increased movement, cold does not tend to make most animals more vulnerable. Hearing is not significantly affected by cold, nor is vision. Bitter cold does somewhat diminish their ability to scent danger, but their sense of smell is still formidable.

HEAT

We made reference earlier to the "October lull," when temperatures are often mild, if not warm. Unseasonably warm temperatures do tend to reduce the activity, especially daytime activity, of most species. And though very high temperatures do not make for optimum scenting conditions, animals with a keen sense of smell can still detect danger, if not from quite the same distance or (in the case of ground scent) for the same period of time. Sound carries all too well in warm weather, and vision is generally not affected. Probably the biggest issue in warm weather, apart from the limited amount of game movement, is the increased difficulty for hunters to control their scent because of perspiration. Scent-free antiperspirants and deodorants can help. A hunting strategy that induces less perspiration can help, too, including hunting from easily accessible ladder stands or ground blinds.

Heat can certainly increase the need for most animals to find water, while decreasing their ability to get it in the foods they eat or in small drainages and puddles. That means they'll have to go to streams, lakes, ponds, or stock tanks. They'll do it at night most often, but the likelihood that they'll be driven to water holes during the day increases as a heat wave continues. How often they go to water during the day depends on the severity of the heat, the perceived safety of a given water hole, and the proximity of the water to a bedding or staging area. The bottom line is: Hunting waterholes can be a good strategy under the right circumstances. Keep in mind that in the case of ponds or stock tanks, animals can be extra wary when approaching a water hole. Camo, concealment, and scent control become critical.

23

TURNING THE
TABLES

Guide Brett Thorpe (yes, that really is his name), patiently remained one step behind as I carefully followed a blood trail down a hill, across a small stream, and into a thicket, but when he suspected we were getting close to the big British Columbia black bear I had arrowed, he insisted we switch places. I was pumped enough to want to stay in the lead, but I knew Brett was just doing his job, so I declined to argue the point. We made our way slowly through the thicket, climbing over downed trees and ducking under tree limbs for another 30 or 40 yards, but as we started up a small hill Brett suddenly put his hand up to stop me.

"He's close," Brett whispered. "Smell him?" I didn't smell anything but a mix of pine trees and swamp, but Brett was confident enough that we backed out and looked for another approach that might offer better visibility. We slipped in from a different direction, and as we approached the area, Brett again signaled a stop. "Smell him now?" he said. Again I had to answer in the negative. "Well, nock an arrow and be ready," Brett said, "because he's very close." We resumed moving ahead cautiously, but had gone less than five steps when Brett stepped aside and pointed up the trail. "He's right there," Brett said, "and he's still moving. Get another arrow in him!" I could see the bear now, not 10 yards away, down but not yet expired, and without wasting any time I drew and released. The big black bear stiffened, raised a leg, and then relaxed.

Only later—when we deemed it safe to approach—did I smell the bear. Bears, like most large animals, produce a fairly strong smell. Rutting bull elk are notorious for their smell, and most elk hunters are familiar with the smell of an elk wallow. Wild hog wallows, too, produce a smell that many hunters can recognize instantly and from some distance downwind. The question is: can human hunters use their sense of smell to detect game at significant distances? There is evidence that some hunters can. We've made the point that the human sense of smell is feeble compared to that of virtually any game animal. On the other hand, we also pointed out that in Vietnam, enemy combatants were sometimes able to smell the presence of U.S. troops.

In December 2006, Nature Neuroscience published the results of a University of California study in which forty-six people aged eighteen to twenty-six, wearing items designed to block their other senses (including masks, earmuffs, gloves, and knee and elbow pads), crawled on their hands and knees in an open field in an attempt to follow a scent trail. The 32-foot trail was produced by a length of twine dipped in chocolate, and included two forty-five-degree turns. The participants were placed approximately 10 feet from one end of the string and given ten minutes to locate the trail and follow it to the end. Thirty-two participants took the test with both nostrils open, and two-thirds of them successfully navigated the scent trail. (Interestingly, the success rate was lower, and the course took longer to complete, for participants with one nostril blocked.) Four participants then trained on the trail, the course of which was changed from time to time to determine if they could improve their skills with practice. These participants were able to cut their times in half, and were observed to wander off the trail less often, suggesting human olfactory abilities can indeed be improved with practice. Further evidence that the human sense of smell can be significantly improved with practice comes from a University of Pennsylvania study comparing the sense of smell of blind individuals with sighted individuals. Surprisingly, the top performers in that test were sighted employees of the Philadelphia Water Department who had been trained to serve on that department's water quality evaluation panel. The researchers concluded that training is the single most important factor in performance on smell tests. In a similar vein, corporate marketing departments that test fragrances of foods, perfumes, shampoos, deodorants, and similar products have learned not to use the same individuals repeatedly in their tests, since continued practice changes the results in a way that no longer reflects the perceptions of ordinary consumers.

It is not only possible, but also probable that we humans have greater olfactory abilities than we normally believe to be the case. It's only speculation, but it seems likely that we have learned to tune out our olfactory abilities to concentrate on our much stronger senses of vision and hearing. Unfortunately, there are some obstacles working against many hunters when it comes to improving olfactory abilities. First, there is an age factor. The sense of smell seems to peak at around age 30 (some experts believe it peaks in childhood or early adulthood), drops off gradually to around age 60, and then deteriorates more rapidly. Individuals with sinus problems usually have significantly reduced olfactory abilities, as do seasonal allergy sufferers, though the latter may regain their sense of smell fully when allergy season ends or even when symptoms are controlled by medication. Other medical conditions, ranging from polyps in the nasal cavities to serious conditions such as tumors or brain injuries, can reduce or eliminate the sense of smell. Smoking reduces olfactory capabilities to such an extent that when smokers give up the habit, they must normally wait at least as many years as they have spent smoking to regain most of their sense of smell. Frequent exposure to various chemicals, not to mention plain old smog, can also decrease olfactory powers. On the flip side, a substance that is widely believed to improve the sense of smell is zinc, which increasing numbers of hunters consume for its deodorant properties.

The notion that human hunters might one day take advantage of the wind to detect the presence of game with consistency at any real distance remains far-fetched. Nonetheless, it does seem entirely possible that healthy hunters who avoid smoking and exposure to noxious chemicals, and who work a little at improving their olfactory abilities, might be able to use their sense of smell to better detect the presence of elk wallows, wild hog wallows, or even some animals themselves, more consistently and at greater distances, than most of us would imagine possible.

24

BOWHUNTING IN THE ZONE

The focus in this book has been on one sense—the sense of smell—but certainly we have addressed the other senses as well, sight and hearing in particular, with some passing references to the senses of taste and touch. We even briefly discussed the possibility of a sixth sense.

I am not a mystically inclined person. My friends will tell you that I tend toward skepticism, and I suspect folks who know me but harbor less friendly feelings toward me would say I am cynical. I do believe, though, that the very best bowhunters are people who become so totally immersed in their surroundings, and so totally engaged in the hunt, that they reach a stage of hyperalertness, in which they see and hear in a way that other people who are not at that level of alertness cannot see or hear. In fact, all their senses are heightened. I don't believe in any sort of extrasensory perception, but hunters operating at this level seem almost to possess it.

Part of it has to do with forgetting the clock. For animals, I suspect, life is pretty much right now. They have memories, and they are capable of learning. Clearly they may be affected by their past. But for the most part, they experience life in the here and now, neither agonizing over past behaviors nor worrying about the future. There is no place they have to be. There is nothing they "should" be doing. We humans—Americans in particular—have elevated the desire for productivity to the level of a moral value, while at the same time turning even the most relaxing and contemplative activities into competitions. (Where but in the U.S.A. would people turn fishing into a competitive sport?) We feel guilty if we're not using every moment productively, and even if we are, we worry that there is something else we could be doing that might be an even more productive use of our time. We have smartphones, pagers, fax machines, and computers—"time-saving" devices that not only enable us to work anywhere, any time, but create the expectation that we will. Then we worry—all too often with justification—that we aren't spending enough time with our families. We work more and more and worry more and more and suffer the consequences more and more. Obesity, diabetes, high blood pressure, heart disease, depression, and other stress-related illnesses reach higher and higher numbers each year.

On top of all that, most of us spend the greater part of our lives in boxes. Our houses are boxes, our vehicles are boxes, our workplaces are boxes. We view the world through glass from what amounts to an artificial womb. For millions of us, caring for our lawns and playing an occasional round of golf is as close as we get to experiencing the outdoors. About eight miles from my suburban home is a 100-acre, fenced-in area called the Nature Center. I've been a member on and off for years. It's a wonderful thing. Busloads of kids come out from the inner city, not to mention the nearby suburbs, to walk around looking at "nature." Signs warn them not to stray from the carefully manicured trail. They wander about like astronauts on the moon, staring at trees and meadows, looking for "wildlife." In the unlikely event they should see a white-tailed deer, they are equally divided between two reactions: those who fear it will attack them, and those who want to go pet it.

Not all of us are quite that removed from nature, but few of us are unaffected by the reality just described. Most of us enter the woods handicapped by a heavy burden, and I'm not talking about our climbing stand, our daypack, our blind, or any of the other paraphernalia we hunt with. I'm talking about our workday stress, about the conflict we're having with a boss or coworker, about deadlines, about bills, about the room we could be painting, the plumbing we could be fixing, or the car we could be repairing. If we are to hunt effectively, enjoy our time afield (and, by the way, fully achieve the health benefits of getting outdoors), we must shuck all that stuff and leave the modern world behind.

Years ago, on an opening day bowhunt out of a lodge in Mississippi, an elderly guide sat behind the wheel of a pick-up truck driving me down a logging road to my stand. He was a quiet old guy who rarely put more than two or three words together at a time, and then only when the need was present. I was eager to get to my stand, and had high hopes for the hunt. Suddenly I remembered something.

"Stop the truck," I said. "We've got to go back to the lodge. I forgot my release aid." He stopped, turned around and began driving back to the lodge. I was frustrated, embarrassed, disappointed, and ticked off. I was sure I had ruined my best opportunity to tag a good buck, and said so. The guide pulled off the road and took the truck out of gear.

"Listen," he said, in a fatherly sort of way. "Never go into the woods worrying that you're getting there too late, or worrying that you have to come back too soon, or that you don't have enough time." It would be a better story, I suppose, if I could say I tagged a big buck that day. I didn't. But the advice was valuable.

Still, saying it is one thing, doing it another. How is it done? One hunter I know has a routine. In effect, he has trained himself to disengage from the work-a-day world by following the same steps each time he goes afield. He leaves his vehicle, walks a hundred yards or so into the woods, sits down against a tree, and remains there with his eyes closed for five or ten minutes. He does this every time he hunts, no matter the time or place. When he resumes walking, he has left the world behind. He is relaxed but alert. Deep breathing helps; don't laugh if you haven't tried it. Doctors, psychologists, shamans and mystics have recommended it and practiced it for thousands of years. It's as simple as stopping and breathing very slowly and deeply for a minute or two. Try it, it works.

I try to avoid carrying a watch with me when I hunt. It's not always possible—sometimes we must coordinate schedules with hunting buddies, or we are fitting in a morning hunt before an afternoon obligation of some sort. When possible, though, I leave the watch behind and do my best not to think about the time. If I must take a watch, I set the alarm for whenever I need to head back. It is unlikely the tiny beep of my watch will be heard for any distance, but I would set it anyway. The freedom to forget about time, even for a few hours, is more important to my enjoyment and my hunting success than the possibility that the alarm going off might spook game that has come onto the scene just as I am about to leave. Shedding worries, relaxing, and forgetting about time is half the battle. Modern lifestyles affect the way we see and hear, too. In a book on turkey hunting, I recounted the story of the time I took a friend and neophyte hunter on a turkey hunt. At one point we flushed a turkey off a roost right over our heads, and he did not see or hear it. By that time, he was only confirming what I already knew: he wasn't going to see a turkey unless it was in the open and close, he wasn't going to hear a turkey unless it gobbled in his ear, and neither of those things was going to happen because he fidgeted and made so much noise that no turkey was ever going to get near him. His case was an extreme example of habits that I think most of us suffer from to varying degrees: the habit of seeing only what is directly in front of us, close up, and in the open, and tuning out most of the sounds around us.

When I was a youngster, my father, whose aging eyes were beginning to fail, regularly impressed me with his ability to spot game long before I could see it. "Don't you see it?" he would whisper patiently as I strained my eyes for the deer or whatever he was pointing out.

"Look just to the left of that shagbark hickory, back in the shadows."

Still I couldn't see it. Eventually an ear would twitch or a tail would wag and I would spot it.

We rabbit hunted with beagles a lot in those days. Most of the rabbits we saw were naturally those we kicked up, or that the dogs jumped or began trailing. On nearly every outing, though, my father would manage to spot a rabbit or two sitting under a cornstalk or tucked neatly into a tuft of tall grass. After a couple of years of practice I discovered that by concentrating, staying alert, and looking in the right places, I could spot them, too. I also discovered over the years that if I didn't practice the skill, I could lose it. I never forgot the lessons I learned from those experiences. Seeing game is not just a matter of visual acuity; it's a matter of knowing where to look, and what to look for. I'm trying to teach my kids the skill. They want to look for a "deer." The trick, of course, is to look for part of a deer. Look for the horizontal line of the back crossing the vertical lines of the trees. Look for an ear, or the white of the throat or the belly. If the deer moves, it's easy to spot—assuming you are looking. Looking is harder than you think, and few of us can do it all the time. Have you ever suddenly noticed a deer right in front of your stand and wondered how it got there? It still happens to me on occasion, and I know there is only one way it got there without being spotted. I wasn't looking. Yes, my eyes were open. That's not the same as looking. Chances are, my mind was elsewhere. Or maybe it was nowhere. The eyes don't see, the brain does.

Most of us are accustomed to tuning out irrelevant noise, and we do the same thing in the woods. The problem with that is that there is no irrelevant noise in the woods, unless we happen to be within hearing range of vehicles on the road, planes flying over, farm animals bellowing, or some of the other routine sounds of domestic life. Natural sounds in the woods are all conveying useful information of some sort, if we are only aware of it. The alert hunter hears the sounds of acorns falling from a white oak, the chuckling of a raccoon, the scraping sounds of a squirrel cutting a hickory nut. He hears the clatter of rocks when something crosses a nearby stream, the alarm putt of a hen turkey when it spots a coyote, the angry squawk of a jay when a hawk circles overhead, and the unmistakable sound of a fawn bleating for its mother. All these sounds and more convey information to the hunter about what might be going on in the woods around him. When the woods grow suddenly quiet, the alert hunter becomes even more alert.

Behavioral scientists talk about the alpha state, a condition that can be measured by observing the electrical activity in the brain of individuals wired to a monitor. This particular electrical activity reveals itself in certain regular brain waves, and these waves invariably accompany a state of relaxed alertness and heightened creativity. We'll never know until a scientist begins monitoring the brain activity of hunters in the woods, but it could be that an "alpha state" is what the best hunters achieve.

How to get there? One way is through comfort. I'm all for discipline, but I suspect it's over-rated. If you can remain alert, fully aware of your surroundings, and hunting effectively when you're cold and shivering, your back aches, or your feet hurt, more power to you. For a hunter, that is an invaluable skill, and one that was second nature to primitive peoples. For the modern hunter, though, I recommend the opposite. Find out what it takes to make you as comfortable as you can be in the woods, and do what is necessary to achieve it, whether that means wearing the right clothes, sitting in the right stand, using the right blind, or looking through the right sunglasses. The tense or uncomfortable hunter is generally the fidgety, distracted hunter. Get comfortable, relax, and focus all your energy, all your senses, and all your thoughts, on the hunt.

However you get there, you'll know when you arrive. Every sense is alive. You feel that you see everything and hear everything that goes on around you. You are relaxed but alert. You are confident. You have forgotten about time, and you are in no hurry, content to be exactly where you are, doing exactly what you are doing. You are in the zone. There is a buck out there with your name on it. He is headed your way.

Still on Fire is a spiritually powerful and remarkably life-transforming book that will positively impact you forever. It is destined to become an inspirational classic.

God bless,
The Publisher, Victory Entertainment

"Delbert McCoy is one of the bravest and strongest individuals I have ever known. When I met him in 1997, he was painfully disfigured as a result of third-degree burns over 90 percent of his body and had endured more than 70 surgeries. Still, he remained upbeat and positive and has never let his injuries keep him from living. He is a true survivor and a wonderful inspiration."

Kate Lawson
The Detroit News

"A remarkable transformation occurs just a minute or two after you've met Delbert. He gets to you and holds you with the way he manages to accept his injuries. His warmth, honesty, engaging conversations, humor, and upbeat personality are contagious. The experience—and it is amazing, unique—is that after you've chatted with him for a few minutes, you forget your troubles and complaints. HE makes YOU feel good!"

Eddie Kean, co-creator of *The Howdy Doody Show*

StillOnFire.com

To bring Delbert "The Real Inspiration" McCoy, one of North America's most inspirational individuals, to your book signing, church, temple, congregation, school, business meeting, conference, seminar, rally, or other event please visit **STILLONFIRE.COM** or call Del Reddy at 1-800-497-1035. God bless.

Please share your story about how this book and/or Delbert McCoy has influenced your life at **STILLONFIRE.COM Thank you.

VICTORY ENTERTAINMENT, LLC PRESENTS

STILL ON FIRE!

FEATURING

DELBERT "THE REAL INSPIRATION" McCOY

Delbert McCoy

You are Still on Fire, too!

God is Great!

ANNE HENNING *and* **DEL REDDY**

Del Reddy

"The Spirit of Detroit" and the Motor City's **ultimate survivor**
Delbert "The Real Inspiration" McCoy.

"THE SPIRIT OF DETROIT"

THE INSCRIPTION ON THE SYMBOL WALL IS FROM
II CORINTHIANS, 3:17 "NOW THE LORD IS THAT SPIRIT AND
WHERE THE SPIRIT OF THE LORD IS, THERE IS LIBERTY"

THE SCULPTURE BY MARSHALL FREDERICKS WAS DESIGNED
TO CONTINUE THE THOUGHT CONVEYED BY THE INSCRIPTION
AND REFLECTS IN ITS CONCEPTION THE SPIRIT UNDERLYING
ALL HUMAN IDEALS — THE RELATIONSHIP OF GOD TO MAN.

THE MAIN FIGURE REPRESENTS THE SPIRIT OF MAN. IN HIS
LEFT HAND HE HOLDS A SYMBOL OF GOD, AND IN HIS RIGHT
HAND, A FAMILY GROUP: FATHER, MOTHER, AND CHILD.
THE ARTIST EXPRESSES THE CONCEPT THAT GOD, THROUGH
THE SPIRIT OF MAN, IS MANIFESTED IN THE FAMILY, THE
NOBLEST HUMAN RELATIONSHIP.

MOTTO FOR THE CITY OF DETROIT:
"Spearamus meliora; resurgent cinerbus"
"We hope for better things, it will rise from the ashes."

Spoken by Father Gabriel Richard after fire decimated
not only the city but his school as well in 1805.

STILL ON FIRE!

FEATURING

DELBERT "THE REAL INSPIRATION" McCOY

ANNE HENNING *and* **DEL REDDY**

Publisher, Victory Entertainment, LLC.

Editor, Anne Henning

Assistant Editor, Ray Glandon

Proofreaders, Lynn Gregg, John Makar

Book Consultant, Janet McKenzie

Book Research Assistant, Dan Stoner

Book Cover Design, Barb Gunia, Sans Serif Designs, and Del Reddy

Book Cover Photo, Lynn Gregg

Book Cover Illustration of Delbert on fire, Brian Remillard

Resource Assistant, Warren Parker

Book and Photo Formatter, Deb Tremper, Six Penny Graphics

Special thanks to: God, Jesus Christ,

Jean Schroeder of Sheridan Books,

Mike Reddy, Sheldon Yellen,

Audiovisual Archivist, Mary J. Wallace of the Walter P. Reuther Library, Wayne State University,

Malgosia Myc, Assistant Reference Archivist of the
Bentley Historical Library, The University of Michigan

Karen L. Jania, Head, Access and Reference Services of the
Bentley Historical Library, The University of Michigan,

Jerry Smith, Kevin Allen, Mo & Al Elfakir, Helen Cottrell, Ted Henning, Aaron Howard,
Dave Story, Don and Pam Howard, Sheila Rogers, Sue Willett, Debbie Nowicki, and Maureen Reddy

Still On Fire! Delbert "The Real Inspiration McCoy" is
Published by Victory Entertainment, LLC.
35228 W. Michigan Ave, Wayne, Michigan 48183
1-800-497-1035

First Edition December 2010

ISBN: 978-0-9830224-1-1

Publisher's Cataloging-in-Publication
(Provided by Quality Books, Inc.)

Henning, Anne.
    Still on fire : featuring Delbert "the real
inspiration" McCoy / by Anne Henning & Del Reddy.
    p. cm.
    LCCN 2010939515
    ISBN-13: 978-0-9830224-1-1
    ISBN-10: 0-9830224-1-0

    1. McCoy, Delbert. 2. Burns and scalds--Patients--
United States--Biography. 3. Accident victims--United
States--Biography. I. Reddy, Del. II. Title.

RD96.4.H46 2010   362.19'711'0092
                         QBI10-600220

CONTENTS

1969

PROLOGUE

*O*akland Baptist Church on Harper Avenue in Detroit, Michigan was overflowing. The spray of white roses stood out in stark contrast to the somber, dark overcoats and dimly lit candles. Every pew was occupied, and mourners spilled out through the double oak doors into the bitter January cold.

All eyes were fixed on the gleaming wooden coffin, as Preacher William Wilson began the eulogy. "Dear friends and family"…

His words were sorrowful and went straight to the heart. Sniffling and soft sobs, along with an occasional raspy cough, echoed off the stained glass windows and reverberated gently back into the cozy chapel.

Albert and Essie McCoy sat in the front row. Daddy, in his navy suit, sitting tall and erect, his shoulders squared to the front and his eyes straight ahead. Mother, wearing her Sunday finest—eyes closed, head bowed, and her body folded into itself, as she rocked gently back and forth. Their children filled the remainder of the front row pew. First the boys—"June," "Ball," and "Slow." They were born Albert, Jr., Luther, and Tony, but nobody ever called them that. As with the rest of the McCoy brood, they were bestowed with appropriate nicknames and would forever remain "June," "Ball," and "Slow." Next to them were sisters "Jackie," short for Jacqueline, and "Skacie," whose given name was Gwendolyn. There were six children born to Albert and

Delbert at age 19.

Essie McCoy. Five were in the front row of the Oakland Baptist Church. The other child lay motionless in the mahogany box.

The rest of the sanctuary was filled with dignitaries. Pearlie and Pauline McCoy, Grandma Agnes, Grandpa Edward and Grandma Sula, Aunt Cristobel, Cousin Clifford, Rodney Reno, Preacher, Regina and Pug. The night shift at the Warren Truck Plant showed up, grateful to have a few hours off. And the 1967 graduating class of Northwestern High School, reunited with their classmates, took up most of the remaining seats. A buzz went through the crowd as mourners recognized their bigger-than-life baseball heroes enter through the heavy doors: Willie Horton, Norm Cash, Denny McLain, Jim Northrup, Mickey Lolich, and the rest of the World Series champs attended wearing their Detroit Tigers uniforms. It was the off-season for the team, as spring training down in Lakeland, Florida wouldn't begin for a few months.

Two little girls were there too. Monique, at 13 months, shyly snuggled up against her mama's waist, while baby Kim slept peacefully in Yvonne's arms. They were so young and innocent, with their sweet cherubic faces and dark curls. The size of the crowd frightened them, and they didn't even understand why they were there. But their mother did.

The long hours of practice paid off, as Nate, the neighborhood talent, pulled his bow slowly across the violin strings. But the soulful melody of "Precious Lord, Take My Hand" did little to drown out the soft sounds of weeping.

Preacher Wilson cleared his throat. "Friends and family, we are gathered here today to honor the memory of one of our own. He was a loving son, a good brother, a faithful husband, and a devoted father...

And at barely past nineteen, Delbert McCoy was just too young to die."

Part
ONE

(Illustration by Brian Remillard)

ONE

In a Flash

It's funny how we take life for granted sometimes, expecting our plans and dreams to come true, especially when we're in the first phase of adulthood. Even though I was barely 19, I had been married for two years and already had a family of two precious daughters and a beautiful wife. I held down two full-time jobs in the auto plants and was working hard to save money to buy our first home. I had big plans for our future. And I wasn't going to work in the factories forever either. My life was good, and it was only going to get better when I would realize my dream of playing outfield for the Detroit Tigers. Those guys were my heroes, and I couldn't wait to jump into a uniform and take my place on the roster. I'd be able to provide a better life for my family, plus it would make my parents so proud. I had great friends, a wonderful, supportive family, talent, and my dad's good looks. I was full of hope, dreams, ambition, love! Look out world…here comes Delbert!

*T*he sound startled me as I shivered at the bottom of a stairway, waiting with a throng of other young people to pay the one dollar cover
charge to enter the Soul Expressions dance club in downtown
Detroit. It was January 12, 1969, and Marvin Gaye's *I Heard it Through
the Grapevine,* the hot single of the previous summer, could be heard
pulsing from the club upstairs. The floor was vibrating to the stomp of
dozens of teenage dancers. My toes were tapping to the beat, and my lips
were singing, as excitement and energy poured from the second floor. I
was a happy, ambitious 19 year old, enjoying a rare night on the town,
anxious to join my friends, Lamont and Napoleon. It was Napoleon's
birthday, and I was meeting them at the Soul Expressions to celebrate.
There were about 25 other teenagers ahead of me in line—all of us cold,
but eager to get upstairs to the party. Life was good in Motown...until,
that is, the instant the stairwell door opened behind me.

The acrid smell of gasoline immediately filled my nostrils, as I simultaneously felt a strange wetness on my pant legs. Sometimes there's a gap
from the time an event happens until it actually registers in your brain,
and that's how it was for me at that moment. I turned towards the door,
but by the time my mind provided a warning, it was too late.

The match was thrown into the explosive liquid below me, and the
bottom of the stairs quickly ignited. A roaring mass of flames swept up
the steps, inciting horror and panic. Dense smoke filled the airspace,
making it impossible to see. The sounds of singing and laughter were
replaced with screams of terror as everyone scrambled, pushing and shov-
ing, to escape from the inferno.

As the last person in line, I was closest to the blaze. My pants immediately erupted in flames, and a rising wall of fire prevented me from
exiting out the door to the safety of the street. My only option for escape
was the wooden stairs in front of me, but they were being devoured by
the ferocious flames. Somehow I had to make it to the club upstairs. But
how? I was already on fire, and like the dozens of others in the stairwell,
I was consumed with unimaginable fear. The gasoline, plus the melting
snow, had made the steps extremely slippery, and it was impossible to
gain secure footing. The heat and smoke were so intense that terrified
teens were slipping and falling in front of me, and I could hear the panic
in their screams as they fought to push up the stairs. The wall of flames

4

behind me and the mass of bodies in front of me prevented me from escaping. There was no way out. I was trapped in the inferno. I kept losing my footing, and the crush of the other bodies repeatedly forced me backwards until I finally landed at the bottom of the stairs. Now my entire lower torso was ablaze.

As I lie in the flames, exhausted, I knew I had two choices: I could give up and die—or get up and fight to live.

Someone at the top of the stairs was yelling encouragement. "Get up…Run for your life," he screamed.

Initially, those at the top, on the dance floor didn't realize they were in danger. When they heard the screaming, some thought a fight had broken out. But when the smoke started pouring in from the stairwell, most of them realized that they too were trapped. There were no flames on the upper floor itself. But smoke and the smell of fire had been enough to inspire terror. In the chaos that followed, many patrons were knocked down as the crowd rushed to find an exit.

When a group of young men threw a chair through a window, many of the teenagers leaped to the ground, two stories below.

When the window had been broken, it aided the escape of those upstairs, but it proved disastrous to my situation. The sudden rush of fresh oxygen fed the flames in the stairwell, igniting an inferno. As I struggled to crawl to the top of the stairs, my body engulfed in flames, my worst fear was that they would collapse, and I would once again tumble back to the bottom, and the source of the blaze. I had no real sense of time or space. My eyes burned painfully from the thick smoke, and it was so hard to breathe that my lungs were working in short bursts. I not only couldn't get any secure footing, but I had nothing to grab onto… nothing to help support me. "God help me," I prayed! I was forced to put my hands onto the burning steps in order to help guide me through the flames. I don't know how long it took for me to climb up the disintegrating stairway…it seemed like an eternity. Each time that I slipped back, the panic intensified, and the adrenalin gave me a new burst of energy.

I thought about my wife, Yvonne, and my two babies—Monique, the toddler, and Kim, our newborn. I had to get out for them. But on the final step, my leg punched through the wood. Terrified, I knew that if I fell back now, I'd never get out. The stairs would probably be gone. I would never see my family again. I'd never hold my beautiful little girls. Somehow, clinging to that image, I summoned all my remaining strength and heaved my body up onto the landing.

But I wasn't out of danger because by now, my entire body was on fire. The gasoline-fed flames had consumed my legs, torso, chest, arms, and now my face, hair, and ears. Suddenly, I realized that although I was out of the stairwell flames, I was still burning, and the horror of my condition renewed my fears and intensified the panic. I began running around the dance floor, slapping at my body and screaming. I wanted to escape, but I didn't know where to go, and I couldn't find the way out.

It was an unimaginable nightmare, and I was at the center of it…a human fireball. When one horrified young man witnessed my terror, he forced me down to the floor, and disregarding further risk of injury to himself, courageously whipped off his coat to beat down the intense flames. To this day I don't know who he was, but I'm sure that he'll live with that terrible image forever.

I could sense others scrambling around me, and I could hear distant cries for help. The smoke was suffocating, as I gulped air for each labored breath. The sound of sirens echoed in the distance, alerting me that help was coming, but I knew it would be too late for me. As I writhed and moaned helplessly on the floor, my body still smoldering under a pile of coats, I was exhausted beyond words and could feel my strength and life slowly slipping away. I don't know how long I lay there, but it seemed like an eternity as I fought to stay alive. I couldn't see, but I was aware that the firemen had arrived and were soon providing me with much needed oxygen and words of encouragement.

"You're going to be all right, son."

"Don't worry, we're going to take good care of you."

They asked for my name, and I gasped out each raspy syllable. "D.e.l.b.e.r.t M.c.C.o.y"

That was the only question that I could answer because, by now my brain had begun to process the severity of my injuries. The horror of what had just happened began to sink in.

"We're losing him!" one of the firefighters shouted.

And I slowly slipped into the void.

TWO

J. T. BOYER

Five-year veteran, J. T. Boyer, was a member of Engine Company 21 of the Detroit Fire Department and first on the scene of the Soul Expressions fire. A Medal of Valor recipient after surviving several days and nights of dangerous duty fighting the blazes of the 1967 riots, J. T. had witnessed some of the darkest hours in Detroit's history and had plenty of experience with the devastating destruction of fire.

*W*hen we pulled up to the scene I could see that a pretty good fire was burning in the front section of a two-story commercial building with a dry cleaners on the lower level. It looked like a routine building fire as we all scrambled out of the rig and I got busy securing the hose to get water started. That was my job and my first priority. When I heard a crash and saw a chair or table that had been thrown out the upstairs window, everything changed. As I struggled to get water up to the second floor, people began screaming and jumping to *the ground below. It was chaos, as more people panicked and leaped to the ground. I was dodging bodies and working the hose at the same time.*

The flames had spread up the stairway into the dance hall and were engulfing the dry cleaners below, where it had already burned off the gas meter to the building. I had to shift the water flow to the meter area to keep the gas from exploding. Two other lines were knocking the flames down on the rest of the building. As we got the fire under control, a couple of my buddies came and got me to see if I could help one of the victims.

I had been a nursing student at Detroit Receiving Hospital before joining the fire department and had seen more than my share of burn victims. As one of the few males on the nursing staff, I got the "dirty" job of debriding burn patients. Nobody wanted that duty because it was so horrifying. We had to use a scalpel to trim down the dead skin as close as possible without actually cutting into the healthy tissue to prevent scarring. The kids were the worst. We couldn't give them any anesthetic because it could kill them, so the procedure was extremely painful. I literally had to "skin" babies. They would be kicking, screaming and sobbing, and I'd be crying the whole time I was trying to help them.

When I scrambled up the ladder and first saw the victim, he was under a pile of coats—his body still smoldering. Everyone else was out of the building, and it was lucky we even found him. I couldn't believe he was still alive. He couldn't scream, or even talk, he just moaned pitifully. He was in terrible shape. His lips were burned off, his nose was gone. He had no ears. No fingers. His eyes were swollen shut, and he didn't look human at all. He was just a gurgling mess. We used to have a rule of thumb when assessing burn victims. If their age plus the percentage of burns reached 100…they were dead. And this guy was way beyond that.

In those days most of the ambulance work was done by a squad company, which provided support for the firefighters. The squad rig would pull up to a scene, put the patient in the truck, and take him to the hospital. It was known as "load and go," and it was the best available rescue service at the time. As the ambulance crew carried him out, I felt really sorry for the poor guy. He was a young man who didn't deserve any of this. He was just a victim.

I looked down at him for the last time and shook my head. I had seen enough and knew enough about the devastating effects of burns from my nursing background. And this was the worst I'd ever seen. "He's not going to make it," I announced, with absolute certainty.

THREE

TWILIGHT ZONE

I was able to hear even before I could see. Faint sounds wafted into my consciousness, but I didn't recognize any of them, as everything sounded muffled from far, far away. A beeping sound... a soft hiss...weeping. I knew I had been sleeping, and I'd probably been dreaming, but as I struggled to wake up, nothing sounded familiar. I strained to open my eyes, and I fought to lift my head, but the blackness of sleep kept pulling me back, and I surrendered to it once again. I don't know how many times I repeated this pattern, but each time that I tried to emerge from my dark world, the effort left me exhausted.

Eventually, it would be the urgency of strange voices that inspired me to slowly focus my eyes. It was difficult to make out shapes. My vision was fuzzy, as if there were a veil over my face. I was covered in white gauze and bandages, with tubes and wires leading from my body. I felt indescribable pain, alternating with complete numbness. As consciousness returned and I focused on the light around me, my mind was filled with questions.

"Where was I?"
"How did I get here?"

"Where was my family?"
"Who was weeping?"
"And why couldn't I move?"

The unbearable answers would come soon enough. And I would ultimately yearn to return to the black void of sleep and pray that I'd never wake up. Because when I emerged from the darkness…I would be in hell.

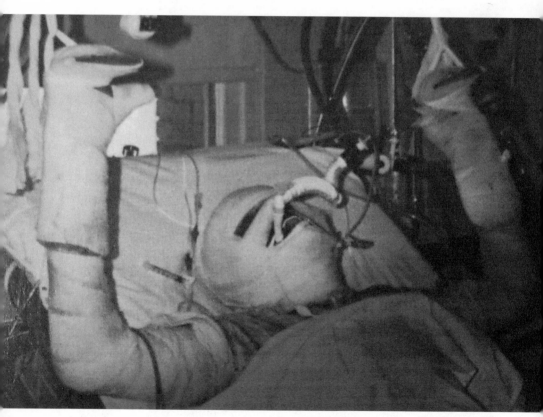

(Photo courtesy of Dr. Irving Feller)

FOUR

DR. THOMAS GRIFKA

In January of 1969 Detroit Receiving Hospital was a city-funded institution with a heavy caseload. Located on Detroit's west side, there were other hospitals in the area, but they usually did not take police cases. So if the police had accident victims or someone with gunshot wounds, they would have to by-pass four or five other hospitals in order to get to Detroit Receiving. Burn units were very rare. The only available burn center in 1969 was in Ann Arbor, some 60 miles away.

Thirty seven year old, Dr. Thomas Grifka, a graduate of the University of Michigan, was the instructor of surgery, having done his residency and internship at Detroit Receiving. In his brief six-year tenure he had witnessed stabbings, gunshot wounds, suicides, and every imaginable kind of trauma. But nothing could have prepared him for the early morning onslaught of January 12, 1969.

11

*T*hat night is vivid in my memory because I was called in to the hospital and put in charge of the burn cases that were swarming in. In a matter of a half hour, ambulances and police had brought in at least 40 patients. Many had suffered smoke inhalation and minor injuries, but we were deluged with burn victims with various degrees of severity. I got on the phone and called other hospitals, urging them to take some of the patients, because we were beyond capacity. But the private hospitals did not take police cases at all.

Doctors, nurses, and any available personnel in the hospital were called to the emergency room to help me assess the injuries and provide treatment. Triage was set up in order to determine in order of importance, those who needed help first, and to prioritize the patients.

Several of the victims had suffered significant burns, and swift response was crucial to their survival. The first thing to do was remove their clothing so that we could assess the nature of their injuries and to prevent further depth of the burns. Sometimes when the clothing was removed, the skin came off with it. The patients with the least amount of burn damage were turned over to the nurses, who would dress the wounds and dispense pain medication. In the more serious cases intravenous catheters were inserted and fluids were administered to prevent dehydration, one of the biggest problems facing burn patients.

One victim stood out in my mind because he was burned worse than any of the others. Delbert McCoy was a young man of 19. With burns over 90% of his body, he was unrecognizable. I had seen a lot of burn cases with varying degrees of trauma, but Delbert was the worst I had ever encountered. It didn't take long to assess his condition; it was evident immediately. The charred, leather-like appearance provided the diagnosis…third degree burns, the worst possible kind. We gave him oxygen to help him breathe, but getting an IV into him was a challenge. With most of his skin burned away, it was difficult to find an entry site. We had to do a "cut down" IV, which meant we had to cut through the charred skin to find a usable vein that still had blood flow.

The emergency room was bursting with activity, and still the cases kept coming in. As I went from patient to patient, surrounded by the chaos and horror of the situation, one thought kept whirling in my mind.

"What kind of human being could do this? How could anyone possibly cause this much pain and suffering to others?"

With very little staff and so many casualties, our duty was to assess the patients and treat the ones that we could save first. Given the massive extent of his injuries, it put Delbert well down the list. Back in 1969, with very little of the knowledge and technology we have today for burn treatment, Delbert would be considered a "hopeless case." My first impulse was to try to relieve the pain and make him as comfortable as possible, because I really, truly did not expect him to survive.

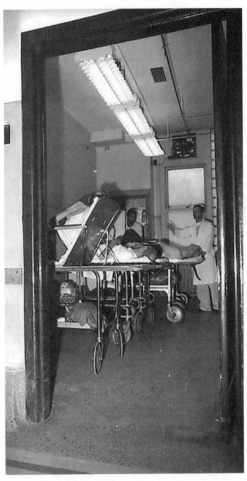

(Photo credit: Walter P. Reuther Library, Wayne State University.)

FIVE

INNOCENT VICTIM

*E*ven though I was only nineteen, I was keenly aware of my responsibilities as a young father and anxious to make my way in the world. I got a job at the Chrysler Warren Truck Plant even before I graduated from Northwestern High School in 1967. In the first days of 1968, I also took on a second job, working at the General Motors Chevrolet Plant. I'd work from 10 p.m. to 6 a.m. at Chrysler and then go to the G.M. factory from 7 a.m. to 3 p.m. Ironically, I didn't even own a car. My brother Ball owned a 1967 Buick Electra 225, and he let me use it to get to work, but sometimes I'd just take the bus.

The work at Chevrolet was tedious and mentally taxing. I was assigned to the line that produced brakes, installing 30 pads in about five minutes, or 360 per hour. So on a daily basis, I was assembling approximately 2,800 brake pads. That's about 17,280 per week...or 898,560 over the course of a year.

My friend, Pug, started working there with me, but he only lasted three days. "This is too hard," he said, "I'm quitting." It really wasn't that the work was difficult, it was simply not challenging in any way. Since I loved sports and yearned to be active, the repetition of assembling brake pads was particularly tiresome.

But whether the work bored me or not, my attitude was always to do what I had to do to support my family. Having inherited my father's work ethic, I was proud of my employment and the three dollar per hour earnings. My take-home pay was $93 from Chrysler and $107 at General Motors. The minimum wage was only $1.60 back then, and the buying power of a dollar was far greater than it is today. By bringing home $200 per week, I was living the American Dream. In 1968, gas sold for thirty cents a gallon and a loaf of bread was only twenty cents. A new car cost just $2,000. What I remember about the early years of my marriage to Yvonne was that we could purchase three baskets of groceries at the local supermarket for less than $30.00.

With my busy schedule, I barely found time to sleep and often worked seven days a week, so I didn't have the energy for parties or other activities that many of my teenage friends did. Besides, I was trying to save money to go to college part-time, with the hope of getting a degree in marketing. Since I'd always been a good student, and schoolwork actually came easy to me, I figured I could handle two jobs plus college as well.

When I did have spare time, I enjoyed watching sports, or reading, or talking about them. I had played sandlot baseball obsessively when I was a kid and played junior varsity baseball in high school as an outfielder on the Northwestern Colts. Baseball was my passion, and I followed it constantly, devouring every statistic. Around Christmas time in 1968, I was already looking forward to the start of spring training. The Detroit Tigers had won the World Series that year, and it had brought the Motor City together, helping it heal from the wounds of the 1967 inner-city riots.

The riots were a very dark chapter for my hometown. I remember walking down the street with some friends one evening when we saw a young kid run out of a store juggling several boxes of cigarettes in his arms.

"What's going on?" I yelled at him.

"Haven't you heard? There's a riot going on," he replied.

As we turned the corner, we saw more looting of the clothing and furniture stores near our house. Soon there was fire, smoke, and police cars everywhere. The city was in such chaos that the governor was forced to call out the National Guard, and army tanks were rolling down the streets of Detroit.

Of course, my father kept his family confined to the house and reminded us of the sinfulness of what was going on outside. To him it was organized insanity. There could be no explanation as to why people were

burning and looting the very stores that they frequented in their daily lives. They were destroying their own neighborhoods. Unfortunately, the images played across television screens throughout the nation, and Detroit was portrayed to the rest of the world as a city of hatred, violence, and crime.

That level of behavior was simply not in my character. Daddy had taught us to respect the property of others and to be responsible for our actions. Even the idea of partying or going out for a night on the town was foreign to me once I was married and my first daughter, Monique, was born.

That's why it was so difficult for my family to accept what happened to me at the Soul Expressions dance hall. I wasn't a risk-taker, and I didn't have a wild streak. As a twelve year old, I'd been captain of the safety patrol, and my high school classmates had even voted me "Most Likely to Succeed." And as a father, responsible for the welfare of two baby girls, I had neither the time nor desire to go dancing or hang out at clubs. But my childhood buddy, Napoleon Ross, had called and asked if I would celebrate his birthday with him that Saturday evening. Since I had the night off, I agreed to go on the condition that we didn't stay out too late. Yvonne, the girls, and I, attended the Oakland Baptist Church every Sunday, so I'd need to get up early.

Another friend, Lamont "Pug" Lawrence, was also going, and picked me up in his 1957 Ford. Since we weren't meeting Napoleon until he got off work at midnight, we decided to stop by the Local 876 UAW hall. A high school classmate, Jimmy Edwards, had a band called the "Superlatives," which was playing that night, and we ended up staying later than expected, dancing and talking to our friends.

Soon I realized it was time to meet up with Napoleon for his birthday. But Pug was busy talking and not quite ready to leave yet, so he told me to go on ahead, and he'd catch up with us later at the Soul Expressions. Since I didn't have a car, I caught a ride downtown with my wife's cousins, who were going by the dance hall on their way home.

It wasn't as if I were heading off to a den of iniquity. The Soul Expressions was an after-hours dance club for teenagers. No alcohol was served, and the club's management instituted a policy designed to keep drugs and alcohol out. There was a one dollar cover charge at the door, and if someone left the club, they had to pay another dollar to return. The rationale was to discourage young people from going out to their car to smoke marijuana or drink alcohol. An intimidating bouncer stood at the door and recited the rule as each teenager entered. There would be no re-entry privileges to the club. Period!

When I got out of the car, I could hear music and laughter coming from the upstairs of a building that housed a dry cleaning shop on the lower level. An enclosed stairwell led up to the second floor dance hall, and there was a group of teenagers waiting to get in the building. As I hurried to join the others in line, a stranger stepped from the shadows and issued a bizarre warning.

"I wouldn't go in there if I were you. Something bad is going to happen," he cautioned.

But the warning gave me no pause. I didn't know what he was talking about, and I really didn't take him seriously. I had promised Napoleon I would meet him, and I was expecting Pug to join us. I was a man who kept his word. I was a man who always tried to do the right thing. But when I found myself engulfed in flames several moments later, I knew that doing the right thing doesn't mean you won't end up in the wrong place at the wrong time.

SIX

DR. GRIFKA

A few hours after arriving at the hospital, Delbert was taken to the operating room to begin the painful and tedious process of debridement; the removal of foreign matter and dead tissue from a wound. The initial procedure is referred to as gross debridement. The skin is so fragile that it literally sloughs or falls off the wounds. The purpose of debridement both initially and thereafter would be to remove dead tissue to prevent infection and allow for blood circulation.

The operating room, which is normally kept cooler, needed to be heated to prevent additional heat loss to the patient's body. Another dangerous condition is fluid loss. With the outer layer of skin burned away, fluid is leaked out of the body, resulting in a condition known as burn shock. After a burn, fluid is lost from the blood, making it thicker. This consequently produces a situation of decreased blood flow, which leads to severe organ damage, renal failure, and death.

An IV was inserted into Delbert's abdomen to facilitate fluid restoration, but it would be several hours before we could get him stabilized and into the intensive care unit.

In order to keep circulation going, we made incisions through the skin to promote blood flow.

The real debridement process doesn't begin until the patient is well stabilized and well hydrated. The procedure is done with the use of a Dermatome, which has an oscillating blade that removes small amounts of skin, similar to cheese slices. The blade keeps going down into the body searching for an area of skin that is still alive, until no more burn tissue is visible. If a patient is lucky, there will be sections where the muscle is still attached. But Delbert's burns were so severe that he had many areas where the muscle was not attached, and underlying tendons and bone had also been damaged.

Delbert survived the initial debridement, but his injuries were so extensive and the burns so invasive, that I really did not expect him to make it. Still I was determined to do everything I could to help him live. But we were faced with a long series of problems, the most important probably being infection. Unfortunately, at Detroit Receiving Hospital at that time, we had nothing even resembling a burn unit. We didn't even have screens on the windows to keep flies out. We had no sterile facilities, plus we had makeshift dressing supplies. There was a product called Silvadene, which was a topical burn cream, but the city could not afford to buy it, so I had our pharmacist make up our own supply. He mixed silver nitrate with a water soluble base called Aquafor, which gave us something similar to Silvadene, and that's what we used for our burn victims.

It was a constant battle to get the supplies and equipment we needed for our patients. The danger of infection was ever present. Once we debrided patients and put them back into bed, even though they had clean linens, they definitely weren't sterile. I wrote several letters to the Detroit City Council, requesting the basic items we needed to treat burn patients effectively. We didn't even have an isolated area for them. They were put in general wards with the other patients—certainly exposing them to infection.

I saw all kinds of burn victims while I was at Detroit Receiving. There was an incident where a woman was mad at her lover, so she mixed up a combination of hot molasses and lye and poured it over his body and genitals. The worst cases were when mothers, angry at their babies for crying, put them in scalding water. The babies would be brought in with half their bodies burned, and most of them died because there was no way to save them. I saw the worst and the best in people during those times.

Since we didn't have a burn unit, we didn't have a burn team. I was responsible for most of the patients care, and I treated them on a day-to-day basis. I had to do it because there was no one else who could. We just didn't have the facilities, equipment, supplies, or personnel to do the things that they can do today for burn victims.

SEVEN

THE ROCK

In our neighborhood our family was known as the "Farmers" because Dad had planted a vegetable garden in the backyard and all of us kids were expected to work in it, weeding, and picking the plants. My parents, Albert Sr. and Essie McCoy, taught me at an early age that it was a parent's duty to nurture the family as if tending a garden, always looking for ways to make the harvest more bountiful.

"Each generation," my father would say, "should do whatever it can to make life better for the next generation."

Working for Chrysler at the engine assembly plant, Dad was able to purchase a modest three-bedroom house on Northwestern Street on Detroit's west side in 1959. Our home was comfortable, but small, especially since there were six of us kids...four boys and two girls. We'd double up for sleeping. My two sisters, Jackie and Gwen, shared one bedroom, my parents had another, and the four of us boys had the third one. June (which was short for Junior) shared a bed with Tony, and I shared with Luther, (but we all called him Ball). It was a little better in the summertime because we could sleep on the screened porch, under the stars.

Times were tough back then, with frequent lay-offs at the auto companies, and it was often a struggle for my parents to feed and clothe the six of us. But we were a team, and therefore, all expected to do our part

ALBERT MCCOY

to raise the standard of living for the family. As soon as we were old enough and able to earn money, we were required to contribute. When I was nine years old, my brothers and I had a paper route, delivering *The Detroit News* and *Detroit Free Press,* the two local newspapers. With my dad driving us around, we had a combined total of seven or eight routes, and all the profits went to help support the family. We also delivered phone books, advertisements and did other odd jobs with my father, especially when he was laid-off from the Chrysler plant. My dad's objective was to eventually become self-employed so he wouldn't need to be dependant upon anyone else. After years of hard work and extra jobs, he finally saved up enough money to buy a party store on Grand River and Livernois in our neighborhood. He would end up owning it for 24 years.

Dad had a military style iron-will about the chores of life. My father is a World War II U.S. Navy veteran, having been one of only 12 African Americans serving aboard the USS Wilson, a 2,250-ton destroyer.

Albert McCoy was proud of his military service, boasting that "the Navy was the first line of defense in those days." He talked about all of the training sailors would receive, and yet no one knew how they measured up until they were in battle conditions—or "the real McCoy" as my father called it. He would tell humorous stories about how the Navy sailors didn't get along with the U.S. Marines and how the Navy men always had the last laugh "because Marines couldn't get anywhere unless we took them there."

Devoutly religious, my father believed strongly that God was looking over him and fellow *Wilson* sailors during World War II. His destroyer was frequently in harm's way, yet always escaped unscathed. He recalls one particularly horrific battle with multiple U.S. warships involved. "And we were the only ship in the harbor that didn't get hit," he emphasized. "We never got hit. We only had near misses." When the war was over, military records revealed that the *Wilson* had eleven battle stars, which means that the U.S. Navy recognized it had been in eleven different significant engagements with the enemy, and that didn't even include the many skirmishes the destroyer had with submarines.

By living through combat in World War II, Albert McCoy developed an enduring sense of what was important and what was not. By the time I reached adulthood, he had instilled in me the importance of work ethic, family togetherness, and God.

That's not to say that I grew up without my share of growing pains. Having six kids isn't easy for any parent, but Daddy kept a tight reign on his children and was unwavering in his style of discipline. Whenever one of us screwed up, we got a "whuppin." Usually his weapon of choice was a belt, but sometimes it would be a switch from the tree in the backyard. Whoever was in trouble would have to go upstairs and bend over the bed. Then our father would dole out as many whacks as the crime demanded.

"This is going to hurt me more than it does you," he'd promise.

But I just couldn't see how that was true, being as I was the one with the sore butt.

I remember one time when I was pretty young and naive, my brothers, June and Ball, got me in trouble. There was a popular dance out that all the kids were doing. They said it was called the *Boogie Woogie*, and they taught me how to do it one day. When Daddy got home from work, I was real excited to show him how good I could dance.

"Look at this Dad," I beamed. Then I got out in the middle of the floor and started gyrating to the music the way Ball and June showed me.

My Dad got that stern look on his face and fire in his eyes and said "You just keep on dancing till I get back." What I didn't know was that my brothers hadn't taught me a dance at all. Instead, I'd been performing a pretty flawless imitation of the mating act. Daddy went to get the belt, and I got a whipping, but so did my traitorous brothers, although it didn't help my situation too much.

Under the guidance of my father, our family went to church on Sunday, gave thanks at meals, and prayed together regularly. He kept a big family Bible on the dining room table, and it was often opened to the 23rd Psalm. Every Wednesday after school, Daddy would hold family Bible study. Each of us kids was expected to read a chapter from the good book, and the passages would change with every reading. Sometimes my normally stern father would be overcome with emotion and burst out in

1949–1968

My amazing mother, Essie, my sister Jackie, brother June, sister Gwen, and brother Ball. I am so blessed to have had the dedication and support of my loving family over the decades since the fire that altered, not only my life, but theirs as well.

Brothers, June, Ball, and Tony, with our father, Albert P. McCoy, Sr. The sacrifices they endured and the love they showed me have been immeasurable.

Beautiful daughters Kim and Monique. I always stressed to them how vital a good education is, and both of my children have done well in professional careers. Kim is an accountant, and Monique is an attorney.

Son-in-law Seth Doyle, daughter Monique, along with precious grandsons Braden and Jalen. Sadly, Monique's first husband, Braden Smith, died of Leukemia.

Son-in-law Aaron Abney, with wonderful grandsons
Aaron and Bryce.

I tutored my nephews, Tony Fortson, Derron Colvin,
and Fred McCoy for many years. During that same
time they helped me with my activities of daily living.
It is impossible to express how much I appreciate
their efforts and sacrifices for my well being.

First Lady of California, Maria Shriver, a legendary name in philanthropy, along with special friend and co-author Del Reddy.

Michelle Lynch, human relations superstar, and long-time pal, Walter Brandon.

Debra Norville of NBC's *Inside Edition* is spreading positive energy through her best selling books *Thank You Power* and *The Power of Respect*.

My fiancée, Renée, and I, with Hall of Famer Mike Ilitch, likely the powerful owner in Detroit sport's history.

Every time I visit Aaron Wiseman, a great kid with nice parents, he shares with me that I inspire and encourage him.

PHOTO BY LYNN GREGG

During the filming of a documentary in Detroit, my life long friends, Napoleon Ross and Preacher (Alan Lawrence), visited the exact spot where the Soul Expressions was firebombed. Forty years after that life-changing tragedy, we buried a symbolic gas can to signify the anniversary. A long time ago I forgave the arsonists. Today, I feel privleged that I can reach people in a unique and powerful way. I am so blessed that through faith, family, friends, and a fraternity of medical personnel that I am doing God's work as a "miracle messenger."

The brilliant Eddie Kean, as *The Howdy Doody Show's* co-creator and chief writer, immeasurably influenced a whole generation of children about right and wrong in the 1950s and was a very good friend before he passed away in 2010.

(L to R) Top Row: Friends, Michigan Film Office Advisory Chairman Er King, Reverend William R. Fleming, and Marcus Sparks. Bottom Row: Fri Bill MacAdams.

(Delbert, ready for Sunday school)

song. Usually, it was *"I love the Lord...He heard my cry,"* which was his favorite. His children would begin to snicker and have to turn their heads and cover their mouths to keep from laughing. Daddy was a good Christian, and he loved the Lord, but he sure couldn't sing.

My father also didn't want to hear any talk about black and white people being separate races.

"There is only one race and that's the human race," he would say. "There are different nationalities, but we are all part of the human race, descended from Adam and Eve."

He didn't just give lip service to his creed either. He followed it up by the way he lived his life and treated others. He was always the strong one...the head of the family, the example we learned from, and the rock we all leaned on. "He walked the walk and talked the talk."

So I guess it was only fitting that he was the first one to walk through the door of the intensive care unit that dismal day in January. He's the one that took the phone call in the middle of the night, receiving the news that every parent dreads. He's the one that had to tell my mother her son had been in a horrible accident, and the one that had to gather the worried family together at the hospital. He's the one who spent the last six hours in the waiting room consoling the others while I was in surgery fighting for my life.

But when I opened my eyes and saw him standing by the bed, he didn't look like a "rock." He looked frightened, horrified, shocked to the core.

"Hi, Daddy," I moaned. That's all I could manage. My mouth was swollen painfully shut, and the thousand questions that were reeling in my brain would have to wait.

EIGHT

ONE OF A KIND

*W*henever I read the Bible story of Jesus feeding a crowd of 5,000 on the shore of Galilee with two fishes and five loaves of bread, I think about my mother. To me it seemed as if she performed that same miracle every single day when her family was young.

With six children to feed and my father frequently laid off, our cupboards were often pretty bare. But Mama was a miracle worker in the kitchen, a creative cook who could frequently turn nothing into something, and there would always be enough to feed friends, neighbors or any family member who happened to be at our house at the time. She would rummage through the refrigerator and dig up leftover potatoes or a chunk of meat, and transform it into a feast. Every neighborhood in those days had one house that served as the gathering place for the kids in the area. The McCoy home was the center of activity for our block.

One of my happiest memories is Mother getting us ready for church and telling us to hurry along "and I will make you something special for breakfast." We would emerge from our bedroom and find pans of biscuits, syrup, and salt pork waiting for us on the table. The biscuits would be made from scratch, and they would melt in our mouth with each bite.

When I was very young, we lived near Belle Isle in Detroit, and my mother's closest friend was Zola Fields, who also had six children. Those

MAMA

ladies would gather all twelve of us kids to walk to the park on Belle Isle for a picnic. We had peanut butter and jelly or bologna sandwiches and Kool-Aid, and it seemed like we were eating like royalty. Mama always had a way of making each meal seem as if it was a major event.

In the afternoons, she would make what she called "tea cakes"—which were essentially sugar cookies—and she would always make enough to feed the friends who were at our house. There was also a mulberry tree and a cherry tree in our front yard, and Mama would pick the berries to bake a scrumptious cobbler.

Mother loved her Sanka coffee, and she would allow each of us kids to have a half a cup with her. We would all sit around the kitchen table and chat while sipping our Sanka and munching our teacakes or cobbler. To her, coffee time was family time.

Mama was as loving as my father was disciplined, and she was the perfect counter-balance to his parental style. As much as our family struggled financially when we were young, my mother always made us feel loved. And she made all our friends feel welcome and special as well.

"Your home was the place you could go to be yourself and be understood because of your mom," Napoleon Ross would often comment.

My father always had the last word, but that wouldn't stop my mother from making a case daily that he needed to ease up on us.

"The kids have been working in the yard all day," she would say, "and they need to go out and play."

"You are too soft on those boys," Dad would reply.

But my mother never changed her approach. She constantly encouraged him to "lighten up" on us kids.

We didn't have the money to celebrate birthdays, but around Christmas mother would make each of us what she called a "birthday Christmas cake," and we each got to choose the flavor we wanted. Gwen and I always picked coconut-pineapple, Ball and Jackie chose chocolate, and June and Tony usually asked for a pound cake. With no extra money available, Christmas was more about family and food than presents in the McCoy household. My Uncle Treetop and my mother would cook up turkey and ham, mashed potatoes, greens, macaroni and cheese, cakes, and pies, and our house would smell like the world's best restaurant.

One of my favorite Christmas memories is when mother bought Tony and me a game of checkers. All of the children, except the two of us, went to North Carolina with the cousins for the holidays. Since there wasn't enough room in the car for all six of us, Tony and I had to stay behind. Mom gave us the checkerboard set to lessen our disappointment. We were so excited; you would have thought she gave us a thousand dollars. We played checkers hour after hour to the point that the colors began to fade on the board.

In the 1960s, children accepted the reality that life was challenging, particularly for large families. We knew that our parents would give us more if they could, and we didn't complain that the car was crowded or that we didn't receive new clothes. We felt blessed when we received a present, and we appreciated it, no matter how small or inexpensive.

My mother understood hardship long before she had children of her own. Growing up in Mayville, North Carolina, she saw her father die when he was just 34, after diabetes blinded him four years earlier. She wanted her children to have a better life than she had and believed strongly in that concept.

In many ways my parents worked perfectly together, and I wouldn't change my childhood for anything. My dad instilled in us the importance of discipline, family, hard work, and the lessons from the Bible. My mother, who had a loving heart, taught us to be kind to one another and charitable in our relationships. She was always there to offer comfort, confidence and strength.

But when she walked tentatively into the ICU, a few steps behind my father, it took all of her courage to look at me lying there.

"You're going to be fine, Delbert," she said bravely. "The doctor says so."

Just as when I was a child, she did her best to give me comfort and strength, but her eyes belied her words, and I knew in her heart that she didn't believe the words either. Her hands were trembling and her lips quivered. She couldn't bear to stay in the room and hurriedly left to go into the hall where I wouldn't be able to see her tears. She tried to spare me, as always, but this time it didn't work. I could hear her mournful sobs through the doorway, and I felt an unbearable sadness for the pain that she was going through.

NINE

LAMONT "PUG" LAWRENCE

here was a bunch of us guys from the neighborhood that hung around together. We all had nicknames, and over the years, grew as close as brothers. My given name was Lamont, but they all called me "Pug." The others were "Napoleon," "Shorty," "Preacher," "John Brown," "Pork n' Beans," "Rodney Reno," and "Boomerang." Delbert had a couple of nicknames. Sometimes we called him "Delray," and sometimes he was known as "Hillbilly." We called him that because he rocked when he walked, and you could tell it was him from a mile away. He also had a thing about hats—and always wore one—even went to bed with it on. Whenever we were wrestling around, his hat stayed on his head, just like the John Wayne movies. When "The Duke" got in a fight, everybody's hat came off but his. And that was how it was with Delray. He never lost his hat.

Delbert was the smartest of all of us, and we would go to him for help with our homework. He was like a leader. He was a good ball player, too. We played sandlot baseball while we were growing up, but in high school we ended up on different teams. His teammates all called him "wrong hand," because he was left handed, but he was really pretty good, and there was a strong competition between us. He was a baseball "nut," and couldn't get enough of it. When we wanted to get a fight out of him, we'd just catch him reading the newspaper and snatch the sports section out of his hands.

Detroit was a tough place to come from, one of the most violent cities in the nation, and often referred to as "The Murder Capital of the World." We lived in the inner-city, the "baddest" part of town, and it was a lot different that it was in the outskirts of the city or the suburbs. A lot of teenagers, many of them we knew, got involved with gangs like the "Whitney Boys" and the "Grand River Boys." But we didn't have a gang. We just liked to hang out together, and you would rarely see one of us without the others. Delray and I even got jobs at Chevrolet together. When we hired on, they always put Delbert on the hard jobs because he was a good worker. I only lasted three days before I decided that it wasn't for me. The work was too darned hard. That got Delray mad at me though.

"Are you going to quit and leave me here alone?" he asked.

"Yep," is all I said, and I was out the door and never went back.

But Delray stayed; he needed the money. He had a wife and kids to support. I didn't have those kinds of responsibilities, so I could leave more easily. He was also persistent and stubborn. When he set his mind on something, he was going to do it, even if it was difficult. I didn't know how he did it, but I looked up to him and respected him for his endurance.

We had some great times together and grew closer every year. You never saw one of us without the other. That's why it's so hard to accept that we weren't together when the fire started at the Soul Expressions. We had started out the evening together by going to the union hall to hear some Motown by a couple of local boys, but we got separated when I ended up hanging out with another friend who was having some family problems. A few hours later Delray wanted to leave to go on over to the Soul Expressions to meet up with Napoleon. But I wasn't ready to go yet, so I told him I'd catch up with him later. I stayed and talked to my buddy, and before long I realized it was too late to go to the dance hall. So I went on home to bed.

The phone woke me up, and it was our pal, Rodney Reno. He was real nervous and anxious.

"Get over to the hospital…Delray's been hurt!"

That's all he knew, and that's all I had to go on as I rushed over to Detroit Receiving Hospital. My mind went crazy with possibilities. Had he been in an accident? Had he been jumped by a gang member? Had he been shot? A year before, one of our friends had been stabbed to death, and I was fearful that Delray had met the same fate. People we grew up with were dying all around us.

As soon as I walked into the emergency room I saw Delbert's brother, Ball. He was crying, and I got a sinking feeling in my stomach. If Ball was crying, it had to be serious—because Ball didn't cry.

"The Soul Expressions got fire bombed, and Delray got caught up in it," Ball explained.

"He's hurt real bad. When you go in there don't tell him how bad he looks, and don't let him see a mirror."

There were lots of people out in the hallway, all Delbert's family and many of his friends. Some had already been in to see him, but only two could go in at a time, so I waited and went in with Napoleon. When we walked into the room the first thing I noticed was his head. I've never seen a man's head that big. It looked like a cartoon because it was so out of proportion to his body. With no room to get any bigger, it seemed like it could explode. It was a terrible thing to see, a horrifying image. Bandages covered his eyes, and he was trying to peek out of the two small slits. When he saw me, he whispered, "Pug, dead." That got me to crying. He thought that I had been in the fire, too and that I was dead, which was typical of Delray. My friend was always worried about somebody else. He was pretty messed up, and his mind was real confused. He had borrowed his brother's suit to wear that night, and he kept apologizing for getting it burned.

"I'm sorry, Ball," he'd repeat. "I'm sorry I ruined your suit."

Then he'd shout "How do I look, how do I look?"

I recalled Ball's warning and tried my best to sound convincing.

"You're fine, Delray, you'll be all right."

But when he wasn't apologizing, or worrying about his face, he was screaming in agony.

"Kill me, I can't stand the pain, take me out," he begged over and over.

Then his mind would go somewhere else and he'd whisper, "Pug dead" again.

I couldn't stand seeing him like that, and the guilt set in real fast. We always did things together and looked out for each other. Maybe if I would have made it to the dance hall, this wouldn't have happened to him. Maybe I could have seen something or helped him somehow. I felt terrible that I wasn't there when he needed me most. And now the doctor told us that he probably wouldn't make it through the night, and I could tell just by looking at Delray's mutilated body and face that it was true. I choked back the tears and said goodbye to my buddy.

But as Napoleon and I shuffled out of the room, our guilt and sorrow were quickly replaced by anger. We both swore that we'd find the guys that did this and make them pay for what they'd done to our best friend.

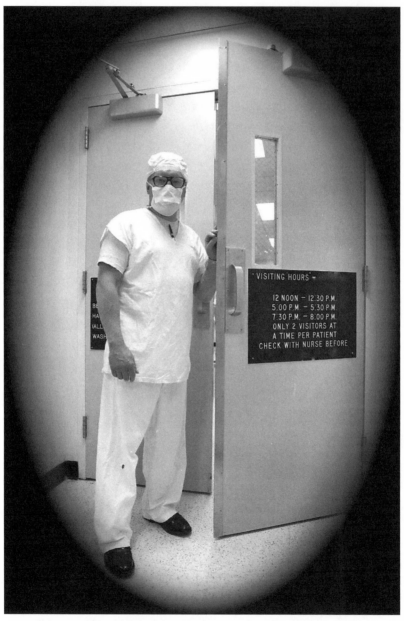

(Photo by Bob Kalmbach, courtesy of Bentley Historical Library, The University of Michigan)

TEN

HARSH REALITY

*J*ust like in Noah's Ark, two by two, my family members trailed into the intensive care unit. That's all that was allowed in at a time—two. They didn't stay long either, just long enough to offer words of encouragement between their mournful tears. "You're going to be okay, Delray. We're praying for you. We love you."

When my parents went back into the hall, my brothers, Tony and June, were permitted to come in. I was shocked to see June because he was living in New York City, where he had a clothing design business. I figured I must not have much time left if he dropped everything to get here so quickly.

I perceived Jackie and Gwen enter the room, but they couldn't contain their tears either and soon rushed back out to the safety of the hallway. My wife, Yvonne, came with her mother, Bernice, but they never even made it past the doorway. Both of them were overcome with grief and had to go back into the hallway with the others. It broke my heart to see my wife so torn up. What was she going to do now? Without a husband, how was she going to support and raise our two little girls?

I was immeasurably relieved when Pug walked through the door, followed by Napoleon. Since I was supposed to meet them both at the Soul Expressions, I was afraid that they too had been in the fire. "I never made

Napoleon Ross

it over there," Pug explained. Napoleon looked pained, as he answered, "Neither did I."

Napoleon, a/k/a Nate, had been my best friend since we were nine years old. We were as different as two people could be. He loved music and took up playing the violin. I loved sports and took up playing baseball. Yet, somehow we forged a bond that made us closer than most friends, and we were ALWAYS together. My best friend looked devastated as he related how he had escaped the fire. After working the afternoon shift at the plant, he went home to change before meeting up with me. But he was so exhausted from a long day at work that he fell asleep. What woke him up a couple of hours later was the sound of sirens piercing the night. By the time he learned what had happened, it was too late to go to the club to find me. He worried and searched throughout the night until his quest led him to the intensive care unit at Detroit Receiving Hospital.

It's ironic that Pug and Napoleon never made it to the teen dance that night. We had been as close as brothers for years, and the three of us hung out with our other friends from the neighborhood, often doing things together as a group. Roughly the same age, we all enjoyed playing ball, listening to records, or just being together. With money tight, every couple of weeks we would take turns having a party at each other's house in the basement. We called them 25-cent parties because we'd charge a quarter to get in. The money was used to pay for the food and beverages. There was always a parent or older sibling at home, and we didn't get into any trouble. We'd just play records, eat, talk, and dance. It wasn't fancy food either. We'd buy cake from the Sanders Bakery, and Mama would make a big tub of spaghetti. And several of us would bring a jug of strawberry Kool-Aid. No beer, not even soda pop, just Kool-Aid punch. Pretty innocent. But sometimes when Mama wasn't looking, we'd spike the punch with cheap Silver Satin wine. We didn't get drunk or drink a lot of it. We just drank a little, enough to give us the courage to ask the girls to dance.

There were lots of dances that were popular at the time, and none of them were hard to do. It's just that us guys were really "cool," and it would take a while before we could get up the nerve to make a fool of ourselves. But once we got started, we were pretty good at showing off our "moves." The "social," "twist," "mashed potato"…those were great dance steps, and with a little help from the spiked Kool-Aid punch, we looked like experts.

We listened to all the popular artists, and most of them were local talent that had been discovered right in our own hometown. The Motown sound was all the rage throughout the nation. The Temptations, Smokey Robinson and the Miracles, Aretha Franklin, Marvin Gaye, Martha Reeves and the Vandellas…they were the celebrities we looked up to, and they were Detroiters just like us.

One night we were having a party in Shorty's basement, and his aunt, who was visiting, came down to chaperone. She was related to Stevie Wonder by marriage, and when she saw how much fun we were having, she decided to surprise us. A short time later the famous entertainer came down the stairs and was introduced all around. What a thrill it was to be in the same company as one of the greats. When he came up to me he put his hands on my face and felt for my features. "You're skinny like me," he announced.

Wow! I was just like Stevie Wonder…He said so. Stevie hung out for a couple of hours, just clapping his hands and moving his head from side to side to the beat of the music. He even played the harmonica for us. That was the best party we ever had, and Shorty was "big man on campus" for a long time after that night.

Every teenager back then wanted to be a singer, and we were no exception, getting together and forming our own group of "wanna-be" crooners. We'd sing all the songs that were popular in that era. *Under the Boardwalk, Tracks of my Tears,* by Smokey Robinson and the Miracles, and *The Way you do the Things You Do,* by the Temptations. We didn't have a bass, or a tenor, or an alto. None of us really sang a special pitch, we'd just change our voice to match the part of the song we needed to sing. And of course, we all wanted to be the lead. That was a joke, since not one of us could carry a tune. So we just took turns. Sometimes I'd get to be Smokey Robinson, and sometimes it would be one of my buddies. It didn't matter. We weren't looking to perform on TV and never had any aspirations of stardom. Our group didn't even have a name. We just liked to sing. It was a way to pass the time and be together. And it kept us out of trouble. The fact that we all banded together in such a tight group kept us from making the same mistakes that so many of our classmates did. A lot of teenage males fought for their identity by joining one of the many gangs that were prevalent in Detroit neighborhoods. Most of them had trouble on their minds, with frequent fighting, stabbings, auto theft, and other dangerous and unlawful activities. Gang warfare was a means of establishing dominance over different territories, and several areas of the city were dangerous due to the sporadic eruptions of violence between opposing members. But those gangs rarely messed with us, and they stayed out of our neighborhood. I guess we didn't have anything that they wanted.

We always felt there was safety in numbers, and that's why we were most often together. Especially Napoleon, me, and Pug. It was just a stroke of luck that kept them from being with me at the Soul Expressions that night. But one person's luck is another's misfortune. I'm guessing that they were hugely relieved, but at the same time feeling guilty. Guilty that I was lying in a hospital bed, with the life draining out of me, while they hadn't even made it to the dance hall. Would either one of them trade places with me if they could? Would I do the same for them if I had the choice?

We never talked much about what could have happened that night. But I thought about it plenty. If things had been different there could have been three beds in the ICU that night. That would have been the worst. But the situation could have turned out for the better, too.

If I wouldn't have agreed to meet Napoleon at the club for his birthday, I wouldn't have been on that stairway.

If I would have stayed at the Union Hall until Pug was ready to leave, I wouldn't have been on that stairway.

If I would have heeded the stranger's warning "Don't go in there, something's going to happen," I wouldn't have been on that stairway.

If I would have had to work that night, like I usually did, I wouldn't have been on that stairway.

And **if** I would have stayed home with Yvonne and the girls, I wouldn't have been on that stairway.

A whole lot of "ifs," but only one truth.

I was the one in the intensive care unit, encased in bandages, unrecognizable, bleeding into tubes, and laboring for my last breaths.

Strangely, I wasn't angry. I wasn't even frightened. I was sad. Sad because of the impact the whole situation had on my family and friends. Sad for the grief and fear that I saw on the faces of my loved ones. They knew I was dying, and they were helpless to save me.

As the morphine took effect, I closed my eyes and let the memories of a lifetime wash over me. I felt calm and peaceful, assured that I would soon be with God in heaven. I was so very tired, I shut the world out and accepted my fate.

ELEVEN

MARLENE STORC

At *21 years old, I had just graduated with a bachelor's degree in nursing from Wayne State University in December. I started working at Detroit Receiving Hospital in January, less than two weeks before the Soul Expressions fire. Since I was university educated, I didn't have as much hands-on experience as some of the other nurses, so I welcomed the opportunity to work at DRH. When I was assigned to the intensive care unit, I was aware that ICU'S were notoriously short-staffed, but I was anxious to gain some of the practical experience that my education was lacking. It turned out to be more than I bargained for.*

We were on rotating shifts, meaning one week I'd work days, then the next would be afternoons, then a week of midnights. It was a difficult schedule to adjust to. In addition, the kind of cases we saw were tough. Coronary patients, accident victims, gunshots, stabbings, beatings, or any other emergency all occupied the ICU. One particularly gruesome case was a man who had been beaten with a baseball bat. When medics brought him in, his head was swollen to three times the normal size. I was shocked at the brutality. But Delbert McCoy was the worst any of us had ever seen.

When a patient is severely injured and has to remain in the intensive care unit for any length of time, they often develop what is called "ICU psychosis." They would experience delusions and paranoia due to the severity of their illness, and disorientation from the bright lights that were on in the unit 24 hours a day, 7 days a week. Delbert had also lost a lot of fluid, so his electrolytes were imbalanced, contributing to his confusion. He would be unaware of how often we gave him his pain meds or changed his IV or catheter line. So he called out for the nurses constantly. Delbert was afraid, in pain, and uncomfortable, and we couldn't do enough to comfort him. He needed constant reassurance and attention, and it was difficult to tend to the other patients while he was experiencing panic episodes and demanding attention.

Not that anybody blamed him. They didn't. His injuries were extremely serious and terribly painful. But sometimes the nurses wouldn't even respond to him, probably because there wasn't much hope for his survival. They detached themselves emotionally in order to do their job effectively. Consequently, he trusted few people. It didn't matter how often we explained something to him, he would be confused and call out for one of us again and again. The minute I walked into the ICU to begin my shift, the first thing I heard was "Marlene,!" "Marlene!"

There was a very high incidence of staff turnover in the ICU. Between the shift rotations, the number of serious injuries, and the shortage of help, trying to be a good nurse was frustrating and exhausting. Three of us hired on together in January of that year. One quit in March, the second one quit in April, and I lasted the longest, until June. After just six months I was completely burned out.

TWELVE

THE UNTHINKABLE

As I drifted in and out of consciousness, I was barely aware of the activities around me. Sometimes I would recognize a familiar voice or a friendly face, but mostly I sensed the presence of strangers. One such time, as I gingerly opened my eyes, a sea of white coats came into focus. A team of doctors had congregated around my bed to examine my injuries and discuss the treatment.

As they all stared down at my mutilated body, one of them was speaking and seemed to be in charge. He was tall, with a confident demeanor and an air of authority about him. I tried to follow the discussion, but I could only understand bits and pieces. Numbers like "90%" and "third degree" peppered his speech. I would learn later that burns covered more than ninety percent of my body, and a high percentage were considered third-degree, or full thickness, which meant the flames had burned through not only flesh, but also muscle. In some areas, the burns had even charred my bones. The only two areas of my body that were not burned were my genitals and the soles of my feet.

I'm sure I looked frightened, lying helpless and exposed in the bed. I felt like a specimen under a microscope while an army of strangers assessed the damages and spoke in a language I didn't understand.

"Hello Delbert, I'm Dr. Grifka," the tall one announced, as he laid his hand gently on my forehead. He looked directly into my eyes and prepared me for the worst.

"You're burned pretty bad, he said.

"You'll need surgery, and you'll be in quite a lot of pain." He paused to let the words sink in.

"It won't be easy, but we're going to do everything we can to help you."

I tried to find comfort in what he was saying, but I knew that if there were this many doctors in my room, I must be in real big trouble. But his words fed me just enough hope to fuel my fight to survive.

"You can make it," he encouraged.

"Hang in there Delbert, just hang in there."

But the scene outside in the hallway was a far different story.

"I've never seen anyone burned as extensively as your son is," Dr. Grifka told my parents.

"There is only one chance in a thousand that Delbert is going to survive," he said sadly. "The odds are stacked against him."

Dr. Grifka was walking a delicate tightrope. He was direct and honest with my parents, but he couldn't offer them much hope. They needed to be prepared for the worst. Yet at the same time, he provided me the gift of strength and encouragement, the chance to survive.

Although Dr. Grifka was honest about my prognosis, that didn't stop him from being relentless in his pursuit to keep me alive. He and his staff worked tirelessly on my behalf, and he made sure that anyone who came in contact with me maintained a positive, upbeat attitude.

A nurse named Marlene was assigned to my case, and she oozed sweetness, warmth, and optimism. With her starched white uniform and little winged hat, she reminded me of an angel, especially when she smiled. She was pretty too, not much more than twenty years old, with dark hair and sympathetic eyes. I liked her immediately, and she would come to be my favorite.

"Hi Delbert, I'm going to take good care of you today," she promised.

Her kind words and gentle touch were just what I needed, and I came to look forward to her shift, always feeling safer when she was on duty. I felt confident that I wasn't going to die on her watch.

Dr. Grifka and Marlene would become my earthly lifelines. Bonding over the many months to come, we became teammates in the game of life. Dr. Grifka was the captain, and I would learn to trust whatever decisions he made to help lead our team to victory. Sometimes we would win, and sometimes we'd lose. But it was okay. Because, just like in baseball, it was the teamwork that was important. I never felt alone as long as my teammates were with me. You can never over-estimate the value of a strong team…and I had the best.

Although it would soon become routine, the first time my bandages were changed was excruciating. When Marlene pulled back my bed covers, I could see that I was totally encased in gauze, including my face. There were only small slits for my mouth and eyes. My entire body was wrapped tight like a mummy. After giving me an added boost of morphine, Marlene and Dr. Grifka gently lifted my leg and began to remove the first blood soaked dressing. Although they had warned me that the procedure would be painful, nothing could have prepared me for the horrific agony that simply removing the bandages would cause.

"Daddy, Daddy!" I screamed when the pain overwhelmed me.

Unable to bear the gore of the process, I closed my eyes tight against the image. I was crying like a baby—the pain was excruciating.

Dr. Grifka ordered another blood transfusion immediately, plus he mercifully increased my pain medication. But with much of my skin gone, my nerve endings were exposed, and every layer of bandage that was removed caused unbearable suffering. I thought about the Christians, who were nailed to the cross for practicing their faith, and I imagined that their pain was as horrific as my own. The last bandage was the worst. Even though an assistant poured water over my leg to help loosen the gauze, the dressing was sticky from the dried blood. When the last bandage came off, it ripped the sticky blood out of the wound, exposing my raw, oozing flesh.

I continued to cry out, and begged them to stop. The pain was more than I could bear. It was agonizing, beyond anything I could have imagined. And we had only done one leg. There was no way I could get through the rest of the bandage changes. Concerned, Dr. Grifka ordered more morphine, and Marlene injected it right into my IV. Soon I drifted into a hazy consciousness. The procedure lasted an eternity, and even though the powerful drug morphine worked its magic, it couldn't completely block the breakthrough of pain as the remaining wrappings were removed.

Marlene tried her best to soothe me, and I know that it grieved her to see me in such agony. And even though he remained calm, and intent on his task, it must have been hard for my doctor as well…having to pull the bandages off, hearing me scream in pain, and knowing that he's the one who was causing it. I knew that he wasn't intentionally trying to hurt me. He was trying to help me. He was doing what he had to do to save my life. I knew all these things, but that didn't prevent me from begging and pleading with him to stop. When he finally finished, I breathed an exhausted sigh of relief, grateful that the horrible experience was behind me. The worst was over. Somehow I had made it through the tortuous procedure, even though it left me weak and fatigued beyond words. Naively, I thought, "If I could make it through that, I could do anything." Apparently, I still had a lot to learn about the nasty business of burns.

The disheartening news depressed me to the core. My dressings needed to be changed twice a day…every day! And just a few hours later, the whole nightmare began again.

The anticipation of that insufferable event was almost as horrifying as the act itself. Even while I was in a morphine-induced haze, I could see the clock on the wall. And as it ticked toward nine o'clock every morning, or four o'clock in the afternoon, I began to suffer severe anxiety, my heart began pounding out of my chest, and I would sweat profusely. I was so terrified that my whole body would shake uncontrollably as the scheduled time approached. Dr. Grifka would try to comfort me as soon as he entered the room, but once he started to unravel the bandages on my legs, I began to weep and cry out for my father, who was always nearby.

The worst pain (if it's possible to measure pain of that magnitude) came when they changed the bandages on my hands. Originally, Dr. Grifka attempted to wrap each finger separately to prevent them from fusing together as they healed. But the pain of separating the fingers each day was simply too unbearable. So Dr. Grifka reluctantly made the decision to wrap the fingers together and accept the fact that my hands would heal fused that way.

The pain of the dressing change would overwhelm me for an hour, or longer after each procedure. Then I would settle down and rest briefly until the anxiety of the next change began to grip me. That was how I spent my days. Enduring the brutality of the bandage removal, only to be left with the fear and anxiety of the next procedure. The cycle was unending. And try as I might, I could not see a light at the end of that dark tunnel.

THIRTEEN

DR. GRIFKA

Skin grafts are performed in order to protect the organs and underlying tissue, but first a patient's body is debrided to keep it free of infection. Small sections of healthy skin were taken from donors and transplanted to Delbert's body in those areas that would accept it. Most of the time, in Delbert's case, the small, two inch by two inch pieces were stretched into place without sutures or staples. Donor skin is not expected to be permanent. If left in place, it will eventually be rejected by the body. We didn't want that to happen, so we would monitor the grafts carefully and debride them before they were rejected. The area would then be replaced with a new skin sample. An autograft is when skin is taken from a patient's own body. With less chance of rejection, the goal is to make it permanent. The graft would take and new cells would eventually grow.

But with the amount of burn damage that Delbert experienced, the grafting process would be slow and deliberate. I was constantly on the lookout for cadaver donors for Delbert, as well as my other burn patients. When patients died from a gunshot wound or accident, we would plead with their families to allow us to harvest some of their skin. First we had to be sure that the victim had died without sepsis or infection, and we were careful not to use any skin that would be visible at the funeral. We would take it only from areas of the body that were covered by clothing.

It was an ongoing problem that we were forced to deal with. Four or five years after the accident, pigskin was introduced as a means of providing temporary grafts. But that discovery wasn't available in time to help Delbert. Fortunately, there have been all sorts of advances in grafting since Delbert was injured. Now doctors can take a little piece of a patient's skin and culture it in a Petri dish. But forty years ago we didn't have the miraculous technology and knowledge that is available today.

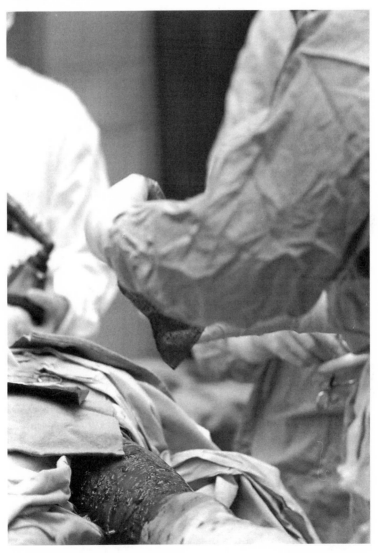

(Photo by Bob Kalmbach, courtesy of Bentley Historical Library, The University of Michigan)

FOURTEEN

THE GIFT OF LIFE

When Dr. Grifka told my parents that I needed multiple skin grafts because of constant bleeding, each of my brothers and sisters and most of my friends volunteered to be donors. My brother, Tony, wanted to be first to give up his skin. Ironically, we had nicknamed Tony, "Slow" because he was always last to finish his chores. But he wanted to be first to help me. Napoleon was disappointed when he was told that an abnormality with his veins made him an unsuitable donor.

My friend, Alan Lawrence, was selected to be second. We called him "Preacher," not because he was more religious than anyone else, but because he had an uncanny resemblance to a preacher at our church.

This was 1969, and skin grafts weren't nearly as common as they are today. Nobody in our circle had ever even heard of the procedure. It took a lot of courage for my family and friends to consent to have skin removed from their body, when they didn't know how it would affect their own health. Ultimately it would be Tony and Preacher who would endure the necessary surgery to become the first round of donors.

According to Dr. Grifka, I would need huge amounts of skin initially, and my body would reject it soon after it was applied. The process would have to be repeated many times until I could regenerate new skin on my own, he warned. The problem was where were we going to get that much skin?

The Detroit Free Press ran two front page stories on January 13, 1969: *Dance Hall Set Ablaze by Arsonist—60 Injured.* And a few columns over— *Suspect in Bank Killings Surrenders to Police.* The two incidents were totally unrelated, and it was purely by chance that they shared the main page that morning. But coincidence became destiny when a man named Eddie Kincannon called my father after learning of my injuries. On the night I was battling the flames at the Soul Expressions, the Kincannon family was experiencing their own personal tragedy.

They had a son named Paul, who was allegedly involved in the armed bank robbery that was featured in the newspaper. Paul had been shot in the head, when he reportedly pulled a gun on police officers.

"We will never know what really happened," a despondent Eddie Kincannon told my father. "But he's in a coma in the same hospital as your son, and there is no hope of recovery."

Paul Kincannon was pronounced "brain-dead," and even though the family was still reeling from the shock and grief of their son's diagnosis, their hearts reached out to me and my family. The Kincannons wanted their son's senseless death to have some meaning. If his skin could help save my life, then Paul's death would not have been in vain.

"They're going to pull the plug on my son as soon as we give them permission," Mr. Kincannon said, sadly. He then told my father that he was instructing doctors to use Paul's skin for my skin grafts.

By the late sixties surgeons had started using the practice of removing skin from cadavers for grafting purposes. However, the idea of organ donation was still foreign enough that families were highly unlikely to agree to allow their deceased love ones to become providers. Yet, this family had actually offered to do just that.

I was wheeled into one operating room, Tony and Preacher were placed in a second, and Paul Kincannon was in a third room. Small patches of skin were removed from inside the thighs of Tony and Preacher, then grafted onto my body. But the majority of the donated skin came from a young stranger.

Doctors removed Paul from the respirator soon after the skin graft was completed, and he died shortly after. A doctor told me later that he had never witnessed a graft as extensive as the one I received from Paul

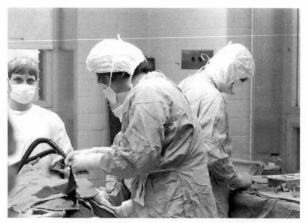

(Photo by Bob Kalmbach, courtesy of Bentley Historical Library, The University of Michigan)

and that surgeons harvested enough skin to cover over half of my burns.

Through their selfless contribution, a family of strangers, even though suffering tremendous pain at their son's death, had given me a chance at life. I never met Paul Kincannon, but I will never forget him. His life will be forever connected to mine, and I am eternally grateful for his sacrifice and that of his family. There's little doubt that I would not have survived without the significant skin graft from another Detroiter. It was a monumental boost to my healing process. But I wasn't out of danger yet.

"I'm still not all that confident that your son will survive," Dr. Grifka told my father. "But we're giving him a chance."

Apparently, it was just one of many dangers that I would face over the coming months. Although the grafting of donor skin greatly reduced the bleeding, it was just a temporary fix. My body would continue to require several plasma transfusions every single day. Dr. Grifka said I would probably need 100 units of blood before my crisis period was over, and that would exceed the number of units the Red Cross would provide for one person. But this time there was an easier solution. My father had been a donor for years through the United Auto Worker's Union, which made him eligible to receive blood for himself and any family members. In addition, his friends at work started a drive in my name, and many of them donated to the Red Cross blood bank. I was assured of having as much as I would need, whenever I needed it. The miracle of having an adequate blood supply could be crossed off the ever-growing list of obstacles to my survival.

FIFTEEN

BASEBALL FEVER

Dr. Grifka believed that I was near death, even though he worked tirelessly to save me. And no one ever told me how bad I really was. My family still had faith, and my father came to the hospital every night at around midnight, after working the afternoon shift at Chrysler. He would sit by my bed until morning, making sure someone would be there when I woke up.

It must have been very tiring for him to sit at my bedside night after night, especially, after working all day. Since I slept most of the time, I wasn't much of a conversationalist, so he'd occupy his time by reading the Bible and praying. But it was a great comfort to know that he'd be there on the brief occasions when I was awake. One night I woke up to the sound of Dad wrestling with a section of the newspaper. Without him being aware, I watched him for a long time, wishing that things could be different. Wishing that I could laugh and joke with him…wishing that we could jump in the car and go out for a burger…wishing that he didn't have to be sitting in this hospital room watching over me…wishing I was any place else, not in this bed wrapped up in gauze with tubes and wires coming out of me.

"What are you thinking, Delray?" he asked when he looked my way.

Ever since I was a kid, my family had called me Delray. My middle name was Ray, so they shortened my first name, then put the two together and came up with Delray.

"I was thinking about playing baseball," I said in the darkness. I didn't know it at the time, but those few words ended up being crucial to my recovery. Sensing that I needed the diversion, my father began talking to me about baseball, the sport that had been my passion since I was a kid.

Every free minute I had as a youngster was spent at the ball field or dreaming about being a major leaguer. I loved the game to the point that each morning I would scramble out of bed and run to Cunningham's drug store to buy the *Detroit Free Press,* so I could pour over the box scores. Even in the winter, I was thinking baseball, and family members were accustomed to me organizing games in spite of temperatures below freezing. I'd gather the neighborhood kids, and we'd sweep the snow off the alley behind the house so that we could get a game in between the snowflakes.

In 1961, when New York Yankees right fielder Roger Maris was chasing Babe Ruth's record of 61 home runs, I followed his season as if he were the most important man on the planet.

"Nobody is going to beat Babe's record," my father predicted. I loved the Detroit Tigers, and didn't like the New York Yankees, but I rooted for Maris that historic season.

Seven years later I had my ear glued to the transistor radio listening to broadcaster Ernie Harwell call the Detroit Tigers' magical march to the World Series championship. The year before had been branded by the riots in Detroit, but the summer of '68 had been marked by pennant fever. Everyone in the city, black or white, young or old, male or female, was talking about the hometown team. If you walked through any neighborhood after seven thirty in the evening, you could hear Harwell's voice coming out of each house. It was as if Ernie was in stereo throughout the City of Detroit. The Tigers came from behind to win the game 40 times in 1968, and Denny McLain had become the first pitcher since Dizzy Dean to win 30 or more games.

When the Tigers made it into the World Series against the St. Louis Cardinals I was delirious with joy. I embraced every pitch, every run, every out...and held my breath whenever the "bad guys" were up to bat. Southpaw Mickey Lolich won three games on the mound in the series and the Tigers erased a three to one deficit to win a dramatic Game seven against pitcher, Bob Gibson. Jim Northrup's triple over the head of Curt Flood is remembered by many Detroit fans because it produced the deciding runs in Game seven. But I personally believe that the series turned around when my hero, Willie Horton, threw out Lou Brock with a perfect strike from left field to catcher, Bill Freehan in Game five.

I idolized Willie Horton. He grew up on the streets of Detroit…just like I did…played for Northwestern High School…just like I did… played outfield…just like I did…and then signed with the Detroit Tigers…just like I longed to do. When I played for my high school team, the Northwestern Colts, I was known as an outfielder who could track down a fly ball as if I had radar. My glove was where base hits went to die. In one game I scaled the home run fence like Spiderman, tearing up my legs to rob some player of a home run. After the game, teammates, friends, and even the coach told me that if there had been a major league scout in the stands that day, he likely would have signed me on the spot. I guess a lot of guys fantasize about professional baseball, but even though I was married with two children, I truly hadn't surrendered my belief that I had the tools to be a major leaguer.

My father understood how much I missed baseball that night when he engaged me in the longest conversation we ever had about the sport.

"Remember how good Mickey Lolich was against the Cardinals?" Dad asked. "Delbert, do you think he can do it again?"

"I do," I said. "The Tigers can win it again. We still have a good pitching staff." My father moved closer to the bed, excited that the talk about baseball gave me something positive to focus on.

Every night thereafter Dad would recite the entire sports section to me until I'd once again doze off. Sharing the sports news gave me a new appreciation of my father and gave us a closeness that we hadn't had previously. Daddy was a stern disciplinarian, a man who wasn't afraid to whip his children if they misbehaved. He demanded respect and imposed strict rules on anyone living in his house. Unlike our friends, the McCoy kids had an early curfew every night. On school nights we had to be in the house when the streetlights came on. In the fall and winter that was about 6:00 p.m. But when he was working, Mama let us stay out a little later. All our friends used to poke fun at us because of our early curfew, and they didn't like coming around much when Daddy was home. He believed in keeping us all busy, and if friends were at the house, he'd put them to work too…painting, digging in the yard, cleaning up. His philosophy was that if we were busy with chores, we couldn't be getting into trouble. He was part of a forgotten generation, when men were raised to be rugged and unemotional.

He was also a devout Christian, and he tried to comfort me the best way he knew how. "Put your faith in the Lord, and he will see you through," he instructed, as we prayed together every evening. He wasn't a "touchy-feely" person who told his children every day that he loved them. Yet he kept a vigil at my bedside during the most critical time of my hospitalization, averaging only about four hours sleep a night. If that isn't love, then what is?

ALBERT MCCOY

SIXTEEN

HEAVEN SENT

So many of the things we take for granted in life come to mean so much more when we can't have them. I hadn't been able to eat or drink anything since the fire, two weeks earlier, and although I was being fed intravenously, my weight continued to drop rapidly. With my body in metabolic overdrive, it required an even greater number of calories than normal, but instead, it was getting less. It's not that I had much of an appetite anyway. All the pain meds and other medications caused my stomach to be queasy, and the nausea was unrelenting. It was difficult for the doctors to keep me hydrated, and the continuous loss of body fluids made me extremely weak, sapping all my energy. But the worst part was the physical thirst. My mother would wet a washcloth with cool water and sponge my bleeding lips, but it offered minimal relief. My mouth was so dry—my tongue swollen, my lips cracked and bleeding. I dreamed of refreshing drinks and water fountains, shimmering streams, rain showers; anything that would diminish the overwhelming thirst.

There was a sink in my hospital room that the nurses, doctors, and visitors all used. It was right next to my bed…tantalizingly close. But it was useless to me, since I wasn't permitted to have anything to drink. Many times I imagined myself gulping sparkling water, taking deep sips into my dry, parched throat, savoring its soothing coolness. Then I would awaken, gasping and straining towards the sound, only to find that I'd been dreaming and someone was using the sink. That was pure torture, and I would cry and beg Marlene, my mother, or anybody in the room to please get me some water.

Finally Dr. Grifka gave Marlene the approval to give me a few ice chips. I was elated. But even the simple process of sucking on frozen fragments came with a price. My mouth was so damaged, the skin so tight, that Marlene had to pry it open with a tongue depressor. It hurt terribly, but the promise of the cool ice and relief from the devastating thirst made it bearable.

However, neither the ice chips nor the antibiotics had much affect on the infection that was raging through my body. Since I was allergic to penicillin, Dr. Grifka had to rely on other types of drugs to stabilize my system, but they didn't seem to be working. I was so weak and exhausted that I dozed off frequently. Then, suddenly, I'd wake up thrashing around in bed and moaning incoherently. Sometime during the night, the chills set in, and even though I was burning up with fever, my body began shaking violently. Dad was with me, as usual, sitting next to the bed. That's the last thing I remember.

I sat by a pond, with my feet dangling in the water, bathing in its refreshing coolness. The burns had disappeared from my body, leaving it mercifully pain free. Peace and serenity enfolded me, and I was mesmerized by the beauty of my surroundings. I was a child again, back in North Carolina, after a day of picking cotton on my Grandpa McCoy's farm. I had no worries, no concerns, and I had a sense of wonder about what would happen next.

There was a bright light directly above me, but when I looked up, there was no need to squint or shield my eyes. The light was soothing, an inviting presence, as if I was looking through a window to heaven. I could see a gorgeous blue sky with one single cloud floating above me, and I felt a sense of relief, as I was being called to heaven. I didn't resist, and I was not afraid. I was weary of the pain and the struggle, ready for release. My body would be healed in that celestial place, and I knew that I would be whole again. The pain would be gone forever. I felt safe, content, and at peace, but slowly an image formed in the clouds. It was a human face, not recognizable as anyone in particular, but it was clear to me that it was a face. When it began to speak softly, the voice was soothing and comforting.

"Pick the watermelon from the vine and suck the juice," the voice said. Then suddenly, the scene disappeared.

I awoke to the image of my father's grief stricken face. But relief flooded over him as I haltingly told him about the vision. "I don't know if I was dreaming, but it felt so real," I explained. He wasn't surprised. It made perfect sense to him. Then he went on to interpret what had actually happened to me in the "real world."

The infection had ravaged through my system. That, coupled with the dehydration, had caused my blood pressure to drop dangerously low. During the night he had watched helplessly as my weakened heart stopped beating, setting off the alarm monitor over my bed. Doctors and nurses rushed into the room, assembling equipment, calling out orders, and making quick decisions. Paddles were applied to what was left of my chest, sending volts of electricity directly into my heart muscle. Drugs were pumped into my veins, as the doctors worked feverishly to get my heart beating again. Watching anxiously from the corner of the room, my father was fearful that this was the end. It horrified him to think about how he would tell my mother her third-born child was gone, especially now, after successfully surviving the debridement and skin graft procedures. The fear and worry came flooding back again, just like the night he first got the call about the fire. Only this time, he was witnessing first-hand the death of his son.

He prayed for a miracle as he watched the scene unfolding in front of him. "God, please save Delbert...help him now Lord," he begged. When the alarm stopped blaring and doctors stepped away from my bed, my father felt the slightest flicker of hope.

"He's stable for now, but he could have another cardiac arrest at any time," Dr. Grifka warned.

Albert McCoy is a very spiritual person, an elder still today in his church in Oak Park, Michigan, and when I told him of my vision, he knew what had to be done. Convinced that God was sending us a message, he asked Dr. Grifka if I could have some watermelon juice in place of the clear nourishment I'd been getting. We both rejoiced when Dr. Grifka answered, "It's worth a try. He needs more fluids, and there'd be vitamins in the juice." The problem was that it was February, and there wasn't any seasonal produce in Michigan in the middle of winter. But I had the solution.

"Just call down to Grandpa's farm," I suggested. "He'll have plenty of watermelons." Of course, I was on heavy doses of morphine and had just come out of cardiac arrest. The doctors even worried that there may be some brain damage. But that didn't stop my father from agreeing with my plan. He didn't try to explain that even though his farm was in North Carolina, Grandpa would have no melons in the dead of winter either. Because he quickly realized that the divine vision had become very important to me. I believed that God spoke to me and told me how I would be saved, and Dad knew that faith was key to my survival.

Faced with the monumental task of finding a watermelon in February, my father threw all his energies into the search. He called Grandpa, just to be sure, but he came up empty. He checked the local markets, and he phoned every produce company in the area. He searched for several days, before he finally located a market just outside the city that had kept a single watermelon in cold storage since the end of summer. For all we knew, that might have been the only watermelon in Michigan in February of 1969.

When my father marched into my room with that big green melon in his arms, I felt as if he had just showed up with the cure for all of my problems. To me, that luscious fruit was a sign that I was going to survive.

"I told you that Grandpa McCoy would have a watermelon for me," I beamed. "You got that from him, didn't you?"

"That's right, Delray," he fibbed. "This is from your Grandpa McCoy's farm in North Carolina. It was flown up here special for you."

Marlene immediately sliced the savory delicacy and squeezed the juice into a little "sippy" training cup, with a covered mouthpiece, that she borrowed from the children's ward. With my muscles burned down to the bone and my fingers unbendable, I couldn't hold the cup myself. Marlene had to hold it for me, but the first taste of that sweet liquid may have been the most delicious drink I've ever had. And although it had been in cold storage for several months, having probably lost much of it's original flavor, to me it was nectar from God. It was far superior to the ice chips I'd been getting. I let it splash around in my mouth, the liquid spilling over my tongue like waves rolling onto the beach, as I savored its wondrous taste and healing powers.

I could only take in small amounts of the juice, but I sucked on that cup like a baby with a bottle, as I felt the strength pouring back into my body, rescuing me with each sip I took. Once my system established that it could handle the juice, I began receiving other substantial liquids, and with nutrients now entering my body, I steadily began to gain weight again.

After contemplating my vision for many years, I'm convinced that I was ready to leave this earth the night my heart stopped beating. Today, I know that I would never have survived without the dedicated work of Dr. Grifka, and the nurses, (especially Marlene), and without the love of my parents and support of my friends. I would have been dead long ago if they hadn't worked together to offer encouragement and give me hope. But I'm also convinced that I would have died without the vision of the watermelon. God had plans for me. Faith is a powerful ally when you are fighting for survival. There is no question in my mind that the gift of the watermelon was truly "heaven-sent."

SEVENTEEN

DR. GRIFKA

*D*elbert was receiving skin grafts now on average of about every three weeks. We tried to use some of his own skin, taking small patches that were viable, thereby eliminating the risk of tissue rejection. We'd expand it as much as we could and slowly cover areas of his body to get the grafts to take. Once the grafted sample attached to the underlying tissue, it effectively closed the wound. A skin graft was deemed successful when new blood vessels and tissue formed in the injured area.

Gauze bandages would be applied to absorb drainage and isolate the wound from infection. When a patient didn't have any skin coverage the normal way of holding fluids in the body was missing. So blood and other fluids would ooze out of the muscle and connective tissue and into the bandages. Whenever we had to change the dressings, I would give Delbert a dose of Ketamine to make him amnesic as to what was happening. The procedure was very arduous and painful. We didn't have enough staff for any individual to do the bandage changes on a regular basis. So the job was divided among many. Sometimes it would be the nurses, sometimes orderlies, and sometimes I'd take Delbert down to the tub myself. I'd just pick him up and carry him. He was very weak and frail.

One of the factors that caused death in burn patients was a bacterial infection known as pseudomonas. It thrived in moist environments and could

infect the blood, bone, eyes, lungs, urinary tract, and heart. We had no an-
tibiotics that could fight this kind of infection, and it was especially danger-
ous to patients with compromised immune systems. And we did almost lose
Delbert on a couple of occasions. With pseudomonas, you could walk into the
room and know that a patient had it because of the characteristic smell. It
was like nothing else you ever smelled. And if that awful infection set in, there
was very little we could do.

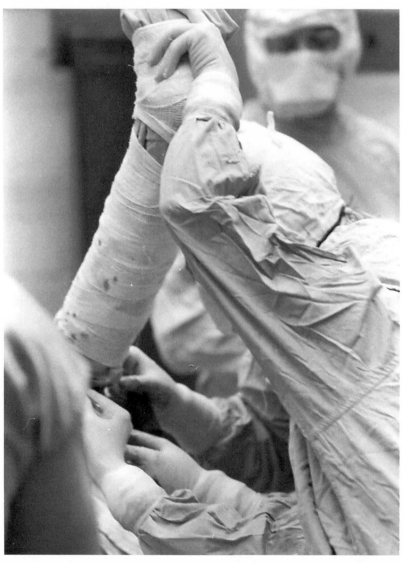

(Photo by Bob Kalmbach, courtesy of Bentley Historical Library, The University of Michigan)

EIGHTEEN

TORTURE

nce the skin grafts began to take hold, Dr. Grifka altered the dressing change routine to assist the healing process. I was relieved because changing the bandages was unbearably painful, and I still hadn't gotten used to it. Dried blood caused the gauze to stick to my body, and when doctors pulled off the covering they would also tear away transplanted skin. That's what caused the intense pain, and more importantly, as far as Dr. Grifka was concerned, that method also created more bleeding.

Dr. Grifka's new plan was to submerge me in a stainless steel tub which was filled with warm salt water. The salt would kill the bacteria that grew on the skin. By soaking in the tub, it would allow the water to loosen the wrappings so they could be removed without tearing off skin and doing further damage. My father walked beside me as I was wheeled on a stretcher for this new saltwater treatment. Dr. Grifka had ordered some kind of special medicine that they injected into my arm, and he promised that it would help with the pain.

But as soon as I was lowered into the water, it felt as if I had been dipped into a vat of boiling oil. The salt seeped into my wounds, setting my body ablaze for the second time. Thrashing and clutching at my father, I called out longingly for him to help me.

"Daddy, Daddy, Daddy!" I sobbed repeatedly.

"Be strong Delray," he said. "These are healing waters. They're going to make you well."

But they didn't feel like healing waters, and they didn't look like healing waters either. The psychological damage of the salt bath was as traumatic as the pain when the once clear water turned deadly red with my blood. It felt like I was immersed in a vat of simmering blood soup, and the experience was the most torture I could imagine.

Slowly and tediously the dressings were removed, one strip at a time, as they were soaked loose. When all the bandages were removed and I was totally exposed, I was lifted out of the tub. Dr. Grifka laid me on a clean white sheet, dried me gently, and poured a solution of silver nitrate over my naked body. It burned as much as the salt water, setting off another round of agonizing spasms and tearful pleading.

Before I was wrapped in fresh bandages, I looked down at my exposed, mutilated torso and was stunned by the level of destruction that the fire had caused. Some wounds were still open, oozing fluids and infection, and in other areas the muscle was gone, leaving several small flaps of decaying skin. I looked like an animal carcass after it had been cooked on a barbeque.

I begged Dr. Grifka to stop the gruesome baths. I couldn't take it. But he just shook his head sadly and said I would need to have it done every day.

Every day? Just the thought of it made me sick with anxiety. "It's healing waters," my father repeated, and he promised he would be there for me every time I had the treatment.

NINETEEN

FACE OF COURAGE

In the midst of all my medical battles, I received my draft notice, ordering me to report to basic training. But when my parents notified the government about my condition, an investigator was sent to the hospital to verify their story. The year was 1969, the war in Vietnam was unpopular, and the country was overrun with draft evaders. When the investigator came to see me, he didn't need to ask questions. It was pretty clear that I was unable to serve my country.

In addition to the skin grafts, blood transfusions, and saline baths, I had another crisis. I was losing weight rapidly. Never very big to begin with, I now resembled a concentration camp survivor. Since my mouth was no more than a thin slit of charred tissue, I could only consume foods that didn't need to be chewed—liquids and pureed mush, which resembled baby food, but tasted awful. I could barely choke it down. Yet, I ate what was given me, in spite of the taste, because I knew I needed nourishment to grow stronger. So I tried to imagine I was eating my mother's home cooking. It was easy to conjure up memories of bacon sizzling and the delicious smell of corn bread or biscuits hot from the oven. But even though I forced down the mush, the weight kept dropping, and there was concern that I would starve to death. My body had plummeted to a dangerous fifty-seven pounds.

My morale was as low as my weight. Yvonne would come by to see me, but she never stayed long. She was only 17, and I was convinced that I was losing her. It was hard for me to stay positive and want to survive when I knew that my life would never be the same again. With my motivation slipping away, the prospect of a recovery grew dimmer than ever.

My mother wasn't going to stand by and watch that happen. When she pleaded with Dr. Grifka and convinced him to let her prepare my meals, it was a real morale booster. He agreed that she could make food at home and bring it to me in the hospital, but it had to be prepared in a specific way. It didn't matter. Mama was thrilled and welcomed the challenge, as she and my sisters would prepare a meal, then grind it up into little pieces that I wouldn't have to chew. The flavors were wonderful, with banana pudding being my hands-down favorite. I would lie in bed those long hours at the hospital and look forward to whatever delicacy they were whipping up for me each day. I know it was a blessing for Mom and my sisters, too. It gave them something useful to do; so they didn't feel so helpless. They put all their love and energy into those wonderful meals, spending hours in the kitchen, constantly searching for new ways of preparing basic foods to make them more nutritious and delicious. They would feel a sense of pride and accomplishment as they created each new culinary masterpiece. I was fortunate to have my very own master chefs, and it was their imaginative cooking that helped my body to eventually grow stronger.

Although it was still very painful to be moved, I was getting up out of bed every day and able to sit in the chair for short periods. By now I was receiving new skin grafts every week or two, and I needed blood transfusions almost daily. But as I started gaining weight, I could feel my strength returning, and it seemed like I'd turned the corner.

Dr. Grifka felt the same way, and he came into my room one morning with surprising news.

"Delbert," he said, "You're ready to move out of ICU. I'm transferring you up to the medical floor." This was definitely "Good News-Bad News."

Good news because it meant that I was getting better and one step closer to going home. But bad news because it meant leaving the security of the only home I'd known for the last six months. I was used to the routine of the unit and knew all the nurses and orderlies. In the intensive care unit there was always someone close by watching over me. I knew it wouldn't be like that on the medical floor. I'd be more alone, more helpless. Plus, I was accepted here. No one judged me on how I looked. Would it be the same in my new home?

I had gradually learned to accept the way my body was disfigured, but I still had not seen my face yet. The thought was always too frightening. If I was going to be moved to the general ward though, it was time for me to look at what the rest of the world would see everyday.

When it came time for the big "unveiling," everyone was there: Mother, Dad, Uncle Treetop, Aunt Pauline, Ball, June, Tony, Jackie, Gwen, Yvonne, and several of my friends. Up until now, no one had seen my face except Marlene and the doctors. We all imagined what it might look like, but we never really talked about it. Nobody wanted to bring it up. Now they were all gathered nearby, waiting fearfully, knowing that this was going to be a pivotal moment in my life, each lost in their own thoughts.

My mind was whirling with possibilities and hope.

Nurse Marlene slowly, methodically unwrapped the bandages, then hesitatingly held the mirror up to my face. I couldn't hold it myself, as my fingers were bound together. Besides, I was shaking too much. At first I couldn't look. I didn't know how bad it would be, but I was terrified to find out. I knew what I looked like six months ago…not a movie star, certainly. Actually, I never really thought much about how I looked. All of us kids came from the same gene pool, with a handsome father and a beautiful mother. So what was there to think about? Other people said I was attractive, and I accepted their assessment. Even in junior high school, I was voted "the best looking" kid in my class. I took pride in my appearance, paying special attention to my dark, wavy hair. I'd spend countless hours applying "Brylcream" and sculpting it into a classic waterfall with a duck's tail in the back, just like every other guy I knew in the '60s. My complexion was smooth, with almost delicate features, and I didn't even have to shave, since my skin was so soft. But my best feature was my brown eyes, with their long lashes. Girls told me they were dark and sexy.

As Marlene brought the mirror up for me to see, I knew that there would be changes. There were bound to be some scars to my face, just as there were to my body. I was prepared to see changes. I was prepared to see blisters and damage from the fire. I was even prepared to be upset. But I was not prepared for what I saw in that mirror. Time froze as I stared horrified at the image before me. It was not my face. It wasn't a man's face. It wasn't even a face at all—just a hairless blob of bloody, raw skin. No eyebrows or lashes. Just slits for eyes, and a swollen obscene pink hole where my mouth used to be. No nose and no ears either. They were completely gone, leaving two holes on the side of the orb that used to be my face.

I turned my head away from the gruesome sight as tears slid down my scarred raw cheeks. Marlene tried to comfort me, stroking my head and soothing me with her words.

"It's going to be all right, Delbert." But her voice cracked, betraying her bravery, as she tried vainly not to cry, too.

"It just looks bad now, but it will get better, you'll see."

But the sobs wouldn't stop. The image was too horrible.

"How can I possibly go through life looking like this? I'm hideous…a monster."

If I couldn't look at my own image, how would others be able to do so?

No wonder my mother was so distraught. Had she seen my face in her nightmares?

My baby daughters would tremble in fear at the sight of me. And my wife? How could she ever want to hold me or love me? My life was over. Why did I survive the fire? Why did the doctors fight so hard to save me?

I sobbed and sobbed relentlessly. For the first time in six months, I didn't feel the pain of my injuries. It had been replaced by a more powerful, excruciating pain that pierced my heart and throbbed with relentless intensity. My hopes and dreams of a happy life were shattered.

"God," I cried brokenly, "Why didn't you let me die?"

TWENTY

TRAPPED

he image in the mirror left me depressed and angry. Dr. Grifka was sympathetic, but he wasn't about to give in to my self-pity.

"Delbert, you're face won't always be swollen and red. There's a lot we can do for you." Even though my future looked dark and bleak, he tried to offer me a flicker of hope. But I wasn't fooled. It wasn't as simple as a little redness and swelling.

"Reconstructive surgery will help you look more normal. But first we've got to get your wounds healed."

I wanted to believe him, to trust in his words, but I couldn't see how any amount of plastic surgery was ever going to make me whole again. I couldn't get the grotesque image of my face out of my mind. It played over and over again, like a broken record. I just wanted to go back to sleep and never wake up.

I didn't care if they moved me up to the ward. I didn't care if people were afraid to look at me. I didn't care if there'd be no one to help me. The reflection in the mirror had taken all hope out of my life. I didn't care about anything anymore. So when the orderly came to wheel me up to the medical floor, I barely noticed. Not even Marlene, walking along side me, could give me any comfort. I hung my head and accepted my fate. My life couldn't get any worse. I was wrong…

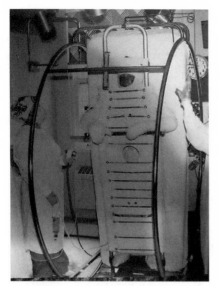

(Photo courtesy of Dr. Irving Feller)

My new room was far different from the old one. Instead of a bed, there was a strange looking device that resembled an amusement park ride.

It was called a "Circoelectric bed," and it was supposed to turn me upside down without having to roll me over, in order to prevent bedsores.

"I don't want to get in it," I declared. With it's two big steel circles and electric motor, it looked claustrophobic and far too frightening. And it sure didn't look safe, either.

"Please don't make me get in it," I begged Dr. Grifka. "Please!"

"You have to get in the bed, Delbert. This will be better for you. It will help your burns to heal more quickly, and it won't be so painful to move you."

He was right about that. I could hardly stand to have anyone touch me. Every part of my body hurt. And rolling me over was unbearable.

Dr. Grifka could be pretty convincing when he wanted to be. I know that he only had my best interest at heart, and he was trying to help me, but still...

Reluctantly, I let the orderly and Marlene lift me off the stretcher and lay me on the lumpy, stiff mattress of the "monster bed." The mattress was much narrower than my old one, barely bigger than my body. Nurse Pfeifer, who would be taking Marlene's place as my main caregiver, buckled two straps across my hips and chest. Now I was really worried. I'd never been strapped into bed before, but she explained that it was because there were no side rails, and they didn't want me to fall out. She then placed a leather strap across my face, covering my chin and forehead, and it hurt when she tightened it. After that, she put a second mattress, just as lumpy as the first, on top of my body. When she tightened some screws at the head and foot of the bed, it pressed me into the two mattresses, one in front and one in back.

I must have looked like a hot dog on a bun, and it would have been funny if I weren't so scared. Marlene stayed right by my side and gave me words of encouragement and reassurance when Nurse Pfeifer pressed the control button. The motor clanged and hummed, and the whole bed started to move. As the foot of the bed dropped, I could feel my head rising. After a few seconds, I was straight up and down. I panicked when I thought I might fall out the bottom, but the nurses both promised me that I was secure. When Nurse Pfeifer was sure that I could handle it, she pressed the button again, and the bed started to rotate once more. When she let go of the button, I was horizontal again, only this time I was lying face down toward the floor. With that, she unstrapped the first mattress that I had been lying on, and pulled it away from the bed. When she covered me with a sheet, the process was complete. I had officially been turned over in bed. Dr. Grifka was right. It wasn't painful. No one had to touch me, and I could be turned over every two hours, without any pain. Maybe this strange bed wasn't so bad after all.

Adjusting to the circular bed would prove to be easier than adjusting to the ward itself. I didn't have a roommate, and it wasn't like the intensive care unit where nurses or orderlies were always looking in on me. Whenever I needed anything in the ICU Marlene or one of the others were right there to help me. But in this isolated room, all I had was the button. Dr. Grifka assured me that someone would look in on me often, but I knew that if I needed help quickly, that call button was going to be useless. Since my hands were bound into a fist, I had no use of my fingers, and I couldn't even reach out with my arm. How was I supposed to push the button?

I soon learned that my personal call button was going to be my own voice.

"Nurse, nurse, help me!" I'd wail, when I couldn't wait any longer for someone to come to the room. But sometimes they didn't show up, and that fueled my anxiety even more. Didn't they know how helpless I was? Didn't they know that I was in constant pain?

There were only two reasons that I would call out to the nurses. One was for pain relief and the other was for bodily function help. Since I couldn't get out of bed to go to the bathroom myself, I had to rely on others for assistance. I had long since surrendered any sense of modesty when it came to my body. Most of the staff in the hospital, as well as my own family members, had seen me naked and exposed. A catheter had been inserted while I was in the ICU, but that had been removed, and I now had control of my own urine. What I didn't have control of was how to get rid of it. I had to wait for someone to come in to my room and hold the urinal for me. That was bad enough, but bowel elimination was worse. In the ICU the nurse would slide a bedpan under me, while lifting me slightly up from the bed, which was excruciating. Naturally, I didn't look forward much to bowel movements. But the Circoelectric bed had an ingenious design to it. The bottom mattress had a hole cut in it where a bedpan could be anchored. I didn't need to be lifted in order to go to the bathroom. But I did need someone to change the pan when it was necessary.

Sometimes my pain medication would wear off before I was due to get another dose, and the pain would be awful. But the nurses seemed reluctant to give me anything. The process wasn't as easy as it was in the ICU where I got it directly into the intravenous line. Here, in the ward, they had to give me a shot in the muscle, or what was left of it. Each injection was painful, and I developed hard sores everywhere that the needle had poked me. They were running out of locations to give me the shot, but it didn't matter. I still needed those shots, and they couldn't come often enough.

It would be several weeks before I got used to my new surroundings and new caregivers. I still missed Marlene terribly, but I was growing fonder of Nurse Pfeifer and the others, and they were getting more comfortable with me. Nurse Pfeifer would tell me jokes to boost my spirits, and sometimes she'd come into the room and we'd just talk. I found out that I actually used to ride to work with her son Michael, when we both worked at the Warren Truck Plant, one of those "small world" stories. Once we got into a routine, we all got along a lot better, and I was more tolerant and less anxious when the staff didn't get to me right away. I guess being in the ward was a good stepping-stone. It was kind of like a look into the future for me. Up until now, I'd had plenty of help in the hospital. But if I was going to get out of here and go back into the real world, I had to learn to do things for myself.

"But how?"

That was the sixty four thousand dollar question. That was the question that fueled my depression by day and haunted my dreams at night.

TWENTY-ONE

BEARING WITNESS

*W*hile I was still fighting for my life, the legal system was pursuing the men who put me in this nightmarish predicament. Little did I know that the young man who warned me not to go into the club had first-hand knowledge as to what would happen next and how my life would be forever altered.

Detectives investigating the case began to develop a suspect list the day after the Soul Expressions was firebombed. Many of the teenagers at the dance hall recalled that two young men had argued with the bouncer after being refused re-admission. One of them had left his jacket inside and was upset about having to pay $1.00 to go back upstairs.

At first, no one knew who they were, but detectives were closing in, and arson investigator, Otto Wandrie, determined quickly that the fire had been started with gasoline. He found pieces of an exploded gas can, and officers were sent to canvas nearby gas stations. At a neighborhood Marathon station, an attendant told police that two customers had borrowed a gas can and had not returned to reclaim the black onyx ring they had used for a deposit. Meanwhile, witnesses had identified the getaway car, and police connected it to the men.

I was too weary and weak to muster enough intensity to hate the men who had done this to me, but even in my pain and confused condition I remember wanting justice. My father had instilled in his children a black-and-white perception of what was right and wrong and that consequences must come to those who break the law. He believed in the American system of fairness and wanted those criminals to be held to the highest standards. My dilemma was that the Bible teaches us about love and forgiveness. Lying helpless and mutilated in a hospital bed, it was hard for me to find any compassion in my heart, and forgiveness would not come easily. But as much as I struggled with the concept, my father experienced it to a higher degree. He had seen the consequences of their selfish act. He had witnessed the devastation they had inflicted on my life and my family. He had stood by helplessly when the pain was so intense, I begged to die. In spite of his spirituality and belief in the power of forgiveness, his anguished feelings were real and honest. "I want to kill them for what they did to you son," he confessed.

The trial was held in May of 1969, more than four months after the fire. I was still in the ICU, too frail to attend, but my father was there, and he listened to every bit of painful testimony. Judge Frank Shemanske presided over the proceedings, and the man who had poured gasoline on the stairway and threw the match was charged with three counts of arson.

The third count was for "placing explosives with intent to destroy property resulting in personal injury." The defense attorney argued that gasoline was not an explosive device and asked the judge to throw the third count out. Judge Shemanske certainly didn't see it that way. Citing the way the cylinders in an automobile engine explode when fueled by gasoline, "It's common knowledge that it is an explosive," he replied.

Another key moment in the trial came when the prosecuting attorney made the defendant admit that when he drove away from the Soul Expressions, he and his passengers could hear people screaming in the burning building. That had to have an impact on the jury, because my father said that even the judge, who presumably would have heard about many heinous and criminal acts in his life, appeared stunned and angered by its callousness.

Back at the hospital, I was told it was time for me to testify. Weighing less than sixty pounds, Dr. Grifka said I was unable to travel to the courthouse. I was too weak and very vulnerable to infection, he advised. He did agree, however, to have the trial come to me. Even though it was painful for me to sit up, I was moved into a wheelchair and taken to the hospital conference center. The jury was already seated there, along with Judge Shemanske and the prosecuting attorney, plus the defense attorney. I can only imagine what kind of impact I had on the jurors when they wheeled me in. I was still covered with gauze bandages, hooked up to IV lines, and obviously weak and in pain. Most everybody in that room felt sympathetic to my condition, and I'm sure they were thinking how lucky it was that this hadn't happened to them.

Once sworn in, the prosecutor asked me questions that simply allowed me to tell my version of what had happened. The most important part of my testimony, as far as the case was concerned, was my memory of two men talking outside the club, and one man warning me not to enter the club because he was "fixing to do something."

"Did these men seem angry?" the prosecutor asked.

"It was hard to say whether they were angry or upset, but they were emotional," I said.

"Then you thought they seemed serious?" he reasoned.

"Yes, it made me hesitate, but not enough to stop me from going in," I admitted.

"Did you see them again?" the prosecutor asked.

"Yes, the two of them came into the vestibule at the bottom of the stairwell and one threw a match that ignited the fire," I answered.

That vision of seeing those men had come to me as soon as I had scrambled up the stairs. It had been seared into my memory.

The district attorney asked if I had identified the defendant's photo out of a group of ten shown to me right after the fire.

"Yes," I said.

"Were you coached to pick that photo?" the judge asked me point-blank.

"No sir—I knew it was him," I replied.

"Can you identify that man in this room?" the prosecutor asked.

As much as I wanted to help, and as much as I wanted justice, I was forced to admit the truth.

"I can't," I said. "Because of the damage to my eyelids, I haven't been able to close my eyes, and they have frequently dried out and become infected. My vision is blurry right now."

The defense attorney seized on my admission and immediately asked the judge to throw out all of my testimony as being unreliable due to my medical condition. I got worried then and feared that I had hurt the prosecution's case. But the judge didn't even need time to deliberate. Instead, he ruled that my testimony was admissible, as was my previous identification of the photo.

When Dr. Grifka and Marlene wheeled me back to the ICU, I felt a sense of accomplishment. After feeling so helpless for the last few months, being able to contribute gave me a sense of purpose, even if I couldn't make a positive identification. I believe that it was important for the jury to see one of the victims of the fire and how much pain and suffering the defendant had caused. Dozens of young people were injured in the Soul Expressions Fire, many of them burned like myself. Although my injuries were more severe than the others, it didn't minimize the amount of pain and suffering that they had experienced. Because of what those cruel men had done, many lives would be scarred forever.

The jury took just over an hour to reach the verdict: Guilty on all three counts.

At sentencing, Judge Shemanske made it clear that he found the defendant's acts to be as despicable as they were criminal. The punishment would be two and one-half years to 10 years on each of the first two counts, and life without parole for the third count.

The trial for the other defendant was held sometime later, but it received less attention. My testimony was not required, and our family did not follow the process, although we learned that the sentence was the same: Life in prison.

It wasn't until many years later that I discovered those lifetime sentences didn't survive appeal. The defense attorneys argued all the way to the Michigan Supreme Court that gasoline poured onto the floor should not be considered an explosive. The higher court agreed with that argument and they overturned the life sentences of both men. The defendants served roughly six years before being released from prison.

My family was very upset when they heard the news, especially my father. He was incensed over the lack of justice. The two men served only six years for causing serious injury to 60 innocent teenagers. Six years for engulfing me in flames and sentencing me to a lifetime of pain and disfigurement. Six years for plunging my family and friends into despair and helplessness.

Initially I felt the same way as Dad. I was angry, hurt, disappointed in the legal system. I could not believe or accept the unfairness of it all. I wanted to lash out at someone, to make those men pay for what they did. But eventually, I began to realize that neither our body nor our soul is nourished by anger. All anger does is stifle our energy or diminish our ability to enjoy the gift of life.

My advice to people who have been severely wronged by others, "Don't let the anger cause mental paralysis." Otherwise, those calloused individuals can continue to hurt you forever. It's bad enough that two men decimated my body and mind over 40 years ago. I would not let them destroy my soul as well.

TWENTY-TWO

MEDICAL PRISON

*L*ife on the ward was a shock to my system in more ways than one. I had fought to survive for over half a year that I was in the intensive care unit, and while there, I developed a comfort level knowing that medical personnel were always around, especially Marlene and Dr. Grifka. This reassurance helped me cope because it was a very frightening environment. There were many days when I thought I was not going to live, and when I did survive a near death experience, those who helped pull me back to life became my greatest allies. The ICU is an intense and fast paced atmosphere because of the perilous condition of all the patients. When nearly everything in your world has been stripped away and you are as helpless as a child, anything that resembles a routine pattern helps you deal with your situation. I knew the sounds of the machines, the footsteps of the staff, the hum of the clock, and the smell of people and medicine. It was a routine I became accustomed to. And as bad as I felt, it was a good secure feeling to know that just a step away, unlike the rest of the hospital, someone was always there.

It was hot on the ward too. As summer came around, I learned that unlike the ICU, there was no air conditioning on the medical floor. With my sweat glands burned away, my body couldn't get rid of the heat, and there was no way for me to cool off. Dad brought in a fan, and that helped, but being as I was sandwiched between two mattresses in the electric bed, I couldn't get much breeze. Some days I felt like I was roasting on a barbecue spit.

My father still came to visit me almost every day. He'd come after work around midnight, go home for a few hours, then return the next morning and stay until he had to be back at work. Sometimes Uncle Treetop came with him. Treetop was my dad's brother, and we called him that because he'd shake all over when he was dancing, just like a tree shakes its leaves. Treetop was married to my mother's sister, Pauline. My dad and his brother married my mom and her sister. I was glad Treetop could come because some days he and Dad had to help me into the salt bath. With fewer staff up on the ward, it was difficult for them to make time to get me into the tub every day. Weekends were the worst, and it was a godsend that my uncle and father could help me into the tank.

They got so that they even learned to change the gauze bandages and give me new dressings. It was a gory task, and they had to get used to seeing the open wounds and blood. But they did it, and they never complained.

While my father brought strength and courage to the hospital every day, my mother brought warmth and love. Now that I was out of the intensive care unit, I think she was less fearful that I was going to die at any minute. Her visits came more and more frequently, and I looked forward to them very much. It was hard to be in a bad mood when Mom was around. She had such an easy manner about her. She'd sit and talk for hours about the neighborhood and the family.

"Everybody misses you, Delray," she'd remind me often.

"You just got to get better so you can come back home real soon."

And, of course, having her bring all my favorite foods made me look forward to her visits even more. The produce was fresh this time of the year, and she'd make collard greens or black-eyed peas that were delicious. She and I would talk for hours about my childhood and the wonderful, happy memories we both had. The hours always went by faster when Mama was visiting.

Sometimes my little sister, Gwen would come, too. Even though she was only 14 years old, and would much rather be giggling with her girl-friends and talking about boys, she still took the time to come see her brother in the hospital. I know it must have been hard for her. At that young age, you feel like you're invincible and nothing bad is ever going to happen. The world looks all rosy, and opportunities are endless. Having to look at me all burned up disfigured, and helpless cast a dark shadow on her bright, happy outlook.

One afternoon she brought in an old record player with a spindle that adapted to the 45-rpm records. Soon all my friends started bringing records when they came to see me. When I was alone after visiting hours, I could lie in my electric bed and listen to my favorite songs for hours.

If I wasn't listening to records, I would be tuned to the radio. I followed every game or sporting event that was broadcast. Of course, baseball was my favorite. But I wasn't choosey. I started looking forward to them all…hockey, basketball, football. It didn't matter. I had plenty of time. I sure wasn't going anywhere. Sometimes I'd doze off in the middle of a contest, and I'd wake up a little later when a different game would be on. I'd fall asleep to baseball and wake up to basketball. At first I'd be confused, but I usually figured it out when the announcer would give the score as 97 to 86. I knew then it wasn't baseball.

Following my favorite teams statistically would prove to be more challenging. For years I had poured over the box scores and tracked the batting average of every major leaguer by reading the newspaper. Now, I needed help to do something even that simple. But Nurse Pfeifer had the answer. She would come into my room, press a button, and rotate the bed so that I was on my stomach facing downward. Then she'd spread the paper out on the floor, after first opening it to the sports section. I don't know how I could see it from that distance, but I did. I'd read the scores and stats over and over again, until she or one of the orderlies came in to turn the page.

As part of my rehabilitation, I was supposed to get out of bed and walk in the hall every day. I had two orderlies, one named Moses and the other named Mr. Johnson. They had the responsibility for getting me up out of bed to exercise. Usually I was a pretty good patient. In spite of the pain it caused, I did all the things I was supposed to do in order to get better.

"Delbert Ray, you just do what the doctor says," mother would remind me frequently. And I always obeyed Mama, especially when she used both my names, back to back.

But as the long days wore on and stretched endlessly into the future, I began losing hope. Depressing thoughts crowded my mind, and I was losing my ability to fight. I just wanted to give up.

"What's the use?" I reasoned.

"I'm never going to have the same kind of life as I used to. I'll never play baseball again, or hang out with my friends, or hold my little girls, or go to work, or drive a car, or..."

The list was endless. There were so many things that I'd never be able to do again, my future was bleak. I would be ugly, useless, and dependent the rest of my life. The futility overwhelmed me, and I determined that it would be easier to just stay in the bed forever. Much easier.

Those were my darkest moments, and although they didn't happen often, it was troubling when they did. The whole family worried that I'd give up. Everyone that is, except Ball. My brother wouldn't let me. He'd stomp into my room, put his face real close to mine, look me square in the eye, and bellow, "Get up...Now"! Next he'd haul me out of the bed, hook his arm under mine, and get me up onto my feet. Nobody messed with Ball. It wasn't that he was mean. He was just firm and determined. If I complained that I was too tired to walk, he'd ignore my whining.

"You didn't come this far to quit now," he reminded me.

Then he leaned my body against his, and we began the arduous walk down the hospital hall. My ankles were so weak that it hurt to put any weight on them, but with Ball's support I was able to shuffle along in a pattern that proved a poor imitation of walking. It was Ball that taught me how to read the newspaper without help, too. When we'd finish our "walk," he'd put me in the chair, and give me the paper. With no fingers, I had to learn how to turn the pages with my fused fist, or bend my head down, put the corner of the section I was reading in my mouth, and turn the page that way. It was awkward and clumsy at first, as I struggled to keep it from falling onto the floor. But after awhile, I got the hang of it. The simple act of reading the newspaper without assistance gave me hope that maybe I "could" have my life back. Maybe I "would" be able to do things again. I just had to learn how to do them differently, that's all.

I was really fortunate in one respect. I had lots of visitors. Some of the patients on the ward didn't get much company, but I had more than my fair share. My family and friends kept me occupied and helped the days to pass while the endless healing process wound forward. The bright spot of my day was always visiting hours, and I was happy about whoever came to see me. But no one put a smile on my face more than the arrival of my little girls.

Kim was just a baby at the time of the fire, barely eight weeks old, and I hardly got to know her before I came to live in the hospital. Now she was almost one. Yvonne said she was a good baby, happy and content. But whenever she came to see me, she stayed in the safety of her mother's arms. I didn't mind. I knew I must look pretty scary to a little baby. Even though I was her Daddy, she didn't know that. To her, I was a stranger, and at that age, she didn't warm up to strangers. But Monique, who resembled me in many ways, was a toddler now. Six months ago, she was crawling all over the house, and we'd laugh at her antics. But now she was walking. She had taken her first steps while I was in intensive care, and it saddened me that I wasn't there to witness it. Those were the milestones in a child's life. Her first steps, first tooth, first words. You never get those events back. They only happened one time, and if you were fortunate, you got to see them first hand. I wasn't lucky with Monique, but maybe it would be different with Kim. Maybe I could get well enough to go home and see my daughters grow up. It gave me something to hope for.

Those visits were a time of joy and a time of sadness. While they were there I was fine, content to be near them, happy to see how they'd grown. But when visiting hours were over and my little girls left, the feelings of hopelessness would return, and I'd sink back into depression. I loved them so much, my heart ached, and I longed to have my life back again. I wanted to be able to provide for them and my wife. To buy them a nice home, nice clothes, all the toys they dreamed of. I wanted to be with them as they grew up, to help raise them, take them to church, play in the park, buy them an ice cream cone. I could almost shut my eyes and see it all happening so clearly. In the darkness, with the power of my mind, I could be whole again, able-bodied, strong, and useful. I could see a future with my family. But when the light poured back in, reality smacked me in the face. I was pressed between two mattresses, strapped down, and helpless. This room was my prison, and an unfulfilled life of pain and misery was my destiny.

TWENTY-THREE

YVONNE McCOY

It wasn't easy going to see Delbert at the hospital. With two babies at home, I couldn't just pick up and go whenever I wanted. I had to rely on someone to watch over the girls so that I could visit their father. I looked forward to, yet dreaded those visits at the same time. I needed to be with my husband, to talk to him, to comfort him, and to see for myself that he was okay. But on many occasions, especially in the early months, he'd be asleep while I was there. As much as I needed to talk with him, I knew that he was better off sleeping. That was the only time he was not moaning in pain, and that was the part I couldn't bear.

I met Delbert Ray McCoy when I was just fifteen years old. Actually, I had a crush on him from the moment I saw him in junior high school, but he didn't know it. His family used to live in the same neighborhood as my aunt, and I would see him and his brothers out in the yard whenever I visited her.

"He's so handsome," I would giggle with my cousin Brenda, when we shared "boy crazy" stories. All the McCoy boys were very good looking, but Delbert just stood out in my eyes. I was so impressed with how he dressed, always immaculate and well groomed. He would wear bright colored shirts with matching slacks, and even his shoes were the same color. I don't think he ever would have noticed me if my cousin hadn't formally introduced us. He *was so shy, and not into girls much, preferring to hang out with his buddies instead. We dated for two years, occasionally going to a movie, but mostly walking, talking, and getting to know each other. Actually, I guess I did most of the talking. He was much more at ease with his guy friends talking about baseball and sports. We had different interests for sure. I liked to go dancing, but he wasn't much good at it. I used to tease him about having two "left feet." But we got along great, and I was happy just to hang out with him, and always felt special to be on his arm. He got a job at one of the auto companies just before he graduated, so we didn't get to see each other as much, but we made the best of it. My family approved of him, and my parents knew he was dependable and was going to make something of himself one day. Unlike a lot of the guys his age, he loved beautiful things and was full of enthusiasm for life. That really impressed my mother, Bernice.*

"That boy's a real go-getter. He's going to make something of himself one day," she declared.

Mother was his biggest fan, often taking his side against mine if we had a disagreement. He could do no wrong in her eyes. She thought Delbert was ter-rific, and she absolutely loved him, especially when I found myself pregnant, and Delbert stepped up and did the right thing.

I was so ashamed, I was barely 16, didn't know much about life, and yet I was going to have a baby. But mother took it all in stride and began mak-ing wedding plans immediately. Delbert and I were married on October 28, 1967 accompanied by family and friends, and Monique was born six weeks later.

We moved into his parent's house on Dexter and shared our bedroom with the baby. There was always room for "one more" at the McCoy house, and Delbert's mother wouldn't have it any other way. She doted on her grandbaby and was good company for me when Delbert was working long hours at the auto plant. We barely had time to adjust to being parents when the stork came calling again. Kim was born November 25,1968, just eleven months after Monique. By now my husband was working two jobs at the factories, eight hour shifts each; so he was home just long enough to sleep at night. We didn't have much time for socializing. Plus, he was making plans to go to col-lege so that he wouldn't have to work in the auto plants for the rest of his life. With two children to support, he was determined to give us a good life, and we were saving our money to buy a home of our own.

I was busy taking care of the babies, and he was busy working two jobs, but we were happy and optimistic about life. Like most newlyweds, we had plans and dreams and a bright future ahead of us.

That dream was shattered the night I walked into the ICU and saw my husband encased in bandages, with wires and machines surrounding his bed. As the agonizing burn treatment progressed, he endured long days of pain and suffering that upset everyone in the family. All of us wanted so much to help him, but there was nothing we could do but be there for him and pray. It was really hard for him to keep a positive attitude and focus on getting well when he was in such excruciating pain. The doctors were doing everything they could, but the pain would not be denied. It consumed him every waking hour. After a while it started working on his mind. He couldn't fathom how he would ever be pain-free again, and he knew he couldn't keep his strength up much longer. He was understandably anxious and despondent, and it seemed like he took out all his frustrations on me when I went to visit. He would be mad at me for not going more often, but when I did go see him, he was angry with me the whole time I was there. I just couldn't win.

Also, the issue of disfigurement began to raise its ugly head. He didn't believe that he could ever be normal again. He felt like he was holding me back and keeping me from finding someone else...someone normal. He began treating me differently when I visited...almost like he was pushing me away. What I didn't understand was that he was probably trying to protect me. I know that he looked forward to my visits, especially when I was able to take the girls to see him. His face just lit up when I'd bring them in. It hurt him that he couldn't hold them or stroke their hair, but it cheered him up just to have them near.

Neither of us knew what the future would hold. The fire had changed the direction our lives would take. But I was determined not to let it take our family. We had two beautiful daughters that we could build a life around. And in spite of Delbert's injuries and disfigurement, he was still the same man inside that I fell in love with. We could still be together. That was the thought I clung to as the days turned into weeks...then months...then years.

While Delbert was fighting to stay alive, I battled my own personal demons at home. With little money coming in and my husband lying in the hospital, I was faced with the task of supporting and raising our girls on my own. I had always been a pretty good seamstress, so I began making all of our clothes, and even took in a small amount of sewing for neighbors. I tried real

Monqiue and Kim

hard to stay upbeat when I was around Delbert and the family, but when I was alone the feelings of doubt, worry and despair took over. I felt so cheated by life, and would often question God. "Why is this happening to us? Why me?" Because everything that happened to Delbert was also happening to me.

The nights were the worst, when the girls were asleep. I had way too much time on my hands, and my mind became consumed with despair. I went to a doctor, who prescribed an anti-depressant, but I didn't like to take it. Besides, no amount of medication could change the facts. The situation would remain the same. My husband was in the hospital fighting for his life. He was horribly disfigured, severely handicapped, and being tortured by pain. Our dreams of a happy, loving family were destroyed. What was I going to do?

TWENTY-FOUR

BLINDSIDED

epression was just one more of a growing list of concerns that Dr. Grifka had to deal with regarding my care. I guess I was following the natural progression. Injury, pain, denial...but I didn't ever think I'd get to "acceptance." That's why it was important that my family and the medical staff worked as much on my mental well being as my physical health. They were certainly inter-connected. Depression had become my new enemy, and its impact threatened my health even more than the injuries. I didn't receive any formal counseling, or psychiatric help while I was in the hospital, but I did have a powerful weapon—my family. They never gave up on me. My father was with me every day, and my mother and sister were there every night. They not only brought me news from home and the outside world, but they were ever vigilant to my mood swings. I was able to talk to them about my doubts and fears, just as if I had a counselor to talk to. We had a daily routine, and prayer was an intricate part of it. They would pray to Jesus to help me heal, to take away the pain, to give me strength, to offer forgiveness, and to accept what had happened in my life.

Those prayers did give me strength, especially when we recited the 23rd Psalm together. I'll never forget the holy words of that comforting prayer. And at the end of each visit, before they left to go back home, we would all say one more prayer together. With my family's unending help, and the faith they helped to instill in me, I eventually did emerge from my funk, and I started to improve…slowly, but steadily.

But challenges continued. As I approached the one-year anniversary of my hospitalization, Dr. Grifka explained that he wanted to transfer me to St. Joseph Mercy Hospital in Ann Arbor because it had a first-rate burn unit. But there was a hitch. The health insurance, which I received from my job with Chevrolet, only covered one year of hospitalization. My provider would stop paying for my hospitalization, even though I wasn't yet recovered, after 12 months. Although I had a second policy through my job at Chrysler, it was with another insurance company, and that policy required me to be hospitalized at Metropolitan, a smaller local hospital.

Dr. Grifka believed he could talk the insurance company into continuing its coverage, but I was going to have to accept a temporary transfer to the smaller facility.

What I didn't know at the time is that Dr. Grifka was extremely concerned about moving me to that hospital because it didn't have a good reputation for caring for burns. He and his staff had dedicated an entire year to caring for my injuries, and I'm sure that he abhorred the thought of turning his patient over to another institution; especially if he felt that the care they provided would be inadequate.

"Keep in touch and let me know what's going on," he advised.

"I'll keep making calls and do everything I can to get you into St. Joseph's."

As upset as I was at the prospect of changing hospitals, I clung to the optimism that Dr. Grifka would figure out a way to get me to a burn center that could treat me as effectively as he did.

My last day at Detroit Receiving Hospital marked a very sad day in my recovery. As the staff came in to say goodbye, we all cried together. I considered people like Marlene, Miss Pfeifer, Nurse Wallace, Mr. Johnson and Moses to be my friends. I was very frightened to leave the safety of the ward that had been my home for the past year. And what would I do without Dr. Grifka? I had relied on him, his knowledge and skills, for all these months. The gifted surgeon had literally saved my life. But I still had a long way to go. How could I leave his excellent care?

I clung to Marlene as the ambulance came to take me away. She had been my lifeline during the worst year of my life. I depended on her for all my needs, physical and mental. I felt like a baby being ripped from his mother's arms. It was so hard to leave her.

Our worst fears about the new institution were realized upon arrival. It was a decaying building with minimal staffing, and an aura of gloom settled over me as soon as I was admitted. But the nurses and staff were kind to me, and they tried to help me feel welcome and secure.

My new bed was different also. Called a Stryker bed, it resembled two metal posts with a hammock type sling made out of canvas. It was also operated electronically, so the nurses were able to flip me upside down with the flick of a switch.

In anticipation of my insurance coverage running out, Dr. Grifka had given me one last skin graft before I had to leave his care. On the second day I was at the new hospital, the surgeon in charge of my case removed it. I had received enough treatments to know that if my body rejected a skin transplant, then it had to be eliminated. But Dr. Grifka's latest graft seemed like it was holding, and I was puzzled and frightened when it was removed. What further fueled my fear was that it wasn't replaced with a new graft like Dr. Grifka always did. The new doctor merely covered the wound with a dressing, and wrapped it tightly.

My sense was that the staff at the new hospital was writing me off as a patient that had no chance of recovery, a waste of time, a hopeless cause. Once again my mind worked overtime, and it was hard to find anything positive about my situation. The hope for recovery that my family and Dr. Grifka had infused in me now seemed like a cruel joke. I laid awake for hours, praying and asking God to help me stay strong...and not to lose hope. It would be a long night, with very little rest.

Then sometime, during the early morning hours, my bandages turned red with blood and fluids. The area where the skin graft had been removed was hemorrhaging. It looked like I was going to bleed to death, and I was terrified. I screamed for the nurse, and by the time she got into the room, I was emotionally devastated.

The nurse was alarmed and tried to calm me down, but the doctor didn't show much urgency. He stopped the bleeding by wrapping the area more tightly. He didn't take me to surgery, and he didn't do a new skin graft, like I knew Dr. Grifka would have done. He didn't assure me that he'd call all over town to get me donor skin, and he didn't say "Hang in there Delbert, you're going to be okay." But he did order another blood transfusion—the first of many.

As the days wore on, it became clear that Metropolitan Hospital didn't have the same dedication to my treatment as Detroit Receiving had. The months of wonderful care that I received at the hands of Marlene and Dr. Grifka had given me a chance for life. Now I felt like I was losing that opportunity.

Even the bath treatments to help loosen the dressings were infrequent, as the hospital didn't have enough staff. My father offered to do them himself, pointing out that he had assisted with the procedure many times, but this facility did not allow non-employees to help as caregivers. So I would wait for hours to be taken to the tub. But no one would come, and then it would be too late and the baths would be closed. So I'd begin again the next morning waiting to be taken to the baths, and the process would repeat itself.

As the previous skin grafts began to heal they would shrink up and itch constantly. The nurses gave me Benadryl, but it didn't help much, and I thought I'd go crazy from the itching. It felt like little ants were scurrying around my wounds, and I just wanted to gouge the skin off my body. But, of course, I couldn't. I didn't have any fingers.

There was no exercise routine either. The nurses or orderlies didn't get me out of bed to help get my circulation going, and they didn't much help me sit in the chair. My mobility decreased as my morale spiraled. Bleeding and infections became more common, and I frequently ran a fever and was losing more weight. It seemed like this dreary place was going to be my last stop in life. I sincerely believed I was dying. My parents were worried sick, and Dad called Dr. Grifka several times to report on my condition. But his hands were tied. He kept battling the insurance company on my behalf and fought to get me into St. Joseph's, but without success.

Several nights later my family was summoned to the hospital because infection had ravaged my body, downgrading my condition to "critical."

"We've done all that we can," the new doctor told my father. "I don't believe your son will be alive in the morning. You better get down here now."

"My son survived one whole year in Detroit Receiving Hospital when he was given thousand-to-one odds," my father erupted. "Since he's arrived here his condition has deteriorated, and now you tell me he's dying? How can that be?"

That night, as we had done on many nights, my family prayed together. We asked God to get me back to the safety of Dr. Grifka and Marlene. We asked him to get me into Ann Arbor, where they had the number one burn unit. I was very weak and very, very frightened. But I knew I wasn't alone. My family was with me, and God would not desert me. "Please don't let me die," I begged, as Daddy paced the floor and Mama tried bravely to hide her tears.

TWENTY-FIVE

JUST IN TIME

*G*od answered my prayers once again, and Dr. Grifka hadn't given up on me either. He contacted St. Joseph's Hospital several times and talked to Dr. Irving Feller, a world renowned burn specialist. Dr. Feller was a pioneer with a superb reputation, and patients were flown in from all over the country to receive his care. In spite of his close association with Dr. Feller, Dr. Grifka had been unable to get me access to St. Joseph's. But when my parents called him on Saturday morning, shortly after my near death experience to report how much my condition had deteriorated, he was shocked.

"If you don't get Delbert in there soon, he's not going to make it," my father implored.

Dr. Grifka came to my rescue once more, as he immediately got on the phone and pleaded our case again to St. Joseph's Hospital. Fortunately, a bed had become available and my insurance coverage was re-instated. But curiously, the carrier wouldn't pay for the ambulance ride from Metropolitan Hospital in Detroit to St. Joseph's Hospital in Ann Arbor, a distance of about 60 miles. That didn't stop my father. He called the ambulance company himself, and when medics showed up at Metropolitan he had cash in his hand to pay them.

Dad took control of my departure, taking advantage of the fact that it was a weekend, to get me out before anyone even knew what was happening. There were no tears, no sad goodbyes. There wasn't time. I was barely conscious, and besides, I wasn't going to miss that place. An hour later, I was admitted to St. Joseph Hospital, where Dr. Feller told my parents that the trip to Ann Arbor had been crucial.

"He was very close to death," Dr. Feller acknowledged. "If you had gotten him here one-half hour later, he'd have been sent to the morgue."

Dr. Feller was the medical world's version of my father. He was stern, strict, no-nonsense, uncompromising in his vision of what should be done. He didn't offer a kind hand on my face as Dr. Grifka had done. He was blunt. But Dr. Feller's disciplined style was helpful in getting me back on the road to recovery. He told me that if I didn't follow his program completely, then I wasn't going to improve. His partner was Dr. Kathy Richards, and they complemented each other, like the good cop and bad cop scenario you see on television. Dr. Richards often joked with me, even though she was just as demanding as Dr. Feller. Their strict, no-nonsense approach worked, and that was important because my problems had once again multiplied and seemed insurmountable.

The staff had a plan for me from the minute I was admitted and hooked up to an intravenous drip. The first order of business was to undo the damage that was done at the previous hospital. My body was raging with infection, and initially Dr. Feller had to change the dressings while I was in bed. He soaked the bandages with some kind of solution, let it sink in for a few minutes, and then unwrapped the gauze. It would be several weeks before I was taken to the tub. In addition to the open wounds on my body, all my joints were locked up. I couldn't use my hands or bend my elbows. After three months in Metropolitan Hospital, I couldn't walk more than a couple of steps, and that came at a painful price.

The quality of care at the new burn unit was first rate in every aspect, including the staff of nurses, therapists, and doctors. It was like a baseball team and everyone had their position to cover and their job to do, and each one of them was an all-star. Even though I still missed Marlene and Dr. Grifka, I felt confident that my new team would help me heal.

My favorite nurse at St. Joe's was Nancy. Whenever she gave me a shot, she'd say, "Delbert, I've got something that's going to make you feel better." She was young, with blonde hair, and she always offered kind words and took good care of me. Marlene was still my favorite, but Nancy ran a close second. Mary Etta was a nurse's aid, and she was special, too. Many times she took my pajamas home and laundered them. Then she'd bring them back the next day, all clean and smelling fresh. I depended on Carol Ann, too. She came in the room often and turned the pages of the newspaper for me. Rob was my physical therapist, who not only helped me physically, but he nourished my spirit as well. He was a deeply religious man, and the two of us would discuss our faith during my many therapy sessions.

The burn unit at St. Joseph's was very different from the one at Detroit Receiving for many reasons. Instead of a ward, the rooms were all semi-private, with televisions and air conditioning. From my perspective this was really high living. Since I was now in the advanced stages of wound care, I was able to spend my days and nights in a regular hospital bed. It wasn't necessary for the nurses to flip me over, as I could move around somewhat on my own. After spending a year in a restrictive, confined bed with mattresses on top and bottom, having a normal bed was a real luxury. I could spread out as much as I wanted to get more comfortable.

I still had a lot of open wounds, and the ones on my buttocks were particularly sensitive; so one of my favorite positions was lying on my side with my rear end hanging over the edge of the bed. I'm sure it must have looked pretty strange, but most of the staff were used to seeing me that way, and they didn't think much of it. But one night a new nurse came on the midnight shift, and when she came in to do her rounds and saw me like that, she would wake me up and place me back in the center of the mattress again. She was worried that I would fall out of bed. She did that several times throughout the night. But every time she came back into the room, she'd find me back in my preferred position.

"Delbert, are you all right," she finally asked.

"Yes, I'm just tired," I mumbled. "I can't get any sleep when you keep coming in and moving me." And I'm pretty sure that she knew I was only half joking. I slept like that the whole time I was at St. Joseph's, and I never fell once.

TWENTY-SIX

HOMESICK

*T*urning twenty-one is a milestone in anyone's life. I spent my twenty-first birthday in the burn unit of St. Joseph Mercy Hospital, surrounded by my family and several friends. Mama prepared made-from-scratch macaroni and cheese, collared greens, and cornbread to go with the roast beef sandwiches she bought at Arby's. I couldn't eat much, but my sisters took turns helping to feed me, and I loved the taste of mother's home cooking.

When visiting hours were over and my family left, I was faced with plenty of time to feel sorry for myself. After a year of being hospitalized, this wasn't exactly how I envisioned spending my entry into adulthood. I wanted to be able to go out and kick up my heels, to have a little fun, to celebrate becoming a "man." As I lay in the bed thinking of all the things I'd miss out on in life, the future looked even bleaker than before.

My thoughts were dark and my mood was melancholic. I could feel the cold grip of depression sneaking up on me once again.

Nurse Nancy must have sensed it and was determined not to let that happen. She rounded up two of the burn technicians who were studying at the University of Michigan Medical School to become doctors. Paul, Bill, and Nancy came marching into my room carrying a little cake with vanilla frosting. They propped me up in bed and insisted that I blow out the candles while they sang *Happy Birthday*. The trio's singing was a little off-key, but it didn't matter. It was such a thoughtful gesture that it made me smile, and my mood improved immediately. It helped to remind me that I was blessed to have so many people that cared about me.

There were two beds in my room, and the other was occupied by a young man named Steve. He worked for the light company, and was electrocuted while working on a utility pole. The electricity shot through his whole body, blowing out his kneecap and severely damaging his arm. He was a real nice guy, a family man with a little baby. His wife would come to visit him often, and I met her as well as his parents.

One night I woke up to see blood spraying all over the curtain between our beds. It was shooting out like a faucet. I screamed for the nurses, and they all came running into the room. The doctor rushed him right down to surgery, and when Steve came back several hours later, he had no arm. An artery had burst and they couldn't stop the bleeding, so they had to amputate his arm to save his life. He was very depressed after that, and we would spend many sleepless nights talking about our injuries and the cards fate had dealt each of us.

Once my body's infection was under control, I was put back on a routine of receiving regular skin grafts and bath treatments. The grafting approach used at St. Joe's was different from Dr. Grifka's. Instead of using cadaver skin, Dr. Feller and Dr. Richards would use skin from my own body. They'd secure small pieces onto my wounds, then wait for it to heal. Once that skin was healed, they would scrape small pieces from the new skin, and use it somewhere else. A lot of tissue was taken from my legs and upper chest, because those areas seemed to produce the best results. Then the skin would be transplanted to my arms, back, buttocks, face…areas that needed it most. This was a big improvement from using donated flesh. By growing and regenerating my own tissue, it greatly improved my chances for successful healing.

As important as the skin grafts were to my recovery, the downside was the healing process itself. When the skin was grafted in an area, it would shrink and dry out as it began to heal. It felt like a million tiny ants crawling all over my body, and it itched so bad I couldn't stand it. Tim was a male nurse on the floor, and he spent a lot of time helping me with the treatments and getting dressed. Whenever he was around, I'd beg him to "scratch my back, scratch it right off." Of course, he couldn't scratch it, but he'd gently rub cocoa butter on the dryness, and I'd get comfort for a little while at least. Then the itching would start up again, and I'd beg Tim or anybody else to help me.

I could hardly bear the pain or the sight of my mutilated body. I couldn't even stand to look at other patients who had injuries less severe than my own. There was a guy on the ward that had been burned all over his back, and had developed ugly raised scars called keloids. His back looked like a roadmap of bumps and deep crevices. Seeing his terrible scars increased the anxiety about my own injuries. I was fearful that my body would look like that when it healed as well. His injuries were only to his back, and it looked awful. "How was I going to look when I had burns all over my body and face?" I couldn't deal with the images that flooded my thoughts; so every time I had a dressing change, I averted my eyes and took my mind somewhere else. I thought of my girls, or my wife, or baseball, or Mama's home cooking. I refused to let my mind think about what the doctor or nurse was doing. I refused to let it think of the pain. And I refused to let it think of what was yet to come. Because if I did, I would be lost.

I also saw a change in my bath treatments. At this facility they were done every day at noon, and they used whirlpool tubs. Instead of salt, they put a chemical in the water which had an unusual side affect. It turned everyone's hair a rusty-red color. When I would go to therapy or pass others in the hall, I could always tell who the burn patients were, even when their scars weren't visible. Every one of them had the signature red hair. The baths were no less torturous though. A designated area of the hospital was used for the agonizing procedure so that the other patients couldn't hear the screams. Those were the times when I'd feel the lowest. It was a daily reminder of what my life would be like in the outside world.

To take my mind off the drudgery of each day, I focused my attention on sports, spending every waking hour listening to games or talking about batting stats. One of the nurses found out about my passion for the game and gave me a gift that really lifted my spirits. She had a sister who knew someone, who was related to someone, who knew someone else, who knew my idol, Detroit Tiger's great Willie Horton. When she told Willie about me, he had the whole Tigers team autograph a baseball. It came on a little stand, and Nurse Liz brought that baseball in and set it on the table next to my bed where I could see it. I was smiling from ear to ear when she read the signatures of the players: Willie Horton, Al Kaline, Jim Northrup, Mickey Stanley, Bill Freehan, Dick McAuliffe, Don Wert, Mickey Lolich, Denny McLain, Joe Sparma, Norm Cash, and Roy Oyler. All my heroes.

And for a long time after that, whenever I went to the baths, I'd think about that special signed ball. It gave me something else to look forward to when I got well—the start of baseball season.

(Photo by Bob Kalmbach, courtesy of Bentley Historical Library, The University of Michigan)

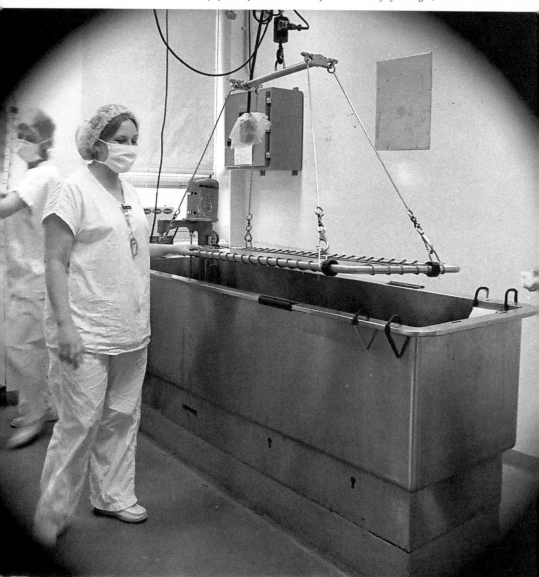

TWENTY-SEVEN

HELPING HAND

With the bleeding and infections under control and my skin transplants flourishing, the doctors could turn their attention to the problems with my arms and hands, instead of keeping me alive. Now my care moved into a specialized area to help me gain important everyday function, and a new player was put on the roster. Dr. Herbertson was an orthopedic surgeon who looked more like an athlete and less like a doctor. With his "win the game" attitude and big strong hands, I felt confident that he was the man who could get it done, and I put all my faith in his abilities.

For more than a year now I had to depend on someone else to help me do everything that most of us take for granted. The biggest loss for me emotionally was the use of my hands. The fire had done so much damage that I was left with useless fused fists. By now, I was actually looking forward to having surgery if it meant giving me mobility in my fingers again. Herbetson would start there. Attempting to get my hands operational would be his first project.

He didn't have much to work with—just flaps of skin, very little muscle, tendons, or nerves. But he tried. I was left handed, and as luck would have it, that was the hand with the most damage. He inserted pins, and made adjustments, but after several surgeries, we were left with

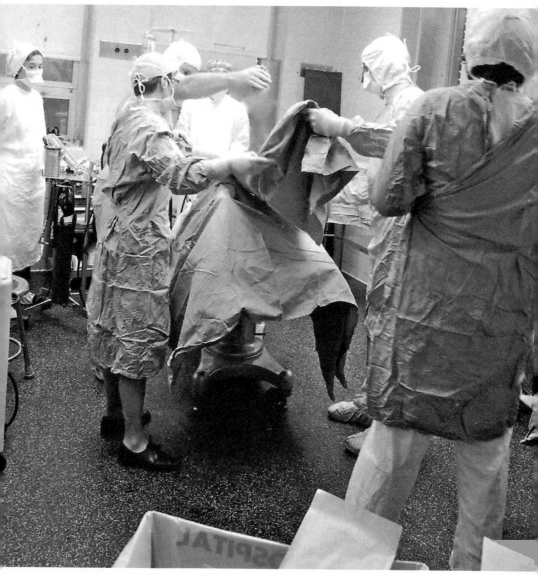

little more than a stub. Instead of a hand, I have two fingers and a thumb, each wrapped in opposing positions, so they're frozen permanently into a crumbled fetal position.

With the loss of my left hand, that made the surgery to my right one even more important. Again, there was a lot of trial and error. Dr. Herbertson was relentless in his efforts to give me working hands, and

95

thereby, some measure of independence. At one point, amputation of my right arm was discussed. Dr. Feller, Dr. Richards, and Dr. Herbertson had a team meeting and came to my room to discuss the procedure. The doctors could fit me with a prosthetic limb with mechanical fingers. I listened carefully to their explanation, but the image of my roommate, Steve, was burned into my memory. I couldn't forget the sight of his blood shooting all over the room and spattering the curtain. In spite of what my body had been through, I didn't think I could adjust to having my arm cut off, too. After much discussion and consideration of my feelings, we decided against amputation. The theory was "don't cut off a body part if it still had some use."

But with nothing else working, Dr. Herbertson had to call on all his creative skills as a surgeon to come up with a solution. Finally, he was able to fashion a modified hand by salvaging my thumb and index finger. Consequently, all the digits on my right hand are much smaller than normal. My thumb is about 1½ inches, and my index finger is almost the same size. The middle finger is just over 2 inches, then the ring finger is 1½ inches, and the little finger is no more than an inch. They, too are frozen forever in a clenched position. The only digits that can move are the thumb and index finger, which I've lovingly dubbed the "pincher."

The task of giving me mobility in my arms proved just as daunting. Both elbows were locked in a bent position, not allowing them to hinge. Dr. Herbertson and his team of surgeons attempted to unlock them so that I could have use of my arms. If I could bend my arms and use my "pincher" I'd be able to dress myself, feed myself, turn the pages of the newspaper, write a letter. It would open up my world dramatically.

But the elbows wouldn't budge. I'd go to surgery, they'd test them successfully in the operating room, and several days later they'd freeze up again. The doctors were frustrated and wanted to do more, but eventually there came a point when they had to accept defeat.

"Delbert, this is the best we can do," Dr. Herbertson admitted.

"You're going to have to find a way to live with what you've got."

I was optimistic, and after having no use of my hands for the past year, I was anxious to experiment. The first task I could do with my "pincher" was pick up a pencil. Then by pushing my locked arms together, I could press my left hand to the right in order to steady the "pincher." Soon, with the help of my occupational therapists, Robbie and Vickie, I was actually able to write letters on a paper using that position. My penmanship wasn't very good, but the technique worked, and I became adept at it pretty quickly. That was a major breakthrough in my fight for independence. I was so proud and happy that I could do such a simple task. It gave me a glimmer of hope; just the smallest little flicker that my life might have some measure of normalcy.

With my elbows frozen at a 90-degree angle, feeding myself appeared to be an unreachable dream. Dr. Herbertson was really disappointed and was always looking for ways to help me adjust. He experimented with a strange looking gadget that strapped onto my arm. It had a slot where I could put a spoon or fork. But there were a few problems with his invention. One…I wasn't able to apply any pressure and couldn't get any leverage on the fork, so the food just kept moving around on my plate. And two…by not being able to move my elbow, it took me forever to get the fork up to my head. And three…by the time I got the fork into my mouth, the food would be all over the floor. I practiced and practiced with this mechanical feeding machine, giving it the old college try, but I just never got the hang of it.

I never gave up the dream though. It's not that I didn't appreciate the help so many people gave me. If it weren't for others taking the time to help me eat, I'd still be hooked up to a feeding tube. I was grateful, yes, but I knew I couldn't go on that way forever. I had to find a way to do it myself. So I came up with my own system. It's routine to me now, after all these years, but back then it took a lot of practice and a lot of patience.

I pick up a napkin with my "pincher," fold it into a triangle and put it over my left elbow. I retrieve the plate of food (any kind of plate—paper, plastic, even glass), and place it on the napkin. Then I raise my shoulders so that my left arm comes up to my face. It provides the perfect angle for my mouth to reach the food. The only thing I can't do is cut up meat. So if I'm having a pork chop, or something that I could choke on, I need someone else to cut it into small pieces.

I'm just as adept with beverages. I lock both arms together, and pick up the bottle or glass with my forearms. Then, using my shoulders, and bending my head, I bring the drink to my mouth, without spilling a drop.

What a gift…to be able to feed myself and drink without help. I can take as much time as I want, savor the flavors and really enjoy the experience of a delicious meal. Just like everybody else.

TWENTY-EIGHT

FAITHFUL SERVANT

When I was transferred to the medical floor, I often had a roommate named Keith. Keith was 24 years old and had bladder cancer. He would spend about a week at a time in the hospital, then go home for awhile, only to return again sometime later. We got to be pretty good friends, and I missed him each time he was released. But whenever Keith had to be re-admitted to the hospital, he'd ask if his "old" room was available so that he and I could be together. He had a real pretty young wife named Sheila, and he was worried about dying and leaving her all alone. We spent many hours talking about our families, worrying about the future, fighting back the pain, and encouraging each other. It was amazing to me how we bonded over our troubles, and we were convinced that unless they'd been in our shoes, no one else could understand our feelings. Keith put up a good fight, but the cancer kept growing, and eventually they had to transfer him up to the 4th floor cancer wing.

One night Rob, the orderly, came in and told me that he didn't think Keith was going to make it, but he wanted to see me. So Rob went up to the fourth floor and brought Keith down to my room. He brought him in, bed and all. I hardly recognized my friend. Keith had been a pretty big guy, about 6'2". But now he looked like an old man in a shrunken, emaciated shell of a body.

"Hi Delbert." It was hard for him to talk.

"I'm bad off," he sighed.

Knowing how weak he was, I carried the conversation for both of us. I told him how much he meant to me and to have faith, but mostly how sorry I was for what he was going through. He was so listless and drugged up on morphine that he could hardly keep his eyes open, but he had wanted to see me, and I was so glad he did. As Rob wheeled him out of the room, I choked back the tears as I said goodbye. My good friend, Keith, died during the night.

The days took on a new routine. Bandage changes, iodine baths, skin grafts, hand surgery, rehabilitation. They all ran together. And after a year of feeling helpless, it was a welcome relief to have so much activity to look forward to.

Since St. Joseph's was a teaching hospital, Dr. Feller would often bring in a group of medical students to look at my injuries. He'd pull back the sheets, and they'd examine me from head to toe, snapping photos, taking notes, and asking questions. I don't remember any of them looking appalled at my appearance, even though they had never seen anyone burned as badly as I was. They were mainly curious about my level of pain. When they questioned me, I answered honestly, "A lot of pain." Still, a year after the fire, my body was not healed, and the pain was constant. I didn't mind them asking, and I didn't mind them examining me as I lay on the bed, exposed. If those young interns could learn something from my case that would help another burn victim, then I was all for it.

When I was able to be moved, Dr. Feller began taking me to his lectures in the big hospital auditorium, where he would display my wounds and explain the treatment he was doing. He even sent me to nearby University of Michigan Hospital, where burn experts asked me questions and reviewed my progress. By getting me out in public and exposing me to the stares and questions of others, Dr. Feller was extending his treatment to my emotional health as well. He tried to reduce my embarrassment over my appearance by pushing me into situations where I was forced to interact with people. And he gave a booster shot to my confidence when he started referring to me as "his star patient." His efforts paid off, as I slowly became more comfortable around strangers. I even started to believe that I could get past my insecurities and return to society. I had been so consumed with my own problems for so long, that it was good to be able to focus on something else for a change.

Dr. Richards, too, could sense that I needed to feel useful in order to heal mentally. That's why she came to me and asked if I would talk to other burn victims to share my experience and offer them support. I'd always been shy, and now, with my disfigurement, I'd be even worse, but her offer appealed to me. I was eager to share what I'd gone through if it would help someone else.

The first person that I reached out to was a man named Gus who had been burned over 30 percent of his body in a motorcycle accident. Dr. Richards said that he was really struggling and couldn't accept his injuries. She took me up to his room and introduced us, then left us alone to talk. Gus was not much older than me and had a real pretty wife. It seemed like every patient I met had an attractive spouse at home. That gave us one more thing in common. I had a pretty wife, too. And I was just as scared of losing her as Gus was about his own wife.

Dr. Richards was certainly right about Gus. He was angry, bitter, depressed…all the emotions I'd experienced. At first I didn't say much to him. I simply listened to him talk about the stress on his family and the fear that he experienced. He was amazed that I was as calm as I seemed. When he saw the extent of my injuries, he realized that the damage to his own body didn't even come close. He had burns that would be covered by clothing. His hands and feet were still useful. He hadn't lost any mobility. His face had been spared and remained untouched. The image in his mirror didn't look like a monster.

"How can you go on living when you look like that?" he asked. "Don't you ever want to give up and die?"

I explained how my heart had stopped on three different occasions, and infection had almost taken me several other times. Certainly I had felt like I wanted to die over the last few months. Too often, to be honest. But now at St. Joseph's, I felt strong and brave. I was determined to live, to be able to hold my babies. I planned to help them with their homework, and watch them go to their first prom. I said I was going to provide emotional support for my family the way they had supported me during these many, many months in the hospital. And I told him that I believed that God had a plan for me and that's why I was still alive.

I saw Gus several more times over the next few weeks, and each time we met, we'd talk about what we each had to be thankful for, and we prayed that God would help him accept his injuries. When he came to say goodbye a month later, I was sorry to see him go. I would miss him, and I told him so. But I was happy for him, too. Happy that he was going home to his family and happy that I'd played a small role in his recovery.

By counseling Gus, I realized that I could provide comfort, encouragement, and tough love lessons to others suffering from medical issues. Perhaps that was going to be my calling. I felt empowered by the fact that the staff was striving every day to improve my quality of life. With my wounds finally healing, could my emotional scars be far behind? I believed I was going to survive, and through the process, I think I had figured out why God had saved me. Within my charred, disfigured body was a man who could help others rediscover their will to live. And maybe that was God's plan all along.

TWENTY-NINE

THE BEST MEDICINE

I'd been in the hospital now for almost two years, and it had become my home...my shelter...my cocoon of safety. The staff and my family were accustomed to seeing my wounds, and they accepted my disfigurement. They knew there was more to Delbert McCoy than just a charred shell and a diminished body. Their acceptance of me in my present state allowed me to forget from time to time that I was different. It was only when outsiders saw me for the first time that I'd get a harsh dose of reality. The look on a stranger's face, the fear and confusion in their eyes, reminded me that what they saw was a far different version of the person I thought I was.

Just before the holidays, Dr. Feller surprised me during his morning rounds.

"Delbert, how would you like to go home for Christmas?"

His suggestion both thrilled and petrified me at the same time. Of course, I wanted to go home. I longed to hold my little girls, to taste my mother's home cooking, to visit with friends. But the thought of leaving the protection of my hospital room left me anxious and frightened.

Dr. Feller was pretty determined though, saying he felt it would be therapeutic for me to be with my family for Christmas.

"Two days is all you can have," he said. "But I think it will do you a lot of good."

I wasn't convinced, however. The fear of rejection from my loved ones and total strangers overwhelmed me. I kept thinking about an incident that happened a few months earlier, and the memory made me skeptical that Dr. Feller's plan would work. I had been sitting in the hallway, outside my room, part of my daily routine to break up the monotony of the tedious hospital stay. I often sat out there and watched visitors go by. Most of them glanced away when they noticed me. A few stared, obviously shocked at my appearance. But this was a hospital, after all, and you could see most anything within these walls. One visitor, an older man who was probably in his seventies, looked right at me as he walked by. He didn't turn away or ignore me, although I wished he had.

"I guess you won't need a mask for Halloween," he joked.

I was stunned. And I couldn't even respond. It certainly wasn't funny to me. It was devastating. It was like a knife driven into my heart. All the things I feared about people's reactions and acceptance of my appearance had come true.

I'm sure he didn't intend to be mean. It was probably just his feeble attempt at humor, when in fact he was feeling extremely uncomfortable. But the harsh words of a perfect stranger would stay with me for the rest of my life. I would learn eventually that my appearance would make many people not only uncomfortable, but fearful as well. The thought of exposing myself to more ridicule and stares crippled me and kept me tethered to the safety of the hospital.

"I don't want to go home," I confided to my father.

But he wasn't going to let me off that easy. He knew I was afraid, and he understood why. He'd sat by my bed for two whole years watching me struggle with the ups and downs of the healing process; so there wasn't much that he didn't know about me. While he appreciated how frightened I was, he also knew that I had to face my fears sooner or later. There was no way around it. I couldn't stay in the hospital forever. So my wise and knowing father ignored my protests, looked directly into my eyes and announced, "Of course you do. You belong at home with us."

Napoleon was equally dismissive of my concerns. "Man, you are the same Delbert Ray you've always been," he emphasized. "Anybody can see that in five seconds. If someone doesn't like how you look, then ignore them. Don't pay them any mind."

My brother Ball also jumped on the bandwagon, promising to personally deal with anyone who had something to say about my looks. Ball had become my personal assistant, confidante, and bodyguard. No one would dare say anything unkind with Ball around. They might think it, but they sure weren't going to say it. Napoleon and my family made it clear that they were taking me home to enjoy Christmas, not to dwell in self-pity.

Since Dr. Feller told me I could only be out of the hospital for two days, I had to pack in as much as I could in a short time. Rodney Reno and Ball came to the hospital to pick me up, and the first place we went to was my parent's store. It had been two years since I'd seen my old neighborhood, and it seemed as if everything had changed in my absence. Dad had purchased the place on Chicago and Grand River while I was hospitalized, and as we drove up to the front door, it tickled me to see the neon sign that read "Al and Mae's Party Store."

People are often perplexed that they can't remember important historical dates or events, but they can remember what kind of cake they had, and who attended their 10th birthday party. But that makes sense to me because you remember what's important to you. The gathering of family and friends and the good times that you have with them are usually the most significant aspects of your life. And that's the way it should be.

What was most vivid in my mind is how wonderfully all those I was closest to treated me on my first trip home. My neighborhood pals all showed up, including Lamont "Pug" Lawrence and his brother Alan, or "Preacher" as we called him. It was meaningful to me that he was there because Preacher had donated some of his skin for grafting right after the fire. The house was constantly full of friends and well-wishers who stopped by just to say hello. My sisters, Gwen and Jackie, were home from school, and Uncle Treetop and Aunt Pauline came over and joined my mother in an around-the-clock cooking marathon.

Nobody cared that I couldn't pour my own beer, or throw a baseball, or even tie my own shoes. We talked, joked, and made fun of each other, just like we always did. It was well past midnight before the party broke up. My brothers and friends all slept on the floor downstairs, and I slept

AUNT PAULINE, UNCLE TREETOP,
AND SISTER GWEN

on the couch because I couldn't climb the stairs to go up to my room. It was easier just to stay at ground level.

In hindsight, it was probably the most memorable holiday I ever experienced, because for the first time in my life I was soaking in every moment as if it might be my last. Once you have cheated death, you enjoy the sound of laughter more than you ever have in the past. You wonder why you never realized how cute your sisters were, or how loving your mother was. You feel bad that you never told your brothers how much you admired them. Once you cheat death, you appreciate the dawning of each new day, and look forward to every beautiful sunrise and the promise of joy that it brings.

That first day at home was so special, so absolutely perfect, it erased all the pain of the last two years, and I didn't want it to end. We all woke up the next morning to the wondrous smells of a big country breakfast. When Uncle Treetop, Aunt Pauline, and Mama had finished filling up the table, they stepped back to admire their culinary masterpiece. With scrambled eggs piled high, along with pans full of large flaky biscuits, thick sausages, steaming pancakes, stacks of bacon, and mounds of grits, the breakfast looked like a work of art to my eyes.

My homecoming was perfect because my family had unconditional acceptance of my limitations. They didn't tiptoe around my injuries. They treated me like Delray, the same guy who had left two years earlier. They acted normal, and I desperately needed normalcy. Ball took charge of my personal care, as he had done many times in the hospital. He helped me to the bathroom, bathed me, and changed my bandages. My family showed me that while my life would be different because of the fire, it could still be rewarding and meaningful. Dr. Feller was right. My trip back home over the holidays in 1970 was without a doubt, the best medicine I could have received at the time.

Yvonne and our little girls were living with her mother, Bernice, a couple of miles from my parents. My family had planned for me to go visit my wife and daughters even before I had convinced myself that I was ready for that step; so my sisters went shopping and bought two baby dolls for me to give to Monique and Kim. I knew everyone was anxious for me to see my babies, and I certainly was, too. I had a photo of them on the wall next to my bed at the hospital, and occasionally they would accompany Yvonne when she came to visit. But I never got to hold them, or sit them on my lap, or put my face against their curls the way I longed to do. I was comfortable in my parents' living room, but I wasn't sure I would feel the same level of ease and acceptance if I ventured over to my mother-in-law's house. My family understood that I needed a push to get out the door, but it was Napoleon who took charge and announced that he was going to drive me over to see the girls.

My fears were renewed once again as I wondered how my children would react to the sight of their deformed father. I wasn't sure how I would respond if they couldn't bear to look at me. But Napoleon gave me no chance to back out. He was sensitive to my fears and accepted that I was worried about how my daughters would handle our reunion. But he wasn't just going to chauffer me over there. He was going with me, to stand by me, to support me, and to make sure that I was comfortable. When we were kids, Napoleon was always with me on the porch, sharing doughnuts, guzzling milk, and reading the newspaper on Sunday mornings. It's certainly true that a man learns who his real friends are during times of crisis and tragedy—who he can count on to stand by him when he needs them the most. Napoleon was that kind of friend. He was with me during my long hospitalization and recovery, and today, as I ventured into "dangerous" territory, he would be my wing man.

THIRTY

A Christmas Angel

lways a man of style and flair, Napoleon returned in his 1967 lime green Cadillac convertible with white leather interior, sporting a joyous holiday attitude.

"I'm going to bring a little Christmas cheer to Yvonne and her family," he laughed, holding up a bottle of Martel cognac.

I had been in my friend's car many times and always enjoyed the ride, but this time was different. I had never been as nervous as I was on that cold, wintry night. I couldn't stop thinking about how Monique and Kim were going to react. Would they be embarrassed or ashamed of me? Would they be able to see beyond my disfigurement and know that I was still their Daddy, who loved them? How would I comfort them so that they wouldn't be frightened? How long would it take before they could accept me this way?

Only the flashing red light of a police car behind us snapped me out of my troubled thoughts. Napoleon had no idea why we were being pulled over, because we weren't speeding. As the two Detroit policemen approached the car, I suddenly realized where we were—at the intersection of Joy and Dexter, a few yards from the Marathon station where two desperate men had purchased the gallon of gasoline and had thrown the match which ignited the fire that altered my life forever. We were only two blocks away from where the Soul Expressions dance hall once stood.

A chill swept over me, a sense of dread, as my buddy rolled down his window to talk to the police.

"What's the trouble, officers?" Napoleon asked respectfully.

"You have a busted tail light," one of them replied.

"Oh, I'm sorry, I didn't know that," Napoleon said, quickly explaining that we were only a short distance from Yvonne's place and that he would fix it in the morning. By then, he had handed the policeman his license and registration, and the other officer was peering into our car with his flashlight. Probing the front seat, he noticed the bottle of brandy, and immediately ordered Napoleon out of the car.

"You're drunk!" He accused.

Despite his protests that he hadn't had a single drink, the officer persisted.

"You're being arrested for having an open bottle of liquor in the car," the officer said, as he forced Napoleon to turn around with his hands behind his back.

"The seal on the cognac isn't even broken," Napoleon insisted. "I was just taking it over as a gift."

The police weren't listening. One officer was patting down Napoleon while the other explored the caddy more thoroughly, probably looking for drugs or weapons. He found neither. We had nothing except one unopened bottle of Christmas cheer and two baby dolls that I was taking to my daughters. It had been only three and half years since the Detroit riots. The two officers were white, in their late twenties, or early thirties, and we were young black men. The undercurrent of racial tension was still strong in one of the city's toughest neighborhoods in 1970. I'm sure that they thought we were up to no good.

"My friend is handicapped, he just got out of the hospital," Napoleon explained. "You can see how messed up he is, he can't drive. He can't even walk."

I tried to raise my locked arms to show them that I didn't have use of my hands, and the cast on my left leg and bandages on my chest were obvious.

"He doesn't have a coat, and he'll freeze to death if you leave him out here," Napoleon argued. "I've got to take him back home."

But the officers appeared to show little concern for my situation, as one of them got into the driver's side, and I pleaded with him to take me home or call someone in my family. I told him about the fire that had occurred just a couple of blocks from where we were and that I had been in the hospital for two years.

"I'm scared to death to be left alone in the dark; I can't help myself," I pleaded.

But he ignored my request, as he drove our car up a few feet so that it wouldn't block the alley entrance. While one officer handcuffed Napoleon, as if he were a hardened criminal, his partner climbed out of the car, put it in park, turned off the ignition and ordered me to "Get home the best way you can."

I couldn't believe what was happening to us. The last thing I saw of my friend, he was put in the back seat of the police cruiser and the officers drove him away. They never wrote down my phone number, or even called in my situation to the police dispatcher. As far as the police were concerned, I didn't exist. I was stunned that the very men who were sworn to protect us would leave me in such a dangerous and life threatening situation, especially on Christmas Eve.

Keys were left dangling in the ignition, but I couldn't drive. I couldn't even start the car to get some heat. It was relatively early in the evening, with a few people out and about, so I was optimistic that someone would stop to help me. But at the same time, I was afraid. I knew the neighborhood. It was dangerous—a high crime area, where drug dealers, gangs, and pimps were the warlords of the territory. I didn't know who I could trust, and the Cadillac had power windows so I couldn't even roll one down to scream for help. As strangers hurried by, most of them paid little attention to me. Even when they heard me banging on the window with my elbow, they simply turned away and kept walking. I was getting more desperate by the minute.

After about an hour, since I wasn't dressed for the extreme weather, and I had so little body fat to provide insulation, the cold became unbearable and the panic level increased. My teeth were chattering and I shivered uncontrollably, just like when I was in the hospital when the infection had ravaged my body.

"Was this the way I was supposed to die?"

After two grueling years in the hospital, recovering from the terrible burns from the Soul Expressions explosion…having survived extensive debridement, horrific pain, dozens of skin grafts, countless blood transfusions, heart stoppage, terrible infections, and a thousand-to-one odds. Was I destined to die alone on a cold, dark, dangerous street on Christmas Eve, simply because I couldn't start the car? The irony didn't escape me. After almost being burned alive, was I now going to freeze to death?

I couldn't believe it. How could I be in the wrong place at the wrong time…again?

"God help me…please," I prayed.

Miraculously, soon after, I saw a young woman walk by the alley. I was so relieved and excited that I began loudly knocking on the window to draw her attention. Startled, she glanced my way, and it looked as if she was going to hurry off, just as the others had.

The fear that she would leave spurred me into action, as I eagerly held up my bandaged arms to show her that I was harmless.

"Please help me," I begged. "I'm freezing."

She was rightfully cautious as she approached the vehicle, but when she saw that I was disabled, some of the fear left her eyes, and she opened the door so we could talk. I honestly can't say that I would have done the same, given the circumstances. But I'm very grateful that she overcame her suspicions and fear to help a complete stranger. Even though I never got her name, I'm convinced that God sent me a Christmas angel that frigid, dark night.

"There's a phone at the Marathon station on the corner," I informed her.

Will you please call my wife, so someone can come for me?" How ironic that the Marathon station, which had supplied the gasoline that nearly killed me, was now going to provide the helping hand I needed to survive.

Naturally, Yvonne was stunned when she got a phone call from a stranger saying that I was stranded in the cold just a short distance from her home. Her brother, Arthur, was visiting at the time, and he literally ran the two blocks to the car. Then he drove me to Yvonne's mother's, where she and Yvonne wrapped me in blankets and gave me hot tea to drink until the warmth returned to my body.

By then, my fear had been replaced by anger and concern over what had happened to Napoleon. My family called his mother, who immediately went down to the station to check on him and make sure he was being treated properly. She called us back to say that he had to spend Christmas Eve in jail, but he would be released the next day.

Although I suffered harrowing moments, courtesy of two insensitive police officers, the Christmas of 1970 still remains one of my favorite memories.

That was the Christmas I learned to fully appreciate the sights, sounds, and smells of the holiday season. It was the Christmas when I realized that family, love, and friendship should never be taken for granted. It was the Christmas when I discovered that there is always hope for a better tomorrow. No matter how bleak a situation may look, a human being can survive if he or she believes that the sun will shine on a new day.

I gained inner-strength and confidence as a result of that two-day reprieve, just as Dr. Feller predicted. My parents, my family, and my friends, made it crystal clear that they wouldn't desert me, and I wouldn't be alone on the long journey ahead. Although my body and face were scarred and forever altered, they looked deep into my soul, beyond the disfigurement, pledging to stand by me, love me, and protect me...even if I wasn't the best looking guy in the room.

Part
Two

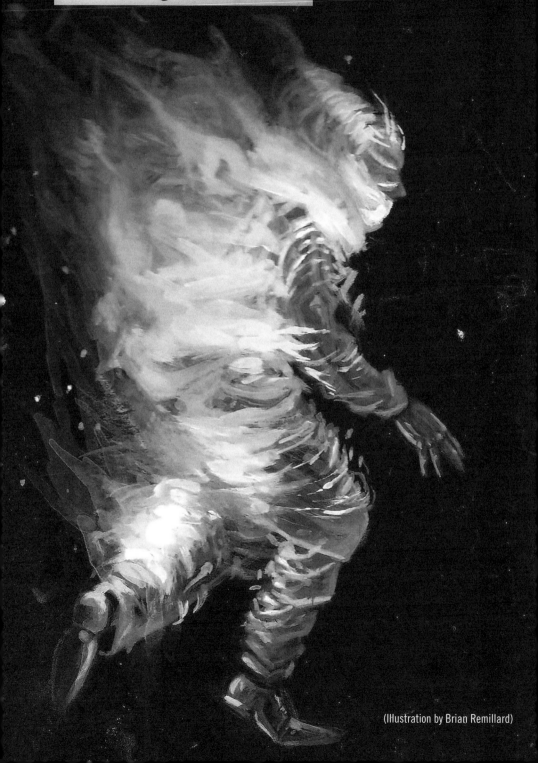

Teen tells of terror
in blazing dance hall

(Illustration by Brian Remillard)

THIRTY-ONE

NEW BEGINNING

*L*ike most people, I don't have any trouble remembering the happiest day of my life. July 21, 1971, I went home for good. I had been in the hospital for 893 days. Two and a half years of my life had been spent in a hospital bed, and the experience left me with mixed feelings.

As a patient, you give up all your individual rights to independence and free thinking. You are forced to rely on your doctors and caregivers for your every need. I had to eat on their schedule, sleep on their schedule, visit with my family on their schedule. I couldn't take a pill whenever I wanted, go for a walk, get a glass of water, eat a sandwich, wash my face, or even go to the bathroom, unless I got permission. The hospital had become my own personal prison, and I had been an "inmate" so long, I almost forgot the everyday freedoms I had taken for granted for the first nineteen years of my life. How was I going to adjust to living without nurses assisting me and doctors directing my care? Who would tell me when to wake up and when to go to sleep? Who would force me to walk everyday or practice bending my arms?

It's not that I didn't appreciate the care I'd received under Dr. Feller's leadership. Certainly I did. The doctors and nurses who had worked tirelessly the past months had saved my life. Plus I had grown fond of every one of them. We spent so much time together that they had become like family, and I knew I would miss them terribly. It had taken an army of health care professionals to get me to this point…doctors, nurses, aides, physical therapists, lab technicians, dieticians, interns, radiologists, and volunteers. I had relied on their expertise and training at a time when I was totally helpless, and couldn't get through one day without them. How on earth was I going to make it on my own?

Those were the doubts and fears I wrestled with as I said goodbye to Dr. Feller and thanked the staff at St. Joseph's Hospital. After being on hold for two and a half years, my life was moving forward, and as I left the sterile safety of the hospital, I went home to the loving environment of a supportive family.

Of course, my family had planned a big celebration for my homecoming. All the women and Uncle Treetop spent the whole day cooking turkey with dressing, sweet potatoes, black-eyed peas, collared greens, plus cobbler and banana pudding. Mama was happy to be able to cook my favorite dishes again, and as usual, she prepared enough to feed the whole neighborhood. Many of them were there anyway, along with most of my friends—Pug, Shorty, Preacher, and Napoleon. Plus Yvonne and the girls, Aunt Pauline, Ball, June, Slow, Jackie, Gwen, and some of the cousins.

The party lasted late into the night, and when the last guests left, Mama made coffee and the family sat around the table and talked …just like old times.

My parents knew that I was nervous about being home on my own, and they understood my fears about being dependant on others for my needs. I didn't want to move back in with Yvonne and my daughters until I was better able to take care of myself. Right then, I was still feeling too vulnerable, and I didn't want to be an added burden to my young wife. I figured she had enough to do with raising two small children.

"Don't you worry about a thing," Mama assured me.

"You've got us to help you now, you're going to be just fine."

I still needed a lot of help with ordinary, everyday tasks. Ball would come over after work to continue my therapy and help me get into the tub every night. Walking exercise was crucial to keep my feet from becoming permanently immobile. As I couldn't use a cane or crutches, since I didn't have the use of my hands, I relied heavily on my brother

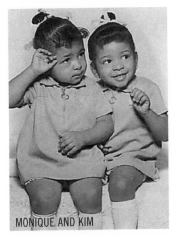

MONIQUE AND KIM

and friends to lead me wherever I needed to go. I couldn't dress myself; so Mama or Gwen had to help me with that task. Getting my pants on and off was difficult, since my one foot was deformed, and of course, with no fingers, I couldn't pull up the zipper. Because my elbows were bowed and locked, my shirt wouldn't go on easily, and it was impossible to do the buttons without assistance.

I hadn't quite conquered the challenge of feeding myself yet either, so it was usually one of the women in my life…Mama, Gwen, or Yvonne who helped with my meals. Supper became a special time when Monique and Kim would shovel potato chips and other treats into my mouth. They got a kick out of feeding "Daddy," and I embraced the times we laughed and shared meals together. They were so young at the time, they didn't have any trouble adapting to feeding me. They didn't even know that it was abnormal. Didn't all children hand-feed their father? And that's how they learned to tie their shoes, too. They got plenty of practice tying mine. They'd make the crooked little loops over and over again, while I sat patiently explaining how to pull the laces through the knot. With inquisitive minds, like most children, they focused on the task at hand, not content until they succeeded. They never tired of trying, but I didn't mind. I wasn't going anywhere.

The one area that would prove to be the most humbling would be using the bathroom. There was no way I could attempt it on my own; so I timed "toilet breaks" to coincide with Ball's visits or if Pug, or one of my friends were at the house. I was too proud and embarrassed to have my sisters or mother assist me. It was humiliating enough to have to rely on help from the males in my life, but I got used to it after a few weeks.

With all my physical needs being taken care of, my emotional needs were being nourished as well. I received repeated reassurance from everyone around me. My friends knew that the adjustment period was going to be a challenge, and they made sure that I was never left alone to wallow in self-pity. I was so fortunate to have the support of my relatives and friends. They never let me down. All those days I was laying in the hospital, their dedication and strength helped me pull through. And now that I was home, they reassured me that they'd always be there for me—for now, and for as long as I needed them. I felt truly blessed to be born into the McCoy family.

As supportive as my family was in every way, there were still some issues that even they couldn't help me with. Two major problems continued to haunt me, and it was a constant battle to keep an upbeat attitude until they were resolved. Finding the means to support my family and discovering how to comfortably go out in public were the two stumbling blocks that became my mental crutches. I had always prided myself as being a "giver," not a "taker," yet now I was not only dependent on others for my physical needs, but I couldn't support myself financially or repay my parents for all that they'd done for me.

Fortunately, I did have a minimal income in the form of government assistance. A new law enacted in 1967, changed the eligibility requirements for social security recipients. It allowed people under the age of twenty-four to receive disability benefits if they had worked one and a half years of the last three years prior to their injuries. Since I had been employed for nearly two years by Chrysler Corporation before the fire, I was one of the youngest people in the nation to be eligible for assistance. The check I received from social security was for $183 per month. And although I was grateful for the monthly stipend, it was less than half the amount I earned in one week when I was gainfully employed with the auto companies. Not being able to work and make an honest living gnawed at my conscience, and I spent many "moody" days and nights worrying about it.

Figuring out how I could earn a living while being disabled was further complicated by the fear I had of being seen by the public. I had become comfortable being around my family and friends, and they accepted my altered appearance and shortcomings, but the thought of leaving the security of my home and exposing myself to the ridicule of others left me paralyzed with self-doubt. As usual, it was those I knew best that helped me overcome this hurdle as well. They had been encouraging me for months to get out of the house and back into the real world, but I wasn't budging from my comfort zone. It was much easier for me to forget how I looked when I was at home surrounded by family. They didn't treat me any different than before. But I knew that others would

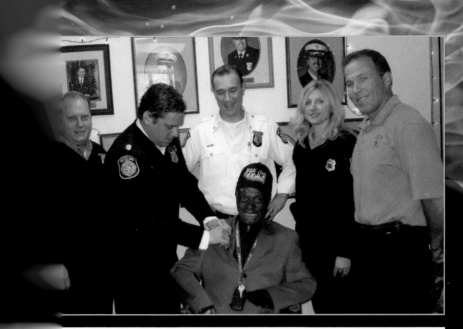

Michael J. Reddy of the Westland Fire Department designated me an ~~rary~~ fireman as he pinned on my badge. Also pictured: Assistant Chief ~~Czpara~~, Scott Lucas, Captain Colleen Fedel, and Captain John Adams.

Former *ABC World News* co-anchor, Bob Woodruff with his wife and business partner, Lee. Their best-selling book, *In an Instant,* a family's journey of love and healing, is something I can relate to very well.

Detroit Tiger great Willie Horton labeled me "an athlete of life."

Joe Girard, "The World's Greatest Salesman," referred as one of the world's most inspirational persons. We grew up in Detroit and are proud of our Motor City he Also pictured is the always helpful Blake Knight.

The Early Show good guy, Mark McEwen, formerly on CBS, is very passion-ate about spreading stroke awareness after suffering his own a few years back.

I hope to be as inspirational a speaker as Hall of Famer Les Brown has been as "The Motivator."

Lion, Hall of Famer, Joe Schmidt, has always been one of my
...letes because of his championship leadership and ability to with-

Celebrating Motown's 50th anniversary with legends: Martha Reeves, Duke Fakir, and Elaine Powell.

Del Reddy and I shared some laughs with "America's funniest multi-talented and versatile Pulitzer Prize winning, Dave Barry.

Internationally acclaimed life-transformer, Dr. Wayne Dyer, and I both grew up in the city of Detroit.

With Senior Pastor Henry Covington of Pilgrim Church/I am my Brother's Keeper Ministries of Detroit, who is portrayed in Mitch Albom's book, *Have a Little Faith*.

For many years I played over in my mind how I was consumed by flames that were never extinguished by water, but as time went on, then and now, I feel I am unbelievably blessed to have lived so long. Every single day I have the opportunity to make an enduring and profound difference in people's lives.

It is very gratifying to annually address Dr. Molly McCelland's University of Detroit Mercy class of nursing students and other such fine groups around the country.

Born without a right hand, major league baseball pitcher, Jim Abbott, is one of the most amazing and inspirational athletes of all-time.

Backstage with Mitch Albom at his fundraising event featuring iconic baseball broadcaster, Ernie Harwell. Like Mitch, I am proud to have created my own foundation, The Fire In My Soul.

Having a great time at the Michigan Sports Hall of Fame with my fiancée, Renée, and television legend, Bill Bonds.

not be so gentle. I didn't want to be reminded of how my appearance had changed, and I couldn't bear the thought of leaving myself vulnerable to the stares and mean-spirited comments of strangers. Simply put, I just didn't want to go through the mental pain of trying to fit into a perfect world while trapped in an imperfect body.

Nate and Ball knew my feelings on the subject, but they were relentless about getting me back to resuming a normal life. One evening they ignored my protests and drove over to take me out to a downtown pub.

"I don't want to go," I pleaded. "Please don't make me."

But my big brother just picked me up and carried me out to the car. I kicked and complained the whole time, helpless to do anything to stop them, and I let them know that I'd never forgive them for kidnapping me.

Not wanting to be literally carried into the club, I leaned against my abductors and allowed them to guide me through the door. We quickly found a table and ordered a round of drinks.

What a strange sensation that was. After two and a half years of hospital restrictions, there I was sitting in a tavern and sipping a beer with my pals. I was still too self-conscious to take my jacket or hat off, but as the minutes ticked by, I noticed something astonishing. No one was paying any attention to me—or the way I looked. No one was staring, or pointing, or whispering, or making rude remarks. As a matter of fact, nobody cared one way or the other that Delbert McCoy was in the pub that night. All the horrible things that I had imagined in my mind didn't happen. For the first time, I began to feel that maybe life in the real world wouldn't be so bad after all.

But sitting in a dimly lit corner with my friends was a far cry from going out in public and actually talking to people that I didn't know. That scenario seemed very unlikely to happen, given that I never left the security of my family and friends. But once again, my father provided me with the opportunity to do just that.

Knowing how important it was for me to earn an income and how equally important it was for me to function in unfamiliar surroundings, Daddy found a way for me to do both. He hired me to work in the party store. Already a family operation, with even Uncle Treetop working part-time, it was just natural that I join the group. My first assignment was to watch the front door, which was probably Dad's way of getting me used to being at the store and around people. My duties were limited to greeting folks as they came in and wishing them a "good day" when they left. And although I was nervous and uncomfortable in the beginning, I eventually became more confident and relaxed around strangers. What a huge leap of faith that was for my father though. Having me work in the store, with my physical handicaps and disfigurement, could have cost him much needed revenue. I'm certain that some patrons were uncomfortable seeing me, and a fair share of them probably took their business somewhere else. But that didn't deter my father. He was going to help his son get acclimated to the real world, and whoever didn't like it didn't need to shop at Al and Mae's Party Store.

I worked hard at being upbeat and confident so that Daddy's faith in me wouldn't go unrewarded. And after a few weeks, when I was just getting comfortable with my position, I received a promotion. This time I was assigned to the counter, where I would need to learn how to operate the cash register. There was a lot of trial and error before I came up with a method that worked, but eventually I was able to deposit the money into the drawer and make change by removing the bills with my "pincher" and a pencil eraser. I couldn't pick up the money, since I didn't have the use of my hand, but I could nudge it out of the drawer and was able to get it to the counter where the customer could retrieve their change. It was a painstakingly slow process initially, but the customers were very patient and accepted the fact that I was doing the best I could. And eventually I became pretty adept as a cashier.

Working at the store was a huge step towards giving me the self-confidence to go out into the world. And it was wonderful to have a sense of independence once again. Al and Mae's Party Store became my "safe haven" where I found a degree of normalcy and happiness in doing something useful. Little did I know that my haven would become the scene of shock and horror that was yet to come.

THIRTY-TWO

MOTOR CITY MAYHEM

On the cold Saturday evening of Jan. 19, 1974, my sister, Gwen, answered the home phone and received the news that turned our family's world upside down once again.

"Ball and Cliff have been kidnapped," she cried, as the receiver fell from her hands.

Cliff was family friend, Clifford Riley, a Viet Nam veteran who was more like a cousin than a friend. We had grown up together. At 6 ft. 10 inches, Cliff had been a basketball star at Western High School, and after a tour in Viet Nam he was still clinging to the long-shot hope of becoming a pro player. In the meantime, my dad had hired him to clerk at the party store.

Crime was on the rise in Detroit in the 1970s. The 1973 energy crisis caused a slowdown in car sales, and Ford, Chrysler, and General Motors had laid off hundreds of workers. The Michigan economy was in a slump, and crime always increases when hope decreases. Gangs were terrorizing the neighborhoods with all manner of criminal activity, especially kidnapping and murder. Although the caller didn't identify himself, he had demanded $25,000 in exchange for the safe return of Cliff and Ball, leading us to believe that the abduction was gang related. They presumably believed that our family had money.

Daddy was at work at the store when we got the terrible news, but Mama was home, and she became hysterical with fear. We were all frightened and phoned our father right away. Daddy immediately called the police and told them that he would pay the ransom. He would use the store as collateral to secure a loan at the bank. But this was a weekend, and he wouldn't be able to get the cash until Monday. Sick with worry, my father and my oldest brother, June, stayed at the party store all night, hoping that the kidnappers would call back.

At the time, Ball was engaged to a lovely girl named Brenda Colvin, and they had a young son together named Derron. Someone had to tell Brenda about the abduction, and it was best to be done in person, so I reluctantly volunteered. My friend, Raymond, came over and drove me to her house. As we pulled out of our driveway, we noticed a suspicious vehicle drive by with three men we didn't recognize. We were in a hurry to get to Brenda's, so didn't pay them much attention, but to this day, I wonder if those three men could have been the kidnappers.

When we arrived at Brenda's home and told her what had happened, she wept uncontrollably. I tried to comfort her, but there was no consoling her. I was just as scared for my brother as she was, but I fought hard not to show it. "We've got to have faith in God," I told her. Before Raymond and I left, we instructed her to lock the doors and not answer to anyone but family members or the police.

Our family stayed up the entire night and waited by the phone. No one got any sleep or even cared to. But even though we waited anxiously, the kidnappers didn't call our home or the party store during the night, leaving us to fear the worst as hope dimmed.

By now, our mother was sick with worry for her son. Although she never would have admitted it, her children all believed she had a special spot in her heart for Ball. He was her favorite. Napoleon often said Ball was "one in a million." My brother was the most understanding guy in our group. He was a man of strong character, willing to stand up for his friends and family, always on our side. How could she not love Ball? He WAS special.

We spent the entire night worrying about Ball's safety, praising his virtues and sharing our favorite stories. When the phone finally rang the next morning, we answered it anxiously; ready to give the abductors whatever they wanted to get Ball and Clifford back. But it wasn't the kidnappers. It was the Detroit Police Department. An officer told my father that they had discovered the body of a young man on the corner of Columbus and Grand River. Judging by the extreme height, the officers had concluded it was Clifford. He had been shot, execution style, by a bullet to the back of the head.

The shocking news rocked us all. If Cliff was dead, then where was Ball? We knew it didn't look good, but we tried to remain optimistic, especially for Mama's sake.

"They'll let him go," I promised her. But she knew better.

"Ball is dead. I can see my son's face. My son is dead," she cried. "His eyes are open, but he can't see."

Although we all tried, none of us could comfort her. She cried for Clifford and cried for Ball, because she was convinced he, too was dead.

Early that afternoon we received the information that we'd all been dreading. Another body had been found. It was Ball. He also was executed. His body had been located in an abandoned house at the corner of Brighton and Chicago, killed in the same brutal manner as Clifford.

Our family was devastated by the reality of Ball's death; our grief more torturous by the knowledge that he had died senselessly and violently.

It would be many days before we learned the circumstances of the murders. It was only after police arrested one of the gang members in connection with another crime. They persuaded him to implicate the others involved in exchange for a lighter sentence. Eventually the entire gang was arrested. Through trial testimony, we found out that the gang had killed Clifford almost immediately because someone had a grudge against him, although we never found out why.

Once the killers shot Cliff, Ball told them that they might as well kill him too, because if they didn't, he was going to hunt them down and make them pay for what they did to Clifford. So they murdered Ball, too. We could all envision Ball reacting that way, even if his life was on the line. Ball was loyal to his friends, and he didn't back down.

The killers received mandatory life sentences, but our family never felt any satisfaction or justice. No punishment, no matter how severe, would ever bring our Ball back to us. We were already serving a life sentence of our own. The grief that my family felt over the murder of Ball was never-ending. My parents couldn't accept the loss of a child, and it was equally unnatural for Ball's brothers and sisters to be without our favorite sibling.

As we prepared for the funeral, we all talked about our favorite Ball moments, most of them related to the mischief we created as youngsters. But what I remembered most was how my brother never gave up on me when I was in the hospital. When I didn't want to get up to do my exercise, it had been Ball who forced me out of my bed. He wouldn't take "no" for an answer.

"You aren't going to get any better if you just lay there all day," he would reason, as he dragged me to my feet.

When he took charge in those situations, his strength became my strength. It nourished me. His positive attitude overruled my objections, and I tried even harder to walk, just so I wouldn't disappoint him. I owed him so much. But now I'd never be able to repay him. My brother was dead.

Luther "Ball" McCoy, November 12, 1948–January 20, 1974

THIRTY-THREE

Yvonne McCoy

*A*fter doing my own battle with depression, I was finally able to get my head on straight and think about the future. I hated being dependent on others, and although I appreciated and loved my mother for taking me in, I knew I needed to be on my own. I found a little bungalow that an elderly lady owned, which was walking distance to mother's. The house had two stories, and the woman lived downstairs while renting the upper level out to the girls and me. I was fortunate to have a steady job working at S & H Green Stamps as a cashier while Monique and Kim were in school. Delbert was still living with his parents, but he came over often to see our daughters.

It started innocently enough, as he would occasionally stay late, spend the night, then get up the next morning to go back to his parents. But pretty soon the overnights got to be more frequent, and it seemed like he was spending more time with us than he was with Albert and Essie. It just seemed right that he move in and we could be a "normal" family again.

The new arrangement proved to be a winner. The kids loved having him with us on a permanent basis, and I enjoyed his company. I had been alone too long.

He was pretty self-sufficient by this time and able to do most things without assistance. He still needed a little help with buttons or buckles, and the *girls helped him tie his shoes, but it was okay. They were happy to be of service, and he appreciated their support. It was good to have a man in the house again. Always a patient person, he would sit with the girls for hours and help them do their homework. Delbert was strict about their schooling, and wanted to make sure that they understood the importance of a good education. I was happy and content. It had been seven years since the fire, and seven years since we'd all lived together as a family. It was about time.*

At first our life was idyllic. We laughed and talked a lot and got along great. And in spite of what he thought about the subject, I never felt like he was a burden. We had high hopes of getting our life back on track. We even opened our own business called McCoy's Records and Boutique Shop. I would take the girls to school before going to work at Singer Sewing Machine Company, and Delbert would go to work at the record store. We weren't worried about money so much anymore, and eventually we were able to buy a nice tri-level home in Southfield. Monique and Kim were thrilled because they each got to have their own room. The house had a nice family room on the lower level, and we spent many happy hours there while my husband helped our daughters with their homework. He seemed happy and content, but I couldn't help noticing that he always had to have his friends around.

Delbert was just like his mother when it came to having a big heart. He was such a giving person, that he never turned anyone away. Many times I would come home from work to find one of his "buddies" sleeping on the couch, and sometimes there'd be a whole family staying with us.

In spite of how much we enjoyed being together, over the years things got worse. We fought a lot. Not about money or another woman, or some of the normal things couples fight about. We argued about his friends. I needed the comfort and security of our small family. He needed the companionship of the guys he had grown up with. I lost a lot of weight during this period, getting down to barely 100 lbs. And although his family and mine loved us both, neither tried to stop the inevitable. They realized that we were just too different. We married way too young, then were separated for too long due to the fire. We never really got the chance to grow together in the early years. And now it seemed too late. We had lots of false starts as far as separating. But when the principal called us to the office one day and told us that the girls' schoolwork was suffering, it was the last straw. We both knew that it wasn't healthy for us to continue living together.

The house was sold, and he moved back with his parents, and I took our daughters and moved back in with my mother. The divorce offered little satisfaction for me. I never wanted it to happen. And neither did he. We both missed being together as a family.

Daughters Monique and Kim

THIRTY-FOUR

A MOTHER'S LOVE

My mother wrote a poem when she was a young girl, and every Christmas she would recite it to the family. And no matter how many times her children heard their mother's words, they never grew weary of them. Mama had a warm smile and a big heart with plenty of love for everyone. But her children meant the world to her, and when Ball was killed, I believe that a piece of her soul died as well. She became a shell of her former self after her son was murdered. Having already been weakened by my suffering after the fire, she couldn't bear the pain of Ball's death and started the slow slide down into depression.

Then when Uncle Treetop died unexpectedly on Christmas morning a few years later, she declined even further. She withdrew into herself, and the simple pleasures of her life, such as watching her favorite television shows, *I Love Lucy* or *Gimme a Break,* didn't excite her much anymore. She would stare at the screen for hours, without hearing or seeing what was playing.

She still cooked for the family, but didn't eat much herself, and began losing a significant amount of weight. The family was worried and begged her to see a doctor, but she resisted vehemently. To this day, I believe that my mother knew, or at least suspected, she had a major health issue. She probably wanted to spare the rest of the family from any more grief and pain, which is why she wouldn't go to the doctor. But eventually she could no longer ignore the weakness that had consumed her and was admitted to Providence Hospital for tests. We were all there with her on her 66th birthday, June 27, 1988. Ordinarily a happy occasion, we were filled with fear and trepidation as we waited for the test results that would give us a definitive diagnosis. When the doctor called us into the hallway to speak to us privately, we knew it was going to be bad. Still, we weren't prepared for the crushing blow that was coming.

"She has pancreatic cancer," he said. "I'm sorry, she only has a short time left. There is no cure."

He told us that chemotherapy would slow it down, but eventually the cancer would consume her. My father, always a tower of strength, looked as if the blood had been drained from his body. He couldn't speak, unable to verbalize how he felt. He just never had imagined his life without mother. The rest of us cried and clung to each other in disbelief and confusion. How could this be happening again? First Ball, then Treetop, and now Mama. The shock of it was too much to bear.

We agreed not to tell Mama about her prognosis, believing it was better for her mental strength to have hope. So instead, we told her that she had a tumor, and that she needed chemotherapy to assure that it wouldn't come back. Over the next few weeks she would undergo several rounds of chemo, with the family always nearby. And when she was at home, there was always someone with her. We never left her alone for a minute. She was extremely weak and needed constant care. But none of us resented having to be there. We wanted to be. We cherished every additional moment that we had with her, and we spent long hours talking about our life together, our childhood, how much she meant to us. Those times were both joyous and melancholic at once. We were happy that we got extra time to spend with her, yet we also knew that the clock was ticking. We simply didn't have any idea of how much time she had left.

A lot of the triumphs I've had in my life were because of the support and encouragement of my biggest fan—my mother. Several years after getting out of the hospital, I received a degree in marketing from Liberty University by taking correspondence courses and pecking at computer keys with my pinched hand. It took four and a half years of staying up

Brothers and Sisters

nights studying, and it wasn't easy, but I did it. Mama always said that I was the smartest of her offspring, and she was determined that I go on to college. I just couldn't let her down. She didn't ask much from her children, but when she did, we wanted to do whatever we could to grant her wishes. That's why I ended up joining the church choir when I was eight years old, in spite of the fact that I couldn't even carry a tune. I knew I couldn't sing, in fact everyone knew it, but Mama wanted me in the choir; so that was that. I spent the next five years humming sheepishly in the front row.

You'd think that by having six children of her own, mother would have her fill of child rearing, but her heart was so big, she opened her arms to everyone else's child as well. She even raised four of her grandchildren: Maurice, Deron, Fred, and Tony, Jr. There was always room for one more, and Mamma and Daddy raised their grandchildren just as they did their own. The boys did the chores, learned the Bible, went to church, and drank Sanka coffee with the rest of us. Mama wouldn't have it any other way.

The memories that she and I shared will always be special to me. We would sit and talk for hours, just like we did when I was in the hospital. Almost every sentence began with the words...."Remember the time...?"

"Delbert, remember the time when you had your first girlfriend?"

I remembered. Her name was Clemetoria, and I was six years old. She lived across the street from us, and I had a pretty good case of "puppy love." I was so smitten, that in an attempt to impress her I would put grease on my head, slick my hair down smooth, stick my head out the window, and croon:

"Oh my darlin...oh my darlin...oh my darlin Clemetoria." I'd serenade her every night after school to the tune of *Clementine*. Maybe that's how Mama got the idea that I should join the church choir. She didn't want to see all that raw talent go to waste.

Nobody would ever have as much enthusiasm for my skills, or lack thereof, as my mother. That's why it was so hard for her to see me suffering when I was in the hospital, and that's why now I would do everything I could to take her mind off the pain and ease her torment. But sometimes it wasn't enough, and on one occasion, when she and I were alone together, she started to cry.

"Delray, I'm dying," she sobbed. "I know I am."

For my entire life my mother had been there for me offering extraordinary love and support. When I was in the hospital her words of comfort gave me strength to want to live. Now she was counting on me to comfort her.

"No, Mama. You're going to get well," I lied. "You have to be strong and put your faith in the Lord, just like you used to tell me to do. I got well, and you will too," I insisted.

But the truth haunted me, and when I was out of the room the tears wouldn't be contained. I cried and cried. Her time was coming, and even though we all knew it would be soon, I wasn't ready to accept it. I loved my mother and didn't want to see her suffer. But the pain of losing her brought back a flood of special memories. One in particular though made me smile through the tears.

Although I got into my share of mischief growing up, mother always stuck up for me. She welcomed my friends into our home, and we shared many happy moments drinking Sanka coffee together. The only time I was ever mad at my mama was the time I got in trouble for eating her banana pudding.

It was a Sunday. Daddy took my sisters to the store, and mother was in the kitchen making preparations for a big family dinner with all the cousins, aunts, and uncles at our house that afternoon. My brothers and I stayed home to clean and get ready for the company. I was about eight years old, and my favorite food in the whole world was my mama's banana pudding. The sweet smell of bananas and vanilla wafers filled the entire house, and it was hard for me to keep my mind on my chores. When the dessert was finished baking, mother put it out on the dining room table to cool. Then she went back into the kitchen to finish preparing the upcoming feast. While my brothers were distracted by their chores, I snuck into the dining room to admire her masterpiece. It was glorious to behold with big mounds of creamy golden pudding and luscious fruit. I had never been able to resist its powerful allure, and today was no exception. I tip-toed into the kitchen to get a fork, but Mama didn't notice. Sneaking back into the dining room, I stuck the fork in the meringue and gulped a mouthful of heaven. Just one bite…that's all I wanted. No one would ever notice. But as the frothy texture melted on my tongue, I knew I was doomed. Giving in to temptation, I grabbed the bowl and slipped under the table, pulling the tablecloth down around me. I knew I didn't have much time, and my heart was racing in my chest. I was living dangerously and could be discovered at any time; so I shoveled scoops of the stolen dessert as fast as I could swallow. The anxiety of being discovered magni-fied my desire for the pudding. Never in my life had it tasted so good.

I didn't have a plan as to what would happen next. I was just going to replace the empty dish and hope for the best. Maybe no one would notice.

At about the same time that I was plotting my escape, my mother came out of the kitchen. She stopped short when she noticed that there was an empty spot where the banana pudding used to be.

"Junior…Luther…Delbert…get in here!"

Clearly, she was not happy. When June and Ball came running into the dining room, minus their brother, she gave it one more try.

"Delbert Ray…where are you? Come here right now!"

She was just about to start the room-to-room search when she heard moaning coming from under the tablecloth. When she lifted it up, there I was, clutching the empty dish and rubbing my stomach in protest.

"Ooohh…I don't feel good," I whimpered. "My stomach hurts."

Obviously, Mama was upset. In a matter of a few short minutes I had single-handedly devoured the dessert that had taken her all morning to prepare and which was meant for the entire family.

"Please don't tell Daddy," I begged, wrapping my arms tightly around my tummy. It was so bloated that I felt like I would burst. "I'm sorry, I won't do it again."

She stared at me for several moments before speaking, apparently moved by my pleas of mercy.

"I'm not going to tell your father, but go to your room, Delbert, and you can't come out for dinner when your cousins get here."

And with that, she marched back into the kitchen to prepare a substi-tute dessert before the relatives arrived.

Relieved that I would escape corporal punishment, I clamped my fingers over my mouth and made a hasty retreat to the bathroom. Choking down the bitter taste, I barely made it before heaving the entire banana pudding into the toilet. Exhausted from all the vomiting, I dragged myself up to my room and lay down on the bed. At least, I thought, I'm not going to get a 'whuppin.' Being sick was punishment enough, I reasoned. But I was mistaken. Because five minutes later, Daddy came up the stairs with the strap, and I had to bend over and assume the position. I couldn't believe it. She told him! Even after promising me that she wouldn't, she still told Daddy. I felt utterly betrayed by my own mother. I didn't think I would ever forgive her. "If you can't trust your mama, who can you trust?" I concluded.

Of course, it never occurred to me that I was the guilty party and should be seeking her forgiveness. Instead, I blamed the whole thing on my mother, and in a way it really was her fault. If she hadn't have been such a good cook in the first place, this never would have happened. Yep, I was convinced. It was her fault, all right. I was mad at her. And it would be a long time before I could even look at another banana again.

I thought of that humorous incident now as I sat next to her bed. She had spent months sitting by me in the hospital while I hovered close to death. And now the tables were turned. She was losing her battle with cancer, and there was nothing I could do but stay by her side. It made me realize how she must have felt when I was hospitalized. The feeling of helplessness was overwhelming, and I wished that somehow I could take her place. I'd gladly go back into the bed and be sick again if I could have her sitting in the chair, happy, and healthy, and smiling.

Instead, she died less than two months after she was diagnosed.

The funeral was at Oakland Baptist Church where we all had attended Sunday school. Reverend Larry Walker captured my mother's kindness with a memorable eulogy. But the real tribute to her value on the earth was the many friends and neighbors who paid their respects and shared their memories. Everyone truly loved her, and she left a big hole, not only in our family, but in the entire neighborhood. The pain of the fire, the surgeries, the death of my brother and my favorite uncle; it seemed like the McCoys had been through so much already. I didn't understand why God had given us yet another tragedy to deal with.

THIRTY-FIVE

GWEN LEE

I *was just twelve years old when I rushed with my family in the middle of the night to the hospital where my brother had been taken. We were given very few details and didn't know what to expect. Was Delray in pain? Was he conscious? Would he recognize us? Would he recover? Would he even be alive when we got there?*

When my parents walked out of the intensive care unit at Detroit Receiving Hospital some time later, Mama was crying uncontrollably, and I had never seen my father look so shaken. By now, most of the family had gathered in the waiting room along with many friends. We all hugged and held each other tightly, as we prayed for a miracle. When it was my turn to go into the room to say "goodbye" to my brother, I was afraid. I could hear Delbert's pitiful screams from the hallway, and everyone around me was caught up in grief and sadness. I could only imagine how horrible it must be to be burned, and how painful the heat must feel on his skin. I was convinced that the hospital was a scary place, where bad things happened to the people I loved, and I desperately wanted to go back home and put the covers over my head.

As I was led tentatively into the room, the first thing I noticed was the machines, pumps, wires, and blood everywhere. Slowly I let my eyes shift to the figure in the bed. I was shocked. It wasn't my brother at all. It was a mummy, wrapped from head to toe in bandages; but they weren't white. A murky rusty liquid oozed out onto the covers. The image burned my eyes and broke by heart, and I quickly ran back to the safety of the waiting room into the arms of my family.

I thought that was the last time I'd ever see Delray again. Surely he wouldn't survive the night. The doctors told us as much. But the outpouring of faith and prayers from our family and friends disproved the doctors' grim diagnosis, and I would visit him at the hospital many, many times over the next two and a half years.

Mama and I would take the bus each afternoon and stay until late at night, well past visiting hours. Then Daddy would go around midnight, when he got off work. Although my parents kept their emotions in check and appeared strong and confident at the hospital, once they got home it was a different story. Mama broke down on a regular basis, and I often witnessed her down on her knees praying to God for help. She even called the church Prayer Line and asked them to pray for her son. She had such a big heart, and she ached so bad to see her child suffering, but she tried her very best to hide it from Delray. Every time we left the hospital she'd say, "Keep the faith, Delray, just keep the faith."

Mama always knew what was best for her children, and when my brother lost so much weight because he couldn't eat, she was the one that stepped in to save the day.

"Delray, you only weigh 57 pounds—the same as your sister. We've got to get some weight on you, or we're going to lose you."

Soon she had convinced the doctor to let us cook food at home and bring it to Delray at the hospital. Mama and I spent many months working in the kitchen and preparing nutritious meals, and I guess that's why I enjoy *cooking to this day. It brings back happy memories of the times I spent with my mother and the love that went into our recipes.*

Taking home-cooked meals to the hospital gave us something useful to do, but once we were there, the reality of the situation set in again each day. Delbert was still in a lot of pain and suffered immensely. I remember the first time I saw him in the circoelectric bed. To my young eyes, it looked like a Ferris wheel, only it wasn't much fun. He had wires going through his ankles and hands, and they would flip him upside down every hour. I thought of how awful it must be to have to stay in bed day after day, for months at a time. It was hard seeing my brother like that. And when the doctors gave him skin grafts, his body itched so bad that he'd beg us to scratch him. We'd try to help, but scratching offered little relief. It disturbed the grafts and soon our fingers would be covered with blood.

Once he was taken out of intensive care and moved to the ward, there were other burn patients in the adjoining rooms, and one in particular caused him much distress. It was a little two-year old girl, who had been severely burned. The baby cried all the time, and it broke my brother's heart. We tried to keep the door to his room closed in order to block out the mournful sound, but it didn't help much. He could still hear her cries, but was helpless to do anything to help her.

Delbert had excellent care while he was recovering, and we got to know all his doctors, nurses, and orderlies because we spent so much time with them. The medical staff all admired him for his courage and strength, in spite of all the obstacles he faced. In fact, there were several serious setbacks during his recovery. Without warning, his heart would stop, and doctors would come rushing into the room, order us to leave, and begin to work furiously at saving his life. Those times were the worst, and each incident reminded us once again how close he was to dying at any moment.

When he came home for good, the whole family and all our friends turned out to welcome him. Mama was so happy to have her son home again, even though there wasn't much he could do for himself, and it meant extra work for her. She didn't care. A bed was set up in the dining room, and that soon became Delray's room. The boys would carry him upstairs to the bath, and Mama would help change his bandages every day. At first he was uncomfortable around outsiders, not only about his looks, but he couldn't feed himself either. He didn't like to have anyone help him eat so he came up with his own method. Since he couldn't move his arms, he would put his head down

136

until his mouth reached the plate and he was able to bite into his food, kind of like bobbing for apples. He often said that the food tasted better when he fed himself, but was quick to explain to his little girls that they shouldn't eat the way he did. As long as just the family was around, he felt safe. He didn't like people staring at him and didn't welcome having my friends come to the house. But eventually he learned that they didn't mean him any harm, and they'd often come over and watch baseball games on television with him.

Delray and I became very close over the years, and sharing his unbelievable journey has given me a better appreciation of the power of faith. When Mama was in the hospital, dying from cancer, she reminded me often of the lessons I'd grown up with. She taught us to be kind to each other, to love one another and that the family sticks together. With our mother gone, now my home has become the family meeting place, where holiday and birthday traditions are carried out with plenty of good food and togetherness. But she'll always be with us in spirit, as a perfect example of someone who's heart was so big and filled with so much love that she selflessly took care of the needs of others before her own. And with the cancer eating away at her and the energy draining from her body, she regretted that she could no longer help take care of Delbert and worried about his comfort and safety. She tried to hang on, but I remember clearly, the last devoted words she spoke to me just before she died.

"Take care of your brother."

THIRTY-SIX

NEVER THE SAME

Our family was never the same after mother's passing. The holidays, which had always been so special to the McCoy family, now provided sadness and gloom. The nucleus of our family, the center of our universe, was gone forever. When she died, the soul of our family died as well.

I continued to live with my father, and we shared the house on Northwestern with my nephews Tony, Fred, and Deron. Just five guys living in the household, without a woman's touch. The boys helped with the chores and assisted me with my personal needs, even as I was becoming more adept at doing for myself. Our life settled into a routine, but we all missed Mama, and I missed the life I had with Yvonne and the girls.

It looked as if I would be a "bachelor" for the rest of my life. Being homebound and reliant on the nephews for most of my personal care, I certainly was in no position to go out looking for companionship. Besides, other than my family and close friends, I didn't really trust being around "outsiders." I was certain that women would not be able to see beyond my disfiguration and physical limitations.

I was wrong. Her name was Renée, and my life was about to change once again.

THIRTY-SEVEN

RENÉE BRANDON

*W*hen I met Delbert that summer of 1992, the first thing that struck me was how friendly he was. In spite of his disabilities, he didn't dwell on his problems or wallow in self-pity. Delbert's nephew, Maurice, had invited me to a family reunion at the McCoy's house, and the party was in full swing when we arrived. The McCoys had a huge family, and many relatives hadn't seen each other in several years. There was lots of laughing, teasing and reminiscing about the past, especially times spent on their grandfather's farm. I was impressed by how much they all cared for each other, and how comfortable Delbert was around his family.

We talked for hours, and he seemed genuinely interested in me. I was a single mother raising four kids on my own, and we shared stories about our children, the music we liked, our favorite foods…all the normal things people talk about when they're getting to know each other. We had so much in common that it seemed like we'd known one another forever. I was raised by my grandmother and went to church every Sunday at the Brown Missionary Baptist Church. Delbert also had a religious upbringing, and I could tell just by talking to him how much his faith meant to him. He loved his family, his daughters, his friends, and the Lord. As far as I was concerned, he was a "great catch."

When we moved in together, he became a wonderful father figure to my children. The youngest was four, but the other three were in school, and Delbert was very strict with them about their studies. He set a good example, since he also was a student at the time, enrolled in college pursuing a degree in marketing.

Over the years, Delbert took an active roll in raising my children and was very influential in teaching them about consequences, and the difference between "right" and "wrong." He was firm, but so kind-hearted, that they really respected him, especially after all he'd been through. And he inspired them to make something of their lives, never letting them forget the importance of schooling. It was a great relief for me to have someone share the burden of their upbringing, and I can't think of anyone better suited for the job. I became very close to his daughters, and we had a good relationship with their mother, Yvonne. In fact, even to this day, she and I are good friends.

The merger of our families has given me a lot of satisfaction and joy, and knowing Delbert has enriched my life in so many ways. He has such a kind heart that he would never turn away anyone in need, and he finds only the best in people. He's extremely good natured and upbeat. And in spite of the tragedies he's endured, he remains optimistic, even when those around him have doubts. I don't know why Delbert has had so much tragedy and disappointment in his life, or why God continues to test him. But I do remember the lessons from my childhood.

"Never question God," my grandmother taught me. "He never gives us more than we can bear."

If that's true, then that makes Delbert McCoy the strongest person I've ever met.

THIRTY-EIGHT

THE CANDY MAN

Renée and I proved to be a good match. I enjoyed the company of her kids, and it was good to have a woman's touch around the house again. She earned extra money as a hairdresser, and she also turned out to be a great cook, often fixing some of my favorite meals, just like Mama used to make. She helped me tend to my personal needs too, especially my hair.

Over the years I'd let it grow to cover my scars, and it got so long that eventually she started brushing and braiding it for me. I sure couldn't do anything with it; so I welcomed having her fuss over my hair and my appearance in general. We usually got along pretty well. Renée was okay with my limitations, and she put up with having my friends over to the house all the time. We rarely quarreled, but on the few occasions that we did have a disagreement, I would withhold the one thing that meant the most to her. I refused to let her braid my hair. Of course, that approach did very little to "punish" her, but it hurt me in a big way. My hair looked like a haystack, wild and so unmanageable that it stuck out everywhere. It covered my eyes and half of my face. But there was nothing I could do about it. So I'd just put on my hat and hope for the best. The hat helped somewhat, but stray strands still managed to escape in all directions. Even though we tried to be discreet, Renée and I could never hide our disagreements from our family or friends. They could tell whenever we had a "tiff" just by looking at my crazy hairdo.

Although Renée was a master at making my hair presentable, she was helpless to improve my overall looks. My face still needed repairs. My eyes were the worst problem. Since I couldn't close them all the way, I had frequent eye infections, which caused constant oozing and tearing. My lips were red and severely swollen, making them unable to close. I had no nose, just a hole where my nose used to be. And I had absolutely no ears. When I first was released from St. Joseph's Hospital in 1971, the doctors told me that I would need extensive reconstructive surgery to correct my facial deformities, but that my body needed time to heal before that process could begin. When I returned several months later to discuss what improvements could be made, I was informed that my insurance company would not cover the expensive surgical procedures. In their eyes the surgery was considered to be "plastic surgery," also known as "elective surgery," and therefore not covered by my policy. It was yet another crushing blow.

The thought of having plastic surgery to give me a more normal face again was the one thing that kept me going when I was released from the hospital and forced back into the real world. The hope of having the revolting mask of scars replaced by a more ordinary face had dimmed to a mere flicker. With four children to support, Renée and I were barely able to make ends meet. There certainly wasn't any money left over for plastic surgery.

But although I knew the odds were against me, I kept that hope alive. And several years later my faith was rewarded once again.

Renée's sons, Spike and Bill, were on the school basketball team. In order to raise money for uniforms and equipment, the team was selling candy at designated locations around the city. We dropped the boys off at the neighborhood shopping center and watched proudly as they learned their first lesson in the subject of high finance and economics. They turned out to be as good at sales as they were on the court and quickly sold all their candy. Bill treated it like a competition and found it to be challenging and a lot of fun.

"Delbert, why don't you try selling candy?" he urged.

"That would be great," his mother chimed in.

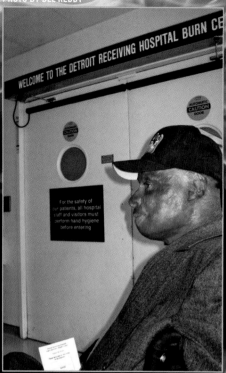

My dream was to join the lineup of the Detroit Tigers. Today, I feel I am doing the Lord's work, positively influencing new people every day.

I get immense satisfaction being a volunteer burn survivor counselor at Detroit Medical Center. Decades ago I entered this same building with an incredibly bleak prospect of surviving.

Great friend Del Reddy and I visit with Nobel Peace Prize winner and human rights activist, Shirin Ebadi.

Enjoying a visit with Television Hall of Famer, Ted Koppel.

I admire Detroit business mogul, Al Taubman, for earmarking millions of dollars to a variety of good causes. My long range goal is to generate hefty sums of money through my foundation to benefit mankind, too.

With business leader Mel Farr, Motown's outstanding and progressive Mayor Dave Bing, former football great Mike Lucci, long-time buddy Walter Brandon, and the "The Supernatural" football hall of famer and minister Lem Barney.

Invited to attend the rededication of the Mike Modano Ice Arena in Westland, Michigan an All-American City. (L to R) Parks and Recreation Director Bob Kosowski, Mayor William R. Wild, and hockey legend Modano.

It is always special to speak to church congregations. Signing books after a presentation with Pastor David and Tuskegee Airmen member Lt. Col. Alexander Jefferson.

Marveling at the "Labor Legacy Landmark" in downtown Detroit, I am proud to be a former UAW autoworker. Known as "Transcending" the art monument celebrates the tremendous contributions by men and women laborers over the years. Nearby is a tile with an inscription from Martin Luther King: "The arc of history bends toward justice."

With Detroit's number one Christian talk radio host, Bob Dutko and the show's producer Jan Foxx at Warren Road Light & Life Church.

Del Reddy and I host the television program, *Still on Fire*, showcasing individuals who have faced severe adversity, but keep going forward regardless of their setback.

My fiancée Renée and her three children: Bill, Marcus, and Nicole, help me everyday with those things I am incapable of doing. We also have a lot of good times with our family dog, Lucky.

Joe Louis won his last World Heavyweight Championship in 1949, the year I was born. My motto is "Life is precious. Never, never give up hope!"

Batting champion, Magglio Ordonez, is as friendly off the field as he is great on it.

Aaron Howard, Marketing & Web Expert of CU Innovative Marketing along with The IT Guy, David Story, were very instrumental in the launch of StillOnFire.com.

Lamont "Pug" Lawrence has been a good friend for over 45 years. In the early days, we cherished the times playing baseball in our Detroit neighborhood and at Northwestern High School.

Popular radio personality "Coco" of WJLB celebrates as she announces another donation to our Fire In My Soul Foundation. On the left is foundation board member Carris Carey.

Besides being one of the greatest bowling champions in history, Eddie "King of the Pins" Lubanski was also an outstanding baseball player. Baseball and bowling have been popular in Detroit for decades.

It is rewarding to share uplifting stories with the friendly people at Biggby Coffee, where I do a number of book signing appearances. (L to R), Former Deputy Police Chief John T. Reddy, Hollywood screenwriter, movie co-producer and Motown native Gordon Michaels, and store owner, the dynamic, Mo Elfakir.

State Representative Marc Corriveau is doing an outstanding job for his District as well as the state of Michigan.

Napoleon Ross wrote the book on being a best-friend. Long-time pals are some of life's greatest treasures.

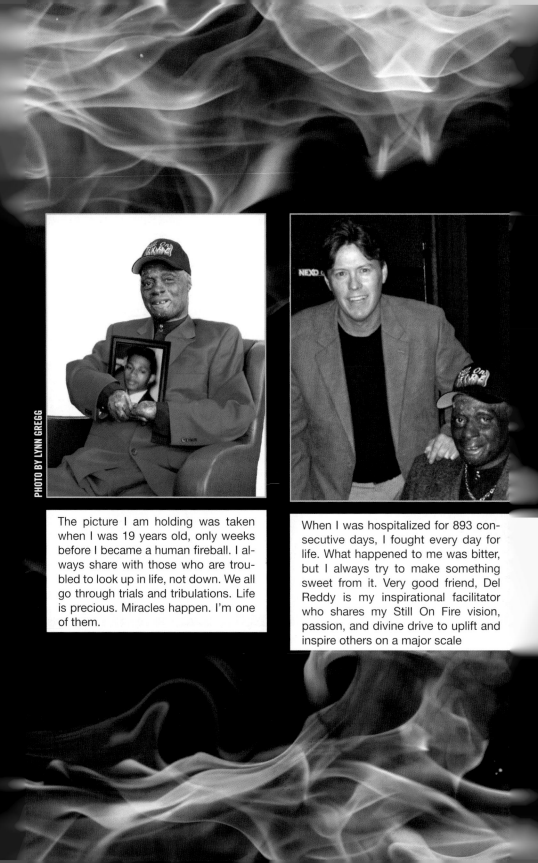

The picture I am holding was taken when I was 19 years old, only weeks before I became a human fireball. I always share with those who are troubled to look up in life, not down. We all go through trials and tribulations. Life is precious. Miracles happen. I'm one of them.

When I was hospitalized for 893 consecutive days, I fought every day for life. What happened to me was bitter, but I always try to make something sweet from it. Very good friend, Del Reddy is my inspirational facilitator who shares my Still On Fire vision, passion, and divine drive to uplift and inspire others on a major scale

It didn't sound like such a brilliant idea to me.

"I can't sell candy," I argued. "Look at me. Who'd buy anything from me?"

"Sure you can," she countered. "You're good with people, and it will give you a chance to get out of the house."

Soon the whole family jumped on the bandwagon, and I was pretty much outnumbered. "I guess I could give it a try."

I had enjoyed working at the party store for my dad, and I'd done all right with the record store, I reasoned. Besides it would help bring in some extra money.

"Maybe I could earn enough to pay for the plastic surgery."

With that encouraging thought in mind I left the comfort of my home and tiptoed into the demanding world of salesmanship.

But it would have to be a joint effort. I would need to rely on Renée, or my friends, now more than ever. We purchased candy (mostly M & M's) from a local wholesale supply warehouse, scouted locations, got permission from management and looked forward to our new business venture.

Even though I was excited about the prospect of being in business again, the thought of going out into the public still made me anxious and fearful, especially now. I wouldn't have the safety of the store and regular customers to fall back on. I'd be more exposed out in the "big" world, among strangers.

The first day was the toughest. Renée and Bill took me to the Oak Park Mall on Nine Mile Road. Since I couldn't stand for long periods of time, Bill helped me into the wheelchair while Renée set up the candy and cash box. Then, after issuing last minute words of encouragement, they left me. I was officially "Opened for Business."

Fighting the panic, I tried to control my anxious thoughts.

What if people won't accept me?

What if they say mean things?

But I stubbornly brushed aside my doubts. I was determined to be the "Best Candy Salesman" there ever was.

Initially most people just walked past me and stared. Sometimes they'd hurry by, not looking my way, as if I didn't exist. Obviously, no one was interested in buying my merchandise. They could get all the candy they wanted inside the store. I felt so vulnerable and uncomfortable, convinced that the whole idea was a mistake.

Forget it, I thought, this isn't going to work, and after all my positive thoughts and bold promises, I was pretty close to giving up.

But gradually, as the day wore on, people started to respond differently.

Some stopped and purchased the M & M's out of pity or guilt, I don't know which—then sprinted away. I guess they were afraid I might be contagious. Or, that my misfortune would somehow rub off on them. Some simply dropped money in the box without taking their candy. I wasn't looking for charity. I wanted them to take the merchandise for their purchase, but many said "No, you keep it."

And some customers, who came to be my favorites, would stop and ask me what had happened. Those were the people I appreciated the most. They were genuinely interested in my situation and had lots of questions. Usually they were amazed and offered me words of encouragement. Others shared their own stories, and I learned that I wasn't the only one in the world with troubles. Lots of people were walking around with heavy burdens. Theirs just weren't visible, like mine were. But that didn't make them any less painful.

I earned $102 that first day selling candy. The income was a blessing, and very much appreciated. But something more important happened that day. I found a new independence and self-confidence that had been lacking for so long. By talking to people and sharing my story, I felt like I was doing something worthwhile, and a small spark of motivation was ignited. I no longer was afraid to go out into the open world, but rather looked forward to what each new day would bring. I enthusiastically approached my candy sales as an opportunity to broaden my life and make new friends. And it wasn't long before I became a regular fixture at neighborhood markets and shopping centers.

Over time I developed a regular route, just like any other salesman. I would go to Oak Park, Southfield, Troy, Blooomfield Hills, and other cities, making many new friends along the way. Often people would tell me that they looked forward to the days I was at their location, and they missed me when I wasn't there. One day I was at a market in Troy, when a police officer approached me and told me I couldn't sell candy in front of the store. Even though I had received permission from the manager, the officer insisted that I pack up and leave. An outspoken customer came to my defense.

"He's not hurting anybody, why don't you leave him alone?"

But the officer remained unmoved by his pleas, and waited as my friend, Keith Thomas, helped me back to the van.

About two weeks later I was at a different store in Troy. This was a Farmer Jack's Super Market, and the same officer drove into the parking lot and approached me again, telling me that I had to leave.

"Why are you bothering me," I asked. "The manager has given me position to be here."

"You can't sell candy in Troy," he explained, "unless you have a permit."

That didn't seem reasonable to me, since I'd been selling my candy for several years by now, and no one had ever told me about a permit. As a matter of fact, many Troy police officers bought candy from me, and they never mentioned a permit either. But I bit back my response and packed up for the day, bewildered as to why that particular lieutenant was so determined to get rid of me.

At first I thought I should just stay out of that city, but I had made many friends there and I really didn't expect it to be a big problem. So two or three weeks later I was back again, this time at a drugstore. I was just finishing up for the day when a police cruiser pulled up. As my "favorite officer" got out of the car, I thought, *Oh, oh, here we go again.*

He looked pretty determined as he approached me with another warning.

"I told you not to sell candy in Troy. People don't want you around. You block the door and get in the way," he insisted.

"Now you can either take what you've earned and give it to the store, or you can go to jail. It's your choice."

In hindsight, I guess the smart decision would have been to give up the money. But I really didn't believe that he would arrest me just for selling candy at a store where I clearly had permission to do so. I felt that I had a right to be there, that I wasn't hurting anyone, that no one had complained, and that people would miss me if I never returned. He was just being mean. I was being picked on, and there was no way I was going to surrender my earnings. It was the principle of the thing. But while I was professing my innocence, and mentally debating the ethics of the situation, the officer and his partner escorted me to the back seat of their police car.

When we arrived at the station, I was charged with "Soliciting without a permit" and placed in a small jail cell, which I had all to myself. They brought me a couple of McDonald's hamburgers, and I laid down on the hard bunk to do my time. *If I could spend two and a half years in a medical prison,* I reasoned, *then one night in jail couldn't be so tough.*

And the hard bunk in the cell was a luxury compared to the Circo bed that kept me captive for so many months. I made it through the night without incident, and Walter and Renée showed up in the morning, posted the $100 bond, and "sprung me."

Rich Fisher, of Channel 50 television, began his newscast that evening with the headline, "Candy Man gets busted for selling M & M's."

Local radio legends, Drew and Mike of WRIF 101, invited me on their number one morning program to share my story with listeners. They too dubbed me "The Candy Man." It wasn't long before the tale of my arrest for selling M & M's reached newspapers and other media. I became somewhat of a folk hero, and it seemed everyone had an opinion about my story. Most people were very sympathetic and came to my defense. They felt, just as my customers had, that I wasn't hurting anyone, and that I should have been allowed to sell my candy. But that wasn't the issue. According to the law, I couldn't sell in Troy…and the case was closed. I've never been back since.

Appearing in studio with number one radio hosts Drew and Mike of WRIF.

THIRTY-NINE

REUNITED

*N*ormally, when a patient leaves the hospital, he never sees his caregivers again. In spite of all that we'd been through together, people like Marlene, and Dr. Grifka, Nurse Pfeiffer, Robbie, and the others were temporary participants in my life. When I left their care and returned to my family, they went on with their lives, and I went on with mine. It never occurred to me that they would remember me, when they had so many patients to deal with every day of every year.

That's why it was such a surprise when in July of 1994 a story about me appeared in the Detroit Free Press. It was titled "Albert and the Angels," but there was no mistaking that it was about my ordeal. Renée suggested I locate the writer, and it seemed like a good idea. He had written the story with such compassion that I felt honored he remembered me. After all, it had been 25 years since the fire.

We called the editor of the paper, and she got us in touch with Tim Sheard, who was then living in Brooklyn, New York. Tim had been the male nurse who took such good care of me at St. Joseph's Hospital. He's the one that rubbed cocoa butter on my brittle skin, and who I shared so many stories and dreams with. I remembered him as a kind and very caring young man, who was close to my own age at the time.

It turns out that Tim was an aspiring author, and after being a critical care nurse for many years, he began writing about his patients. One of those stories was submitted to the newspaper and featured in the magazine section. He didn't know if I was still alive, but he hoped that someone would recognize the accounting and link it back to me. He was both surprised and thrilled when I called him. And a few months later he flew to Detroit for a reunion at my home. He met Renée and her boys, and I bragged about Monique and Kim, who were only babies when I knew him.

That meeting turned out to be another turning point in my life. From Tim's story in the paper, a small seed of an idea grew. His passion for writing was fueled by my passion to share my story. It appeared we had the makings of a great team, and after much collaboration, *The Fire in My Soul* was published.

(photo courtesy of Tim Sheard)

FORTY

EYE OPENING

*T*he moment I was able to close my eyes for the first time in almost 30 years, I knew God had performed another miracle. Through all of the examinations, tests, and surgeries that I endured for many years after the fire, no member of the medical community was ever able to offer a solution for the problem that plagued me the most. Scar tissue had formed on my eyelids, and they wouldn't close completely. For almost three decades I was forced to sleep with my eyes partially open, and more importantly, I suffered from frequent eye infections because I couldn't blink properly.

Blinking is an important aspect of our daily lives because it provides moisture to the eyes. Really our eyelids should be thought of as windshield wipers. Each blink coats the eyelid with lubricants from nearby glands, keeping them from drying out and preventing foreign matter from entering. My eyes were constantly dry and irritated, in spite of antibiotics, and sometimes I would get two or three infections a week. It seemed like each infection had to run its course before I'd get relief.

In 1997, Kate Lawson of *The Detroit News* wrote a powerful article about my recovery from the fire in 1969. The day it was published, I received a phone call from Dr. Sandra Brown, a physician with expertise in skin research.

"I think I can help you close your eyes, and it won't require surgery," Dr. Brown advised.

Those words seemed too good to be true, but I wanted to believe them more than anything. A Wayne State University trained physician with a caring spirit, she specialized in the treatment of severe acne, burns, scars, and especially keloids. Dr. Brown believed that a technique she had developed, using acids, would loosen up the eyelids and allow them to blink.

When we met at her office for the examination, we were surprised to discover that we had been in the same class several years ago in school. I felt like I was in good hands, and the Good Lord had sent me another angel. Just as she had predicted, the acid relaxed the eyelids, reducing the scarring substantially, and after only two treatments I was able to close my eyes fully for the first time in 30 years. The relief I received from Dr. Brown's procedure was indescribable. The infections finally halted, and thankfully, I was able to sleep more soundly than I had in decades.

That same year *The Detroit News* selected Dr. Brown as one of the "Michiganians of the Year" in recognition of all the life-altering work she did for people who often had run out of hope. Many of her patients, just like myself, were unable to pay for her services, but she treated them anyway.

"I have been blessed with a gift," Dr. Brown told *The Detroit News*. "I am able to bring hope. You couldn't pay me enough money to give me the feeling I have when I see a person bloom in front of me."

Dr. Brown treated me for an entire year without ever charging me a penny. She is an amazingly talented, generous, and spiritual woman, and I am so grateful to her for improving the quality of my life and showing me once again that people do care.

Most people assume that before I met Dr. Brown I had given up all hope of closing my eyes again, but they'd be wrong. I have always maintained a strong faith that God would provide the solution to my needs. The Soul Expressions tragedy was just the beginning of my journey into the realm of pain and suffering. Since that night in 1969, I've endured more than 100 surgeries and countless procedures. Ironically, not all of them were a result of the fire. In 1998, my faith would be tested once again.

Our children were grown up and on their own, Renée and I were living quietly and modestly, and life had fallen into a comfortable routine.

One day a friend of mine, Keith Thomas, asked me to go with him to Pennsylvania. Some of his relatives had enjoyed a successful hunting season, and they had more venison and small game than they could use, so they offered the excess to Keith. Not wanting to make the long trip alone, Keith said "Come on with me, Delbert. I'll share the meat with you." It sounded good to me, and I looked forward to getting away for a while.

We arrived late in Pennsylvania, packed up the meat, chatted with his relatives, and then grabbed four or five hours sleep before starting back home early the next morning. About halfway through the trip, Keith got drowsy and pulled over at a rest stop to shake out the weariness. After resting for a short time, we started back up, and I recall putting my feet up on the console on the passenger's side.

"I'm going to get a little more sleep," I said, dosing off. That was the last thing I remember until I woke up some time later moaning in excruciating pain. The van we'd been traveling in was completely destroyed, and I was trapped in the wreckage. Fortunately, Keith was not hurt, and he kept assuring me that help was on its way, but it couldn't come soon enough. I couldn't feel anything from my waist down. My legs had been crushed, and when I tried to move them, I screamed out in pain. What frightened me most was the thought that I might be paralyzed.

Two paramedics climbed into the van, and I begged them not to touch me because the pain was so bad. They did a quick assessment and found that my right leg was discolored and swollen and my left leg was broken at the femur. "There's gasoline leaking from the tank, and we have to get you out of here," they urged. I couldn't believe that I was in a situation where I could once again burn to death, but the pain was so severe that the thought of being moved made me forget the horror of the fire. "Please don't touch me," I cried.

One of the paramedics was female, and she put her hand gently on my forehead trying to comfort me. "I'm sorry," she said, "but you have to trust us." Just then I heard the whirl of helicopter blades, and I knew I was in pretty bad shape. Despite my pleas, the paramedics turned me over and carefully placed me on a stretcher. I screamed again and again, over and over. The pain was unbearable. I didn't pass out, even though I prayed that I would.

Originally, the helicopter took me to a small hospital in Salem, Ohio, but doctors there quickly decided that they were not equipped for the severity of my injuries. So I was reloaded on the helicopter for a short flight to the Cleveland Clinic, which had a world famous trauma center. X-rays showed that my right leg was broken at the tibia, but it could be healed with time and a cast.

However, the left leg required an extensive operation. After interviewing me about my medical history, the doctors realized I had a pretty good understanding of the surgical process. They offered me spinal anesthesia rather than general so that I could be awake for the procedure. I can vividly remember watching the monitor as the surgeon cut my leg open. Even though I was intrigued by the image on the screen, sometimes I had to close my eyes when the likeness was too graphic. But watching the actual surgery was inspiring. And when they hammered a pin into my bone with a rubber mallet, successfully stabilizing the leg, I was filled with relief.

"Your bones are very brittle because of your burns," explained the surgeon, "but you're strong and I know that you'll fight hard to get well."

My stay in the Cleveland hospital lasted for five days, and then I was transferred to Providence Hospital in Southfield, Michigan for rehabilitation. The staff there told me that restoration of my legs would take at least 30 days. But it was only two weeks before Christmas, and I desperately wanted to be home for the holidays, so I worked extra hard at the exercises.

My therapist was named Gloria, and she gave me a device that would enable me to transfer my body from the bed to the wheelchair. I had to hoist myself up onto the board, which would temporarily support me so that I could slide into the wheelchair.

"You can't go home until you can successfully use the support board," Gloria challenged. I practiced using the board almost every waking minute. Even when she wasn't helping me, I kept on trying. It was very difficult at first, but eventually I got the hang of it. I'd been through plenty of therapy after the fire; so I knew what had to be done, and I was determined to speed up the process.

I completed the rehab program and was able to go home after a record-setting nine days. Gloria and the rest of the hospital staff were stunned at how quickly I had progressed, but I wasn't surprised.

"I've got plenty of experience in exceeding medical expectations," I replied proudly.

Part
Three

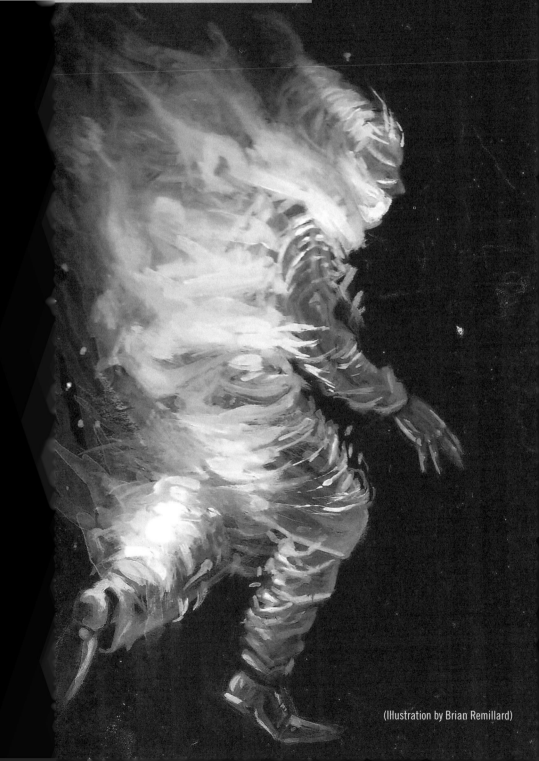

Dance hall set ablaze by arsonist; 60 injured

(Illustration by Brian Remillard)

FORTY-ONE

MONIQUE SMITH

In *spite of the fact that my father was unable to be a part of my life in some areas because of his physical limitations, it didn't matter. He more than made up for it in other ways. Since he needed help with personal tasks, my sister and I would often help him button his shirt, or tie his shoes, or even brush his hair. We loved to fuss over him. I have many happy memories of the time we spent together when I was growing up.*

Since he couldn't do much of a physical nature, we would spend hours watching sports together on television, especially the Tigers' games. He loved baseball and passed that love on to me. While other girls "wasted" their time experimenting with makeup or hairstyles, I was memorizing statistics, batting averages, RBI's and knew all the best players of the American and National Leagues. If we weren't rooting for the Tigers, we'd play a game of cards, usually Spades, and on weekends the whole family would go to a drive-in movie.

But mostly, I remember the exhaustive amount of time he spent helping me with my homework. Never one to let anything get in the way of our studies, he would sit with me for hours tutoring me in any subject, but mostly math. That was his specialty. Mom helped me with book reports and writing assignments, but Dad was the "go to guy" when it came to math. He was a real taskmaster, always stressing the value of a good education. His emphasis on schooling planted a seed of determination in my young mind, and by the time I reached middle school, I no longer needed his encouragement for inspiration. By then I had started setting personal goals and was pushing myself to excel in all subjects. My intent was to never have less than a "B" on my report card—no "C's."

I began envisioning what I'd like to do with my life as well. When I was very young, I wanted to be a schoolteacher, but then I became interested in the medical field and had aspirations of being a doctor. I wasn't sure exactly what I wanted to do when I grew up, but I was certain of one thing. I knew I wanted to help people. My father always had a need to help others, and I guess he passed that on to me too, along with the baseball gene. Eventually I settled on the practice of law and am currently an attorney for the City of Detroit, in the Government Affairs Division.

Dad has been a huge influence in my life, not just in the area of education, but by the example he has set spiritually. His faith has kept him strong and enabled him to endure the many hardships he's been burdened with. When my first husband was stricken with leukemia in his early forties, I watched helplessly as he battled the disease for two and a half years before his death. Many times I was overcome with sadness and grief and questioned my ability to go on. My father was there to comfort me. His soothing words and gentleness eased my sorrow, but it was his own remarkable journey that inspired me the most. Knowing what he had endured and how he had suffered reminded me that there would be light at the end of the tunnel, and I learned to rely on my faith in God, just as my father had, for his entire life.

Now Dad helps another generation of McCoys to be the best that they can be. He teaches his grandchildren about baseball, team stats, and batting averages, and he motivates them to do their homework. Braden, age 13, and Jalen, eight, are crazy about their granddad. They don't see him as a victim—or know him as a survivor. They don't find his appearance frightening or even unusual. They just know that he's the "Best" grandpa in the whole world.

FORTY-TWO

KIM ABNEY

*M*y *father treasures being a granddad. With four grandsons to share his passion for sports, he's able to do what makes him most happy. After all these years, he still enjoys cheering on his Detroit Tigers and following their progress each season. My son, Aaron, who's seventeen, played little league ball for several years with the Rosedale Park League, and one of his biggest thrills was going with Dad to a book signing event and receiving an autographed edition from Tiger's superstar, Willie Horton. Aaron and Dad love to talk baseball, players, and statistics, and my youngest child, four-year old Bryce, will undoubtedly be a fan as well. It must be bittersweet for Dad to watch the pro teams, knowing that if he hadn't been severely injured, he might have been a professional player himself. His dreams*

157

died in the flames of the Soul Expressions fire, but he isn't bitter or angry. He's channeled his energies into other areas and long ago accepted the fact that instead of playing for the Tigers, he can be their "biggest fan."

Education continues to be very important to him, and as a child growing up in the McCoy household, I received the full value of his strong beliefs. As early as elementary school, he began laying down the foundation for Monique and me to be the best we could possibly be, not letting us forget for a second how important education was to our future. When I was in college, struggling with the demands of a heavy schedule and adjusting to a grown-up lifestyle, he was there for me. Always a good listener, I was able to talk to him about anything and could go to him with any kind of problem, no matter how difficult. He never passed judgment or showed disapproval of my actions, making me comfortable confiding in him. He seemed more like a best friend than a parent. And when I had relationship issues or boyfriend troubles, he was there to offer much appreciated guidance and advice. His mother was like that also. I never hesitated to talk to Grandma McCoy about any subject either; so I guess it's in his DNA.

There were a lot of experiences my sister and I missed out on as a family because Dad couldn't be a part of them. Simple things like enjoying a bike ride or taking a family vacation were absent from our childhood. Traveling more than a short distance was very difficult for him, as was walking or standing for any length of time. So carnivals and amusement parks were out of the question. It's unfortunate that he was unable to attend our school functions, never got to see me perform with the theatre group, or twirl the baton as a majorette. Although now he is very comfortable appearing in public, initially he lacked the confidence to do so. Maybe he was worried about embarrassing us, or maybe he was afraid of what people might say. He was probably more concerned about how the comments of strangers would affect his children than he was for himself. And yes, it did bother me for a time. It wasn't that I was embarrassed or ashamed, I was just a little uncomfortable. Sometimes strangers would make rude comments or ask a lot of probing questions. Other times they would ignorantly stare at him, as if he were an oddity. He wasn't particularly sensitive to their hostility, but I took offense to it. In my mind there was nothing to stare at. He was my father. I'd never known him any other way, and the way he looked was "normal" to me. Why couldn't they see past that?

With his big heart, wisdom, strength, and compassion, he has so much to offer. Yet, many people are under the misconception that because he's different externally, they need to treat him differently. Some people shun him, avoiding all contact or conversation, as if by doing so, he doesn't exist. Yet others are overly gentle with him, as if he were fragile and would easily break. They don't realize how incredibly strong and resilient he really is. With all that he's been through, there should be no doubt that he's a fighter and a survivor. And that's probably what's brought us closer over the years. Being around him has taught me to appreciate a person's inner beauty. Spirituality, love of God, kindness to others, are all ingrained in his character. It's not important how we look on the outside, but rather how good we are on the inside. My father is indeed special. Not because of his crippling disfigurement, but because of his unique spirit. On the inside, where it really counts, he has a beautiful soul.

FORTY-THREE

DEL REDDY

We *never know when someone very special will enter our lives and alter it dramatically and forever. I've witnessed some astounding occurrences that seem to defy mere coincidence and believe via God that it was divinely driven that I would befriend Delbert in 2001. I had just come out of the Farmer Jacks market in Bloomfield Hills when a young man approached me to buy some candy. As I reached in my pocket for a five-dollar bill, I asked him what the candy sales were for. I'd been involved in many fundraising and promotional events and was keenly interested in what foundation or cause was the benefactor. I always admired those working at a grass roots level to generate income for their particular focus. When the fellow told me it was for Delbert McCoy's surgeries, my curiosity was peaked.*

"I've always wanted to meet him," I said. In fact, I had a newspaper article about him that I'd saved over the years. His incredible saga impacted me the day I read his story, and it seemed too amazing to be true.

"Where is he?" I inquired.

When the young man (Walter Brandon) told me he was across the street in front of the Rite Aid drugstore, I immediately headed over to see him.

I was fairly sure I knew what to expect, because the news story had included a haunting picture of Delbert sitting alone in a chair. His extensive facial scarring and mutilated ears, nose, and lips were evident in the photo, and I remembered thinking how much suffering he must have endured in all the years since his own personal holocaust. But still, I had never known a severely burned victim, and actually seeing him for the first time was quite a shock, even though I tried hard to conceal it.

"Hi Delbert. It's great to meet you. I'm a Del, too. We've got the same name."

He was seated in a wheelchair, and my right hand was already in motion to shake his, when I suddenly realized that he had no way to return the greeting. His fingers were molded into half stumps—it was impossible for him to reciprocate. I snatched my arm back quickly, a little embarrassed at my miscalculation and then patted him on the back. But he didn't seem to mind.

"How ya doing?" He smiled broadly to put me at ease.

Normally not at a loss for words, I was a little uncomfortable and afraid I'd say the wrong thing, offending him. He had a portable radio, and it appeared he was listening to the ball game when I walked up; so I asked him about the Detroit Tigers. He instantly became animated about his favorite team, and I could tell he was a true enthusiast. We talked of old players from past years and I impressed him right away when I recalled in the seventies who Eddie Brinkman's infield partner was—Gary Sutherland. We discussed many other hometown sports and their respective personalities. He was extremely knowledgeable about the Motor City's elite athletic teams and very passionate about the subject. We connected immediately.

He was so engaging, laughing, smiling, and personable that I forgot about his facial disfigurement and crippling deformities. Historically, radically burned victims have been kept isolated because of the public's ignorance and lack of sensitivity about their condition. Society has portrayed them in a negative and unflattering manner. "Monsters" and "villains" often have severe burn scarring, and Hollywood has created characters such as The Phantom of the Opera and Freddie Krueger. They, and many others, are depicted as lonely,

161

evil rogues who prey on the world's innocents. Witches were burned at the stake; the association of Hell with eternal damnation and fire are terrifying images for people. With public discrimination already against him, it took a tremendous amount of courage for Delbert to expose himself to the outside world at a time when few like him did so. He didn't hide in the shadows or retreat to the safety of his home. He's right out there, front and center...forcing us to confront the absurdity of those misconceptions.

I could have spent the whole day talking to him and couldn't believe how positive he was in spite of the unfathomable tragedy that he had endured. I watched other people approach him, stopping to talk, and witnessed the happy expressions they too had after they shared time with Delbert. It was evident that many others were drawn to him, just like myself.

It occurred to me that his demeanor of cheerfulness and openness with those he encountered—in spite of his nightmarish ordeal—was very special. He had a "Spiritual Magnetism."

Before leaving, we exchanged information, and I told him I would be in touch. He raised his permanently locked right arm and smiled, "God bless," just as I've seen him do hundreds of times since.

A few weeks later I called him and said I had purchased a couple of extra tickets and wanted to invite him to The Michigan Sports Hall of Fame dinner that was being held at the Detroit Marriott Hotel. He was excited because he had never before been to the event that showcased the greatest athletes in our state's history. I met him and his fiancée, Renée, at the ballroom, which was packed with local celebrities, and before dinner was served, I took him around the room and introduced him to some of the featured guests. He talked with Mike and Marion Ilitch, legendary owners of the Detroit Red Wings and Tigers, as well as local television icon, Bill Bonds. It was great to see him say hello to new inductee Bill Davidson, who owned the Detroit Pistons, and pose for a photo with Mr. Detroit Lion, Joe Schmidt. We spoke with Mike Abbott, father of Jim Abbott—the famous one-armed major league pitcher—who was also being inducted. Mike had suffered a burn years ago and was very empathetic and touched by Delbert's amazing triumph over adversity. It was terrific to see him having such a good time and personally connecting with so many of the stars he had read about in the sports section, heard on the radio, or seen on television during those long, lonely days in the hospital.

Delbert has become one of my closest friends. We have had hundreds of conversations, and he and I have attended many other noteworthy functions.

At Morel's restaurant, I introduced him to my long-time friend, Joe Girard, Automotive Hall of Famer and recognized as," The World's Greatest Salesman." He gave Delbert a signed copy of his internationally famous book, "How to Sell Yourself," in which Joe penned: "Delbert, A great inspiration to all." We've spent time with football star, Lem Barney, known as the "Supernatural" who continues to spread his powerful Christian message around the country today. Debra Norville, Ted Koppell, Maria Shriver, and Nobel Peace Price winner, Dr. Shirin Ebadi, are just a few of the luminaries we have shared experiences with. Most of them are awed by Delbert's unbelievable story of perseverance and his indomitable will to overcome incomprehensible challenges.

Delbert was especially excited when he personally met Detroit Tiger's great, Willie Horton, during the private launch of Willie's book, "The People's Champion," held at Comerica Park. They both shared fond memories of their days attending Northwestern High School and reminisced about the 1968 World Series team. Afterwards, Willie described Delbert as "an athlete of life."

While spending a lot of time with Delbert, I became more impressed with his exceptional outlook on life and the mind-boggling number of difficulties he had experienced first hand. He and I have been to the University of Michigan Burn Center and the burn unit at Detroit Receiving Hospital compiling research for this book. I have read a number of medical textbooks that describe the treatment during that time period for severely burned patients and the reconstruction of their ravaged bodies. Dr. Irving Feller and Claudella A. Jones penned a book in 1973 that became the standard in the industry for a number of years and was used by thousands of nursing students. After talking with experts from that period, and culled from voluminous research, it became even more apparent that the odds of Delbert surviving his horrendous trauma was more like a million to one. An important fact is that he was the last victim to be removed from the dance hall, and as firefighters battled the inferno, Delbert's entire body was smoldering, continuing to burn from the inside while decimating his flesh, tissues, muscles, and bone. It wasn't until the blaze had been extinguished that he was transported to a hospital. The firemen on the scene were convinced that he would not live, the doctor's believed he had no chance to survive, and the nurses were of the same mindset. Because they had never seen someone with burns so extensive, and to spare him the agony of a grueling recovery, a number of people even prayed that he would die.

Sharon Klein, who worked as a social worker at the time Delbert was admitted to Detroit Receiving Hospital, offered her perspective to Kate Lawson of The Detroit News: "You couldn't tell what he looked like—a mass of charred, rotting flesh. Worst I had ever seen. I can't tell you why he survived because it wasn't modern medicine that sustained him. His mouth was severely burned, he could barely talk, but he never complained. He had an incredible will."

Students in the health profession are often told that if you want to know medicine, study burns. In the severely burned victim, all organ systems are affected. Wearing clothing at the time of the initial incident also makes the injury and recovery much more difficult. The skin of an adult is roughly the size of a bed sheet, around 21 square feet, and weighs several pounds, including miles of blood vessels, millions of sweat glands, and countless specialized cells. Even today, there is still a lot of mystery of how excessive thermal trauma affects people. Fat cells ignite and explode, flesh melts from the body. It is metabolic mayhem—chaos within. Toxic gases are released inside the heat-abused victim; the body goes into hyper-drive, attempting to deal with the impossibility of containing the massive and evolving wound.

Delbert was burned over 90% of his total body surface area, with full-thickness or third degree destruction of about 75%. He became one of the first people in the history of mankind to survive such massive thermal injuries. As late as the 1950s, many of those with 20% overall body burns simply died. Historically, infection and shock (burn shock) led to the demise of millions and millions of people.

The initial care for a patient with severe burns is among the most difficult to treat in the realm of medicine, and some knowledgeable experts have claimed that surviving is the easiest part.

There is an endless list of possible complications that can occur at any moment—pneumonia, kidney shutdown, respiratory distress, septicemia, and organ failure—any of which can be fatal. Additionally, there is a constant battle against bacteria in the burn unit, as experts estimate there are more than 500 million trillion bacteria in the world, and they outnumber human cells ten to one. Back in the time of the fire in 1969, sterile precautions were not as stringent as they are today. Delbert could easily have died from infection...especially since he's allergic to penicillin.

During his many months in the ICU, Delbert encountered multiple major complications, each of which was life threatening, while being sustained by dozens of different medications with serious side effects. With the severity of his condition he was always an anesthesia risk, forcing him to undergo procedures which would normally be performed in the operating room, but instead he endured them without proper sedation.

He likely suffered inhalation injury from the lengthy exposure to toxic fumes originating in the dry cleaners below the dance hall. He could have expired after a wave of fluid flooded his lungs or died from complications of cerebral edema—swelling of the face. He could have died from the threat of nearly every known cardiovascular complication or even suffocated from the swelling in his larynx. His immune system was overwhelmed to an indescribable degree, and the lymph system was ambushed, making severe ulcers a major threat to his recovery. Stress-diabetes, hemorrhaging, and blood clots were also possible major problems.

The pain he suffered was excruciating, and at the time of his hospitalization, there were concerns that patients could become drug dependent after being released. His father, Albert McCoy recalls, "The doctors didn't want to give him too much morphine, afraid of making him a drug addict. He suffered every day in agony. Sometimes he cried; sometimes he screamed."

Blindness and deafness were serious threats during his journey to healing as well. He still suffers today from the effects of hypertrophic scars, massive fusion of all his joints, and severe skin contractures. During his treatment, he was blatantly told that he would not reach the age of 50 because of the enormous amount of radiation he was exposed to during the hundreds of x-rays he was given.

He could have died any of the three times that his heart stopped during his hospital stay. He could easily have died as a result of any single one or a combination of factors. Sadly, one of the most common known truisms about extensive burns is that, "you can be fine one hour, and dead the next."

But six decades ago Delbert didn't read what the experts wrote, or realize he was establishing medical history as a world pioneer, while showcasing what the human body and mind can overcome.

His family prayed, his friends prayed, his church congregation prayed. And when he was able—Delbert prayed, attributing his remarkable recovery to "Dr. Jesus, nothing but the Lord." And Dr. Grifka, the compassionate and skilled surgeon who battled to save his life, recalls Delbert's incredible youthful fortitude proclaiming. "Even today, someone with that extensive of burns is not expected to live, because they are going to succumb to something along the way. Sure some survive, but it is still almost a death warrant when you have that much of your body burned."

Delbert fought to live every single minute of every single day. He defied the experts and medical journals, ignored the mortality charts, and overcame astronomical odds in order to survive—because he willed himself to do so. He simply refused to give up, even when faced with the horror of his situation daily and the innumerable reminders of the destruction he had endured both physically and emotionally. The endless painful procedures, and the sleepless nights when he was alone in his 10 x 10 room—a medical prison—left to imagine how he would relive the same grueling ordeal again and again, did not diminish his will. Like the stars he admired in the sports world, the athletes who entertain the masses with their God-given talent, Delbert waged his own personal World Series contest, and he triumphed. He is certainly a medical miracle, a super survivor, with extraordinary mental toughness.

Over the years, I've had the opportunity to witness how people are drawn to him, first through curiosity, then through inspiration, as they learn the story of his survival and the incredible odds that he was forced to overcome. The more they become aware of his personal history, the more they admire him and draw strength from him. Many, just like myself, are at first hesitant to talk to him, not knowing what is appropriate to discuss. But he puts everyone at ease, and no question is off limits. On rare occasions, someone may be a bit offensive or even rude, but it doesn't bother Delbert. He keeps everything in a very positive perspective. Having endured the worst possible pain and humiliation, on all levels, he doesn't allow a few insensitive comments or blatant stares to get him down. "I loved people before and love them now even more," he reasons.

Most of us are inherently frightened of being burned alive and can't imagine how terrifying the experience would be. Some people believe "if I don't see it or know about it, it can't happen to me." So when they meet Delbert, it brings the whole question of their own vulnerability into focus. "There but for the grace of God go I." If it could happen to him, it could happen to them. But once they get past being uncomfortable, people are open to his kindness, gentle manner, and radiant humor. Knowing him becomes an emotional journey—evoking curiosity, disbelief, fear, amazement, gratitude, awe, and admiration. But above all else, he provides true inspiration—the Real McCoy. I've seen people pray for him, and I've witnessed them ask for his prayers for their own problems, as well. He is a teacher, a counselor, and an ambassador for Jesus. How he affects people for the better and literally changes their lives is amazing. He reminds us instantly, sometimes without even saying a word, that we all have so much to be grateful for and that our problems may not be as serious as we think they are.

Having Delbert as one of my best friends has changed my life profoundly, and it is a blessing to witness his dramatic effect on people every day. If he could endure all the pain, mental suffering, humiliation, loss, and crippling disfigurement that he has dealt with for over 40 years, then certainly I can deal with whatever life throws at me. When times are tough, or something bothers me, I think of Delbert—of what he goes through on a daily basis—and I am humbled. My problems shrink in comparison to his, as I'm reminded of just how fortunate I truly am, and I count my blessings.

I have such a deep respect for all that he's gone through and all that he's accomplished. Delbert doesn't let anything defeat him. He assures us that he "was burned up, but not burned out," and has an extraordinary fighting spirit and determination to live. I witness that determination almost everyday when he sits for hours out in the cold and rain, selling his wares to help make ends meet. He is always smiling, always grateful to be able to share with people, and always positive. I call him God's right hand man, for he truly is a "Miracle Messenger."

Co-author and very good friend, Del Reddy, along with
Nobel Peace Prize winner and human rights activist, Shirin Ebadi.

FORTY-FOUR

THE MIRACLE MESSENGER

Most people have never known a severely burned person, so when they first meet me, they are usually nervous, often not knowing what to say. They don't want to stare, but I know they're likely apprehensive, so I attempt to put them at ease and make them feel comfortable.

Usually, they ask what happened to me. Although my injuries are obvious, they're curious as to how they occurred and what the long-term effects are. I'm happy to share my story because it means I'll be making a new friend. I explain the reason I'm in a wheelchair. I use the old black, foldout style, since it's more convenient for my family and friends to compact and place in the trunk of the car. It makes it a lot easier for everyone who drives me to my many destinations, since I'm on the move every day.

For several months after the fire, doctors could find no place on my body to insert the IV. The only available tissue was in the bottoms of my feet. That caused calluses and sores to develop; so surgery was performed and part of my heel was removed, leaving my left foot turned over at an awkward angle. I was told I would never walk again, but even though my feet are weak and wobbly, I am able to take a few steps. My left knee is locked, and I have hardware in place of bone—plates and screws. During my 2½ years in the hospital, I had many procedures where the surgeons had to re-break several of my bones and nearly all my joints. At one time, I had pins and splinters sticking out of all my fingers and toes in an effort to make them functional. Unfortunately, in most cases, the positive outcome did not occur.

My elbows are fixed at a 90-degree angle, which basically means they are locked permanently into position. Thus, I can't bring my hand to my mouth, and I haven't been able to extend either arm outward or open my hands for nearly four decades. My left hand in most instances is useless, in spite of having multiple amputations. I've been left with bone deformities and massive fusion, unable to rotate either wrist. "There's nothing we can do," the doctors have declared. I keep the left hand covered because it's so unsightly. My right hand doesn't move up and down or sideways. It's permanently fused also, with the fingers gnarled and twisted in different directions, then molded back into each other, upside down. My "pincher" is the closest thing I have to a real hand.

In our society, appearance is judged to be very important, and we place a premium on how we look on the outside. The beauty and youth business is a multi-billion dollar industry. I understand this. That's why I've spent years trying to make my looks more acceptable to others, with countless surgeries and re-constructive procedures. My deformed hand is kept covered with a sock, and I wear pants and long-sleeved shirts to obscure my scarred body. I've even grown my hair long so that it hides the damage on the back of my scalp and neck.

Shielding my body was the easy part. But there's not much I can do about my face. For the typical person, the slightest imperfection may cause anxiety. Pimples, moles, wrinkles, or any minor abnormality could be the trigger. But for years I didn't even have a face. I suffered from complex facial deformity, abnormal contour, and extensive scarring. It took many painful reconstructive surgeries to give me the image I see every day in the mirror. I endured over 108 operations, and most of the procedures were to re-establish a nose, mouth, ears, and facial skin. There are very delicate and specialized muscles and tissues that comprise the nose and mouth areas, and most of mine were destroyed. Because of that, my ability to convey emotion is limited, and it's harder for me to be as expressive as most people. But I do my best to always smile as broadly as I can. On the plus side, one advantage to my condition is that I never have to shave. Not only that, but no one guesses my age—61!

Being deprived of calcium after the fire resulted in the loss of several of my teeth, and I couldn't close my mouth completely, as my lips were mangled and for many years remained swollen and deformed. Three years ago doctors removed multiple layers of skin from each lip, which finally enabled my mouth to function better. Amazingly, my tongue and throat suffered no permanent damage. But my voice is raspy due to the build up of scar tissue from the breathing tubes that inhabited my throat for so many months.

Since my eyes had been compromised due to inadequate tissue, they suffered many infections throughout the years, and I wasn't able to completely close them for over three decades. The left eye was badly damaged, leaving it virtually sightless, and Dr. Feller recommended a corneal transplant. I know that the surgery would have helped my eyesight, but I decided against it, because at the time, I had had enough. Eventually, after additional operations and Dr. Sandra Brown's remarkable topical treatment, I would finally enjoy the relief of completely shutting them.

I now have ears, thanks to new advances in plastic surgery and my talented surgeon, Dr. Ian Jackson. He and other doctors removed part of my rib, fashioned the bone into the shape of an ear, then grafted skin from my body to cover the curved bone. As part of the reconstruction process, small balloon-like bags were inflated and the skin was stretched over them. A drainage tube hung downward on each side of my head during the healing process. The hole in each ear is small, but my eardrums weren't affected; so I hear pretty well. Fortunately, in this era of tremendous technological advances, many of the setbacks I sustained long ago are greatly minimized for patients today.

If I could wave a magic wand, or have just one wish, it wouldn't be for a handsome face or a stronger body. I'd ask for a "real" hand. Of all my injuries and disfigurement, the loss of my hands has caused me the most torment, because it robbed me of the ability to do things for myself.

I still rely on the kindness of others for help every day, and it will be that way for the rest of my life. I can take a bath myself, but I can't button my shirt. I can't comb my hair, or brush my teeth, or drive a car, or buckle my own seat belt. I can't blow my nose or shake a friend's hand.

I'll never hold a baseball bat again, and I need help to go to the bathroom and getting up and down stairs. Everyone has a sense of pride, but mine has been stripped away. I used to feel humiliation and anger about needing assistance from others. I would dwell on the unfairness of it all. But over time, I've learned to let go of the bitterness, and I used my energy to get well and heal my body and mind. But I couldn't have done it alone. I've witnessed the BEST and the WORST behavior of the human race.

I've known the compassion and dedication of hundreds of highly skilled doctors, nurses, and medical personnel and have experienced the extraordinary strength and love of my family, together with the unwavering loyalty and support of so many friends. I've even born witness to the kindness, generosity, and sympathy of strangers. But also at the hand of strangers, I've been exposed to intolerance and disrespect from those who refused to treat me with dignity. And I've felt first-hand the evil and abuse of men who have little regard for anyone, or anything, outside themselves.

Recently, I appeared in a documentary that was being filmed in my old neighborhood of Detroit. Along with my lifelong friends, Preacher and Nate, we re-visited the exact location where the dance hall inferno (now a vacant lot) had taken place almost forty years ago. My two buddies dug a hole in the ground, as I took a gas can, along with a dollar bill (the amount used to enter the club) and placed it in the freshly carved pit. Although I had made a conscious decision much earlier to let go of the negative emotion, the intensity of being in the same exact location, and reliving that horrifying night in 1969, that had affected my family and friends and changed all of our lives forever, made the task more difficult. After they covered the hole symbolically with dirt, I proclaimed with sincere emotion…"This is the past. I forgive those who did this to me. I'm going forward."

I've long ceased being a victim. Whatever happened to me is yesterday. Even though the physical scars are always present, the emotional ones have healed. It's been a very painful and frustrating journey, with so many people to thank for my survival and for my very existence. I can never adequately express my gratitude to everyone who helped me get to this point in my life. Every day gives me new reasons to count my blessings.

Through faith, family, and friends, I've accepted my limitations. I've become a better person and have moved forward into a new chapter of my life. People frequently ask me if I'm mad at God. "No, I'm not mad at God." I strongly believe that the inferno that scarred me forever was the devil's work. Whenever I was depressed, or feeling sorry for myself, I would recall how Jesus was nailed to the cross. I knew I was no better than him, and my suffering was no worse than his. My thoughts were, *if he could do it, I could do it.* It was through faith in God and our Savior that I survived. Like my father always says," Nothing but the Lord."

The last few years have been very exciting. The most rewarding part of my life now is that I'm able to reach out and help others who are suffering, not just physically, but emotionally, as well. The world is full of people who have a heavy cross to bear, and the burden can be overwhelming. The pain, depression, anxiety, fear, abandonment, loneliness—can be unbearable. Sometimes just having someone who understands can make all the difference in the world. I know. I DO understand. I've been there. Thousands of people have conveyed their most traumatic personal struggles along with their bleakest moments to me because they feel that I can relate. After talking and sharing life experiences, they wish we had connected long ago. Friends tell me I am always upbeat and I love sharing positive proclamations with them such as "you can't get too depressed about anything that goes on in your life, we all go through trials and tribulations." It is extremely gratifying that I can reach people this way and often affect their outlook. Nearly every day, I share with so many people "to look up in life—not down." Miracles happen. I'm one of them.

The reaction I've received from others has inspired me to create *The Fire in my Soul Foundation, a* non-profit organization. It's mission is to assist the physically, psychologically, and emotionally scarred victims of senseless acts of violence, or unfortunate circumstances, as they persevere and continue highly functional lives. In a few short years, we have been able to help everyone from a courageous young woman, who had acid thrown in her face, to a terminally ill teenager. Along this same line, my good friend Del Reddy and I host a new television program on Comcast's WLND, which features heroic individuals who have overcome severe adversity.

Besides the continuing growth of the foundation, I've been lucky to have a music tribute CD in which all the songs chronicle different phases of my life, the most popular being "Delbert's Rockin Tonight."

I've been highlighted in many media outlets both locally and nationally. The City of Westland even named me their first ever- honorary fireman. Understandably, I have a soft spot in my heart for those everyday heroes and have spoken in support of the dedicated service and work they perform.

I believe that my mother would be proud of her son today. She always told her children to "Be nice to everybody, say our prayers, and be thankful." Essie McCoy's life was all about helping people, and that's what my life has come to mean as well. She'd probably be amused that her bashful little boy, who was too shy to sing with the church choir, now makes speeches in front of thousands of people. As timid as I once was, I no longer get nervous when I'm around others, and I must have shared my tale of struggle and triumph hundreds of times. In the ensuing years, people have cried with me, prayed with me, and regularly tell me that I inspire them. Students have written book reports about my experience, and I've spoken to church audiences, inner city youth groups at massive Cobo Hall in Detroit, corporate audiences, and to large gatherings of medical personnel. Just hearing their feedback and being called an "inspirational pioneer" helps keep me motivated.

Recently, I had the privilege of reuniting with Dr. Irving Feller, the surgeon who treated me at University Hospital in Ann Arbor. I hadn't seen him for many, many years, and he was surprised to see how well I'm doing. We reminisced about all the months I'd spent in the hospital and talked about the new improvements in burn care since I was a patient and about the ways I'm now able to help others learn from my experience. When it was time to say goodbye, he hugged me warmly. "Keep pushing, Delbert," he said. "I'm proud of what you're doing."

Seeing Dr. Feller again was as if my life had gone full circle. He knew me when I was helpless—at the lowest point in my life. Now, after 40 years, he saw me at the best time of my life. Ironically, I have defied all the expectations of experts and beaten the odds. I should have died when my heart stopped on three different occasions, or when my body was riddled with infection, or any number of other reasons. I was supposed to be in the mahogany coffin. I was supposed to be dead in 1969. But instead, I've lived a long and fulfilling life. I received a college degree, watched my two daughters grow up, and even became a grandfather. Along the way, I became an author, entrepreneur, inspirational speaker, youth counselor, mentor, grief advisor, and burn survivor specialist. And I found my purpose. I've been chosen to share my message with the world—*Life is precious. Never, Never, Never Give Up!*

My hope is that my story of survival can provide inspiration to others who are facing great hardships, trials, or tragedy. May it serve to be a beacon in the darkness of their lives. And I truly believe that was what God had in mind when he carried me up the flaming stairway of the Detroit dance hall over 40 years ago.

The horrific flames that consumed me that January night, so long ago, have long since been extinguished. Even though their searing heat left my body forever altered and disfigured, they didn't char my heart, and they didn't destroy my soul. Because, in spirit I am, and always will be... STILL ON FIRE!

Part
FOUR

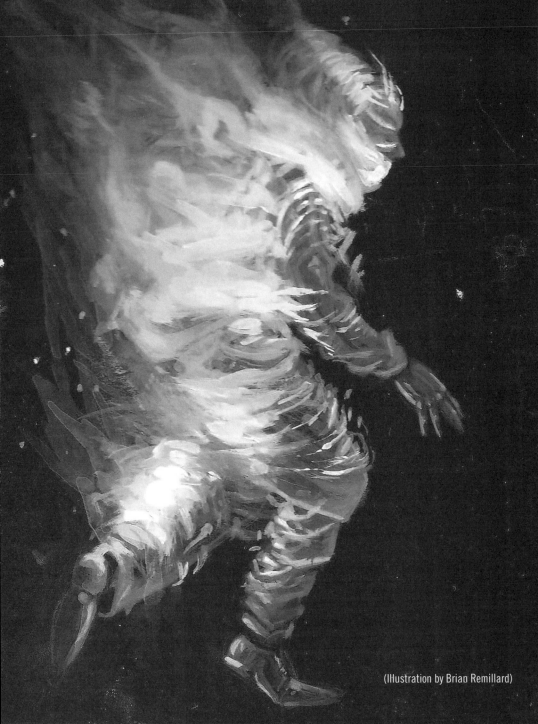

Fire Bomb Hurts 60
In Dance Hall Here

(Illustration by Brian Remillard)

FORTY-FIVE

THE REAL MCCOY

I have been privileged to have a dual ministry in the business world and several churches. I've seen many examples of courage, but Delbert McCoy is the most amazing I have ever experienced in my life and ministry. Delbert is a miracle unto himself. I met him some time ago through two good friends, Bill MacAdam and Emery King. Many people ignore him because of the way he looks. Yet he has an incredible purpose and the spirit and will to move on and dedicate his life to helping others.

Often asked to counsel other victims, and help kids facing adversity, he tells them it's what inside that counts, not what they look like. Delbert has undergone 108 surgeries, and his survival is considered a medical miracle.

Winston Churchill said courage is the first of all human qualities because it guarantees all the others. Yes, sometimes courage is shaken, but turning to God with all our hearts give us a courage that can never be taken away.

Delbert's love of life, strong heart, unquenchable courage and refusal to be bitter contributes to his courageous attitude. He has counseled many who have suffered and remain bitter, but he always tells them to go forward—to look up, not down. This advice applies not just to Delbert, but also to you and me. Our strength and courage is a God-given truth.

Delbert's presence is constant and reassures us that we too can carry on our lives, no mater what life has dealt us. This is not Delbert's story. It is our story. Yours and mine. It reminds us of the courage we had in Jesus, when he was crucified on the cross. God and Delbert have done wonderful things together.

> Reverend William R. Fleming
> Christ Church Cranbrook
> Birmingham, Michigan

I was going through the darkest and most challenging time in my life when I first met Delbert. I walked out of the CVS drugstore completely drained, feeling hollow inside, and there he was. An indescribable feeling of peace washed over me the minute our eyes met. Delbert was selling his book and I eagerly bought a copy, somehow aware that it was going to change my life.

Immediately, I got in the car physically shaking on the outside, but calm on the inside. I called my friend to tell her about my experience. I explained that it felt as if I was lost, and God placed Delbert there at that very moment to remind me that He was with me. I read Delbert's story and was completely inspired by the tremendous faith that carried him through the most unimaginable events and challenges in his life. Reading his memoir altered my perspective on struggles and reconfirmed my trust in God.

Delbert's strength, courage, and acceptance should be a lesson to all of us. His faith and trust in God are exemplary, and I feel blessed and honored to have met him. His story is a constant inspiration in my life. Delbert is an angel on earth!

> Elaina Kielbaso
> Elementary school teacher
> Plymouth, Michigan

Delbert, you are one of the most courageous individuals I have ever met. I admire you more than any athlete I had the privilege to coach throughout my career. You are very special.

> Rick Forzano
> Head Coach Detroit Lions 1974–76

I work in the advertising industry and attended the Adcraft Club's annual luncheon where Ted Koppell was the guest speaker for the Discovery Channel. I can't tell you what the topic was, because once I met Delbert McCoy, he captured my full attention. I was so immersed in his story and how he overcame so much tragedy that I couldn't get enough of him, asking him some pretty tough questions, as I helped him with his meal. The answers certainly weren't what I expected. I was amazed at his calm demeanor and how gracious and accepting he was. Most of us have had some kind of misfortune or sadness in our life. I was no exception. It puts you in a dark place, and it's hard to find the light. But in spite of all that he'd been through, Delbert held no malice or resentment. He had forgiven the men who had disfigured him, altering his life forever. He didn't wallow in self-pity, or hide in the shadows, but was at peace with himself and all that had happened. His story was incredible and impacted me at a pivotal point in my own life. It was like he crawled inside of me and opened up the doors in my head. Meeting Delbert inspired me to look in the mirror and ask myself some difficult questions. Suddenly my burdens didn't seem so heavy. My mind became clearer, and I was able to make important decisions that have transformed my life. And how many people who meet him don't have their life altered in some way? He is such an inspiration. It's impossible not to be affected by knowing him. He truly is a remarkable and unforgettable individual.

Bill Donahey
Michigan Entrepreneur

I hadn't seen Delbert in nearly 40 years, since he was first discovered smoldering under a pile of coats at the Soul Expressions fire. He was such a young man with horrific injuries, and through no fault of his own. He was just a victim of a fire set for revenge. I couldn't believe he was still alive after all these years. His burn injury left a lasting impression on me and was part of what motivated me to join the Detroit Fire Department arson squad.

J.T. Boyer
Detroit Fire Department (retired)

With every generation it seems that there are a handful of people in the world with the remarkable ability to not only overcome adversity in their own lives, but to also inspire others to do the same. Delbert McCoy is one such person. I am grateful for having met Delbert several years ago and consider him a personal friend. Knowing him has changed my perspective on life. His story has gotten me through several very tough life situations, but just as importantly, it has caused me to truly appreciate and make the best possible use of my time on Easy Street. Whether you are experiencing extreme difficulty in your life and are ready to give up hope or are looking for a positive uplifting book to boost your enthusiasm for a wonderful life, Delbert's story is a must read!

Jack A. Stein
President, INCOSE Michigan Chapter

"It is with profound gratitude and happiness today, as I seek to address you as a brother. Delbert, you are one in a million. Your courage and love for life are extraordinary. Your fortitude and forcefulness have taught millions…to learn how to capture the essence of life. The true love and veneration that you have shown, and shared with your family and fellow man, makes me stop to think that you are really special. You have given your very soul, your wisdom, your long suffering, your faith, and your kindness without measure. You have the strength of Samson, the faith of Abraham, the braveness of David, the willingness of Peter, and the courage of Daniel…"

Vancia Robinson Smith
New York University student

I once was blind, but now I see, thanks to Delbert's quiet determination and persistent presence at our corner shopping mall. With a nod of his head at each passer-by, the sounds of Tiger baseball at his side, and a gentle "God bless," Delbert is changing the hearts and minds of people like me who live in affluent suburbia—far removed from poverty and the real needs of the world. I once chose to be blind to his plight, fearful of his presence. Now he is a fixture at our mall, blessing us much more than we could ever bless him. God has opened my hardened heart and sent an Angel, named Delbert, who changes the world one shopper at a time and who gives us hope.

Sally
Bloomfield Township, Michigan

Delbert McCoy is an inspirational force. His presence is a reminder of the value of life. Delbert talked to my franchise store owners and our employees as if they were life-long friends, leaving them appreciative of what gifts God has given them. He reminded them of how lucky they were and inspired them to be better people in all aspects of their life. Delbert's story is life changing.

> Lou Toarmina
> President—Toarmina's Pizza

(Toarmina's Pizza Franchisee meeting)

All I could see was the smile. It was a bleak winter day, as I waited in the Westland Biggby coffee shop to finally meet Delbert. Yet, when he came through the door, his smile blazed with light and warmed the room. As he told his story, focusing always on his appreciation for God's multiple blessings, others came to listen as well. We were humbled and inspired. As the story moved to the present time, we learned of continued miracles that are happening daily in his life and in the lives of those he meets. By the end of the day, we were all planning a movement where we work together to lift others up with love, respect, and the help of God.

> Gail Witt
> Founder of Eachofusmakesadifference.com

I am a Nursing Professor with the responsibility to teach my students about a wide variety of medical and surgical issues. One of my course objectives is to train these nursing students how to care for patients who have suffered burns. Recently, I had the privilege of meeting Delbert, a man who not only impacted my life but the lives of my students as well. Delbert sustained considerable and severe burns throughout most of his body 40 years ago, nearly costing him his life. However, Delbert's strength, faith, determination, and resilience allowed him to not only live, but also thrive. He is truly an inspiration to everyone he comes into contact with.

Delbert did not hesitate when I asked him to come speak to my classroom of nursing students. He has also been instrumental and collaborative in helping to work with an interdisciplinary group of nurses and engineering students build assistive devices for disabled people. Each time Delbert talks to a classroom of students, they leave moved, encouraged, and motivated by his experience. Numerous students cried and told me how much Delbert's speech impacted them to become better nurses.

Delbert has a remarkable story and has used his tragedy to help others. He is an excellent motivational speaker and a truly remarkable human being. I look forward to having Delbert come speak to many other students, to teach them what it means to care for a severely burned patient. It has been my honor and privilege to have Delbert as my friend. My students will be better nurses because of his interaction with them in my classrooms.

Molly L. McClelland
RN, MSN, PhD
Assistant Professor of Nursing
University of Detroit Mercy, College of Nursing

WELCOME TO THE DETROIT RECEIVING HOSPITAL BURN CENTER

AUTOMATIC CAUTION DOOR

AUTOMATIC CAUTION DOOR

For the safety of our patients, all hospital staff and visitors must perform hand hygiene before entering.

I get immense satisfaction being a volunteer burn survivor counselor at Detroit Medical Center. Decades ago I entered this same building with an incredibly bleak prospect of surviving.

DELBERT MCCOY

FOUNDATION

As I reflect on my life and the extremely disturbing change it took on a cold January day in 1969 I realize that my terrible experience was simply a part of my preparation to do something great for others. I understand more and more each day that *my story* though unique in its twists and turns could have been the fate of anybody, but I endured this tragedy for the express purpose of moving closer towards my purpose in life. So, it was personally satisfying for me to introduce to my friends and associates my organization: T**he FIRE in my SOUL foundation**.

My foundation is dedicated to assisting physically, psychologically, and emotionally scarred victims of senseless acts of violence or unfortunate circumstances as they persevere and continue living highly functional lives. Our goal is to provide financial provisions when needed, create a network of survivors who will act as a support group that exemplifies the human spirit, and we also wish to provide access to information on resources available to assist individuals in getting their lives back in order.

My foundation has been instrumental in assisting a few individuals, families and organizations, since our inception in 2007. We were able to assist Kristin's Heart Fund, whereby a teenage girl, with terminal cancer, had one last wish to raise money to build a home for orphans in

Zambia. We also contributed to The Martin Luther King Band in their quest to raise funds to attend the Summer Olympics in China. This was a once in a lifetime opportunity for these youths who had worked so hard and were very dedicated students, so our foundation felt compelled to rally with the community and offer our support, as well. I attended a benefit for a young lady that had been a random victim of a senseless crime, whereby a man threw acid in her face and on her body, which resulted in severe burns, disfigurement and blindness to this courageous young woman. I was very honored to meet and speak with her and to contribute towards her well being. This situation hit very close to home because it took me back to my tragedy in 1969, but I was able to share my personal experience with her and she was an inspiration to me, as well. Finally, we helped a young family whose house had been burned down, leaving a single mother with three children homeless and without the daily essentials that they needed. These are just a few of the individuals that my foundation has been able to assist and we look forward to helping countless others in the future with a percentage of my book proceeds going to the Foundation. My cup runneth over and my heart is full if my tragedy can help change the lives of others.

MISSION STATEMENT

To exemplify to people of every age, race, gender, and culture that the human spirit can help them survive any obstacle they are confronted with in life.

Fire in my Soul is committed to providing moral, emotional, mental, and financial support to victims of severe physical, psychological, and emotional trauma as the result of violence, with an emphasis on victims of senseless acts of arson.

185

ABUNDANT APPRECIATION

elbert, Anne, and Del would like to thank all those who helped contribute to *Still On Fire*. Without you, this project would not have been successful. We would like to offer our heartfelt appreciation to the following: God, Jesus Christ, Dr. Thomas Grifka, Marlene Storc, J.T. Boyer, Albert McCoy, Sr., Napoleon Ross, Monique Smith, Kim Abney, Renée Brandon, Lamont "Pug" Lawrence, Drew Lane, Mike Clark, Kate Lawson, Helen O'Neill, Timothy Sheard, Rich Fisher, Emery King, William R. Fleming, Bill Sparks, Marcus Sparks, Nicole Sparks, Walter Brandon, Gert McCoy, Yvonne McCoy, Kevin Allen, Marcella Lee, Laura Berman, Shaunna Kelley, Flip Willson, Joe Menard, Mike Wiseman, Carris Carey, Chuck Roberts, Ted Henning, Dr. Irving Feller, Mary J. Wallace, Karen Jania, Bill MacAdams, Dr. Molly McClelland, Lou Toarmina, Gail Witt, Vancia Robinson Smith, Jack Stein, Bill Donahey, Dr. Sandra Brown, Coach Rick Forzano, Elaina Kielbaso, Joe Schwartz, Angelo Plakas, Jim Plakas, Bob Kosowski, Mayor William R. Wild, Brain Remillard, Lynn Gregg, Michelle Lynch, John Makar, Deb Tremper, Jean Schroeder, Bob Resch, Jim King, Ian Smith, Dr. Ian Jackson, Sharon Klein, Claudella A. Jones, Marc Corriveau, Joe Girard, Bill Bonds, Barry Sanders, Craig Welkenbach, Dave Monak, Mo Elfakir, Al Elfakir, Dan Stoner, Mark

Solomon, Eddie Kean, John T. Reddy, Keith Thomas, Sheila Rogers, Reverend Larry Walker, Kincannon family, Maurice Williams , Derron Colvin, Fred McCoy, Tony Fortson, Luther McCoy, June McCoy, Clifford Riley, Gwen Lee, Mike Reddy, Allan George, Kevin George, Ebony George, Rick Forzano, Jr., and family, Chief Michael J. Reddy, the McCoy family, Tammy Campbell, Sue Willett, Mark and Mike— producers of the Drew and Mike show, Dr. Kathy Richards, Dr. James Herbertson, Bob Kalmbach, Tony McCoy, Gwen Lee, Meriem Kadi, Residents of Bloomfield Hills, Rite Aid-Maple and Lahser, Kroger-Long Lake and Telegraph, Sav-On-Drugs—Telegraph and Maple, Blockbuster Video, CVS, Aaron Howard, Ebony George, Shutterstock, Ray Glandon, Dan Stoner, Sheldon Yellen, Malgosia Myc, Bentley Historical Library, University of Michigan, Walter P. Reuther Library, Wayne State University, Detroit Receiving Hospital Burn Unit, Detroit Medical Center and all those whom we failed to mention.

God bless all of you.

PRAISE FOR ANNE

Thank you, Anne, for your terrific writing during our collaboration for *Still on Fire*. You never wanted any credit or recognition for your talented work, but you definitely deserve it. This has been a great team effort overall, and I am deeply honored that this divinely inspired book will help others for many years to come. Anne, you did a Hall of Fame job!

God bless, Delbert McCoy